Scarcity and Growth Reconsidered

Scarcity and Growth Reconsidered

Edited by V. Kerry Smith

Published for Resources for the Future
by The Johns Hopkins University Press
Baltimore and London

Copyright © 1979 by Resources for the Future, Inc.
All rights reserved
Manufactured in the United States of America

The Johns Hopkins University Press, Baltimore, Maryland 21218
The Johns Hopkins Press Ltd., London

Originally published, 1979
Second printing, 1982

Library of Congress Cataloging in Publication Data

Main entry under title:
Scarcity and growth reconsidered.

    Includes index.
    1. Natural resources—United States—Congresses.
I. Smith, Vincent Kerry, 1945—   II. Resources
for the Future.

HC103.7.S25   333   78-27236
ISBN 0-8018-2232-7
ISBN 0-8018-2233-5 pbk.

Resources for the Future is a nonprofit organization for research and education in the development, conservation, and use of natural resources and the improvement of the quality of the environment. It was established in 1952 with the cooperation of the Ford Foundation. Grants for research are accepted from government and private sources only if they meet the conditions of a policy established by the Board of Directors of Resources for the Future. The policy states that RFF shall be solely responsible for the conduct of the research and free to make the research results available to the public. Part of the work of Resources for the Future is carried out by its resident staff; part is supported by grants to universities and other nonprofit organizations. Unless otherwise stated, interpretations and conclusions in RFF publications are those of the authors; the organization takes responsibility for the selection of significant subjects for study, the competence of the researchers, and their freedom of inquiry. RFF support was provided by the Ford Foundation.

This work was begun in RFF's natural environments program and completed within the quality of the environment division, Walter O. Spofford, Jr., director. It was funded by Resources for the Future, the Ford Foundation, and the John Simon Guggenheim Memorial Foundation. V. Kerry Smith is a Senior Fellow at Resources for the Future. The book was edited by Ruth B. Haas. Charts were drawn by Federal Graphics.

RFF editors: Joan R. Tron, Ruth B. Haas, Jo Hinkel, Sally A. Skillings

Contributors

HAROLD J. BARNETT
Professor, Department of Economics, Washington University, St. Louis, Missouri

DONALD A. BROBST
Chief, Eastern Mineral Resources Branch, U.S. Geological Survey, Reston, Virginia

GARDNER M. BROWN, JR.
Professor, Department of Economics, University of Washington, Seattle, Washington

HERMAN E. DALY
Professor, Department of Economics, Louisiana State University, Baton Rouge, Louisiana

BARRY C. FIELD
Associate Professor, Department of Economics, University of Miami, Coral Gables, Florida

ANTHONY C. FISHER
Professor, Energy and Resource Program and Department of Economics, University of California, Berkeley, California

NICHOLAS GEORGESCU-ROEGEN
Distinguished Professor of Economics Emeritus, Vanderbilt University, Nashville, Tennessee

H. E. GOELLER
Senior Engineer, Oak Ridge National Laboratory, Oak Ridge, Tennessee

BRUCE M. HANNON
Director, Energy Research Group, Office of Vice Chancellor for Research, University of Illinois, Urbana, Illinois

JOHN V. KRUTILLA
Senior Fellow, Resources for the Future, Washington, D.C.

V. KERRY SMITH
Fellow, Resources for the Future, Washington, D.C.

JOSEPH E. STIGLITZ
Professor, All Souls College, Oxford University, Oxford, England

Contents

Foreword

In recent years, a renewed interest has emerged in the availability of natural resources for continued material well-being and economic growth. Sharply rising energy costs, increased prices of natural resources generally, widening popular support for a clean environment and improved health, the current uncertain state of the economy, and a genuine concern for the future have all contributed to the public's recent questioning of whether or not it will be possible to provide and maintain a reasonably high material standard of living for all while ensuring that the overall quality of life remains unchanged.

Despite a history of research in this area and the current resurgence of this activity, a number of fundamental issues concerning natural resource scarcity remain both controversial and unresolved to this day. While the main concern involves the continued erosion of a finite natural resource base and whether or not technological improvements can keep pace with rapidly increasing demands for goods and services, it does not represent the whole story. A spectrum of other related problems confronts our society as well. An increasingly important set involves the detrimental side effects of production technology. These byproducts range from despoiled landscapes and pollution to toxic materials in the environment. Although some effects are limited to local degradation, others are more global in character and may even threaten natural systems which are essential for the support of life. The latter, more severe, impacts appear to be associated with some of the new technologies. Material well-being and the quality of the natural environment are integrally related, and policies established to address one will ultimately have an impact on the other. Clearly, the provision of goods and services and the uses and quality of the natural environment must be considered as a whole, and tradeoffs will be necessary.

The conference upon which this volume is based addressed some of these issues by bringing together in a single forum a wide range of professional opinion covering three principal areas of current research on resource availability.

In the first area, dealing with economic modeling of the role of natural resources, Joseph Stiglitz presents an overview of the neoclassical perspective on the contribution of natural resources and stresses that for the most part natural resources are not sufficiently different from other inputs to production activities to require amendments in this type of analysis. Herman Daly and Nicholas Georgescu-Roegen disagree completely with Stiglitz. They maintain that physical laws imply that natural resources are essential for the maintenance of human well-being and therefore conventional economic models must be substantially amended to reflect this.

In the section on geological appraisals of the limits of resource availability, the second area of research, H. E. Goeller evaluates resource availability from the perspective of several hundred years, ignoring any of the impediments—economic, legal, and political—that might prevent the realization of these ultimate prospects. By contrast, Donald Brobst points out that it is essential to both recognize and take account of these impediments in any assessment of the physical quantities of resources available for future use by mankind.

In the third section, on economic measures of resource scarcity, Gardner Brown and Barry Field question past measures of resource scarcity and offer some guidance as to how one might approach the problem under idealized conditions. While the data necessary for carrying out their suggestions currently do not exist, the authors do suggest ways in which construction of these more desirable measures might be undertaken. On the other hand, Harold Barnett maintains that the same tools and measures that were used in his and Chandler Morse's now classical study of resource scarcity published by Resources for the Future almost two decades ago (*Scarcity and Growth: The Economics of Natural Resource Availability*, 1963), are still capable of being used today. Moreover, Barnett uses a wide array of more recent international data with these measures to develop the original thesis of *Scarcity and Growth* that natural resources, with the possible exception of timber, do not appear to be becoming increasingly scarce. Fisher's paper reviews both of these arguments and provides a link between cost, price, and rent-based measures of resource scarcity.

If the continuing debate over natural resource adequacy is to be finally resolved, the underpinnings of each position's arguments must be understood. The literature has been dominated for too long by the rhetoric from each school without substantial progress toward an appreciation of the reasoning responsible for their conclusions. The objective of this volume is to identify the sources of the differences in each group's arguments and, in so doing to direct attention to avenues for future research.

Indeed, the conference has already led to a program of research at RFF supported by the National Science Foundation and the Electric Power Research Institute. It is our sincere hope that this first product of this program at RFF will stimulate research that will both enhance our understanding of the issues surrounding judgments on natural resource adequacy and contribute to the public policy initiatives in the area.

March 1979

Walter O. Spofford, Jr.
Director, Quality of the
Environment Division

Preface

The objective of this volume is to report on an effort to reconsider the long-run importance and availability of natural resources for economic growth and material well-being. These concerns were among the contributing factors which motivated the founding of Resources for the Future. It is not surprising, then, that they formed the basis for some of RFF's first research efforts. One of the most influential products of this research was the work supervised by Harold Barnett. Indeed, the volume to which the title of this book refers summarizes this research. For nearly two decades, Harold Barnett and Chandler Morse's *Scarcity and Growth: The Economics of Natural Resource Availability* has had a significant impact on the attitudes of economists and policy makers toward natural resource availability.

A renewed questioning of the adequacy of our natural resources as conventionally defined; increased popular interest in preserving our environmental resources and improving their quality; and a more cautious, if not somewhat skeptical, view of technological change and economic growth made this seem an appropriate time to take stock of current views on natural resource availability. The papers in this volume were presented at a forum sponsored by the Ford Foundation in the fall of 1976. Larry Ruff was instrumental in initiating this effort. Prompted by the general concern over the need for a reevaluation of the Barnett–Morse work and a series of meetings with Harold Barnett, Herman Daly, Bruce Hannon, and Toby Page, Larry arranged for the funding which permitted organizing a research forum on these issues.

My own interest in this area was initiated eight years ago when John Krutilla first discerned that the treatment of the role of natural resources in economic activities made it necessary to reconsider the Barnett–Morse findings. I have been generously assisted in this task by support from Resources for the Future, before and after joining the staff and by a fellowship from the John Simon Guggenheim Memorial Foundation for the 1976–77 academic year. Since most of my own thinking on these problems has been influenced by John Krutilla, I was exceptionally pleased when he agreed to join with me in preparing the overview and concluding essays for this volume.

The forum was organized around three broad aspects of *Scarcity and Growth:* (1) the role of natural resources in economic modeling; (2) the nature of the physical constraints on the availability of natural resources; and (3) the ability of empirical methods to gauge the potential for stringencies in our natural resource endowments. The topics and research papers were selected to highlight the range of intellectual perspectives on natural resources in each case. This volume includes these papers, along with the remarks of the chairpersons of each session and introductory and concluding essays by John Krutilla and myself. While Tony Fisher's paper arose from his remarks on the third topic, it extends beyond comments on the papers by Harold Barnett, Gardner Brown, and Barry Field to a complete treatment of many of the issues central to evaluating scarcity measures which might be applied to appraising the availability of natural resources.

We were fortunate to have a distinguished group of natural scientists and economists participate in the forum. Their remarks and the overall discussion significantly influenced John's and my treatment of the problems associated with summarizing their views and more generally, in defining anew the questions which must be considered before a judgment on natural resource availability can be made.

The individual papers in this volume were reviewed by a number of persons, who are acknowledged by the authors. Special mention should be given to John R. Moroney of Tulane University and William D. Schulze of the University of Southern California for their most thoughtful and constructive reviews of the entire volume.

My editorial tasks were assisted immeasurably by the tireless efforts and thoughtful insights of Ruth Haas of the RFF editorial staff. I am sure all the authors share my appreciation for her significant input to the volume. Mary Kokoski served as research assistant and assisted me in numerous details associated with the final research product.

The introductory and concluding essays and related materials went through numerous revisions, all of which were patiently and cheerfully typed by John's and my secretaries over the period. Thus, I would like to express our collective appreciation to Mae Barnes, Cassandra Madison, Virginia Reid, and Diana Tasciotti.

Finally, I would like to thank my wife, Pauline, and son, Timothy, for their continuing support, which is so important to all that I do.

All responsibility for any remaining shortcomings with this volume rests with me.

March 1979

V. KERRY SMITH
Resources for the Future

Scarcity and Growth Reconsidered

1

The Economics of Natural Resource Scarcity: An Interpretative Introduction

V. Kerry Smith and John V. Krutilla

I
Introduction

It is doubtful that any country has been more richly endowed with natural resources than the United States. The diversity and abundance of its resources contributed to America's rapid industrial development and emergence as a paramount world power. New supplies were forthcoming at rates equal to demands and at almost continuously falling supply prices, so that not until the mid-1900s was any general concern expressed regarding the adequacy of supplies of raw materials to sustain continuous economic growth.[1]

The heavy demands of World War II led, in the early 1950s, to a review of the nation's agricultural potential and mineral resource stocks by two presidential commissions. The President's Materials Policy Commission (Paley Commission, 1952) found that over the next twenty-five years it was unlikely that there would be any general exhaustion of resources. However, there was concern about the apparent change in the trend of prices and particularly about some critical commodities. Indeed, it was felt that a continuous reexamination of materials policy was needed

V. Kerry Smith and John V. Krutilla are Senior Fellows in the quality of the environment division, Resources for the Future. A number of individuals have generously commented on earlier drafts of this paper. We would especially like to thank K. J. Arrow, H. J. Barnett, W. J. Baumol, E. N. Castle, R. C. d'Arge, R. Day, B. C. Field, A. C. Fisher, F. M. Fisher, G. Heal, A. V. Kneese, C. Morse, P. Portney, V. Ruttan, T. Sandler, T. W. Schultz, W. D. Schulze, M. Sharefkin, R. M. Solow, J. Sonstelie, and W. Spofford. Thanks are also due the conference participants since many of their remarks have influenced our thinking on these issues. Smith's research was partially supported by the John Simon Guggenheim Memorial Foundation.

[1] This concern is to be distinguished from that of the early conservation era's reaction to the wanton disregard for land manifested in the extraction activities of the times.

1

because of the expected rising relative costs of important industrial materials.[2]

Resources for the Future was established twenty-seven years ago, largely in response to this concern over the continued adequacy of natural resources. The most profound analysis of this issue, *Scarcity and Growth: The Economics of Natural Resource Availability,* by Barnett and Morse, had its origin in these events. Their evaluation of the trends in "real unit costs" and relative prices over the period 1870 to 1957 concluded that resource scarcity had been avoided by advances in technology which allowed the progressive substitution of lower grade resources, with corresponding increases in *effective supplies.*

Much of the thinking about natural resources policy has been influenced by the reasons advanced to account for the apparent increase in effective supplies. Basically, four factors were adduced to be involved. *First,* as higher grade sources are exhausted, lower grade sources are found in greater abundance. Moreover, the qualitative differences among various stocks diminish as the grade of the materials declines. *Second,* as a particular extractive resource becomes more scarce, continued increases in the rate of appreciation in its price tend to be offset by substitution of other resources. That is, users seek alternatives with more favorable cost relationships and all but the more insistent demands for the resource are reduced or eliminated. *Third,* increases in prices stimulate exploration for new deposits and provide incentives for increased recycling, which can reduce the pressure on sources of virgin materials. *Fourth,* technical change reduces the costs of providing natural resource commodities either by reducing the extraction costs for existing deposits or introducing methods which make previously uneconomic resources a part of the effective reserves at current or short-term future prices.[3]

Of these four factors, one involves the frequency and characteristics

---

[2] Cooper [1] recently evaluated the Paley Commission's predictions after twenty-five years. He found the commission underestimated the growth in the U.S. economy and *over*estimated the associated consumption of materials. He offers several potential explanations: (a) Mineral prices rose, contrary to the projection's assumption of no change in relative price. (b) There was improved secondary recovery of metals, thereby reducing the need for new primary production. (c) There was very large expansion in the imports of manufactured goods between 1950 and 1972, at a rate faster than the growth in GNP. This tendency would seem to indicate that the U.S. economy was satisfying resource needs through imports of finished goods rather than direct consumption of primary materials. He concludes, noting: "The ratio of material input to output fell faster than the Commission allowed for, reflecting technical and material changes, many of which may well have been induced by the threat of scarcity. Such developments are certain to continue in the future. . . ." [p. 245]

[3] This expression of the reasons is taken from Herfindahl [2]. However, equivalent statements of this tendency can be found in Morse [3], Landsberg, Fischman, and Fisher [4], and a variety of other studies following in the tradition established by the Barnett–Morse work.

of resource occurrences. The others are related to the technology of conversion and the characteristics of markets. Accordingly, any evaluation of natural resource scarcity must address all three aspects: the physical constraints of the resource endowment, the production technology or state of the art for conversion, and the character of the markets in which outputs exchange.

The oil embargo of 1973 and other materials shortages of the period,[4] the emergence of activist environmental groups, and popular predictions of secular stagnation have all rekindled interest in whether our supply of natural resources is adequate to sustain current patterns of production and consumption. The current debate over the adequacy of materials resources offers the widest range of opinion of any recent policy issue. Judgments range from Houthakker's statement that "the ancient concern about the depletion of natural resources no longer rests on any firm theoretical basis" [5, p. 12], to the completely opposite conclusions of Georgescu-Roegen [6] which draw on principles from the natural sciences in support of his position. His paper in this volume observes that:

Neoclassical economics . . . has paid practically no attention to natural resources. To be sure, legions of production functions in the neoclassical literature contain the factor land, by which is meant, however, only Ricardian land. But Ricardian land raises no issue for the intergenerational allocation of resources. And this is *the* problem of natural resources. [chapter 4, p. 95]

These differences in opinion are not limited to theoretical approaches, but extend to empirical appraisals of the resource picture as well.[5] Accordingly, there appears to be some justification for organizing within a single volume statements representing these views in order to understand why there is a divergence of opinion on such an important problem. This is the purpose of this volume. It is the outgrowth of a forum sponsored by Resources for the Future on the economics of natural resource scarcity. Its objective was to help identify what questions need to be investigated so that we can begin to resolve the issues underlying differing views of resource adequacy.

In the following sections we provide background and an overview of the papers presented at the forum and included in this volume. In doing so, we attempt to show their relationship to earlier literature, as

[4] See statement of George C. Eads, Executive Director of the National Commission on Supplies and Shortages before the House Committee on the Budget (July 28, 1976) for discussion of the factors influencing the 1973–74 shortages of specific materials.

[5] Appraisals of Kahn [7] versus Meadows and coauthors [8] can offer the widest possible range of opinion. However, one can avoid the Meadows work and use the current U.S. Geological Survey's report, "Demand and Supply of Nonfuel Minerals and Materials for the United States Energy Industry, 1975–90—A Preliminary Report" (Geological Survey Professional Paper 1006-A, B 1976) to make the same point.

well as to each other. We begin with a definition of natural resources, and what is meant by reference to their scarcity. The third section of this introduction reviews how the role of natural resources in production and consumption is modeled under various definitions. This discussion considers the role of society's purposes in governing the allocation of a nonrenewable resource as well as constraints on the allocation process. Section IV discusses the deficiences of formal modeling and empirical analyses in this area in order to provide a setting for the papers that follow as well as an outline of the issues which a research agenda must address. The concluding section reviews some unanswered questions which we will return to in the concluding chapter of this volume.

II
The Definition of Natural Resources and the Meaning of Scarcity

For the most part, earlier analyses of the adequacy of our natural resources have represented them as the basic sources of primary commodities produced by extractive activities. They are the raw material inputs into production and consumption. While these studies have clearly distinguished between renewable and nonrenewable extractive outputs, the definition of natural resources in total has been sufficiently restrictive so that *materials policy* could be construed as addressing the problems of natural resource scarcity.

The conception of resources as a source of materials inputs leads one to consider the environmental side effects of extraction and conversion activities as phenomena to be distinguished from resource utilization and depletion. Such a view is explicitly advanced in Barnett and Morse's *Scarcity and Growth*. Resource commodity extraction and conversion might be attended by environmental degradation and may influence the quality of life, but these authors hold that this phenomenon is independent of the issue of resource scarcity in the classical sense. Their view is even more clearly stated in Barnett's reappraisal of the trends in scarcity indexes in this volume (chapter 8). He contends that environmental damage can be treated separately from scarcity measures by evaluating the costs associated with meeting air and water pollution standards.[6]

[6] In a recent evaluation of the effects of pollution abatement costs upon output per unit of input, Denison [9] concluded that his estimates of the index indicate an increasing effect over time. Specifically he argues that: "The index shows that the increasing diversion of labor and capital to pollution abatement was impairing the growth of measured output per unit of input importantly by the mid-1970's and that the amount was growing. From zero before 1967, the amount of impairment increased to an annual average of one-twentieth of a percentage point from 1967 to 1969, one-tenth of a point from 1969 to 1973, and nearly one-fourth of a point from 1973 to 1975." [p. 32]

In later sections of this essay we argue that such a separation may not adequately address the issue and is a matter which must be evaluated critically. For the present, what is important is the definition of natural resources. Treatment of resources as industrial raw materials eliminates, by definition, consideration of alternative final consumption services which such resources could provide. Since these alternatives are frequently incompatible, and use of resources for one purpose may foreclose irretrievably the option for an alternative use, such restrictive definitions can bias evaluation of resource adequacy.

Accordingly, we shall argue that the most appropriate definition of natural resources can be taken as a direct extension of Ricardian concepts to be all the *original* elements that comprise the earth's natural endowments.[7] In a broad sense, they may be thought of as the life support system. However, when they are considered in terms of the earth's endowments, we can readily identify both the early and current analyses of natural resource problems with a specific subset of these endowments. For example, the work of Hotelling and much of the concern of current neoclassical models has been directed to mineral endowments. It is our contention that a more general viewpoint will identify an array of economic issues associated with the use of these endowments which are overlooked when the focus is too narrow.

To begin with, all natural resources are assets which yield service flows. The literature has focused, for the most part, on a subset of the natural resources and uses of their services. A broadened definition that includes common property or open-access resources provides for diversity of uses and the corresponding complexities for economic analysis. Even within the traditional framework, we wish to distinguish different types of nonrenewable natural resources—those which can be recycled and those which cannot. An example of the former might be metallic minerals, while the latter might be any of the conventional energy commodities.

Because private property resource services may be increased at the expense of common property resources, this general framework identifies the potential for conflict in alternative allocations of natural resources and provides one dimension on which it is possible to differentiate the analyses in the papers which follow.[8] In neoclassical economics, atten-

---

[7] We are grateful to T. W. Schultz for this suggestion.

[8] Our use of the terms private property and common property resources should not be interpreted as being related to a specific institutional framework. Rather, it is the result of the features of the goods involved. In some cases, it is possible to exclude others from using the good or service and hence there is the possibility, in principle, of vesting the property rights in private parties. This does not imply that the problems considered can be removed under alternative mechanisms for assigning ownership rights. We are grateful to Tjalling Koopmans for calling this issue to our attention.

tion is directed to goods and services that exchange on organized markets while Daly's work can be viewed as concerned more directly with the conjunctive effects of these use patterns, that is, their implications for the common property amenity and life-supporting natural resource services. Any restriction on the definition of natural resources will affect the view of resource adequacy that is derived from the associated models.[9]

Assume, for the moment, that we accept the more restrictive definition of natural resources as industrial raw materials exchanging on primary commodities markets. Two questions must then be addressed. The first of these concerns what we mean by scarcity and the second focuses on why the scarcity of natural resources would present more of a problem than scarcity of any other resource.

With universal abundance of all resources—that is, in the absence of scarcity—there is no role for economics, nor do we encounter any realistic situation known to human history. However, with insufficient means to satisfy all of society's ends, we must distribute the "deficiency," that is, allocate the scarce resources among competing ends. But the substance of the resource rationing problem depends on society's goals as well as the resource endowments and the state of the technology that converts natural resources into final consumer goods. We have a set of criteria by which it is possible to evaluate these choices, and they involve selecting those methods which allocate resources to their highest valued use. This process seems straightforward enough until one realizes that the values themselves are influenced by previous "efficient" allocations which determine, in part, the distributions of income and wealth. Since economic judgments on the efficacy of institutions which allocate resources to achieve predefined ends depend on the process defining these ends, it is proper to inquire as to how effectively society's larger purposes are met by the marketplace and its distribution of property rights. There is the related basic question of whether scarcity of means is increasing in severity over time relative to demands for them.

Once we broaden the definition of natural resources to include all services provided by our natural endowments, it becomes necessary to evaluate whether the set of interrelated markets is sufficiently comprehensive and discriminating to function satisfactorily in distributing scarcity. There are some ends which require resources that are not allocated through the established markets, or for that matter through any markets which could be established. Accordingly, it is reasonable to question whether all legitimate claims to our natural and man-made endowments are adequately mediated through existing markets motivated solely by the sovereignty of the consumers existing at any given moment.

---

[9] This point complements that raised by Fisher in his overview of the Barnett and Brown–Field papers in this volume (chapter 10).

Daly (chapter 3) begins his essay with a philosophical discussion of the relations between means and ends and the role of natural and social sciences in determining these means and ends. Moreover, he argues that there are unique problems associated with nonrenewable resources and their role in production technology which make it imperative to consider carefully the process which defines society's ends.

Once there is an explicit definition of these ends and the mechanisms by which they are pursued, it is possible to be more specific in defining measures of scarcity and discussing their meaning. The different consequences of natural resource scarcity compared with scarcity of any other input are also fundamental to anyone's interest in the availability of sufficient supplies of natural resources (however they might be defined). One of the attributes of the mechanisms by which means are combined to satisfy ends involves the extent to which alternative means can be used to satisfy the same ends. In his Richard T. Ely lecture, Solow makes this point directly by considering as the means labor, produced capital, and natural resources. He observed that, "If it is very easy to substitute other factors for natural resources, then there is in principle no 'problem.' The world can, in effect, get along without natural resources, so exhaustion is just an event, not a catastrophe" [10, p. 12]. Thus, to answer the question of the effects of natural resource scarcity, an analysis must go beyond either a physical inventory of available natural resources, an investigation of the nature of the production technologies (i.e., means–ends associations) which involve natural resources, or an appraisal of the pattern of demands for final goods. It must include all of these dimensions.

It seems, as we noted, that the answer to the importance of natural resource scarcity rests with the significance of natural resources in the ends–means relationship. Those economists adhering to a neoclassical framework resolve the issue in terms of the potential for substitution for natural resources in production. While their discussion is generally cast in appropriately qualified logical arguments, the quote above is an apt summary. By contrast, Georgescu-Roegen tells us that "the issue does not even concern elasticities at all. It concerns the physical finitude and irrevocable exhaustibility of natural resources" [chapter 4, p. 97]. His reasoning rests with the physical laws that govern the production activities economists seek to model. The difficulty with a strict adherence to neoclassical production function is that we are led into solutions which are inconsistent with these physical laws. More specifically, Georgescu-Roegen suggests that:

Solow and Stiglitz could not have come out with their conjuring trick had they borne in mind, first that any material process consists in the transformation of some materials into others (the flow elements) by some agents (the fund elements), and second, that natural resources are the very sap of the economic process. They are *not* just like any other production factor. A change in capital and labor can only diminish the amount of waste in the production of a commodity; no agent can create the material on which it works [chapter 4, p. 98].

Is the resolution of this divergent view merely a matter of faith?[10] We think not and will argue in what follows that it may be one must judge both the degree and scope of the quality of the approximations offered by neoclassical production functions. Therefore evaluation of prospects for resource substitution cannot proceed without a clear understanding of the limitations of these approximations.

The definition of natural resources can also be seen to be important in judging the relevance of any answer to the question of whether these resources are growing progressively more scarce. There are two approaches one might take to answer this question or to evaluate the commonly held answer to the question. One could attempt to understand the complete ends–means association and the role of natural resources in it. Or, alternatively, one might argue that since scarcity implies that the availability of a natural resource is not sufficient to satisfy the demands for it, and we do not need to know the reasons underlying any given shortage of resources in order to evaluate resource adequacy, then indirect methods will be sufficient to answer this question. It is this rationale which underlies the empirical aspects of the Barnett–Morse work and Barnett's update of it in this volume. In short, progressive increases in an index of the scarcity of natural resources, which are perceived as the source of primary commodities by Barnett and Morse, would provide indirect evidence that the outputs of the extractive sector are increasingly inadequate for the prospective pattern of economic activity. However, if research indicates that the scarcity of natural resources, as measured by the given indexes, is not changing over time, then it could be argued that there is no need to be concerned about the matter.

Such an approach presupposes that we can develop measures of scarcity which will be capable of reflecting the ends–means relationship and the role played by natural resources. It is this general issue which

---

[10] The preface to the late C. E. Ferguson's book, *The Neoclassical Theory of Production and Distribution,* suggested that placing reliance on neoclassical economic theory must be "a matter of faith." Under this view one must rely on the opinion of other distinguished economists to determine the usefulness of neoclassical models.

We prefer the view developed in Marsden, Pingry, and Whinston [11] suggesting that the production function should be tied to the engineering features of the production activities rather than to convenient functional forms with "desirable" economic properties.

underlies the Brown–Field analysis of scarcity indexes (chapter 9, this volume). Implicitly accepting the Barnett–Morse research strategy to skirt the fundamental issue of the significance of natural resources, Brown and Field review the properties of alternative indexes of scarcity and their individual ability to reflect resource availability.

This approach also assumes that the scarcity index reflects all the subtleties associated with all potential uses of the services of natural resources. That is, over a range of use levels, the marginal cost of additional services from some endowments may well be zero. However, once the level of use exceeds such a capacity threshold, additional services may only be rendered at increasing cost. It is quite proper to inquire in these circumstances if the property rights and institutions governing the allocation process register the effects of total use in the costs of each increment.

In some cases natural resources are irreversibly depleted by use, while for others the process may be reversed. Agricultural land can be regenerated within limits through crop rotation and augmenting investments. However, there have been suggestions that the use of nitrogenous fertilizers depletes the ozone layer of the atmosphere and therefore has long-term effects.

Without the benefit of a formal model, it is difficult to fully understand the extent to which scarcity indexes can or cannot reflect these factors. Accordingly, in what follows we consider the formal models of economic activities involving natural resources and describe the role of each of the papers in this volume in terms of its relationship to this formal structure.

III
Modeling the Role of Natural Resources in Extraction and Production Activities

Neoclassical Models: A Taxonomy. The economic modeling of natural resource use has a long history. In describing this research it is important to distinguish those efforts directed toward depicting the behavior of a firm engaged in extractive activities, from models of a simple economy (i.e., neoclassical growth models) which include natural resources in the production process.[11] As a general rule, research in the first category has been directed toward analyzing in a *positive* context the effects of a variety of influences such as market structure (i.e.,

---

[11] We have deliberately excluded a review of the economic models for the allocation of renewable resources. These models are considered in detail in Peterson and Fisher [12].

Hotelling [13], Stiglitz [14], Schulze [15]), taxes (i.e., Burness [16], Stiglitz [chapter 2], or uncertainty (Heal [17]) on the patterns of extraction selected by the firm.[12] The second type of study has attempted to evaluate the *normative,* or welfare implications, of different extraction patterns or the allocation systems leading to different extraction paths (see Solow [10, 18], Dasgupta and Heal [19], Dasgupta [20]). In both cases we find that natural resources are identified in terms of their uses as raw materials.[13] In all cases these models are confined to what might be considered a neoclassical tradition that *implicitly assigns a dominant role to a classically well-behaved production function,* for their results.[14] Accordingly, it is appropriate to review their principal findings and outline the research issues they suggest as significant.

This is the objective of the paper in this volume by Stiglitz. In the literature reviewed by him, use is made of two different neoclassical models, one involving behavior of the firm engaged in extractive activities, and one involving behavior of consumption (and welfare) patterns over time in the face of nonrenewable resources, using a simple aggregate growth model. It is perhaps useful to note the distinction. In the first case, firms are assumed to maximize profit subject to a variety of external influences. For example, Stiglitz has shown within a partial equilibrium setting that a (mining) firm facing a constant elasticity demand curve (for its extractive outputs) will supply the same amounts of extractive output regardless of the market structure (i.e., competitive or monopolistic) in which it operates. His analysis requires a number of simplifying assumptions, among the strongest of which is negligible extraction costs. Moreover, he argues, based on earlier research [24], that the competitive firm offers an intertemporally efficient use profile for a nonrenewable resource (chapter 2). Intertemporal efficiency, in this context, means that "the present discounted value of the net marginal product will be the same at all dates..." [chapter 2, pp. 50–51].

There are any number of questions one might pose concerning the applicability of these conclusions to natural resource policy. However, we shall defer these for the moment and attempt to use this framework to illustrate the nature of the problems associated with modeling the allocation process for natural resources. There are two aspects of the debate surrounding this class of neoclassical model that should be considered. The first of these concerns the nature of the demands for extrac-

---

[12] For a complete review of these efforts, see Peterson and Fisher [12].

[13] Notable exceptions to this view include Arrow and Fisher [21], Henry [22], and Rausser [23].

[14] It is important to recognize that these relationships were developed as convenient abstractions. We shall consider later in this paper the relationship between the engineering-process model and conventional production functions, with special reference to the work of Marsden, Pingry, and Whinston [11].

tive outputs. Kamien and Schwartz [25] have recently extended the Stiglitz results to show that if one accepts the neoclassical tradition, that is, that natural resources are basically no different from other factors of production, then the isoelastic demand functions facing these mining firms must be derived demands because of the use of the resources in some activities. The Kamien–Schwartz results indicate that the necessary and sufficient conditions for monopolistic and competitive extraction rates to be identical (in the absence of extraction costs) are the sector using the extractive outputs in its productive activities is characterized by a Cobb–Douglas production function. Further, they have extended [26] the equivalence of monopolistic and competitive firms' extraction choices to a general equilibrium setting, again with a Cobb–Douglas function representing the production activities of the sector using the extractive outputs.

Thus we must ignore incompatible uses (e.g., the conflict between extractive activities such as mining on public lands and the recreational use of the same land) in deriving the demand for the services of natural resources. This observation is crucially important to the properties we attribute to market solutions and to our analysis of the behavior of scarcity indexes based on such models. We develop this further subsequently.

The second and equally important aspect of the models of firm behavior concerns the implications of such an inquiry into the origins of the demand for extractive outputs, and the implied desirability of market-induced behavior. It leads to some interesting questions concerning the nature of activities using extractive outputs. Simply stated, the models require that the activities of all economic units involved in using extractive outputs be represented by a *modus operandi* which assumes cost minimization subject to an aggregate Cobb–Douglas production function. As with so many economic problems and the models used to analyze them, we squarely encounter a substantive aggregation problem. If a wide variety of extractive outputs are used as raw materials in many different manufacturing activities,[15] it can be mischievous to represent them as a single productive factor for our purposes. The issue, of course, is the extent of the error introduced by using the model as an approximate guide to economic behavior and policy.

There is no need to develop anew here the arguments associated with the existence of an aggregate production function for all of the activities using extractive outputs.[16] Rather, what should be recognized is that the

[15] In evaluating the hypothesis that natural resource intensive industries are also capital intensive, Moroney [27] recently used a sample based on 104 industries.
[16] Detailed treatments of these issues are available in Fisher [28], Johansen [29], and Sato [30].

results of such analyses must be interpreted with particular care. For example, Houthakker [31] has shown that an economy with fixed coefficient microlevel production relations can give rise to an aggregate production function which is Cobb–Douglas. While this finding has been extended in several ways by recent authors (see Levhari [32], Sato [30], and Johansen [29]), we can use this specific example to illustrate a set of issues. First, aggregate production is an abstraction constructed to summarize diverse forms of microbehavior. In the case of our example, aggregate substitution takes place through substitution of processes with different capital–resource intensities. Thus the difference in functional forms is not what is at issue. *Rather, it is whether the micro responses implied by aggregate substitution over the full range of labor, capital, and natural resource combinations are feasible.*

Equally important, the use of an aggregate relationship to characterize a diversity of microtechniques and to estimate the role of various natural resources in the ends–means relation may be subject to misinterpretation. Returning to our example again, the Cobb–Douglas aggregate (or any consistent aggregate function) will give a completely accurate picture of the response behavior only so long as the underlying distribution of capital over firms (micro units) does not change.[17] Thus the response to changes which give rise to alterations in this distribution may not be accurately represented within an aggregate framework. This observation suggests that the policy implications of these models may be quite limited. Moreover, estimates of the characteristics of the technology may bear no resemblance to the actual micro features. Recent stimulation experiments by Fisher, Solow, and Kearl [33] with micro CES and aggregate CES functions suggest this is indeed the case. In summary, then, the use of an aggregate framework to represent a diversity of microbehavior patterns implicitly constrains both the nature of the microtechnologies and their distribution across micro units. The closing comments of Fisher, Solow, and Kearl are particularly relevant here. They observe, "Our parting advice is to handle them [aggregate production functions] the way the old garbage man tells the young garbage man to handle garbage wrapped in plastic bags of unknown provenance: 'Gingerly, Hector, gingerly' " [33, p. 319]. This observation is important both to the modeling of the firm engaged in extractive activity and to the economy-wide models, because in both cases a single (generally simple functional form, either Cobb–Douglas or CES) production function is used to describe output-producing activities, and thus the role of extractive resources in them.

In his paper in this volume, Stiglitz defends the use of the Cobb–

[17] We are grateful to Franklin Fisher for calling this point to our attention.

Douglas function on the grounds that it represents an extreme view of natural resources. They are "essential" to production activities. This view might appear to be quite conservative. However, the Cobb–Douglas function assumes all factor inputs are essential. It also allows for ready substitution of these individually essential inputs. At first these two observations may seem at odds, but they are not. *The point is simply that production requires at least some small amount of each input (infinitesimal if one wishes), and irrespective of how small an amount we have, the remaining inputs can be used to maintain output levels.* These two attributes are indeed unusual and should be considered in judging whether the Cobb–Douglas specification actually offers a conservative viewpoint on the role of natural resources in the ends–means relationship.

Turning to aggregate models of the economy, Stiglitz has established that it is possible to sustain a constant per capita income if one of three conditions is satisfied: (1) the elasticity of substitution among natural resources, capital, and labor is greater than unity; (2) the elasticity of substitution among natural resources, capital, and labor is unity, and the elasticity of productivity for capital exceeds that of natural resources; or (3) there is a strictly positive rate of resource-augmenting technical progress [34 pp. 123–138].[18] Moreover, in a utilitarian framework, Dasgupta [20] has recently noted that if the production function exhibits either of two properties, it will not be desirable to exhaust the natural resource in finite time. These conditions are: (1) some finite amount of the natural resource is essential for production [i.e., if $F(K, N)$ is the production function, with K produced capital and N the natural resource, $F(K, 0) = 0$], or (2) the marginal product of the natural resource is unbounded for vanishing levels of use. These conditions, together with the results available from other analyses of the role of natural resources in programs that are designed to either maintain constant per capita income or maximize discounted utility, clearly indicate that the properties of the specified production function at the extreme levels of resource use (Dasgupta and Heal [19] refer to this issue as the properties in the corners) are central to the outcomes of the models.

Does substitution continue indefinitely, as some of the models appear to suggest? Is it possible to produce some output without any input of natural resources? It is important to recognize that since all the models use aggregate production function to provide the answers, the relevance of their findings to real world conditions, in part, resides with the ability of these aggregate specifications to accurately reflect the behavior

---

[18] This is an assumption that these conditions underlie the Houthakker [5] conclusion cited at the outset of the paper as well as Solow's [10] own view of the natural resource problem.

of the microtechnologies at the extremes. Unfortunately there are *no* guarantees the patterns will be consistent.

Cummings and Schulze [35] have recently raised an issue that bears on the question of unlimited substitution. They have argued that production functions may not accurately reflect the materials balance required by physical laws and thus they implicitly support, in part, the views advanced by Georgescu-Roegen in his paper in this volume. That is, it is possible that substitutions implied by conventional production functions indicate a level of material output that is incompatible with the flows of material inputs. They suggest that conventional natural resource models be amended to reflect the constraint that the ratio of output to materials (natural resource) inputs cannot exceed one. Thus their approach would call for the use of conventional production functions together with this constraint. However, the failure to meet this materials balance requirement is a direct criticism of the use of the production function as an abstract representation of the underlying production technology. Therefore, such amendments can be considered indirect reflections of the need to consider the limits to the substitutions indicated in conventional production functions.

Thus on theoretical grounds there are several reasons for caution in using these models for evaluating policies that are suggested by prospects of increasing scarcity of nonrenewable resources. It must be admitted that the aggregation issues we have considered are not restricted to the case of natural resources and are present any time policy implications are drawn from a simple aggregated formulation. But they are of critical significance for a realistic evaluation of the resource adequacy issue.

Accordingly, it appears that rather than reconstructing neoclassical models with only the names of the inputs altered, it would be useful to inquire whether there are unique features of the processes using the services of extractive resources that make the conventional neoclassical formulation ill equipped to deal with the problems for which it is being employed.

Thus far we have discussed the assumptions and potential theoretical limitations of these models on their own terms. That is, we have accepted implicitly the narrow definition of natural resources as those goods which exchange on primary commodity markets. Once the definition is expanded to be consistent with the definition we stated at the outset, a reexamination of the conclusion of the model and the associated policy implications is further justified.

There are two problems raised by ignoring the role of the nonpriced services of common property resources in neoclassical models involving natural resources. Quite aside from the inability of such limited formulations to portray all aspects of behavior, this partial view of the character of natural resources can introduce both theoretical and empirical biases in the results. Consider the analysis of a mining firm. Improvements in the state of the art governing the firm's ability to extract larger quantities of a constant quality ore or to tap lower grade deposits may be made at the expense of greater use of the services of common property resources. One of the methods used in measuring the effects of technical change in production processes calls for allocating the gains in productivity to all measured inputs for the process involved. Since the services of common property resources do not exchange on organized markets, they are omitted in these methods and thus such an evaluation contains theoretical biases associated with the underlying model as well as biased empirical analyses of the determinants of reductions in unit extraction costs. While one might call for the use of shadow prices in making such calculations, this will not change the fact that the market transactions do not reflect the use of the services of common property resources as components of the full extraction costs.

For the aggregate models, the difficulties introduced with the expanded definitions are equally striking. Omitting consideration of the services of common property resources as a type of natural resource input implicitly assumes either that: (1) these services make no contribution to the production of measured outputs, or (2) these services can be estimated from the levels of raw material inputs by assuming their use levels are proportional to those of the materials.

Consider the first of these assumptions. One might argue that we could treat common property resources in either of two ways in modeling the production process for fabricated goods. If their function is to serve as receptacles for the residues of production processes, then we might attempt to measure their use as inputs or identify dispersal medium-residual combinations as joint outputs with marketable products. Under certain conditions, the two will offer compatible descriptions of the underlying production technology. However, this specification assumes that the services of common property resources are used only as receptacles of industrial wastes, which is clearly unacceptable in such an aggregate context. It ignores their amenity, recreational, and, for that matter, life support services.

Consider the second set of assumptions implicitly underlying these models. Separability in production technology implies that the marginal technical rate of substitution between the raw materials and common property services of natural resources is independent of the levels of usage of all other factor inputs at all levels of output. In simple terms this implies that we can construct an index of the two inputs and use it to measure the production technology. The proportionality assumption assumes that the correct weights are constants. Even with this assumption, the estimated characteristics of the technology will differ from the true by a scaling factor (i.e., the unknown factor of proportionality).

However, we cannot leave the issue at this. One must inquire as to how likely these assumptions are to be satisfied. Here again even casual empiricism suggests that judgments can be made. Common property resources' services are generally different from raw materials, and their functions in the production technology may be quite different from those of materials inputs. Accordingly, it seems quite unreasonable to maintain that such restrictive conditions will hold.

Unfortunately if we abandon the restrictive assumptions, we must then admit all past estimates are biased in an unknown way. That is, the previous production technology estimates have been based on models with the specification error of omitted variables. If we assume that the level of use of the services of the common property resource (or resources) varies over the sample, then the estimates of the remaining parameters associated with priced inputs can be biased and inferences drawn from the results may be erroneous. Moreover, we might expect from a simplified view of the process of technical change, as conceptualized under an induced innovation framework, that new techniques will be selected which substitute the nonpriced services of common property resources for those which are priced. This behavior seems to suggest that a failure to account for the role of common property resources in the description of the technology can impart progressively more serious biases as a result of the induced changes in this technology over time. Accordingly, we should support Houthakker's [5] implicit call for more econometric work in this area since most of the past work has been deficient in the respects discussed above. Of course, we hasten to add that the problems which must be dealt with represent no easy task. If the services of common property resources were easily and conveniently measured, and they are not, there still would remain considerable problems. This issue does not, however, eliminate the need to evaluate seriously the shortcomings of the conventional neoclassical framework being used to make deductions regarding natural resource adequacy.

The Neoclassical Model's Physical Constraint Set. Both of the types of models described earlier have tended to accept one of two conceptions of the physical occurrence of natural resources. The first of these assumes a fixed stock of the resource, which cannot be augmented. The second assumes, as we noted in discussing the proposed explanations for the Barnett–Morse findings, that there are increasing supplies available for progressively lower grade stocks of the materials. One might reasonably inquire as to which view offers a more accurate representation of the availability of materials. Equally important, there is a need to broaden the issue considerably so that account is taken of our more general definition of natural resources.

Consider the more conventional view. In order to understand the issue of availability of materials, it is necessary to appreciate the difficulty of quantifying the unknown. That is, while our knowledge of the geological structure of the earth's crust has improved dramatically with advanced exploration techniques and the accumulation of information, there remain substantial gaps in our knowledge. It is therefore not surprising to find a diversity of accounting schemes and estimation methods for projecting the available quantity of a given material. We have included two quite divergent views of the problems involved in this area in the papers by Brobst (chapter 5) and Goeller (chapter 6). The Brobst paper provides an overview of the issues associated with defining, in a systematic way, the quantities of a resource available at a given time. Figure 5-2 in his paper describes the taxonomy adopted by the U.S. Geological Survey to classify the kinds of information available about material stocks.

Two aspects of this classification scheme are of central importance to the use of this information. They involve the factors which influence the estimates of the available supplies of a material in a given time period. The first of these issues relates to the state of knowledge concerning the physical composition of the earth's crust. In simple terms, how much do we know generally about the location, amount, and quality of various deposits of materials? Equally important, what are the characteristics of the earth's crust where these deposits occur and to what extent can we expect similar occurrences elsewhere? This latter issue is particularly important when one recognizes that all areas of the earth have not been completely explored for deposits of minerals. Moreover, those which have been investigated may not represent an ideal sample on which to base projections. Since economic motives were largely responsible for the information we have, it seems reasonable to conjecture that the most likely sources of deposits have been considered first.

Despite the improvements in technique and the increase in knowledge associated with greater exploration and extraction activities, our basis for estimates of what is available as resources is quite limited.[19] This problem is particularly acute for the data used by Goeller (chapter 6) in his

[19] The term resources is used to denote materials that occur in a particular geologic volume without consideration of whether or not the deposit is commercially exploitable. See Brooks [36] pp. 144–149 for further discussion.

analysis of the natural resource scarcity issue from the perspective of crustal abundance. Brobst noted in this regard that, "Defining accurately and precisely the chemical composition of the earth's crust becomes difficult at best, considering the problems of inadequate sampling and the variety of analytical and computational methods available" [chapter 5, p. 121]. The variation in estimates and maintained hypotheses concerning the physical disposition of materials is great. One of the most important of the accepted tenets of conventional wisdom (the first explanation of the Barnett–Morse results) is not as secure as conventional economic analysis of these issues might lead us to believe. As Brobst noted, *there is now some evidence which suggests an alternative hypothesis that conflicts with the view that progressively greater quantities of lower grade materials are always available.* Rather, there may be significant differences in the distribution of the geochemically abundant metals compared with the scarce elements. That is, several prominent geologists now suspect that the less geochemically abundant metals, the ones for which increasing demands may pose serious problems, follow a bimodal distribution. This view implies that after the richest grades are exploited, the quantity available at lower grades will decline rather than increase. Equally important, this hypothesis concerning the availability of minerals means that we may reach a level of ore concentration where a scarce element occurs only as "an isomorphous substitute" and cannot be easily concentrated.

At this stage this argument is simply a competing hypothesis. Further geological research will be necessary to discriminate between this view and the more traditional viewpoint. *However, the existence of such an alternative hypothesis and the fact that it is adhered to by growing numbers of scientists suggest that the first of the four reasons for complacency over the adequacy of materials supplies (i.e., increasing supplies of lower grade ores) must be reconsidered.* This is why we need additional evidence to discriminate between these competing hypotheses.

The second component of any forecast of available supplies of materials is based on economic considerations. That is, the reserves of a given mineral are defined both on the basis of the technical data regarding availability and physical characteristics of deposits for the element in question as well as the economic feasibility of its extraction. In other words, given existing technology and the implied extraction costs, together with current and anticipated prices, does extraction represent an economically viable activity (i.e, yield a return to the investment comparable to other competing uses for the resources)? Thus, estimates of reserves for a particular mineral can be potentially as diverse as the expectations of future price patterns. They represent one point on the long-run supply curve for the element in question. Accordingly, it is difficult to judge the consequences of alternative demand projections in terms of the reserves available in a single period. Technological change and increases in demand will likely affect both the extraction costs and future prices of minerals. Both of these considerations, together with the known characteristics of ore deposits, influence estimated reserves.

In order to assess the adequacy of our materials base, it is necessary to project how the upper left-hand corner of Brobst's figure 5-2 will change. As we have argued, this involves analyses of the geological and economic conditions underlying the extraction activities for a given mineral.

Unfortunately, the detailed analyses of these problems are limited and cannot be readily generalized. In the past, research has attempted to forecast additional reserves as a physical relationship to the elemental composition of the earth's crust.[20] There is no reason to believe that economic and geologic factors will behave in such a manner as to preserve what is a rather arbitrary statistical measure. In fact, there may be good reasons to believe such a physical relationship will be quite misleading. If one believes, as we noted earlier, that the most accessible, higher quality deposits tend to be exploited first, then past estimates of reserves related to a fixed measure of the proportion of the earth's crust that includes a given element will be subject to considerable upward bias.

The Neoclassical Model's Value System. Can the market be relied on to take into account the interests of the future? When we consider the results of present allocation decisions associated with an exhaustible resource, can we be assured that markets will fully reflect future interests? Stiglitz's answer is yes, given: (1) we assume the existence of perfectly functioning futures markets, and (2) accept the prevailing distribution of income. Moreover, on the first count his earlier [34] work (again with a Cobb–Douglas production technology) argues that:

Two kinds of problems were noted:

(a) A long-run instability associated with the inability of the economy to foresee infinitely far into the future, and, thus a tendency either to use resources too slowly or too quickly. Although we could establish no convincing bias in either direction, we did note that excessive rates of exhaustion would become apparent in finite time, while too slow rates of exhaustion might never be detected; the consequences of the former are, of course, far more serious than the latter.

[20] See McKelvey [37] and Erickson [38].

(b) An exogenous increase in the expected rate of increase in the price of natural resources might require large changes in the price of natural resources and/or might result in large disturbances in other markets as the capital market attempts to return to equilibrium.

This is about as far as our analysis can take us without explicitly taking into account uncertainty about the rate of change in prices, and the differences among individuals about the likely rate of exhaustion of natural resources. [24, p. 151]

On the interests of the future as they are associated with the distribution of income, he would argue that the appropriate way of reflecting these concerns is through monetary policy to alter the rate of interest and the intertemporal allocation of resources.

By contrast, Page [39] has stated that these arguments are based solely on the preferences of the current generation. The present value criterion discounts all benefits and costs back to them. It does not resolve conflicts between generations over resource allocations, but rather, in Page's view, assumes them away, considering allocations as reversible in the sense that increased accumulation of produced capital always more than compensates for the losses of natural resources. He observes that:

Markets can be expected to allocate resources more or less efficiently relative to a given distribution of wealth or market power (a hypothetical ideal market would actually achieve efficiency). But markets cannot be expected to solve the problem of what is fair or equitable distribution of wealth, either among different people at a point in time (intratemporally) or among different generations (intertemporally). *The questions of depletion and generation of long-lived wastes are fundamentally questions of equitable distribution of burden across generations.* The problem of a fair intertemporal distribution arises because the material resource base is potentially long-lived, as are some wastes. . . . Thus the same materials must be shared among many generations. [39, p. 9; emphasis added]

What are the alternatives and what are their implications for resource allocation? Any number have been proposed, ranging from a revival of interest in Ramsey's [40] egalitarian principles to a generalization of Rawl's [41] max-min principle, to intertemporal allocations (Solow [18]). Markets will only reflect the desires of the groups that can express their preferences. One must remember, of course, that such an expression requires want plus *ability to pay*. (And parenthetically, if future generations are deprived by the present of the wherewithal to pay, the market may not appear to them to have served their interests!)

Markets, when sufficiently comprehensive and perfectly functioning, satisfy the Stiglitz criteria for efficient intertemporal resource allocation. The problem of registering the interests of the future in current transactions is important, as we have just noted, even when natural resources are considered to be the same as any other input. However, with the broadened definition one might well suspect that there are values and costs associated with certain uses of these resources which are *not* reflected in their market prices.[21] Accordingly, they cannot be relied upon to establish efficient resource allocations. It follows then that the system used to value the outputs of a neoclassical model is deficient for a number of reasons. Perhaps the most obvious of these arises out of considerations of intertemporal equity.

Somewhat less apparent, though of at least equal importance in evaluating the conclusions of neoclassical models, is the question of the external effects of the extraction, production, and consumption activities that use natural resources for materials inputs. Under our general definition it might be argued that the changes in the patterns of extraction over the past three decades have increased the effective supply of the material inputs components of natural resources while reducing the amenity and life support services of these same resources.

Rosenberg's [44] description of the characteristics of the progression of technological changes in the American economy during the nineteenth and twentieth centuries, compared with earlier periods, lends some support to this viewpoint. He observed that:

A major thrust of twentieth century technology as it has been based upon the knowledge revolution has been to reduce dependence upon specific natural resource inputs. . . . industrial technology since the seventeenth and eighteenth centuries has been preoccupied with liberating productive enterprise from severe constraints imposed by dependence upon *organic* sources. . . . The more recent materials revolution may be regarded as carrying this liberation process to an entirely new level. Not only are metals being produced and alloyed in ways which make them more "finely tuned" to specific human purposes . . . but entirely new products are being synthesized which bear only the remotest relation to materials occurring in nature. [44, pp. 141–142][22]

Rosenberg did not explore the potential detrimental implications of this progressive substitution from organic to inorganic to synthetic substances. However, there is accumulating evidence that there may be significant and pervasive externalities associated with many of them.[23]

Thus, rather than augmenting the range of our production possibilities, we may have simply substituted one type of resource for another.

[21] For a discussion of the relationship between discounting and intertemporal efficiency, see Sandler and Smith [42, 43].

[22] It should be noted that the economic historians were not referring to the scientific definitions of organic. Rather they meant organic as having to do with living matter, and inorganic as nonliving sources of raw materials.

[23] See Kneese and Schulze [45].

Moreover, the reason such substitutions become a matter of concern is that the values of the latter services are not readily reflected in market transactions that, in the main, guide decisions regarding natural resource (in the larger sense of the term) use.

Daly's concern over the definition of ends and selection of means to achieve them in part reflects these issues. He noted:

As stocks of artifacts and people have grown, the throughput necessary for their maintenance has had to grow also, implying more depletion and more pollution. Natural biogeochemical cycles become overloaded. Not only has the throughput grown quantitatively, but its qualitative nature has changed. Exotic substances are produced and thrown wholesale into the biosphere— substances with which the world has had no adaptive evolutionary experience, and which are consequently nearly always disruptive. . . . [chapter 3, p. 75]

IV
Measuring Resource Adequacy

Theory. As we noted at the outset, the concept of scarcity of a resource requires some standard of comparison if it is to have meaning. Similarly, in order to appraise alternative scarcity measures, it is reasonable to ask what properties an ideal scarcity index would have. Fisher's paper in this volume answers this question directly. He observes that, "A measure of a resource's scarcity should have just one essential property: it should summarize the sacrifices, direct *and indirect,* made to obtain a unit of the resource" [chapter 10, p. 252]. If the allocation problems associated with natural resources could be fully analyzed within a comparative static framework, then the real rates of exchange could provide such a measure. Given the fact that we treat natural resources under a narrow definition as exhaustible stocks, the problem becomes somewhat more complex, as Fisher, Brown and Field, and Barnett all agree. However, their individual appraisals of the appropriate measure are not entirely consistent. Accordingly, it seems reasonable to evaluate each paper's perspective on the properties of alternative scarcity indexes.

The original Barnett–Morse study began its analysis by focusing on the *classical* concepts of scarcity and sought a measure of scarcity independent of "values." In many respects Barnett's paper in this volume continues in this classical mode. Scarcity measures, in this view, must evaluate the real resources necessary to extract a unit of material output and should not be influenced by the differential opportunity costs attached to the uses of these resource inputs. Barnett and Morse proposed two measures (but noted a preference for the first): (1) an index of "real unit costs" and (2) relative prices of extractive to nonextractive outputs. They define strong and weak scarcity using the level of their real unit costs and a relative cost measure to isolate the movements in each. Barnett and Morse did not develop a formal rationale for each of the alternative scarcity indexes. Rather, they relied on a discussion of each measure within the context of the classical views on natural resource adequacy and its measurement.

Both the Brown–Field and Fisher papers formally address these measurement problems. These authors do find agreement on two issues. First, if concern is directed to the natural resource in the ground, then rents are very likely a good scarcity index. Second, the behavior of rent as a scarcity measure is affected by stock depletion effects and the prospects for a "backstop technology." Both the Brown–Field and Fisher papers also note the importance of the definition of the resource in making these judgments. If the natural resource were defined as an extracted resource product, then these judgments would not hold. Moreover, each paper highlights difficulties involved in evaluating scarcity.

In his analysis of depletion effects, Fisher observes that while there appears to be a type of duality between cost and rent measures, with the former a good scarcity indicator with depletion effects and the latter good without them, prices seemed to be the only index which consistently increases as the resource stock is depleted. However, Fisher does argue in favor of attempting to estimate rent, noting that, "It turns out that rent on a mineral resource can be estimated, at least to a first approximation, by the marginal replacement cost, that is, the cost of discovering new deposits. This is not a bad measure of scarcity, at least of the resource 'in the ground,' in that it reflects the sacrifices required to obtain the resource" [chapter 10, p. 273].

While Fisher's analysis did not consider the Barnett–Morse definition of real unit costs, Brown and Field do. However, they choose to evaluate it in a partial equilibrium setting. As we noted, their analysis concludes that site rents reflect the actual scarcity of a resource. In an argument reminiscent of earlier work by Vickrey [46],[24] they argue that depending upon the fraction of the price accounted for by extraction costs versus rent, prices may not increase at the rate of interest, while rents will. These issues are readily illustrated with an adaptation of the price behavior of a competitive mining firm facing nonzero extraction costs devel-

[24] Vickrey [46] noted: "Attempts have been made, on occasion, to judge the degree of depletion of natural resources by studying the trend of market prices of the products. This type of analysis must be used with caution, since in most cases the prices available include processing in addition to the value of the resource in its original state. For such prices, it is not a relatively steep rate of increase in the price that indicates scarcity or impending exhaustion, rather the contrary: it is, in fact, the slowing down of the rate of increase of price in the central market that indicates increasing scarcity." [p. 320]

oped recently by Heal [47] (and also noted in a slightly different form in Stiglitz's paper). This result is given in equation (1) below:

$$\hat{P} = \left(\frac{P - MC}{P}\right) r + \frac{MC}{P} \widehat{MC} \tag{1}$$

where P = price of the natural resource
MC = marginal extraction costs
r = rate of interest
$\wedge$ = rate of increase $\left(\text{i.e., } \hat{P} = \frac{dp/dt}{P}\right)$

The rate of increase in price is thus seen to be a weighted average of the interest rate and the rate of change in the marginal extraction costs. In the special case where $MC = 0$, the model reduces to the conventional result. However, when extraction costs are not inconsequential, we find that the contribution of the interest rate to the rate of price increase is weighted by the fraction that rent $(P - MC)$ comprises in the price of the resource. In addition, changes in the marginal extraction costs also affect price movements with a weight corresponding to the proportion extraction costs (MC) bear to the price. In Brown–Field's view, this weighting system "hides" true scarcities. We have argued that the most appropriate interpretation of their results is in terms of what is defined as the resource.

Unfortunately, neither of these analyses fully captures the Barnett–Morse objectives. Barnett and Morse sought to evaluate the role of natural resources within a general equilibrium setting rather than in terms of the micro responses of the representative mining firm. Thus one might argue, as Barnett does in his paper, that they have not fully addressed the questions raised in *Scarcity and Growth*. We have selected two simplified general equilibrium models to illustrate the relationship between the Barnett–Morse real unit cost index and what would correspond to Fisher's ideal scarcity measure for an extracted natural resource —the real rates of exchange (i.e., relative prices). The first of these models was developed out of a concern for sectoral imbalances similar to that of Barnett and Morse, by Baumol [48] some four years later. Our second framework is developed directly from Jones's [49] model to analyze the comparative static properties of prices and wages in response to changes in factor supplies, technology, and income within a general equilibrium framework.

The central elements of each structure are available in Baumol [48] and Smith [50]. In what follows we have summarized briefly the insights each model provides. Consider first the Baumol model. This framework assumes the production technology is characterized by fixed input requirements. Therefore, demand influences (the effects of willingness to pay identified by Fisher, chapter 10) do not influence real rates of exchange. As a result, both the relative prices and the Barnett–Morse unit cost measure are completely determined by supply factors. Thus there is a direct relationship between the two measures, as in equation (2).

$$\frac{P_{Et}}{P_{NEt}} = a \frac{L_{Et}}{E_t} \tag{2}$$

where P_{Et} = price of extractive outputs in t

P_{NEt} = price of nonextractive outputs in t

L_{Et} = resource inputs used in obtaining extractive outputs in t

E_t = level of extractive outputs

a = technical coefficient

Once the production conditions are generalized to allow for a concave transformation function between extractive and nonextractive outputs, as with the Jones model, then both demand and supply factors will influence the behavior of real rates of exchange.[25] Equation (3) provides the relationship between the rates of change of two indexes—relative prices and unit costs in this case.[26]

$$\left(\frac{\hat{P}_{Et}}{P_{NEt}}\right) = \frac{|\theta| T_L}{\theta_{KE}\sigma_E} - \frac{(\hat{\pi}_E - \hat{\pi}_{NE})\theta_{KE}\sigma_E}{|\theta|} - \frac{|\theta|}{\theta_{KE}\sigma_E} \frac{\hat{L}_{Et}}{E_t} \tag{3}$$

where $\quad T_L$ = nonnegative measure of technical change's effects in reducing demands for labor in the production of $E(T_L > 0)$

θ_{KE} = share of the total cost accounted for by the capital (K) used in production $E(\theta_{KE} > 0)$

σ_E = elasticity of substitution between L and K in the production of $E(\sigma_E > 0)$

$|\theta|$ = the determinant of a matrix containing the share of the total costs accounted for by each factor in each sector $(|\theta| = \theta_{LNE} - \theta_{LE})$

$(\hat{\pi}_E - \hat{\pi}_{NE})$ = the relative rate of change in technology's effects on the outputs $(E$ and $NE)$ produced in the economy

[25] The Jones model which is the basis for these results makes the following assumptions: (a) There are two final goods—extractive (E) and nonextractive (NE) outputs. (b) There are two factor inputs in the production processes for each output—labor (L) and capital (K). (c) Production functions in these activities exhibit constant returns to scale with diminishing returns to factor proportions. (d) There is full employment of resources, perfect mobility, and no factor market imperfections. (e) Each commodity is intensive in the use of a given factor at all levels of factor prices and no two commodities have the same factor intensities. (f) There is perfect competition in product and factor markets.

[26] A good summary of the Jones model is available in Batra [51].

Using the simple model [i.e., equation (2)] with supply determination of the real rates of exchange, the Barnett–Morse unit cost and relative price measures of scarcity move together at the same rate. Equation (3) clearly indicates that once (1) substitutions taking place among the factor inputs used in the two sectors (extractive and nonextractive), (2) demand influences on relative prices, and (3) the pattern of technological change are taken into account, then a general conclusion on the direct correspondence between the Barnett–Morse real unit cost and the relative price measures of scarcity is not possible.[27]

The extent of agreement between the two will depend upon: (1) the relative effects of technical change in the two sectors (i.e., $\hat{\pi}_E - \hat{\pi}_{NE} \gtrless 0$), (2) the relationship between the share of the total costs accounted for in the labor in each sector (i.e., $|\theta| = \theta_{LNE} - \theta_{LE}$), and (3) the effects of technical change on the labor (L) requirements in the extractive sector.

Unfortunately this is not the end of the story on the measurement of relative scarcity. We have ignored the special features of the extractive sector that would lead to further modifications in these results, since our intention was to illustrate the problems associated with measuring scarcity of extractive outputs in several simple frameworks. One cannot ignore the effects of institutional elements affecting allocation decisions. For example, the tax treatment of extractive outputs will affect the extent to which both indexes of resource scarcity actually reflect changes in the real rates of exchange for the resources involved. Changes in tax laws governing minerals have a long and involved history (see Page [39] for some discussion of these issues) making it difficult, if not impossible, to separate the institutional effects from those associated with the conditions of physical availability. For example, favorable tax treatment (i.e., depletion allowances and the expensing of intangible costs) can be expected to reduce prices for minerals outputs. Alternatively, price supports for agricultural commodities, demand prorationing, and the mandatory oil import quota system for petroleum offer opposing distortions.

Since such influences are present in many markets in the United States, and their existence alone would not be sufficient to dismiss any efforts to measure relative scarcity, it becomes necessary to appraise their potential effects on the observed prices at a moment in time and the pattern of change in these prices with the passage of time. Here again, the information is limited, but what evidence there is indicates the problems

---

[27] See Stiglitz (chapter 2) for further discussion of these issues.

introduced by differential taxes and subsidies across sectors must be given serious consideration.[28]

One final technical issue arises with measurement as with modeling. That is, aggregation affects our ability to evaluate the implications of any change in the index. Simply stated, the movement in an index can be the result of changes in the real rates of exchange or of changes in the composition of goods involved in the index over time. Clearly this issue is not a new one and plagues any attempts to evaluate price movements at an aggregate level. While Barnett and Morse did examine alternative base years for their weighting system without apparent effects on their findings, this problem is more fundamental and concerns not only the stability of the constructed indexes but also their interpretation.

Practice. Harold Barnett's updated analysis (chapter 8) of the Barnett–Morse real unit cost and relative price trends in the United States and in selected other countries using aggregate and disaggregated data does not offer any reasons to consider amending the conclusions expressed in *Scarcity and Growth*. A review of the results of his regression analyses of the trends in a variety of relative price series would lead one to the conclusion, on the basis of the evidence presented, that for the most part there does not appear to be a growing scarcity of extractive materials (using the narrow definition). Moreover, if one accepts his arguments concerning our ability to treat environmental quality issues separately from those associated with scarcity of natural resource commodities, then little has changed since the publication of *Scarcity and Growth*.

However, this view may overlook some important issues associated with the statistical analysis of these data. The hypothesis underlying the statistical trend analysis is that there is either no association or a constant negative association between the relative prices of extractive outputs and time. If the regression analysis indicates an insignificant relation or one which is statistically significant with a negative trend coefficient, then the implication is that the hypothesis of increasing relative resource scarcity can be rejected. Unfortunately, given the time spans involved as well as the factors noted in section I of this paper, yet another plausible explanation of the behavior patterns for relative prices, which would invalidate the whole testing procedure itself, is possible. That is, there

---

[28] Brannon's [52] evaluation of the effects of tax treatment on the inputs to energy industries suggests that they are substantial. His analysis indicated that the net value of tax benefits as a percent of the delivered price of the resource input to electric power companies ranged from 2.8 to 12.9 percent in 1971, with uranium receiving the smallest benefits and oil the largest.

may be no *constant* association between relative prices and time. The relationship may well vary from subperiod to subperiod within a given sample. Without prior knowledge of these periods, it is difficult to apply conventional methods of hypothesis testing. Smith's [53] analysis of Manthy's [54] updated Potter–Christy [55] data (those used in the original Barnett–Morse study) indicates that there appears to be considerable instability in such simple trend models when used with the indexes of extractive sector prices relative to both the wholesale price and consumer price indexes over the period 1900 to 1973. *Accordingly, the rejection of a hypothesis of increasing natural resource scarcity that is based on the results of simple statistical tests using these data alone must be viewed as not substantiated.* We should be clear on this point. Smith's evidence does not necessarily indicate that materials are growing increasingly more scarce. Rather, it suggests that one cannot obtain a reliable answer from simple trend analysis with relative price data for the aggregate components of the extractive sector.

V
Some Unanswered Questions

When the views presented in this volume are considered from their most general perspective, they seem to offer questions as to the validity of the four factors we presented at the outset as tempering influences on materials scarcity in the future. Brobst's work identifies a hypothesis competing with the conventional wisdom that lower grade minerals are always available in greater quantities. He argues that there is increasing evidence of a difference between the patterns observed for the abundant versus the scarce elements. Goeller's paper does not necessarily contradict this view. Rather, it suggests that from a very long-term perspective assuming continuous technological improvements, it should be feasible eventually to rely on the content of the earth's crust. In effect, he implicitly assumes away the problems associated with extracting elements in silicate structures. He may be correct if time poses no problem, but increasingly we are coming to recognize that the time constraints within which "backstop technologies" have to be on line are potentially quite limiting. It is difficult to deal meaningfully with his speculations. Nonetheless, he does agree with Brobst that energy will be critical to the adequacy of both short- and long-term material supplies and we know that there are time constraints to be met in developing backstop technologies in the energy field.

It is at this juncture that a part of the Daly argument drawn from the work of Georgescu-Roegen [6] and our classification of natural resources should be reconsidered. Even with technical advances, can we indefinitely continue to convert low entropy energy resources to higher entropy forms?[29] The answer seems to be no. However, what is of central importance to resource allocation is the time horizon over which this constraint might be considered binding. It seems unlike the case of the physical availability of materials in that here the time horizon could conceivably be bounded by eons, not years. Therefore one's view of the problems introduced by entropy turns on an individual's philosophical view of man's activity and his role in the universe. As Wiener [56] noted over twenty-five years ago:

[T]he question of whether to interpret the second law of thermodynamics pessimistically or not depends on the importance we give to the universe at large, on the one hand, and to the islands of locally decreasing entropy which we find in it, on the other. Remember that we ourselves constitute such an island of decreasing entropy, and that we live among other such islands. The result is that the normal prospective difference between the near and the remote leads us to give far greater importance to the regions of decreasing entropy and increasing order than to the universe at large. [56, pp. 39–40]

The Georgescu-Roegen (chapter 4) and Daly (chapter 3) discussions do raise an important issue associated with the conventional modeling of production processes. Unfortunately it seems that much economic research has lost sight of the original role of the production function in economic analysis. This function was developed to facilitate the modeling of firm behavior. It offered a simplified view of the relationship between inputs and outputs in a more complex underlying technology. As a shorthand, then, it can yield considerable insight into the influences on firm behavior. However, one must not lose sight of its abstract character. The validity of the production function construct with natural resources treated as an input goes to the heart of the second factor advanced as mitigating natural resource scarcity. Stiglitz and most neoclassical modelers treat natural resources as if they were "conventional inputs." While this view may be suitable for those natural resources which function as raw materials inputs to production over limited ranges of prospective substitution, it is not necessarily valid for addressing the problem when it involves services of nonpriced common property environmental resources also required in production and consumption processes. In order to understand the difficulties involved here, it is necessary to inquire into the adjustments taking place in a given production process which underlie the substitutions an economist estimates with the pro-

[29] Georgescu-Roegen [6] defines entropy as "an index of the amount of unavailable energy in a given thermodynamic system at a given moment of its evolution" [p. 351].

duction function abstraction. For example, consider the case of a process using capital, labor, and fuel inputs. An observed substitution of fuel for labor (say in response to changes in their relative prices) may involve the use of a different type of fuel which requires less labor input in the production activities. Alternatively, we might observe changes in the processes used to manufacture products. Here again, there may be a limited range of alternative processes available at a given time and for given final outputs. The adjustments to these processes implied by the factor substitutions represented in an abstract production function may well violate physical laws. Marsden, Pingry, and Whinston [11], in comparing the relationship between production processes with the specific physical reactions involved and their abstract representation by production functions observe that:

A basic dichotomy in the emphasis of the engineering and economic production functions becomes readily apparent here. When models of the type introduced earlier in the paper [mass energy balance relationships] are applied to processes including significant relative amounts of labor, it becomes increasingly difficult to meaningfully quantify equations of the form (3) [an explicit relationship for reaction rates] . . . in the more highly technical processes, which are becoming more and more prevalent, where labor does not enter as a substitutable input, the engineering formulation is directly applicable. Indeed, we argue that this approach is preferable since it provides a basis for important direct technical analysis. [11, pp. 136–137; bracketed notes added]

These implied adjustments must be consistent with certain basic physical laws. If the production process involves combustion of fossil fuels, the source of the carbon (i.e., fuel used) can be changed or the manner in which it is exposed to oxygen altered within limits (i.e., change in process used), but the chemistry of combustion determines the fixed proportion in which carbon and oxygen combine in the joint production of heat and carbon dioxide. Implied substitutions in a production function can be deceiving. They are principally *local approximations* of discrete changes in a technology, and do not necessarily imply that substitution can continue indefinitely, as the abstract generalization suggests.

The third factor tending to reduce the effects of increased demand for materials is the incentive to recycling and further exploration provided by price increases. Some natural resources cannot be recycled regardless of the inducements offered. In other cases, however, in which the services of the resources exchange in markets and recycling is technically feasible, price increases can offer incentives. We do not understand well enough, as the Brobst paper (chapter 5) notes, the relationships between exploratory activity and the creation of new reserves. So there may be scope for these types of adjustments. However, where the resource services do not exchange in markets because of their inherent characteristics, we cannot be sure the inducements will move in the correct direction. Moreover, for certain uses of these resources, it may be well to treat them as nonrenewable. Disposal of long-term, nondegradable substances into the ambient environment is limited by the capacity of the environment to receive them and still continue to sustain life forms as we know them.

Finally, technical change can be a mixed blessing. While it is true that innovations are viewed, in the most popular models of endogenous technical change, as motivated by cost reduction objectives, it is also true that these models offer unsettling descriptions of firm behavior in the use of nonpriced factor inputs. Microeconomic models of induced technical change suggest that the profit-maximizing firm will select its innovations to economize on the use of factor inputs according to their respective share in the total costs of production. Thus as raw material inputs to production processes account for an increasing fraction of total costs, the firm is induced to explore those avenues which will use the factors accounting for a smaller fraction of total costs. While these models do not offer insights into behavior at "corner solutions," it seems reasonable to conjecture that this type of behavior favors the use of the nonpriced services of common property resources. That is, these resource inputs, which function as receptacles for the residues of production and consumption processes, have been used extensively without adding to the total costs of production. Accordingly, it is not unreasonable to argue that technical change may have been induced to substitute the nonpriced services of natural resources for those generally associated with raw materials which exchange on organized commodity markets.

In summary, we find the issues raised in the papers which follow sufficiently convincing to merit a fresh look at the definition, modeling, and measurement of the role of natural resources in production and consumption processes. Since the papers are diverse and their recommendations in some cases specialized, we have reserved until the end of the volume discussion of the central elements that in our judgment should be reflected in the research agenda in this area.

References

1. R. N. Cooper, "Resource Needs Revisited," *Brookings Papers on Economic Activity* no. 1 (Washington, D.C., Brookings Institution, 1975).
2. O. C. Herfindahl, "Can Increasing Demands on Resources be Met?" in D. B. Brooks, ed., *Resource Economics: Selected Works of Orris C. Herfindahl* (Baltimore, Johns Hopkins University Press for Resources for the Future, 1974).

3. C. Morse, "Depletion, Exhaustibility and Conservation," in W. A. Vogely, ed., *Economics of the Mineral Industries* (3rd. ed., New York, American Institute of Mining, Metallurgical and Petroleum Engineers, 1976).

4. H. H. Landsberg, L. L. Fischman, and J. L. Fisher, *Resources in America's Future* (Baltimore, Johns Hopkins University Press for Resources for the Future, 1963).

5. H. S. Houthakker, "The Economics of Nonrenewable Resources," Paper No. 493 (Cambridge, Mass., Harvard Research Institute, 1976).

6. N. Georgescu-Roegen, "Energy and Economic Myths," *Southern Economic Journal* vol. 41 (January 1975) pp. 347–381.

7. H. Kahn, W. Brown, and L. Martel, *The Next 200 Years: A Scenario for America and the World* (New York, Morrow, 1976).

8. D. H. Meadows, D. L. Meadows, J. Randers, and W. W. Behrens, III, *The Limits to Growth* (New York, Universe Books, 1972).

9. Edward Denison, "Effects of Selected Changes in the Institutional and Human Environment upon Output per Unit of Input," Reprint 335 (Washington, D.C., Brookings Institution, 1978).

10. R. M. Solow, "The Economics of Resources or the Resources of Economics," *American Economic Review* vol. 64 (May 1974) pp. 1–14.

11. J. Marsden, D. Pingry, and A. Whinston, "Engineering Foundations of Production Functions," *Journal of Economic Theory* vol. 9 (1974) pp. 124–140.

12. F. M. Peterson and A. C. Fisher, "The Exploitation of Renewable and Nonrenewable Natural Resources," *Economic Journal* vol. 87 (December 1977) pp. 681–721.

13. H. Hotelling, "The Economics of Exhaustible Resources," *Journal of Political Economy* vol. 39 (April 1931).

14. J. Stiglitz, "Monopoly and the Rate of Extraction of Exhaustible Resources," *American Economic Review* vol. 66 (September 1976) pp. 655–661.

15. W. D. Schulze, "The Optimal Use of Non-Renewable Resources: The Theory of Extraction," *Journal of Environmental Economics and Management* vol. 1 (May 1974) pp. 53–73.

16. H. S. Burness, "On the Taxation of Nonreplenishable Natural Resources," *Journal of Environmental Economics and Management* vol. 3 (December 1976) pp. 289–311.

17. G. Heal, "Economic Aspects of Natural Resource Depletion," in D. W. Pearce, ed., *The Economics of Natural Resource Depletion* (New York, Wiley, 1975).

18. R. M. Solow, "Intergenerational Equity and Exhaustible Resources," *The Review of Economic Studies*, Symposium on the Economics of Exhaustible Resources, 1974.

19. P. Dasgupta and G. M. Heal, "The Optimal Depletion of Exhaustible Resources," *The Review of Economic Studies*, Symposium on the Economics of Exhaustible Resources, 1974.

20. P. Dasgupta and G. H. Heal, "Resource Depletion, Research and Development and the Social Rate of Discount," Paper presented at Resources for the Future Conference on Energy Planning and the Social Rate of Discount, March 1977.
21. K. J. Arrow and A. C. Fisher, "Preservation, Uncertainty, and Irreversibility," *Quarterly Journal of Economics* vol. 88 (May 1974) pp. 312–319.
22. C. Henry, "Option Values in the Economics of Irreplaceable Assets," *The Review of Economic Studies*, Symposium on the Economics of Exhaustible Resources, 1974.
23. G. C. Rausser, "Technological Change, Production, and Investment in Natural Resource Industries," *American Economic Review* vol. 64 (December 1974) pp. 1049–1059.
24. J. Stiglitz, "Growth with Exhaustible Natural Resources: The Competitive Economy," *The Review of Economic Studies*, Symposium on the Economics of Exhaustible Resources, 1974.
25. M. I. Kamien and N. L. Schwartz, "A Note on Resource Usage and Market Structure," *Journal of Economic Theory* vol. 15 (June 1977) pp. 394–397.
26. M. I. Kamien and N. L. Schwartz, "The Optimal Resource Capital Ratio and Market Structure," Discussion Paper No. 233 (Evanston, Ill., Center for Mathematical Studies in Economics and Management Science, Northwestern University, August 1976).
27. J. R. Moroney, "Are Natural Resources Capital Using? A Microanalytic Approach," *Southern Economic Journal* vol. 43 (January 1977) pp. 1203–1217.
28. F. M. Fisher, "The Existence of Aggregate Production Functions," *Econometrica* vol. 37 (October 1969) pp. 553–577.
29. L. Johansen, *Production Functions* (Amsterdam, North-Holland, 1972).
30. K. Sato, *Production Functions and Aggregation* (Amsterdam, North-Holland, 1975).
31. H. S. Houthakker, "The Pareto Distribution and the Cobb–Douglas Production Function in Activity Analysis," *Review of Economic Studies* vol. 23 (1955–56) pp. 27–31.
32. D. Levhari, "A Note on Houthakker's Aggregate Production Function in a Multifirm Industry," *Econometrica* vol. 36 (January 1968) pp. 151–154.
33. F. M. Fisher, R. M. Solow, and J. M. Kearl, "Aggregate Production Functions: Some CES Experiments," *Review of Economic Studies* vol. 44 (June 1977) pp. 305–320.
34. J. Stiglitz, "Growth with Exhaustible Natural Resources: Efficient and Optimal Growth Paths," *The Review of Economic Studies*, Symposium on the Economics of Exhaustible Resources, 1974.
35. R. Cummings and W. D. Schulze, "Ramsey, Resources, and the Conservation of Mass-Energy." Paper presented at Conference on Natural Resource Pricing, Trail Lake, Wyoming, August 1977.

36. D. B. Brooks, "Mineral Supply as a Stock," in W. A. Vogely, ed., *Economics of the Mineral Industries* (3rd. ed., New York, American Institute of Mining, Metallurgical and Petroleum Engineers, 1976).
37. V. E. McKelvey, "Relation of Reserves of the Elements to their Crustal Abundance," *American Journal of Science* vol. 258-A (1960).
38. R. L. Erickson, "Crustal Abundance of Elements and Mineral Reserves and Resources," D. A. Brobst and W. P. Pratt, eds., in *United States Mineral Resources*, Professional Paper 820 (Washington, D.C., U.S. Geological Survey, 1973).
39. R. T. Page, *Conservation and Economic Efficiency* (Baltimore, Johns Hopkins University Press for Resources for the Future, 1977).
40. F. P. Ramsey, "A Mathematical Theory of Saving," *Economic Journal* vol. 38 (December 1928) pp. 543–559.
41. J. Rawls, *A Theory of Justice* (Cambridge, Mass., Harvard University Press, 1971).
42. T. Sandler and V. Kerry Smith, "Intertemporal and Intergenerational Pareto Efficiency," *Journal of Environmental Economics and Management* vol. 2 (February 1976) pp. 151–159.
43. T. Sandler and V. Kerry Smith, "Intertemporal and Intergenerational Pareto Efficiency Revisited," *Journal of Environmental Economics and Management* vol. 4 (September 1977) pp. 252–257.
44. N. Rosenberg, *Technology and American Economic Growth* (New York, Harper & Row, 1972).
45. A. V. Kneese and W. D. Schulze, "Environment, Health and Economics —The Case of Cancer," *American Economic Review, Proceedings* vol. 67 (February 1977) pp. 326–332.
46. W. Vickrey, "Economic Criteria for Optimum Rates of Depletion," in Mason Gaffney, ed., *Extractive Resources and Taxation* (Madison, University of Wisconsin Press, 1967).
47. G. Heal, "The Long-Run Movement of the Prices of Exhaustible Resources." Paper presented at International Economic Association Conference on Economic Growth and Resources, Tokyo, Japan, September 1977.
48. W. J. Baumol, "Macroeconomics of Unbalanced Growth: The Anatomy of Urban Crisis," *American Economic Review* vol. 57 (June 1967) pp. 415–426.
49. R. W. Jones, "The Structure of Simple General Equilibrium Models," *Journal of Political Economy* vol. 73 (December 1965) pp. 557–572.
50. V. Kerry Smith, "A Note on Baumol's Unbalanced Growth Model," *Public Finance* vol. 30 (1975) pp. 127–130.
51. R. N. Batra, *Studies in the Pure Theory of International Trade* (New York, St. Martins, 1973).
52. G. M. Brannon, "Existing Tax Differentials and Subsidies Relating to the Energy Industries," in G. M. Brannon, ed., *Studies in Energy Tax Policy* (Cambridge, Mass., Ballinger, 1975).

53. V. Kerry Smith, "Measuring Natural Resource Scarcity: Theory and Practice," *Journal of Environmental Economics and Management* vol. 5 (May 1978) pp. 150–171.
54. R. Manthy, *Natural Resource Commodities 1870–1973: Prices, Output, Consumption, and Employment* (Baltimore, Johns Hopkins University Press for Resources for the Future, 1978).
55. N. Potter and F. T. Christy, Jr., *Trends in Natural Resource Commodities* (1870–1957) (Baltimore, Johns Hopkins University Press for Resources for the Future, 1962).
56. N. Wiener, *The Human Use of Human Beings* (New York, Doubleday, 1954).

2

A Neoclassical Analysis of the Economics
of Natural Resources

J. E. Stiglitz

I
Introduction

The oscillations in the general views on the prospects for the future, alternating between the despair of imminent and inevitable doom and the euphoria of an impending new millenium, have a remarkable regularity about them, perhaps matching that of the long business cycle. The nineteenth century concern about the implications of the second law of thermodynamics, as represented, for instance, in the work of Henry Adams, has its twentieth century counterpart in Georgescu-Roegen, and Malthus's worry about food scarcity has its twentieth century counterpart in Meadows and Forrester. There are those who would suggest that the nineteenth century preachers of inevitable progress have been replaced by the modern neoclassical economist who, if he does not believe that we are on the verge of the new millenium, finds it difficult to take seriously the prognostications of imminent doom.

What are we to make of these continuing controversies? How could what appears to be essentially the same controversy continue for so long (not always, of course, with the same intensity)? Those who forecast imminent disaster in the nineteenth century were clearly wrong. Why were they wrong? Were they wrong only in the time predicted for disaster but correct in their long-run analysis?

There are, I think, two reasons for the failure to resolve these disputes. The first is that the issues have not been posed in such a way as to admit an unambiguous answer. The second is that, when properly posed, it becomes clear that some of the more important issues cannot be answered on the basis of presently available evidence.

This paper attempts to pose what I consider the appropriate ques-

The author is indebted to V. Kerry Smith for his helpful comments on an earlier draft.

tions and to suggest what kind of evidence might resolve them. There are, of course, important policy issues in which one's position inevitably depends on the answers to these unresolved questions. What is one to do until these are obtained? Some preliminary thoughts on this question constitute the third objective of this paper.[1] However, there are a few distinctions which will help clarify the scope of my subject.

First, it is obvious that continued exponential growth is impossible, if only because eventually, at a strictly positive growth rate, the mass of people would exceed the mass of the earth. I am not concerned here with such very long-run problems. (Similarly, I am not concerned with long-run problems arising from the laws of thermodynamics.) I am concerned here with the more immediate future.

Second, it is important to distinguish between natural resources which can be treated as *private goods,* such as coal, oil, and iron, and those which are basically *public goods,*[2] such as air and water. Whether public intervention is required in the allocation of the former is at least a moot question about which we shall have much to say later; but in the case of the public goods, appropriate allocation inevitably will require some type of government action. There is a third category of natural resources— those which are normally publicly managed but which are really private goods, as for example, forests. A clear distinction has to be made between these resources and true public goods.

Although it is often clear whether the good is a public good, a private good, or a publicly provided private good, there are some ambiguous cases. The fish in a lake are often thought of as a public good although fish caught by one individual may reduce the amount available to others, and property rights for fishing in a lake could be given to an individual. The appropriate method of organizing the allocation of such goods is one of the more important issues in the economics of natural resources.

Third, I have not yet defined what I mean by natural resources. Presumably a natural resource is any commodity or factor which is provided by nature and not produced, or producible, by man. Although such a definition is not very precise, it will suffice for our purposes. (Most of what we think of as natural resources, such as oil, require human activity

---

[1] I was asked by RFF to present a survey of the neoclassical view of the problem of the scarcity of natural resources. I have chosen to provide an "interpretive review" rather than an exhaustive review of the literature; for the latter, see Peterson and Fisher [1].

[2] The distinction I have in mind is based on the traditional definition of public goods: those involving difficulties in appropriability and those in which the marginal cost of an extra person enjoying the benefits of the good is zero. Thus coal can be marketed just like any other produced good and if one person burns a unit of coal, it is not available for use by any other individual. It would be hard to charge for the use of air.

to convert them into a useful form and indeed to extract them from the ground. Moreover, the supply of many natural resources, say fish, can be affected by human activity.) It will, however, be useful to consider some polar cases. These are *exhaustible natural resources,* the supply of which is fixed and cannot be augmented; *renewable natural resources* such as fish, the supply of which can be increased (renewed) after utilization; *inexhaustible but nonaugmentable resources,* for example, land; and *recyclable resources.*

In fact, many cases do not fall into these neat categories; land—at least arable land—can be augmented as well as depleted. A resource which was perfectly recyclable would essentially be inexhaustible but nonaugmentable, while so long as some of the resource cannot be recovered for reuse, a recyclable resource is like an exhaustible natural resource.

We used to think of air as an inexhaustible resource. Clean air, we now recognize, is a resource which can be exhausted, but in most cases it should be viewed as a renewable natural resource: by taking appropriate action, a dirty atmosphere can be changed into a clean one if there is sufficient time.

I am primarily concerned here with the first category of natural resources, that is, exhaustible, nonrenewable, natural resources, since they are considered to pose the most serious problem. Much of what I shall have to say is, however, applicable with appropriate modifications to the other categories as well.

The paper is divided into eight sections. Section II identifies the major issues; sections III–VI are concerned with each of the major issues in turn; section VII is concerned with a brief discussion of two important recent policy issues, and our concluding remarks are contained in section VIII.

II
The Issues

There are several distinct issues which have become confused in many of the popular discussions of resource availability. This section is intended to help identify and distinguish them.

Viability.   Is it possible to have sustained economic growth? This is concerned not with the question of whether it is likely that we face imminent doom if we do not take remedial action soon (the forecasting issue), but with whether doom is *inevitable.* Is there anything we can do? This is one of the questions to which neoclassical economics has provided a clear answer. There are conditions under which growth cannot be sustained and conditions under which it can. In section III we identify these conditions.

Forecasting. Forecasting is concerned with predicting what the world will be like in twenty-five, fifty, or a hundred years. One might be interested in a forecast to satisfy one's curiosity by gazing into a crystal ball. But information is valuable mainly to the extent that it leads to alteration in behavior, and usually the forecasters have some policy prescription in mind. Thus their forecasts have a qualification, "unless a certain prescribed course of action is taken." Forecasting usually entails an extrapolation of past events into the future; this extrapolation requires certain, usually quite strong assumptions, and a great deal of the disagreement concerning predictions is concerned with precisely those assumptions. We talk about these assumptions at greater length in section IV.

There are two distinctive issues on which the forecasts of the future are supposed to provide us with some information. (1) The more popular versions focus on some cataclysm; the economy, in any form similar to that which we presently know, is not viable. "We shall be unable to sustain current energy consumption rates." "The temperature of the earth will increase by $x°$ and New York City will be under water." "We shall suffocate from . . . poisoning." (2) The more mundane versions are concerned with estimating the magnitude of the increase in natural resource prices and gauging the effect of this increase on our standard of living.

Efficiency. The question of whether we are wasting our resources is quite separate from the question of whether doom is imminent or inevitable. We might not be facing imminent doom, yet we could still be misusing our resources. Much of the popular literature seems to take the position that doom is not inevitable but because of wastage of resources, it is nevertheless likely to occur, perhaps soon, and it is in this sense that the three issues are closely linked.

There are a number of reasons that the economy might not allocate natural resources efficiently, some arising out of peculiarities of the private market, and some arising from particular government actions. These are discussed in section V.

Intertemporal Equity. The economy could be efficient, resources might be being used efficiently, but still, because of the rate at which we use our resources, our descendants will be poorer. There is a tradeoff between our consumption and that of our descendants, and the market solution may be inequitable. We shall have a few words to say on this in section VI.

III
The Viability Issue: Is Sustained Growth Possible in the Presence of Exhaustible Natural Resources?

Any analysis of the economics of natural resources should, I think, begin with the question of why the scarcity of natural resources is different from the scarcity of any other factor of production (or any commodity, for that matter). The layman's response to this question would probably be that if we run out of corn we can produce more corn. With natural resources there is simply nothing we can do. This, of course, is not a completely satisfactory answer.

For there to be a meaningful natural resource problem, several conditions need to be satisfied:

1. A resource must be in limited supply relative to current usage rates; thus, if there are several hundred years' worth of reserves[3] of some natural resource, there is, at most, a very long-run problem.

2. It must be nonrenewable and nonrecyclable. Natural resources (such as metals) do not disappear after they are used; rather, they become available for reuse. Only that part which is not renewable—or more precisely, that part, for which the cost of renewing to a marketable state will exceed the market prices—is exhausted in economic terms. The net utilization rate of natural resources may thus be considerably less than the gross.

3. It must be essential, that is, it must be required for production (or consumption).

4. There cannot exist substitutes for it; for example, capital cannot be substituted for it in production.

5. It must be impossible to improve the efficiency with which the resource is utilized beyond some point; for there to be an immediate problem, we must be near that point. Technical change which increases the productivity of a resource is referred to as "resource-augmenting technical progress," since its effect is equivalent to an increase in the stock of the resource.

---

[3] I have used the term "reserves" in the casual way that it is usually used; it is important to observe, however, that the natural economic definition of reserves is not that conventionally employed, for example, by geologists. Since the amount of a natural resource which can be extracted depends on the expenditure on extraction, reserves is an economic, not a geological concept. The appropriate definition entails an analysis of how much can be extracted, not at current market prices, but at market prices that will prevail as the supply becomes smaller; there is some presumption that this may be significantly larger than that implied by the conventional definitions.

6. It must be impossible to develop a substitute for the given resource.

Several of the recent articles on the economics of natural resources have attempted to make more precise the conditions under which it is possible to sustain a constant per capita consumption [2–4]. Most of these conditions are fairly intuitive.

The assumption that the natural resource is essential implies that the isoquants (between the natural resource and the other produced factors of production) never hit the axis of the produced factor. (See figures 2-1 to 2-7 where the other factor of production is taken to be capital. In figure 2-1 natural resources are essential; in figure 2-2 natural resources are not essential.) Note that what is crucial for the question of whether the natural resource is essential is not any property of the production (isoquant) function when there is a large input of natural resources. If the isoquant has relatively little curvature (i.e., is flat, as in figure 2-3) we might be tempted to extrapolate the curve and to infer that the natural resource is nonessential, but the curvature could easily be changed as the resource input becomes small, so that although at present it is easy to substitute, say capital, for resources, eventually it becomes quite difficult. Conversely, it may be quite difficult to substitute now (the isoquant can still be quite curved) but when the resources become sufficiently scarce, we may be able to switch to a completely different technology, for which the substitution is relatively easy, and the isoquant does hit the axis (figure 2-4).

The concept that economists usually use for measuring the ease of substitution is the "elasticity of substitution," which gives the percentage change in the input ratio (say, of natural resources to capital) which would be engendered by a percentage change in the relative price of capital to natural resources.[4] If a 1 percent change in relative prices does not give rise to a change in factor inputs (figure 2-5), the elasticity of substitution is zero; if we discontinue using the factor whose price has risen, we say that the elasticity is infinite. The central case where a 1 percent change in factor prices gives rise to a 1 percent change in factor inputs is called the Cobb–Douglas production function.[5] If the elasticity of substitution between natural resources and capital and/or labor is

[4] The production function $Q = \phi([aK^\rho + (1 - a)R^\rho]^{1/\rho}, L)$ where Q is output; K is the stock of capital; R is the flow of natural resources used in production; L is the labor supply has a constant elasticity of substitution between K and R: $\partial Q/\partial K = \phi[aK^\rho + (1 - a)R^\rho]^{1/\rho-1}aK^{\rho-1}$; $\partial Q/\partial R = \phi[aK^\rho + (1 - a)R^\rho]^{1/\rho-1}(1 - a)R^{\rho-1}$

$-1/\sigma \equiv$ elasticity of substitution $= \dfrac{d \ln [(\partial Q/\partial K)/(\partial Q/\partial R)]}{d \ln K/R} = \dfrac{1}{(\rho - 1)}$.

[5] The Cobb–Douglas production function can be written: $Q = K^{\alpha_1}R^{\alpha_2}L^{\alpha_3}$, $\alpha_1 + \alpha_2 + \alpha_3 = 1$. With a constant population, a sustained per capita consumption is possible if $\alpha_1 > \alpha_2$.

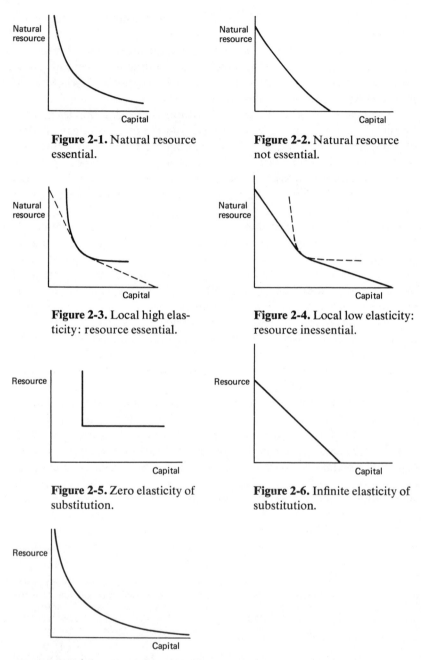

Figure 2-1. Natural resource essential.

Figure 2-2. Natural resource not essential.

Figure 2-3. Local high elasticity: resource essential.

Figure 2-4. Local low elasticity: resource inessential.

Figure 2-5. Zero elasticity of substitution.

Figure 2-6. Infinite elasticity of substitution.

Figure 2-7. Unity elasticity of substitution.

constant, then a sustained constant per capita consumption is feasible if (1) the elasticity is greater than unity, or (2) if the elasticity is unity and if the share of capital exceeds that of natural resources.

If the elasticity of substitution is not constant, what is crucial is what happens to the elasticity asymptotically as resource input goes to zero. In these cases the produced input is sufficiently substitutable for the natural resource that the decrease in supply of the natural resource can be compensated for by an increased supply of capital. Of the two cases, the Cobb–Douglas case is clearly the most interesting for there natural resources are essential in the sense that some input of the natural resource is required for production (the isoquants never do hit the axes). But a small input of natural resource can be compensated for by a sufficiently large input of capital, and whether that is feasible for the economy depends simply on the relative shares of the two.

The conditions under which technical change makes sustained per capita consumption viable are also easily interpretable. The development of a produced substitute can be interpreted as changing the isoquant so that in fact it does hit the natural resource axis. The other condition is that there be a strictly positive rate of resource-augmenting technical progress.[6] If the input of the natural resource were to decline at the rate of the resource-augmenting technical progress—clearly a feasible policy —the effective input would be constant, and with a constant population a constant per capita level of consumption would thus be viable.

IV
The Forecasting Issue

The way we have posed the problem makes it easy to see what is required if we are to forecast the future: we need to know to what extent it will be possible to substitute produced goods for natural resources and we need to know the likelihood of technical changes which will lead either to the development of substitutes or to an increase in the efficiency with which we use what resources we have.

This problem can be approached in several different ways. The "engineering approach" examines the set of presently available techniques and attempts to assess the difficulties associated with developing new technologies. There seems to be an "informed consensus" that within the next 100 years technologies for the production of essentially a boundless supply of energy at "reasonable cost" (for example, solar energy)

---

[6] A production function with factor-augmenting technical progress may be written: $Q = F(K, R, L, t) \equiv F[\mu(t)K, \gamma(t)R, \lambda(t)L]$.
One unit of resource at t is a perfect substitute for $1/\gamma(t)$ units at time zero.

will become available. On other issues, for example, whether the atmosphere will be affected by certain technological developments, there seems to be less of a consensus. The economist, I suspect, has relatively little to say on these technological issues. The economist's approach is, in some sense, much cruder. He attempts to look at the past and to extrapolate from that into the future. It is not, however, obvious what the appropriate method of extrapolation is. The crucial question is what is to be taken as a constant. For instance, is the average *rate* of growth of the input of oil and the *stock* of presently discovered oil to be taken as given? If so, we are probably indeed in trouble. Or is the rate of increase of discovered resources to be taken as given, in which case prospects are not quite so bleak. And if the rate of growth is to be calculated, over what period should we make the calculation? How is one to choose among these alternative hypotheses and calculations?

Economists approach this problem by formulating a model which is sufficiently general to encompass the entire range of competing hypotheses as special cases and then subjecting the model to empirical testing. In principle then, we should be able to ascertain, at least by extrapolating from past experience, which hypothesis is more reasonable.

If this were as easily done as said, there would be far fewer disputes. Three problems are repeatedly encountered. (1) The data may not be able to distinguish among hypotheses; that is, two alternative hypotheses could be equally consistent with past observations, yet have very different implications for the future. (2) Most tests involve some kind of parameterization; thus, the actual test performed is not of the hypotheses in their most general form. (3) The structure of the economy may have changed, making "testing" of alternative hypotheses on the basis of past data inappropriate.

Let me illustrate these points with the issue at hand. We identified in our earlier discussion two parameters determining the future viability of the economy: the elasticity of substitution and the rate of technical progress augmenting natural resources. I focus my attention here on attempts to measure the former. The question, as we noted earlier, is whether the elasticity of substitution between natural resources and, say, capital, is greater or less than unity (again, recall that what is crucial is the limiting elasticity as the input of natural resources goes to zero). Note that no simulation exercise will ever resolve the question of the correct value of a parameter such as the elasticity of substitution. Moreover, if we know the value of the elasticity, analytical methods can completely answer the question of whether the economy is viable in the long run; we do not need to resort to simulation. What simulation can do—if we have a reasonable model with reasonable estimates of the parameters—is to give us some feel for how long the long run is (for example, if there is a "long-run natural resource problem," is it likely to make itself evident in 50 or 500 years?). Simulation may also enable us to identify the crucial parameters but, here as elsewhere, direct analytical methods are likely to be less ambiguous.

The easiest way of obtaining an estimate of the elasticity of substitution entails introducing one further assumption: that of competitivity, that the prices of (returns to) factors of production equal the value of the marginal productivity of the factor. With this additional assumption, if the elasticity of substitution were much less than unity, then we should expect the share of various natural resources in national income to have changed dramatically; those which have become relatively scarce should have a rapidly increasing relative share, those for whom unexpectedly large supplies have been found (and hence, whose scarcity had previously been overestimated) should have a falling share. In fact, at least in the aggregate, such dramatic shifts do not for the most part seem to have occurred if we take as our period of calculation the past 100 years; obviously if we look only at the past few years we could obtain quite different results. In the one case—land—where there has been a marked change in the share over the past several hundred years, it has been in the wrong direction. The share of land, for instance, in the past was as high as 50 percent; today it is much less in spite of a much larger ratio of population to land.

Resource optimists might argue that the share, say of land, has declined either because the elasticity of substitution is not low and/or because the effective supply of natural resources (land), taking account of technical change, has increased.

Resource pessimists might argue against these results in a number of different ways. (1) The competitive assumption on which the analysis was based might not be true, but for them to argue that the elasticity is low, they must argue further that the degree of monopoly in natural resources has changed in a significant way. (2) The future may not be like the past: it is at this point then that recourse has to be made to the "engineering approach" discussed earlier. (3) The particular parameterization implicit in the above calculation that the elasticity of substitution is constant is not correct: for example, they might argue that as resources become scarcer, the elasticity declines.

I am not aware of any convincing test of this hypothesis; my own guess is that the data are consistent with the hypothesis of a constant elasticity of substitution, but that if some parameterizations involving nonconstant elasticities were employed, nonzero point estimates of the rate of change of the elasticity would be observed. I am not sure whether the point estimates would side with the pessimists or optimists, but the value might well vary according to the parameterization adopted. My own suspicion is that the standard errors would be large enough to allow pessimists and optimists to continue arguing their case.

No matter how the test turned out, either side could argue against the result on the grounds that the analysis had been carried on at too high a level of aggregation. A real test, it might be argued, entails an analysis at a much more disaggregated level, taking into account different productivities of different firms within the industry, elasticities of substitution within each sector, and intersector elasticities of demand. Thus, for instance, changes in the distribution of firms within a sector (say, the difference between best practice and average practice) would result in the aggregate elasticity of substitution appearing not to be constant, although the "best practice" production function does have a constant elasticity.[7] Similarly, even if the production of neither commodity A nor commodity B allows the substitution of capital for natural resources, if commodity A uses less of the resource relative to capital than does commodity B, by substituting commodity A for commodity B, we can reduce our utilization of natural resources. Thus, estimating the full potential for substituting other factors for natural resources requires an understanding of all the possible patterns of substitution available in consumption and production.

Once we recognize possible methods of substituting produced for nonproduced goods, a further kind of technological adaptation becomes possible: tastes may change to reflect the changing environment. Although there is a widespread feeling that tastes are "endogenous," that they respond to changing circumstances, the extent to which changed patterns of consumption reflect a rational response to changing prices (the changed patterns of consumption reflect the changes in the best method of obtaining the "basic wants" but the underlying utility function

---

[7] For a more extended discussion of the relationship between micro and macro production function see K. Sato [5, 6].

Many of the attempts to estimate the elasticity of substitution are based on cross-sectional data, rather than the heuristic time series approach that we have employed above. There are a number of problems involved in using these cross-sectional estimates as a basis of predicting the long-run elasticity of substitution; this is not the place for an extended discussion of these econometric problems except to note one that has not received sufficient attention in the literature. Consider the traditional method of estimating constant elasticity functions, originally introduced by Arrow and coauthors [7], entailing regressing marginal product (wage) on average product. Assume that labor is not homogeneous and one cannot observe how many "efficiency units" are associated with any particular individual. Then, if some firms hired mostly efficient workers and paid them a high wage, and if some firms hired mostly inefficient workers and paid them a low wage, it would appear as if there were a positive elasticity of substitution, even though the elasticity might have been zero.

remains unchanged) rather than a change in basic attitudes and preferences remains a moot question.

Where does this leave us? The kinds of tools economists have used in the past are not likely to resolve this issue for those who are firmly committed to one side or the other in this debate. Yet it seems that what economic theory does remind us of is "that there is more than one way to skin a cat." If the resource pessimists are correct that we are going to be facing a serious resource problem in the immediate future, they must convincingly show that (1) within each sector the elasticity of substitution is low and the demand elasticities are also low, so that as resources become scarcer we do not, or cannot, substitute less resource-intensive commodities for more resource-intensive commodities; (2) the prospects of adapting tastes to the new set of economic circumstances are poor; and (3) the prospects are bleak for technical changes that would enable us better to use what resources we have.

The more mundane forecasting problem of estimating the likely impact of increasing scarcity of natural resources on our standard of living not only requires a knowledge of some of the same critical parameters, but also entails information concerning a few other parameters.

Elasticity of Demand.   If the elasticity of demand for natural resources is high (either because there are readily available substitutes in production or because there are readily available substitutes in consumption which are less resource intensive), then increasing scarcity will not be a serious problem. Note that while for the question of viability we needed to know what happened to the elasticity as the resource input became arbitrarily small, here we only need to know the elasticity associated with levels of input not too different from those at present—a far easier question.

Costs of Extraction.   There is, however, an argument that to assess the impact of increasing scarcity in the short run we need not know the demand elasticity; in competitive markets prices will be rising in such a way as to make net royalties (price minus cost of extraction) rise at the rate of interest.[8] The level of prices and the patterns of consumption are affected by the nature of the demand curve, but not changes in the price level.[9] Thus, to forecast real price movements all we need to do is fore-

----

[8] Consider a competitive firm. It must decide whether to extract a unit of oil today, receiving net $p_t - c_t$ where p is the price and c_t is the extraction cost; or to extract it tomorrow, receiving net $p_{t+1} - c_{t+1}$ whose present value is $(p_{t+1} - c_{t+1})/(1 + r_t)$ where r is the rate of interest. In equilibrium, it must be indifferent, that is, $(p_{t+1} - c_{t+1})/(1 + r_t) = p_t - c_t$ or in continuous time $(\dot{p} - \dot{c})/[p(t) - c(t)] = r(t)$.

[9] Of course, changes in the consumer surplus, that is, welfare, associated with given changes in the price will depend on the elasticity of demand, so that the impact of a given increase in prices will be greater the lower the demand elasticity.

cast real interest rates and movements in real costs of extraction. The former are not likely to vary much in the immediate future (if anything, the increased scarcity of natural resources will lower the real return on capital and the rate of increase in prices). Thus, predicting future price movements comes down to predicting movements in the cost of extraction. There are two offsetting effects here. On the one hand it is in general optimal to first extract natural resources from deposits with lower extraction costs; as these are used up, extraction costs increase. Now, if natural resources were not scarce so that the price were determined by the extraction costs (as for a conventionally produced commodity), then this would raise the price. But for a natural resource, the increased extraction cost actually leads to a lower *rate* of increase of prices.[10] The second effect, which in the past has dominated, is that technological change has lowered the cost of extraction.[11] The lowering of the cost of extraction enables royalties to rise, even with a constant consumer price. As a consequence, in the recent past, there has been no significant increase in the real costs of extraction for many commodities, and a decline for several. If this trend continues, then it is not likely that an increase in resource scarcity will significantly lower standards of living.

New Deposits. The third factor which is important in determining the likely movements of prices in the short run is discoveries of new deposits. To the extent that such discoveries are anticipated (in a probabilistic sense), they should have no effect on price movements; but to the extent that the actual discoveries are greater or less than anticipated, prices will rise or fall (or rise at a faster or lower rate than they otherwise would have). Since by definition it is only the "unanticipated" discoveries which affect the price path, there is no way that we can say anything about the direction of these effects (similarly with respect to the discovery of substitutes for natural resources).

Finally, it should be noted that exhaustible resources constitute a small fraction of national income so that even a significant rise in price will have only a small effect on standards of living. (This is not to say that there might not be costly adjustments associated with significant price rises.)

[10] $\dot{p}/p = (1 - c/p)r$ so an increase in c lowers $\dot{p}/p$. This argument assumes that c is not changing over time.

[11] One ought really to include in the costs of extraction the total costs associated with discovery, bringing the resource from below ground to above ground, refining, and delivering the resource to the user. The "consumer price" may be lowered because of a reduction in any of these costs. Note that much of the technological change has resulted from better methods of extracting the mineral of interest from the ore. Some technological change may be indistinguishable from "returns to scale": as the economy grows, it may be possible or economical to have larger mines and refineries.

In short, it is not likely that resource shortages will lead to a significant lowering of standards of living in the immediate future. The arguments are reinforced if one believes that there are incentives within the market for estimating resource scarcities (as we shall argue in the next section), so that prices reflect the judgments of those participating in the market concerning the scarcity of resources. To argue that we will face, in the near future, a significant lowering of the standard of living requires arguing that the market systematically underestimates future demands and overestimates available supplies. A fuller analysis than we have been able to present here would recognize more explicitly that there is uncertainty associated with forecasts of demand and supply; it would then calculate the consequences, say, of underestimating demand by one standard deviation and overestimating supply by one standard deviation. If demand elasticities are low, such errors may be associated with large welfare losses. The market, however, presumably at least partially takes these risk considerations into account. The extent to which it does this is discussed more fully in the next section.

V
The Efficiency Issue

There is, admittedly, something satisfying about knowing whether the economy, as we know it, will come to an end in fifty years or so, or not. But there are those who seem to feel that establishing the fact that the economy faces dire problems with respect to natural resources has obvious implications for the role of the government. On the contrary, I would argue that the existence of a natural resource problem has no immediate implications: it is neither a necessary nor a sufficient condition for governmental intervention in the markets for natural resources. The market could be doing as well as could be done, and the economy could still be facing a doomsday; and the market could be doing a quite bad job of resource allocation, and yet there might be no doomsday in store.

This section is concerned with the *efficiency* issue as opposed to the equity issue, which we treat in the next section. Efficiency has a very precise definition: Is it possible to increase the consumption (welfare) of any individual (consumption at any date) without decreasing it at any other? If it is, we are clearly wasting resources. Efficiency is not, of course, the only objective of economic policy; we are also concerned with the intertemporal distribution of income. A pattern of growth which left our grandchildren with few resources might be efficient, yet very undesirable.

The object of this section is to analyze the efficiency with which the market allocates resources; the role of the government in resource markets (as in other markets) is customarily justified in terms of some kind of market failure. We consider here the major possible sources of market failure.

In the discussion below we show that there are a number of reasons to expect that the market allocation of natural resources might not be efficient; some of the effects lead to excessively rapid rates of resource utilization, others lead to excessive conservation; in still other cases we are able to show only that the market may not be efficient but are, in general, unable to argue whether the market is too profligate or too conservation minded. The conclusion of the analysis is that there is no overriding case that we are using our resources too rapidly, but that there are a number of actions which the government could take which would probably lead to a more efficient utilization of our natural resources.

We first show that the problems associated with monopoly are probably less important than for other commodities, while the problems associated with imperfect risk and futures markets, and costly information, are perhaps more important. The most convincing case for government intervention is in the area of support for research and development.

The government has, of course, intervened extensively in the market for natural resources; these interventions have probably been the most important source of inefficiency in the allocation of resources, and although one perhaps should not infer from this that future interventions would be equally as unsuccessful, there is little reason to believe that the efficiency with which the government allocates resources would be drastically better in the future than it has been in the past (we do not present any argument for why there should be systematic inefficiencies associated with governmental regulation; these have been discussed elsewhere in the literature). We now turn to a detailed discussion of each of the major sources of market and nonmarket failure.

Monopoly. In the wake of the oil embargo there developed a widespread belief that the noncompetitive nature of the oil industry raised prices and led to resource inefficiencies. For conventional *commodities,* monopoly results in the raising of prices and a decrease in consumption. For natural resources the effect is less clear, for if fewer natural resources are consumed today, there will be more to consume in the future; thus, raising the price today means that the price will be lower at some date in the future.

The fundamental principle defining efficient intertemporal allocation of resources is that the present discounted value of the (net) marginal product[12] must be the same at all dates, that is, the value of the marginal product rises at the rate of interest. This is ensured in a competitive economy by having the price rise at the rate of interest. A monopolist will equate the present value of *marginal revenue* at all dates, so marginal revenues rise at this rate of interest.[13] Thus, if price is proportional to marginal revenue, that is, for a constant (over time as well as for different levels of consumption) elasticity demand function, the *monopoly and competitive allocation are identical.* If the elasticity increases over time, as one might expect with development of substitutes, or if there are positive extraction costs, then the monopolist adopts an excessively *conservationist* policy.[14]

Absence of Futures Markets. The presumption that the market allocates resources efficiently follows from the more general result that, under certain conditions, a competitive economy provides efficient (Pareto optimal) allocation of resources. One of the conditions is that there be a full set of markets, including markets for trading into the future and trading different risks. These are obviously absent and their absence may have important implications.

Before discussing these, there is one fallacious argument which does need to be disposed of: it is sometimes argued that because our children

---

[12] Net of extraction costs. For simplicity we assume here that extraction costs are negligible.

[13] These basic principles of the intertemporal allocation of resources were originally discussed by Hotelling. They are just the application to this problem of the fundamental principles of efficient resource allocation. A unit of, say, oil must have the same *value* in all its uses. Among its alternative uses are its consumption today versus its consumption next period. Postponing consumption by a unit lowers output this period by the marginal product of oil today MP_{t+1}; it raises it by the marginal product of oil next period MP_{t+1}, but a unit of output next period is worth less than a unit of output today, if the rate of interest is positive. We require: $MP_t = (MP_{t+1})/(1 + r)$ where r is the rate of interest.

[14] These results are discussed in greater length in Stiglitz [8]. They apply only for the case of an elasticity of demand exceeding unity (which it must be at the point at which the monopolist is operating since otherwise revenues could be raised by lowering output). Gilbert [9] has analyzed models in which the elasticity is less than unity, but there is a limit price, that is, a price above which a substitute is introduced or developed. Gilbert [9], Salant [10], Stiglitz [11], and Cremer and Weitzman [12] have analyzed the behavior of a single large producer facing a competitive fringe. They have employed different models, entailing slightly different solution concepts; Salant has analyzed a Nash equilibrium, while Gilbert and Stiglitz have used a Stackleberg equilibrium with the monopolist acting as the leader; the monopolist knows the response of the competitive fringe to his actions. Gilbert has shown that the behavior of the large producer depends critically on whether the competitive fringe is supply constrained. If it is, it can be shown that as the supply of the competitive fringe is increased, the supply of the large producer will be increased. Newbery [13] has shown how the argument of Stiglitz [11] for random taxation can be reinterpreted in this context as establishing that under certain conditions it is optimal for a monopolist facing a limit price to randomize his prices.

and grandchildren are not present today, the market will systematically underrate their importance; that it will be reluctant to undertake investment decisions lasting longer than the lifetime of the typical investor (for example, planting and harvesting hardwood trees). (One guise in which this argument sometimes appears is that the social rate of time preference ought to be lower than the market rate of interest.) This overlooks the fact that the investor can sell the asset (for example, the hardwood forest) to another investor (say, in the next generation) to obtain his return; the forest does not have to be felled for him to get a return on his investment.

The consequence of the absence of futures and risk markets is that investors have to *guess* about future prices and have to absorb the risks associated with the uncertainty. Thus, whether the market pursues an excessively conservationist or excessively profligate consumption policy depends on whether there are systematic errors in the forecasts of future prices (demands); but even if it turned out that in some past period there were systematic errors, that does not imply that there is a need for government intervention, or indeed that government intervention is desirable. There are strong incentives within the market for discovering systematic errors—incentives which are, in general, lacking within a bureaucratic framework. Because the rewards obtained within the private sector depend on the accuracy of their forecasts, speculators and firms will strive to obtain better forecasts; and when they fail they bear the brunt of the costs. This is not so with a government allocation.

Moreover, when individuals differ in their judgments—as they are likely to—the market provides a systematic way of aggregating their beliefs, although it may be objected that the beliefs of the wealthy carry more weight than those without financial resources. On the other hand, little is known about how a bureaucracy would aggregate their beliefs.

Although it does seem to me that these considerations strongly suggest that the basic responsibility for the intertemporal allocation of our resources remains with the market, the absence of futures markets does result in at least three distinct problems for which remedial action by the government might be desirable.

The first is the case of the individual who believes that the market is underestimating the magnitude of resource scarcity. This person purchases the resource (or claims on the resource), holding it until the date (which he believes will surely come) when the scarcity is recognized. At that date the price rises and he will have made a capital gain. In effect he transfers resources that would have been consumed today to some date in the future, capturing the difference in (present) prices as his return. But if the shortage is not recognized within his lifetime, then there will be no way in which he can capture the returns; thus the individual has no incentive to enter the market.

Similarly, if an individual believes that the market overestimates future demand (underestimates supply), he would engage in a long-term contract for future delivery; he believes that eventually the market will recognize that prices are too high, so that prices will fall and he will make as his profit the difference between the contracted price and the lower spot price then prevailing. There are two difficulties with this. First, the long-term contracts required may not (generally do not) exist. (There is an apparent asymmetry in the market associated with holding positive and negative quantities of an asset.) Second, in order to capture the returns, the error in market forecasts has to be recognized within the individual's lifetime.

In fact, in the case where the market is excessively conservationist, the error might never be reflected in market price. The price of the natural resources may be rising at the rate of interest so that over the short run there is an efficient allocation of natural resources, but the initial price may be too low or too high. In the former case it can be shown that in finite time with a Cobb–Douglas production function the price will become infinite, but if the initial price is too high, nothing will happen except that we will never use up all our resources; thus short-run perfect foresight (short-run efficiency) can be consistent with an excessively profligate consumption policy for a finite time, but it can be consistent with an excessively conservationist policy forever [15].[15]

These considerations do, I think, provide a convincing argument that the market allocation may not be efficient, but it is not clear whether there is a bias for or against conservation.

Second, the efficient intertemporal allocation of resources requires the acquisition of information concerning future demands and supplies. Although the fundamental theorem of welfare economics establishes the Pareto optimality of the market allocation of resources with a given information structure, there is no theorem establishing its optimality when information has to be acquired. On the contrary, it can be established that the market may not be Pareto optimal [9, 16]; there may be excessive expenditures on information (arising from unnecessary duplication, as when different individuals attempt to acquire the same piece of information, for example, about the value of some lease) or there may be too

---

[15] Indeed, the problems associated with excessively high rates of capital accumulation (savings) which were the center of so much of the discussion in the pure theory of growth in the 1960s (see, e.g. [14]) are resolved by the presence of natural resources: there can never be a problem of oversaving in capital since with very low rates of interest, lower than the rate of growth, resources will be exhausted in finite time; but there can be a problem of oversaving of resources [15].

little expenditure because information is partially a public good. In particular, if the market prices adjust to reflect information, then individuals who do not do the research themselves may, by observing the market prices, obtain the information indirectly (thus part of the total benefits of obtaining information accrue to individuals other than those who purchase it directly) [17].

Third, many natural resource markets seem to be characterized by excessive instability, and this instability may in part be a result of the absence of future markets. There are strong a priori reasons to believe that adjustment processes for natural resources may not work well; we showed earlier that equilibrium in the market requires the expected rate of change of (net) price to be equal to the rate of interest. If for some reason price rises slightly faster than the rate of interest (for example, because some individuals believe that there is an impending resource scarcity and hold back supplies), then that has two effects: those who base their expectations of future price movements on past movements will extrapolate the high rate of price increase into the future, and thus expect the price to rise faster than the rate of interest; they will then hold back their supplies as well, leading to further increases in price in a destabilizing way.[16] Second, the reduced supplies will lower the rate of interest if resources and capital are complements in production (as one would normally expect); thus the gap between the expected rate of price increase and the rate of interest is again increased. (For a fuller discussion, see Stiglitz [15].)

These considerations suggest that there may be a role for the government in indicative planning in helping to forecast future demands and supplies, but it should be emphasized that this role is far different from one of actually allocating the resources themselves.

Absence of Risk Markets. The absence of risk markets means that those who hold stocks of natural resources may not be able to insure themselves against the risks of a price fall because of the discovery of a substitute or of a new supply of the resource.

The effect of this is actually very hard to analyze. There is a simple intuitive argument: viewing the holding of a resource (not extracting it) as a risky investment, an increase in uncertainty makes it less attractive, thus increasing the rate of consumption.

But this misses the fact that the risk depends on the stock (the amount by which the price falls when a substitute is discovered depends

---

[16] Note that the instability arises from individuals having to forecast future prices; futures markets, were they to exist, might equilibrate the process. The expectations formation process may, under not unreasonable conditions, be very destabilizing.

on the stock available at that date) and that what is critical for the inter-temporal allocation of the resource is how the risk varies over time.

In one simple model in which the probability of discovery of a substitute is constant per unit time and there is risk neutrality [with respect to income but not with respect to consumption of oil, i.e., the indirect utility function is of the form $V(p, Y) = V(p)Y$], for large stocks of the natural resource, uncertainty leads to greater conservationism, whereas for small stocks, it leads to a more profligate policy.[17] In another model where the stock of the resource is unknown and the only information that is acquired over time is that one had at least as much as one had consumed, it has been shown that uncertainty always leads to more conservation [18].

Uncertainty undoubtedly has an effect on intertemporal allocation, but for some purposes this is not as important as the question of what policy implications this has. For policy purposes it is inappropriate to compare an allocation of one market structure with an allocation which would emerge from another, except if the policy to be considered is a change in the market structure; the risks associated with uncertain future supplies and demands borne by private individuals in imperfect risk markets are real "costs"; and the fact that under some idealized world in which these risks are not borne by these individuals the intertemporal allocation of oil would be different is of interest, but of no direct policy import. An appropriate question to ask, for instance, is whether a Pareto optimal improvement could be made within our market structure by taxing or subsidizing the return to holding oil; or to put it another way, to ask whether the intertemporal allocation of natural resources arising from a stock market provides a "constrained" Pareto optimum. The answer, in general, is no, but the magnitude and direction of bias depend on a number of factors, for example, on differences in attitudes to risk in the economy [11]. A full analysis of this problem is presently under way. Until this is completed, it is difficult to ascertain how important this potential inefficiency of the market is.

Common Resource Problems. As we noted earlier, there are several distinct categories of natural resources; most of this paper is concerned with private exhaustible natural resources. Many of our most

---

[17] One might have thought that the effect of uncertainty is to raise the effective interest rate, thereby increasing the rate at which the price of a natural resource increases, hence leading to a lower price (more consumption) today. Although there is an effect going in this direction, there is another effect, which may be called the precautionary effect. Because one does not know when the substitute will arrive, one must hold back a supply of the resource as a precaution against the contingency that it does not arrive until some date far in the future.

important natural resources are, however, "public"—such as atmosphere—and for these the presumption that the market provides an efficient allocation of resources is reversed; only under the most unusual circumstances would one expect the market solution to be efficient. Individuals and firms will not, for instance, take into account the effect of their activities in lowering the quality of the air.

Most of these resources are "renewable": a stock of fish can be maintained, provided fish aren't consumed too rapidly; a "reasonable" quality of air may be maintained so long as the flow of pollutants is not too high. We are concerned here, however, only with three aspects of the problem: whether this will lead to an "exhaustion" of our natural resources and, even if it does not lead to exhaustion, whether it will lead to a significant lowering of the standard of living of succeeding generations, and whether there are any simple remedies for these problems.

There are some cases where the failure to charge for "common resources" has led to near exhaustion of a renewable natural resource: for example, whales, and there is evidence that if governments had not taken action, the air in certain cities would have become so polluted as to be almost unbreathable.

Most of the resources with which we are concerned here are renewable resources; hence there is a sustained level of per capita consumption which can be maintained with these resources with a constant population. Whether a sustained per capita level of consumption can be maintained with a growing population depends on exactly the same kinds of parameters we discussed in previous sections, for example, the substitutability between the given natural resource (now viewed as a constant flow) and other factors of production, the development of new substitutes, and the continuation of technical progress that augments resources.

There are, however, strong reasons to believe that with common resource problems the rate of extraction will be too rapid. Consider, for instance, a pool of oil which is available to anyone who wishes to take from it (or who purchases some land over the pool). Clearly, the intertemporal tradeoff of the individual is considerably different from when the resource is completely privately owned. For now the individual does not ask what will he get if he sells a unit today or tomorrow. He observes that if he does not extract it today, someone else will, and there will be no oil available for him to extract tomorrow. Thus market equilibrium will be associated with excessively rapid rates of extraction.

There are a variety of remedies for these problems. For many common resource problems a simple solution is to put the entire pool under a single management (for example, unitization of the oil pools, or giving a monopoly for fishing within a lake; obviously where there is more than one governmental jurisdiction involved, as for fishing in international waters, arriving at a solution will be more difficult). For other resources, such as "atmosphere," either governmental regulation or taxation is required. The relative merits of alternative methods are too broad to be discussed here.

Nonmarket Failures. The market failures discussed above appear to be the major ones. There are, in addition, a number of sources of nonmarket failure, of government interventions leading to inefficiencies both in the rate and pattern of extraction. These inefficiencies are perhaps even more important than those discussed above because they result in what appears to be shortages, when in fact they would not exist were it not for the government's actions; this is particularly true of the regulatory practices described below.

Taxation. There are several provisions of the tax code which may have an important effect on the allocation of natural resources.

Depletion Allowances. The impact of a depletion allowance at a constant rate may be less than is generally thought; if extraction costs were zero and the sector were competitive, it would have no effect. The reason for this is simple: the depletion allowance only changes the pattern of resource extraction to the extent that it changes the intertemporal tradeoffs between extracting today and extracting tomorrow. A depletion allowance increases receipts today but it increases receipts tomorrow by exactly the same percentage, and hence has no effect on intertemporal tradeoffs. If extraction costs were positive and constant, they would lead to faster extraction (than in the absence of the depletion allowance).[18] If the sector were monopolized, it would also lead to a faster rate of extraction if the monopoly was excessively conservation minded (as it would be with positive extraction costs and a declining elasticity of demand), offsetting the effects of the monopoly. If the monopoly were excessively profligate, the depletion allowance would lead to a still faster rate of consumption.

Although the effects of a constant depletion allowance may be smaller than is widely assumed, the effects of the gradual removal of the depletion allowance are larger than is widely assumed; if a depletion allowance is to be removed, it should be removed as quickly as possible. For again, the gradual removal of the depletion allowance means that it

[18] See Stiglitz [16]. Let the depletion rate be d. Assume extraction costs are constant, then equilibrium with the depletion allowance requires $[(1 + d)\dot{p}]/[(1 + d)p - c] = r$ or $\dot{p}/p = r(1 - [c/p(1 + d)])$) from which it is clear that the depletion allowance raises the rate of price increase and hence must lower the price initially.

is more profitable to extract now than later, and this encourages depletion.

Other provisions of the depletion allowance probably have serious implications for the structure of the industry; what implications this has for economic efficiency is not clear. For instance, any provision which assigns a depletion allowance for some categories of firms and not for others ought to result in most of the extraction being conducted by those who receive the depletion allowance. Limiting the amount of the depletion allowance as a percentage of profits, unless computed on a well-by-well or mine-by-mine basis, will also affect the structure of the industry.

Although the depletion allowance would have no effect on the pattern of extraction from known reserves with zero extraction costs, it does affect the incentive for discovering oil. The total stock of oil which is likely to be discovered is greater, and because of that, present prices are lower and consumption rates higher. Similarly, if there is a positive extraction cost, oil, which it would never pay to extract without a depletion allowance, will be extracted. But, apart from considerations of monopoly, the cost of discovery and extracting this oil will exceed its benefits, and so such a policy is undesirable.

If the removal of the depletion allowance has not been anticipated, the immediate effect of the removal will be to raise the price of oil, both because of the slower rate of extraction and the smaller stock of oil that will eventually be extracted. These effects may be disguised at present because the short-run effect of a gradual removal of the depletion allowance is to increase the supply of oil.

Immediate Write-Off of Drilling Expenses. With immediate write-off of capital expenditures, the corporation tax can be viewed as a pure profits tax, and is thus nondistortionary.[19] But since other sectors are not so treated, there is a relative distortion; investment in oil exploration is encouraged relative to other kinds of investment. There is no justification for this favorable treatment.

Inability to Write Off Immediately Expenditure on Lease (or Land) Acquisition. For expenditures other than drilling, the oil sector is treated like any other sector. But this symmetric treatment does induce a distortion in the rate of extraction relative to what it would be in the absence of taxation. Consider a firm which purchases land under which there is oil. After the oil has been extracted, the land will be worth less. The firm can take a capital loss on the reduction in land value, and thus reduce its tax liability. The present value of the tax write-off is increased by accelerating extraction. It would probably be desirable to allow imme-

---

[19] Without interest deductibility of debt. Immediate write-off with interest deductibility would appear to act like a capital subsidy.

diate write-off of these expenditures. In order to discourage excessive allocation of resources to this sector relative to others, other taxes would have to be imposed.

Special Treatment of Capital Gains. Since the return to holding oil is the increase in its price, if this increase in price is subjected to capital gains taxation, the return to holding oil will exceed the return to holding conventional assets, and there will be excessive conservation. This effect could be significant because the difference in rates is large. Since the sale of oil is treated as ordinary income, this distortion requires that firms that do the exploration hold on to the land until the date of extraction. They then sell their land; the purchaser extracts the oil, the income from the oil being perfectly offset by the reduction in the value of the land.

Of the various provisions discussed above, several have been introduced to offset the tax-induced biases of the general tax structure (or so proponents of the provision argue). The depletion allowance is justified as a simple alternative to depreciation, but the present tax code essentially allows triple depletion; immediate write-off of drilling expenses, depletion allowances, and write-off of the loss in value of leases or land after extraction is completed. Other proponents of these provisions admit that it constitutes favorable treatment but argue that the, favorable treatment is required to offset the distortionary effects of the corporation tax structure, which unduly penalizes risky and capital-intensive sectors. Elsewhere it has been argued that the sector is not more risky than other sectors, that the corporation tax does not discourage (but rather encourages) risk taking, that it does not penalize capital-intensive industries, and that there are second-best arguments for taxing the oil industry at a higher rate than other industries because the share of rents in that sector is larger.

Leasing Policy. The terms on which the government leases oil probably have a significant effect, not so much on the total rate of extraction as on the pattern of extraction. Efficiency requires that oil be taken from tracts of land with low extraction costs before it is taken from tracts with high extraction costs. (Similarly, tracts with low exploration costs should be explored before tracts with high exploration costs.) One of the provisos in government leases is the so-called diligence clause, requiring some development of the tract within five years. It pays the firm to extract at the end of five years so long as price exceeds extraction costs; but in the absence of the clause it would pay the firm to postpone extraction on tracts with high extraction costs.

Moreover, in models of competitive bidding it can be shown that the return in excess of extraction costs is a function of the number of bidders; this, it can be shown, leads to too little expenditure on exploration in areas in which there are a large number of "informed" firms, that is, firms who have extensive information about the tract; and it induces firms to nominate for leasing and explore fringe areas where there are likely to be few bidders and high exploration costs. This is inefficient.

In addition to these inefficiencies, there is an inefficiency arising from excessive and, from a social point of view, misdirected prebidding exploration, the object of which is not to discover oil but to ascertain how much should be bid for the lease. This has a private but not a social return. (It leads, for instance, to inefficiencies in the location of wells; for example, locating wells at boundaries of tracts to find out about neighboring tracts.)

It is not easy to devise more efficient policies. Recent proposals for developing pools as a single unit avoid the obvious inefficiencies arising when there are several tracts within a pool owned by different firms (the usual common-pool problem, where each firm fails to take account of its effect on the extraction of others; this normally leads to excessively rapid rates of depletion). The royalty bidding experiments showed that firms would bid very high royalty rates, but the consequence was that the well would be abandoned if the extraction costs as a percentage of price plus the royalty rate exceeded unity. Since these would be tracts with high extraction costs from which extraction should be postponed, provided they could eventually be leased again, this is not as great a disadvantage as it might seem.

Regulatory Policies.   The government has engaged in both long-term and short-term attempts at price regulation. In the case of natural gas, the government has attempted to keep the price low; in the case of oil, following the embargo, they have attempted to keep it from rising to its scarcity value. Both policies have serious effects. Because the price was not allowed to rise with the rate of interest, there was an incentive to extract as quickly as possible. Because the price was kept at a very low level, consumers had little incentive to conserve on natural resources.

The effects of price regulation in the oil embargo are not as apparent. The immediate effects were the usual inefficiencies associated with prices which are fixed below a market-clearing level, for example, lines at gas stations. It might be thought that because the supply was inelastic, there would be no effects on the total rate of consumption; although this is true in the short run, it is not in the long run. If firms and individuals come to believe that when there is an event such as an oil embargo prices will be kept below their market-clearing level, they will not have the incentive to take the efficient precautionary policies; firms will extract too much oil today (since they obtain a return on holding a precautionary stock that is less than its social value) and individuals will adopt technologies of consumption involving less flexibility than is socially optimal.[20]

VI
The Intertemporal Equity Issue

One of the major issues underlying the debate concerning natural resources is whether, with present policies, our descendants will be left in an impoverished state, without natural resources. What is of concern here is an equity issue—the welfare of our descendants versus the welfare of the present generation. There are two important observations to be made in this respect.

First, one should not view equity in a narrow sense of simply looking at the division of natural resources between present and future generations; the present generation may give future generations fewer natural resources (this is inevitable in the case of exhaustible natural resources), but it will give future generations a higher level of technology and more capital. One has to look at the relative welfare of the different generations and there is a strong presumption that future generations may be better off than the present generation. On grounds of equity it might be argued that we should consume even more now (including more natural resources).

Second, the appropriate instrument to use for obtaining more equitable distribution of welfare (if one believes that the present distribution is not equitable) are general instruments, for example, monetary policy directed at changing the market rate of interest. These do not lead to an inefficient allocation of resources. (Obviously, prior to using such general instruments, policies directed at correcting inefficiencies in the allocation of resources, as discussed in the previous section, have to be adopted.)

There has been an extensive recent literature concerned with the optimal pattern of consumption of natural resources. Although the models employed in this literature are obviously overly simple, they do give us a method of obtaining a rough check on whether the present allocation,

---

[20] Indeed, recent regulatory policies have punished those who have adopted flexible technologies: electricity generating plants which were convertible to coal were required to do so, forcing those who had adopted the flexible technology to pay more for their fuel than those who had not.

with all its market distortions, is different in a significant way from an optimal allocation. We solve for the optimal rate of extraction, using the utilitarian criterion, that is,

$$\max \int U(c)e^{-\delta t}e^{nt} \, dt$$

where $U(c)$ is the utility associated with a per capita consumption flow of c, n is the rate of growth of population, and δ the rate of discount, subject to the national income constraint,

$$C + \dot{K} = F(K, R, L, t) = K^{\alpha_1}R^{\alpha_2}L^{\alpha_3} \, e^{\lambda t}$$

(where F is a constant return to scale production function, which we have specialized as the Cobb–Douglas production function, with λ being the rate of technical progress; K is aggregate capital; L is labor; R is resource flow; and C is aggregate consumption), and to the resource constraint

$$\int R(t) \, dt = S$$

where S is the stock of the resource today.

The exact nature of the optimal consumption path (which, unlike the case without resources, may not be monotonic) depends on the elasticity of marginal utility, the rate of time preference, the rate of population growth, and the rate of technical change.[21] If the utility function is logarithmic $U = \ln c$, then it can be shown that the optimal rate of extraction is just equal to the pure rate of time discount minus the rate of population growth $(R/S) = \delta - n$. If $\delta - n$ is a number around 3 percent, this means that we should use up 3 percent of our remaining stocks each year, that is, at *current* rates of consumption, we have approximately thirty-three years' supply left, a number which is certainly smaller than our stock of energy-producing materials.

VII
Two Policy Issues

In the preceding two sections we discussed several policy issues in the context of whether a sustained level of per capita consumption growth is feasible and whether there are systematic misallocations of natural resources arising from market failure. In this section I wish to look at two further policy questions which have received widespread discussion.

---

[21] The general formula is that, asymptotically: $R/S = ([\delta(1 - \alpha_1) - \nu\lambda])/(1 - \alpha_1 - \alpha_2\nu) - n$ where ν is the elasticity of utility [4].

Operation Independence.   A careful analysis of the costs associated with attaining energy independence (autarchy) would likely lead to a realization of the undesirability of that policy. Here, I wish to draw attention to two aspects of the debate.

The first question that ought to be posed is whether there is any reason to believe that the market has taken insufficient precautions for the contingencies of an embargo or a large price rise. The fact that individual economic agents have not "fully" insured against these contingencies is to be expected, given the high cost of such insurance. Our previous analysis suggested that in the absence of government regulatory policies (which do not allow the price to rise when scarcity values rise), there is no particular reason to believe that the market will make insufficient provision for these contingencies.[22]

Second, with respect to measures designed to obtain greater independence through increasing domestic supply, there is really a question of the intertemporal allocation of dependency; increased extraction today may reduce the costs of an embargo today, but would increase it in the future. Indeed, the argument of nondependency was one of the main ones used in support of the oil quotas in the 50s and 60s; this led to a higher level of consumption of our domestic supply, leaving us now with less domestic oil than we would have had then. (Thus, although we were better "protected" then we are less well protected now.)

R and D Policy.   It has recently been suggested that some kind of price guarantee is required in order to elicit the appropriate levels of investment in R and D. The patent system is probably not an effective instrument in encouraging investment in R and D for energy (or natural resource) substitutes; the immediate effect of a discovery is to lower the price of the natural resource,[23] hence there is likely to be a long delay

[22] Obviously, if the market's assessments of the probabilities of an embargo or price rise are wrong, then it will take incorrect precautionary actions. If it underestimates these probabilities, then it will take insufficient precautionary actions. This can be corrected (assuming that the bureaucracy has reason to believe that it has better information about the probabilities, and that releasing this information to the market will not affect the market allocation, presumably because they refused to believe the bureaucrats) but tariff policy may not be an effective instrument. If individuals have point estimates of the price next period and production is not capacity constrained, then they always wish either to extract everything this period, everything next period, or are indifferent. Hence, with elastic foreign supplies, tariffs cannot control the intertemporal domestic supply allocation (although they do control domestic consumption). However, quotas will work.

[23] In a recent unpublished paper, Steinmuller [19] has reinterpreted the introduction of coal in Britain: it is not that the exhaustion of the forests led to the introduction of coal, but rather that less expensive methods of extracting coal made wood uneconomic as a fuel; although coal extraction was cheaper than planting and cutting a forest, it was not cheaper than cutting a forest; hence the immediate effect was to exhaust the forests and it was only later that it became economic to extract coal.

between invention and innovation. In addition, the lowering of the price is a social benefit which (apart from engaging in speculative activity) the inventor cannot capture. Although this does suggest that some kind of government price support program might be desirable, the price support should take the form of long-run contracts rather than a price support for the market as a whole.

VIII
Concluding Remarks

In this paper we have taken the view that natural resources are basically no different from other factors of production. There are presently extensive possibilities of substitution between resources and other factors (capital) and, with further research, there are likely to be further ways of substituting other factors for natural resources and making what resources we use go further. There is not a persuasive case that we face a problem from the exhaustion of our resources in the short or medium run, and although there are undoubtedly market failures leading to inefficiencies in resource allocation, there is no reason to believe they are worse here than elsewhere. Indeed, in the case of the effects of monopoly there is reason to believe that they are significantly less. In addition, a number of sources of inefficiency arising out of government intervention have been identified.

Although this is the conclusion that I, and I think many other economists would come to, I should emphasize that many of the points raised are moot. Although the economics of resource allocation in a static environment without uncertainty are well understood, there are many gaps in our understandings of dynamic economies with imperfect information, imperfect risk markets and imperfect futures markets, and these limitations are probably more important here than for conventional commodities. Further, at a number of points we have had to make empirical judgments (for example, about the value of the elasticity of substitution) about which there clearly can be disagreement. Perhaps more important than reaching agreement on the answer is reaching agreement on how we might resolve our disagreements. It is my hope that in this paper I have presented a framework within which this may be done.

References

1. F. M. Peterson and A. C. Fisher, "The Exploitation of Renewable and Nonrenewable Natural Resources," *Economic Journal* vol. 87 (December 1977) pp. 681–721.

2. P. Dasgupta and G. M. Heal, "The Optimal Depletion of Exhaustible Resources," *Review of Economic Studies,* Symposium on the Economics of Exhaustible Resources, 1974, pp. 3–28.
3. R. M. Solow, "The Economics of Resources or the Resources of Economics," *American Economic Review* Papers and Proceedings (May 1974) pp. 1–14.
4. J. E. Stiglitz, "Growth with Exhaustible Natural Resources: Efficient and Optimal Growth Paths," *Review of Economic Studies,* Symposium on the Economics of Exhaustible Resources, 1974, pp. 123–138.
5. K. Sato, "Micro and Macro Constant Elasticity of Substitution Production Functions in a Multi-firm Industry," *Journal of Economic Theory* vol. 1 (1969).
6. K. Sato, *Production Functions and Aggregation* (Amsterdam, North-Holland, 1975).
7. K. Arrow, H. Chenery, B. Minhas, and R. M. Solow, "Capital Labor Substitution and Economic Efficiency," *Review of Economics and Statistics* vol. 43 (1961) pp. 225–250.
8. J. E. Stiglitz, "Monopoly and the Rate of Extraction of Exhaustible Resources," *American Economic Review* vol. 66 (1976) pp. 655–661.
9. R. Gilbert, "Imperfect Competition and the Allocation of Oil," Working Paper No. 87, Department of Economics, University of California at Berkeley, 1976.
10. S. Salant, "Nash-Cournot Equilibrium for an Exhaustible Resource Like Oil," Federal Reserve Board, mimeo, 1975.
11. J. E. Stiglitz, "Utilitarianism and Horizontal Equity: The Case for Random Taxation," Institute for Mathematical Studies in the Social Sciences, Report, Stanford University, 1976.
12. J. Cremer and M. Weitzman, "OPEC and the Monopoly Price of World Oil," *European Economic Review* vol. 8, no. 2 (August 1976) pp. 155–164.
13. D. Newbery, "Feasible Price Stability May Not be Desirable," Institute for Mathematical Studies in the Social Sciences, Working Paper 68, Stanford University, April 1976.
14. P. Diamond, "National Debt in a Neoclassical Growth Model," *American Economic Review* vol. 55 (December 1965) pp. 1126–1150.
15. J. E. Stiglitz, "Growth with Exhaustible Resources: The Competitive Economy," *Review of Economic Studies,* Symposium on the Economics of Resources, 1974, pp. 139–152.
16. J. E. Stiglitz, "Information and Economic Analysis," unpublished monograph.
17. S. J. Grossman and J. E. Stiglitz, "Information and Competitive Price Systems," *American Economic Review* vol. 66, no. 2 (May 1976).
18. R. Gilbert, "Resource Depletion Under Uncertainty," Department of Economics, Stanford University, mimeo, 1975.
19. W. E. Steinmuller, "The Seventeenth Century Energy Crisis: a Critique of the Timber Famine Theory," unpublished paper, Department of Economics, Stanford University, July, 1976.

Bibliography

Barnett, H. J., and C. Morse. *Scarcity and Growth: The Economics of Resource Availability* (Baltimore, Johns Hopkins University Press for Resources for the Future, 1963).

Dasgupta, P. "Some Recent Theoretical Explorations in the Economics of Exhaustible Resources," in H. W. Gottinger, ed., *Systems Approaches and Environmental Problems* (Göttingen, Vandenhoek and Ruprecht, 1974) pp. 193–214.

———— and J. E. Stiglitz. "Uncertainty and the Rate of Extraction under Alternative Institutional Arrangements," Department of Economics, Stanford University, mimeo, 1975.

Herfindahl, O. C. "Depletion and Economic Theory," in Mason Gaffney, ed., *Extractive Resources and Taxation* (Madison, University of Wisconsin Press, 1964).

Hotelling, H. "The Economics of Exhaustible Resources," *Journal of Political Economy* vol. 39 (1931) pp. 137–175.

Nordhaus, W. "The Allocation of Energy Resources," *Brookings Papers on Economic Activity* no. 3 (Washington, D.C., Brookings Institution, 1973).

Pindyck, R. S. "Gains to Producers from the Cartelization of Exhaustible Resources," World Oil Project Working Paper, Massachusetts Institute of Technology, 1976.

Salant, S. W. "No End to the Age of Zinc: The Length of the Optimal Program when Depletion Affects Extraction Costs," International Finance Discussion Paper 73, Board of Governors, Federal Reserve System, 1976.

Solow, R. M. "Intergenerational Equity and Exhaustible Resources," *Review of Economic Studies,* Symposium on the Economics of Exhaustible Resources, 1974, pp. 29–45.

Stiglitz, J. E. "Tax Policy and the Oil Industry," report prepared for the Energy Policy Project sponsored by the Ford Foundation, partly published as chapter 3, "The Efficiency of Market Prices in Long Run Allocations in the Oil Industry," in G. Brannan, ed., "Studies in Energy Tax Policy" (Cambridge, Mass., Ballinger, 1975), pp. 55–100.

————, P. Dasgupta, R. Gilbert, G. Heal, and D. Newbery. "An Economic Analysis of the Conservation of Natural Resources," Federal Energy Administration Report (forthcoming).

Sweeney, J. "Economics of Depletable Resources: Market Forces and Intertemporal Bias," Department of Engineering Economics, Stanford University, mimeo, 1974.

3

Entropy, Growth, and the Political Economy of Scarcity

Herman E. Daly

Debts are subject to the laws of mathematics rather than physics. Unlike wealth, which is subject to the laws of thermodynamics, debts do not rot with old age and are not consumed in the process of living. On the contrary, they grow at so much per cent per annum, by the well known laws of simple and compound interest . . . as a result of this confusion between wealth and debt we are invited to contemplate a millenium where people live on the interest of their mutual indebtedness.

Frederick Soddy (*Wealth, Virtual Wealth, and Debt* pp. 68, 89)

I
Introduction

Chemistry has outgrown alchemy, and astronomy has emerged from the chrysalis of astrology, but the moral science of political economy has degenerated into the amoral game of politic economics. Political economy was concerned with scarcity and the resolution of the social conflicts engendered by scarcity. Politic economics tries to buy off social conflict by abolishing scarcity—by promising more things for more people, with less for no one, forever and ever—all vouchsafed by the amazing grace of compound interest. It is not politic economics to point out, as the Nobel laureate chemist and heretical economist Frederick Soddy [1] did in the above quote, that compound interest is the law of

This paper was presented at the RFF Conference on Natural Resource Scarcity on October 19, 1976 in Washington, D.C. I wish to acknowledge the benefit of comments received at that time from N. Georgescu-Roegen, B. Hannon, C. Morse, T. Page, and V. Kerry Smith. I have also benefited from comments by my colleagues, W. Culbertson, S. Farber, D. Johnson, and A. Toevs. Of course none of the above are to be held responsible for the views expressed, or for any errors committed.

debt, and that wealth is subject to the law of entropy, the law of moth, rust, accident, and decay. It is not politic to remember with John Ruskin:

the great, palpable, inevitable fact—the root and rule of all economy—that what one person has, another cannot have; and that every atom of substance, of whatever kind, used or consumed, is so much human life spent; which if it issue in the saving present life or the gaining more, is well spent, but if not is either so much life prevented, or so much slain. [2, p. 96]

Or as Ruskin more succinctly put it, "there is no wealth but life." Nor is it considered politic economics to take seriously the demonstration of the same insight by Georgescu-Roegen who has made us aware that

the maximum of life quantity requires the minimum rate of natural resources depletion. By using these resources too quickly, man throws away that part of solar energy that will still be reaching the earth for a long time after he has departed. And everything that man has done in the last two hundred years or so puts him in the position of a fantastic spendthrift. There can be no doubt about it: any use of natural resources for the satisfaction of nonvital needs means a smaller quantity of life in the future. If we understand well the problem, the best use of our iron resources is to produce plows or harrows as they are needed, not Rolls Royces, not even agricultural tractors. [3, p. 21]

Significantly, the contribution of Georgescu-Roegen is not so much as mentioned in the *Journal of Economic Literature's* 1976 survey of the literature of environmental economics [4]. The first sentence of that survey beautifully illustrates the environmental hubris of growth economics: "Man has probably always worried about his environment because he *was once* totally dependent on it" (emphasis supplied). Contrary to the implication, man's dependence on the environment is still quite total, and is overwhelmingly likely to remain so. Nevertheless, Robert Solow [5, p. 11] assures us that, thanks to "the productivity of natural resources increasing more or less exponentially over time," it is to be expected that, "the world can, in effect, get along without natural resources." In view of such statements it is evidently impossible to insist too strongly that, in Soddy's words:

life derives the whole of its physical energy or power, not from anything self-contained in living matter, and still less from an external diety, but solely from the inanimate world. It is dependent for all the necessities of its physical continuance primarily upon the principles of the steam-engine. The principles and ethics of human convention must not run counter to those of thermo-dynamics. [6, p. 9]

Lack of respect for the principles of the steam engine also underlies the basic message of the influential book *Scarcity and Growth* [7]. We are told that, "nature imposes particular scarcities, not an inescapable general scarcity" (p. 11). We are also asked to believe that:

> Advances in fundamental science have made it possible to take advantage of the uniformity of matter/energy—a uniformity that makes it feasible, without preassignable limit, to escape the quantitative constraints imposed by the character of the earth's crust. . . . Science, by making the resource base more homogeneous, erases the restrictions once thought to reside in the lack of homogeneity. In a neo-Ricardian world, it seems, the particular resources with which one starts increasingly become a matter of indifference. The reservation of particular resources for later use, therefore, may contribute little to the welfare of future generations. [p. 11]

Unfortunately for the politic economics of growth, it is not the uniformity of matter-energy that makes for usefulness, but precisely the opposite. If all materials and all energy were uniformly distributed in thermodynamic equilibrium, the resulting "homogeneous resource base" would be no resource at all. It is nonuniformity, differences in concentration and temperature, that make for usefulness. The mere fact that all matter-energy may ultimately consist of the same basic building blocks is of little significance if it is the *potential for ordering those blocks* that is ultimately scarce, as the entropy law tells us is the case. Only a Maxwell's Sorting Demon could turn a lukewarm soup of electrons, protons, neutrons, quarks and whatnot, into a resource. And the entropy law tells us that Maxwell's Demon does not exist. In other words, nature really *does* impose "an inescapable general scarcity," and it is a serious delusion to believe otherwise.

The differences cited above could hardly be more fundamental. It seems necessary therefore to start at the very beginning if we are to root out the faddish politic economics of growth and replant the traditional political economy of scarcity. The standard textbooks have long defined economics as "the study of the allocation of scarce means among competing ends." A reconsideration of ends and means will provide our starting point. Modern economics' excessive devotion to growth will be explained in terms of an incomplete view of the total ends-means spectrum. The arguments of two main traditions of criticism will be discussed —the "scarce means arguments" and the "competing higher ends arguments." The concepts of entropy, scarcity, and growth are brought into relationship with the ends-means spectrum, and it is argued that a holistic view of the spectrum leads away from growth mania and toward something like John Stuart Mill's [8] vision of a "stationary state" (here called a steady-state economy, or SSE for short). The basic concepts used to elaborate this alternate paradigm are set forth, drawing on the work of Mill, Irving Fisher [9], Kenneth Boulding [10] and Nicholas

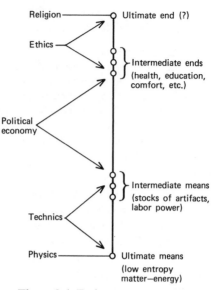

Figure 3-1. Ends-means spectrum.

Georgescu-Roegen [3]. Policies for a noncatastrophic transition from a growth economy to a SSE are suggested, including a prescriptive institutional model for the social rationing of low entropy.

II
The Ends–Means Spectrum

In the largest sense, man's ultimate economic problem is to use means wisely in the service of the Ultimate End. Stated so generally, it is not hard to understand our tendency to divide up the single, unified problem into a number of smaller subproblems, as indicated in figure 3-1. This is a good procedure as long as we do not forget about other parts of the spectrum in our zeal to solve the problem of one segment.

At the top of the spectrum is the Ultimate End—that which is intrinsically good and does not derive its goodness from any instrumental relation to some higher good. At the bottom is ultimate means, the useful stuff of the world, low entropy matter-energy, which man can only use up and cannot create or replenish, and the net production of which cannot possibly be the end of any human activity. Each intermediate category in the spectrum is an end with respect to lower categories and a means with respect to higher categories. Below the Ultimate End we have a hierarchy of intermediate ends which are in a sense means in the service of the Ultimate End. Intermediate ends are ranked with reference to the

Ultimate End. The mere fact that we speak of priorities among our goals presumes a first place, an ordering principle, an Ultimate End. We may not be able to define it very well, but logically we are forced to recognize its existence. Above ultimate means are intermediate means (physical stocks) which can be viewed as ends directly served by the use of ultimate means (the entropic flow of matter-energy, the "throughput").

On the left of the spectrum line are listed the traditional disciplines of study that correspond to each segment. The central, intermediate, position of economics is highly significant. In looking only at the middle range, economics has naturally not dealt with ultimates or absolutes and has falsely assumed that the middle range pluralities, relativities, and substitutabilities among competing ends and scarce means were representative of the whole spectrum. Absolute limits are absent from the economists' paradigm because absolutes are encountered only at the poles of the spectrum, which have been excluded from the focus of attention. Even ethics and technics exist for the economist only at the very periphery of professional awareness.

In terms of this diagram, economic growth implies the creation of ever more intermediate means (stocks) to satisfy ever more intermediate ends.[1] Orthodox growth economics, as we have seen, recognizes that particular resources are limited, but does not recognize any general scarcity of all resources. The orthodox dogma is that technology can always substitute new resources for old, without limit. Ultimate means are not considered scarce. Intermediate means are scarce, it is argued, only because our capacity to transform ultimate means has not yet evolved very far. Growth economists also recognize that any single intermediate end or want can be satisfied for any given individual. But new wants keep emerging (and new people as well), so the aggregate of all intermediate ends is held to be insatiable, or infinite in number, if not in intensity. The growth economist's vision is one of continuous growth in intermediate means (unconstrained by any scarcity of ultimate means) in order to satisfy ever more intermediate ends (unconstrained by any impositions from the Ultimate End). Infinite means plus infinite ends equals growth forever.

A consideration of the two poles of the spectrum, however, gives us a very different perspective. It forces us to raise two questions: (1) What, precisely, are our ultimate means, and are they limited in ways that cannot be overcome by technology? (2) What is the nature of the Ultimate End, and is it such that, beyond a certain point, further accumulation of intermediate means (bodies and artifacts) not only fails to serve the

[1] Qualitative change in physical stocks is "development." Growth refers to quantitative change. The distinction will be developed in section V.

Ultimate End, but actually renders a disservice? It will be argued below that the answer to both sets of questions is "yes." The absolute scarcity of ultimate means limits the *possibility* of growth. The competition from other ends, which contribute more heavily at the margin toward the Ultimate End, limits the *desirability* of growth. Moreover, the interaction of desirability and possibility provides the *economic* limit to growth, which is the most stringent, and should be the governing limit.

Paradoxically, growth economics has been both too materialistic and not materialistic enough. In ignoring the ultimate means and the laws of thermodynamics it has been insufficiently materialistic. In ignoring the Ultimate End and ethics it has been too materialistic. There are impressive intellectual traditions that criticize standard growth economics from each of these two perspectives. Table 3-1 gives a brief outline, with some of the representative members of each tradition.

The classification into ends-based (moral) and means-based (biophysical) critics of growth is in terms of emphasis and starting point only. Many writers to a considerable extent belong to both traditions. This is to be expected because the two traditions are not really so logically independent as may at first appear. For example, many moral issues regarding distributive justice and intergenerational equity hardly arise if one believes that continual economic growth is biophysically possible. Likewise, if one's arena of moral concern excludes the poor, future generations, and subhuman life, then many biophysical constraints are no longer of interest. To crack the nut of growth mania, it is not enough to hammer from above with moral arguments because there is sufficient "give" underneath supplied by optimistic biophysical assumptions. Hammering only from below with biophysical arguments leaves too much room for elastic morality to absorb the blow. (The interest rate automatically looks after the future, growth itself is the Ultimate End, or as close as we can come to it, man's manifest destiny is to colonize space— the earth is a mere "dandelion gone to seed," etc.) Growth chestnuts have to be placed on the unyielding anvil of biophysical realities, and then crushed with the hammer of moral argument. The entropy law and ecology provide the biophysical anvil. Concern for future generations, subhuman life, and inequities in current distribution of wealth provide the moral hammer.

Man is both a material creature in absolute dependence upon his physical environment, and a rational being who has purposes and strives to become better. These two aspects must be consistent with each other. Improvement presupposes survival, and survival in an entropic and evolving world is impossible without continual striving for improvement. Biophysically based conclusions about economic growth, or any other

Table 3-1. Intellectual Traditions of Growth Criticism

Biophysically or Means Based		Ethically or Ends Based	
Physical or bio-economists	Frederick Soddy Kenneth Boulding N. Georgescu-Roegen John Ise A. J. Lotka	John Ruskin Thomas Carlyle Henry Thoreau William Morris	Early critics of industrialism
	J. Culbertson R. Wilkinson	G. K. Chesterton H. Belloc	Distributism
Ecologists	Rachel Carson Paul Ehrlich Garrett Hardin Barry Commoner *Blueprint for Survival* Eugene Odum	Narodniki American agrarians Kropotkin Tolstoy Gandhi	Rural agrarian critics of industrialism
Systems ecologists	Howard Odum Kenneth Watt	J. S. Mill E. F. Schumacher E. J. Mishan D. Goulet	Humanist economists
Geologists	M. K. Hubbert Earl Cook	H. Daly	
	Harrison Brown Preston Cloud	Lewis Mumford Ivan Illich Jacques Ellul	Critics of technological society
Systems engineers	Jay Forrester Dennis Meadows	Theodore Roszak	
	Bruce Hannon Mesarovic and Pestel 1930s Technocracy, Inc.	Thomas Derr John Cobb Frederick Elder	Emerging theology of ecology
Conservationists	G. P. Marsh William Vogt David Brower Denis Hayes	William Ophuls Richard Falk L. K. Caldwell	Political science of survival
Demographers	K. Davis N. Keyfitz		
Physicists	A. Lovins D. Abrahamson J. Holdren H. Bent		

Note: See bibliography for references to representative work of each author.

subject, should be in accord with morally based conclusions. If there is a discrepancy it must indicate a flawed understanding of the natural world or a warped set of values. That ends-based and means-based arguments should converge in their rejection of growth mania is both comforting and not unexpected. Let us consider each line of argument, beginning with the means-based, biophysical arguments.

III
Means-Based Arguments

From a basic branch of physics, thermodynamics, we learn that for man's purposes the ultimate usable stuff of the universe is low entropy matter-energy.[2] What is low entropy? In terms of materials, low entropy means structure, organization, concentration, order. Dispersed, randomly scattered molecules of any material are useless (high entropy). In terms of energy, low entropy means capacity to do work, or concentrated, relatively high-temperature energy. Energy dispersed in equilibrium temperature with the general environment is useless (high entropy).

We have two sources of low entropy: terrestrial stocks of concentrated minerals, and the solar flow of radiant energy. The terrestrial source (minerals in the earth's crust) is obviously limited in total amount, though the rate at which we use it up is largely a matter of choice. The solar source is practically unlimited in total amount, but strictly limited in the rate at which it reaches the earth. Both sources of ultimate means are limited—one in total amount, the other in rate of arrival. These means are finite. Furthermore, there is an enormous disproportion in the total amounts of the two sources: if all the world's fossil fuels could be burned up, they would provide the energy equivalent of only a few weeks of sunlight. The sun is expected to last for another five or six billion years.

This raises a cosmically embarrassing economic question: If the solar source is so vastly more abundant, why have we over the past 150 years shifted the physical base of our economy from overwhelming dependence on solar energy and renewable resources, to overwhelming dependence on nonrenewable terrestrial minerals? An important part of the answer is that terrestrial stocks can, for a while at least, be used at a rate of man's own choosing, that is, rapidly. The use of solar energy and renewable resources is limited by the fixed solar flux, and the rhythms of growth of plants and animals, which in turn provide a natural constraint on economic growth. But growth can be speeded beyond this constraint, for a time at least, by consuming geological capital—by using up the reserves of terrestrial low entropy. If the object is high growth rates now, then it can be most easily attained by using up terrestrial sources rapidly. Such growth permits us to achieve population and per capita consumption levels that are beyond the capacity of renewable resources alone to support—thereby creating a strong vested interest in the continuing consumption of geological capital.

---

[2] The following paragraphs draw heavily on the pioneering work of Nicholas Georgescu-Roegen [3, 11].

The difficulty is twofold. First, we will eventually run out of accessible terrestrial sources. Second, even if we never ran out we would still face problems of ecological breakdown caused by a growing throughput of matter-energy. Even if technology were able to double the incident flow of solar energy (by far the cleanest source), the millions of years of past evolutionary adaptation to the usual rate would make a doubling of that rate totally catastrophic. The whole biosphere has evolved as a complex system around the fixed point of a given solar flux. Modern man is the only species that has broken the solar income budget. The fact that man has supplemented his fixed solar income by rapidly consuming terrestrial capital has thrown him out of balance with the rest of the biosphere. As stocks of artifacts and people have grown, the throughput necessary for their maintenance has had to grow also, implying more depletion and more pollution. Natural biogeochemical cycles become overloaded. Not only has the throughput grown quantitatively, but its qualitative nature has changed. Exotic substances are produced and thrown wholesale in the biosphere—substances with which the world has had no adaptive evolutionary experience, and which are consequently nearly always disruptive (e.g., DDT and plutonium).

But are we not giving insufficient credit to technology in claiming that ultimate means are limited? Is not technology itself a limitless resource? No, it is not. All technologies, nature's as well as man's, run on an entropy gradient, that is, the total entropy of all outputs taken together is always greater than the total entropy of all inputs taken together. No organism can eat its own outputs and live, and no engine can run on its own exhaust. If the outputs of a process were of lower entropy than the inputs, once *all* inputs and outputs were accounted for, we would have a process that violates the second law of thermodynamics, and so far no such process has ever been observed. Technology itself depends on the ultimate means of low entropy. If low entropy sources are not unlimited, then neither is technology. If the technological optimist really believes in "exponentially growing resource productivity" and in a world that can "get along without natural resources," then he should not object to quantitative restrictions on the resource throughput, as will be urged in section VI. If resource productivity can really approach infinity, then that is reason for using fewer resources, not more!

It is especially ironic to be told by growth advocates that technology is freeing man from dependence on resources [7, p. 11]. It has in fact done the opposite. Modern technology has made us *more* dependent on the *scarcer* of the two sources of ultimate means. It has also made us more dependent on each other, on remote experts, and more vulnerable to systemic breakdowns and sabotage by small groups. In view of the popular belief in the omnipotence of technology, it is even more ironic to recall that the most basic laws of science are statements of impossibility: it is impossible to create or destroy matter-energy; it is impossible to have perpetual motion; it is impossible to exceed the speed of light; it is impossible to measure anything without in some way interfering with the thing being measured, etc. The remarkable success of physical science has been in no small measure due to its intelligent recognition of impossibilities and its refusal to attempt them. Paradoxically this success has, in the popular mind, been taken as "proof" that nothing is impossible!

The entropy law tells us that when technology increases order in one part of the universe, it must produce an even greater amount of disorder somewhere else. If that "somewhere else" is the sun (as it is for nature's technology and for man's traditional preindustrial technology), then we need not worry. If "somewhere else" is here on earth, as it is for technologies based on terrestrial mineral deposits, then we had better pay close attention. The throughput flow maintains or increases the order within the human economy, but at the cost of creating greater disorder in the rest of the natural world, as a result of depletion and pollution. There are limits to how much disorder can be produced in the rest of the biosphere and still allow it to function well enough to continue supporting the human subsystem. There is a limit to how much of the ecosphere can be converted into technosphere.

Although technology cannot overcome these basic limits, it could achieve a much better accommodation to them, and could work more in harmony with nature's technology than it has in the past. There are enormous possibilities for artful technological finesse and elegant frugality [12]. But arbitrarily cheap energy has given the edge to brute force, and has driven really clever technology off the market. An improved technological accommodation to limits, while certainly possible and desirable, is not likely to be forthcoming in a growth context, in an economy that would rather maximize throughput than reduce it. Such improvement is much more likely within the framework of an SSE, where profits would be made from development, not growth, as will be elaborated later.

IV
Ends-Based Arguments

The temper of the modern age resists any discussion of the Ultimate End. Teleology and purpose, the dominant concepts of an earlier time, were banished from the mechanistic, reductionistic, positivistic mode of thought that came to be identified with the most recent phase of the evolution of science. Economics followed suit by reducing ethics to the level of personal tastes. No questions are asked about whether individual priorities are right or wrong, or even about how they are formed. The same goes for collective priorities. Whatever happens to interest the mass public is assumed to be in the public interest.

Our modern refusal to reason about the Ultimate End merely assures the incoherence of our priorities, both individually and collectively. It leads to the tragedy of Herman Melville's Captain Ahab, whose means were all rational, but whose purpose was insane. The apparent purpose of growth economics is to seek to satisfy infinite wants by means of infinite production. This is about as wise as chasing a white whale, and the high rationality of the means employed cannot be used to justify the insanity of purpose. Rational means simply make insane purposes all the more dangerous. Among our presumed "infinite" wants is there not the desire to be free from the tyranny of infinite wants? Is there not a desire for finite wants, for only good wants? If the assumption of infinite wants includes the desire for finite wants (and how could it be excluded except as a moral commandment that "thou shalt want more"?), then we have a kind of liar's paradox—one of our "infinite" wants is the want for finite wants! And even if wants were infinite, it does not follow that infinite production, even if possible, would be capable of satisfying more than a finite subset of our "infinite" wants. Some logical cracks thus appear in one of growth mania's cornerstones.

What is the Ultimate End? The question is logically unavoidable. But only a minimum answer to such a maximum question is likely to command much consensus. As a minimum answer let me suggest that whatever the Ultimate End is, it presupposes a respect for and continuation of creation and the evolutionary process through which God has bestowed upon us the gift of self-conscious life. Whatever values are put in first place, their further realization requires the continuation of life— the survival of the biosphere and its evolving processes. It may be a noble act to sacrifice the remaining years of one's own life to a higher cause. But to sacrifice, or even to risk sacrificing, most of creation to some "higher cause" is surely fanaticism. This minimum answer begs many important questions. What direction should survival and evolution take? To what extent should evolution be influenced by man and to what extent should it be left spontaneous? For now, however, the only point is that survival must rank very high in the ends-means hierarchy, and consequently any type of growth that requires the creation of means that threaten survival should be forbidden. The nuclear-powered "plutonium economy" is a prime example of the kind of growth that must be halted. The long-run survival costs of extravagant luxury (Rolls-Royces rather than plows), must also be allowed to temper our enthusiasm for growth. No one doubts that the basic needs of the present must take precedence over the basic needs of the future. But should not the trivial wants of the present yield at some point to the basic needs of the future?

But what about other kinds of growth? Are *all* kinds of physical growth subject to desirability limits? Is there such a thing as *enough* in the material realm, and is enough better than "more than enough"? Is "more than enough" inimical to survival? Certainly all organic needs can be satisfied and to go beyond enough is usually harmful. Satisficing[3] should play a larger role in economic theory, and maximizing a correspondingly smaller role. The only want that seems insatiable is the want for distinction, the desire to be in some way superior to one's neighbors. Even the want for distinction need not cause problems except when the main avenue of distinction in society is to have a larger income than the next fellow and to consume more. The only way for everyone to earn more is to have aggregate growth. But that is precisely the rub. If everyone earns more, then where is the distinction? It is possible for everyone's *absolute* income to increase, but not for everyone's *relative* income to increase. To the extent that it is higher relative income that is important, growth becomes impotent. As British economist E. J. Mishan put it:

> In an affluent society, people's satisfactions, as Thorstein Veblen observed, depend not only on the innate or perceived utility of the goods they buy, but also on the status value of such goods. Thus to a person in a high income society, it is not only his absolute income that counts but also his relative income, his position in the structure of relative incomes. In its extreme form— and as affluence rises we draw closer to it—only relative income matters. A man would then prefer a 5 per cent reduction in his own income accompanied by a 10 per cent reduction in the incomes of others to a 25 per cent increase in both his income and the incomes of others.
>
> The more this attitude prevails—and the ethos of our society actively promotes it— the more futile is the objective of economic growth for society as a whole. For it is obvious that over time everyone cannot become relatively better off. [13, p. 30]

Aggregate growth can no more satisfy the relative wants of distinction than the arms race can increase security. When society has reached a level of affluence such that at the margin the relative wants of distinction are dominant, then aggregate growth becomes either futile, or the source of increasing inequality. At some point growth becomes undesirable, even if still possible.

The effective limit to growth, however, is neither desirability nor

---

[3] Satisficing, as used here, means to seek enough rather than the most. The concept of enough is difficult to define, but even more difficult to deny.

possibility, but the interaction of the two, that is, the *economic* limit. It is not necessary that the marginal benefits of growth should fall all the way to zero, nor that the marginal costs of growth should rise to infinity, but only that the two should become equal. As growth continues we know that marginal benefits fall, and marginal costs rise and at some point they will become equal. We do not satisfy our ends in any random order, but strive always to satisfy our most pressing needs first. Likewise, we do not use our low entropy means in any order, but exploit the highest grade and most accessible resources first. This elementary rule of sensible behavior underlies both the law of diminishing marginal benefit and the law of increasing marginal costs, which are the very keystones of economic theory, and which apply to aggregate output as well as to individual commodities. The fact that growth-induced disruptions of ecosystem services cannot be arrayed to occur in increasing order of severity is a major obstacle to economic calculation, and leads one away from maximizing and toward "satisficing" strategies.

Once one has convinced one's self that absolute scarcity is real, and that growth should be a means to some end rather than an end in itself, then the next question is: What is a feasible and desirable alternative and how could it be attained? How can we move away from the politic economics of growth and toward a political economy of scarcity? The next section presents the alternative of a steady-state economy, and the following section offers some policies for making the transition.

V
The Concept of a Steady-State Economy

The steady-state economy (SSE) is defined by four characteristics:

1. a constant population of human bodies,
2. a constant population or stock of artifacts (exosomatic capital or extensions of human bodies),
3. the levels at which the two populations are held constant are sufficient for a good life and sustainable for a long future,
4. the rate of throughput of matter-energy by which the two stocks are maintained is reduced to the lowest feasible level. For the population this means that birth rates are equal to death rates at low levels so that life expectancy is high. For artifacts it means that production equals depreciation at low levels so that artifacts are long lasting, and depletion and pollution are kept low.

Only two things are held constant—the stock of human bodies, and the total stock or inventory of artifacts. Technology, information, wisdom, goodness, genetic characteristics, distribution of wealth and income, product mix, etc., are *not* held constant. In the very long run of course nothing can remain constant, so our concept of an SSE must be a medium run concept in which stocks are constant over decades or generations, not millenia or eons.

Three magnitudes are basic to the concept of an SSE:

1. *Stock* is the total inventory of producers' goods, consumers' goods, and human bodies. It corresponds to Irving Fisher's [9] definition of capital, and may be thought of as the set of all physical things capable of satisfying human wants and subject to ownership.
2. *Service* is the satisfaction experienced when wants are satisfied, or "psychic income" in Fisher's [9] sense. Service is yielded by the stock. The quantity and quality of the stock determine the intensity of service. There is no unit for measuring service, so it may be stretching words a bit to call it a "magnitude." Nevertheless, we all experience service or satisfaction and recognize differing intensities of the experience. Service is yielded over a period of time and thus appears to be a flow magnitude. But unlike flows, service cannot be accumulated. It is probably more accurate to think of service as a "psychic flux" [3, 11].
3. *Throughput* is the entropic physical flow of matter-energy from nature's sources, through the human economy, and back to nature's sinks, and is necessary for maintenance and renewal of the constant stocks [3, 10, 14].

The relationship among these three magnitudes can best be understood in terms of the following simple identity [15].

$$\frac{service}{throughput} \equiv \frac{service}{stock} \times \frac{stock}{throughput}$$

The final benefit of all economic activity is service. The original useful stuff required for yielding service, and which cannot be produced by man, but only used up, is low-entropy matter-energy, that is, the throughput. But throughput is not itself capable of directly yielding service. It must first be accumulated into a stock of artifacts. It is the stock that directly yields service. We can ride to town in only one of the existing stock of automobiles. We cannot ride to town on the annual flow of automotive maintenance expenditures, nor on the flow of newly mined iron ore destined to be embodied in a new chassis, nor on the flow of worn rusting hulks in junkyards. Stocks may be thought of as throughput that has been accumulated and "frozen" in structured forms capable of satisfying human wants. Eventually the frozen structures are "melted" by entropy, and what flowed into the accumulated stocks from nature then flows back to nature in equal quantity, but in entropically degraded quality. Stocks are intermediate magnitudes that belong at the center of analysis, and provide a clean separation between the cost flow and the benefit flux. On the one hand stocks yield service, on the other hand stocks require throughput for maintenance. Service yielded is benefit; throughput required is cost.

The identification of cost with throughput should not be interpreted as implying a "throughput or entropy theory of value." There are other costs, notably the disutility of labor, and the accumulation time required to build up stocks. In the steady state we can forget about accumulation time since stocks are only being maintained, not accumulated. The disutility of labor can be netted out against the services of the stock to obtain net psychic income or net service. In the steady state, then, the value of net service is imputed to the stocks that render the service, which is in turn imputed to the throughput that maintains the stocks. It is in this sense that throughput is identified with cost. The opportunity cost of the throughput that maintains artifact A is the service sacrificed by not using that throughput to maintain more of artifact B. The throughput is a physical cost which is evaluated according to opportunity cost principles. However, the opportunity cost of the throughput must be evaluated not only in terms of alternative artifact services forgone (which the market does), but also in terms of natural ecosystem services forgone as a result of the depletion and pollution caused by the throughput (which escapes market valuation). Depletion reduces the service of availability of the resource to future people who cannot bid in present markets, and pollution reduces the ability of the ecosystem to perform its life support services. The true opportunity cost of an increment in throughput is the greater of the two classes: artifact service sacrificed and ecosystem services sacrificed. Thus throughput is better thought of as a cost-inducing physical flow rather than identified with cost itself, which by definition must always be a sacrificed benefit, not a physical magnitude. In like manner the stock is a benefit-yielding physical magnitude and should not be identified with benefit or service itself.

We can arrive at the same basic result by following Irving Fisher's reasoning. Fisher [9] argued that every intermediate transaction involves both a receipt and an expenditure of identical magnitude which cancel out in aggregating the total income of the community. But once the final user has obtained the asset, there is no further exchange and cancelling of accounts among individuals. The service yielded by the asset to the final consumer is the "uncancelled fringe" of psychic income, the final uncancelled benefit left over after all intermediate transactions have cancelled out. Subtracting the psychic disservices of labor, Fisher arrived at *net psychic income,* the final net benefit of all economic activity. It is highly interesting that Fisher did not identify any original, uncancelled, real cost against which the final value of net psychic income should be balanced. Here we must supplement Fisher's vision with the more recent visions and analyses of Boulding [10] and Georgescu-Roegen [3, 11], concerning the physical basis of cost. As everyone recognizes, the stock of capital wears out and has to be replaced. This continual maintenance and replacement is an unavoidable cost inflicted by entropy. Fisher treated it as cancelling out in the aggregate: house repair is income to the account of the carpenter and an identical outgo to the account of the house. But Fisher did not trace the chain all the way back to any "uncancelled fringe" at the beginning which would correspond to uncancelled final costs in the same way that net psychic income corresponds to uncancelled final benefits. If we do this, we come to the unpaid contribution from nature: the provision of useful low-entropy matter-energy inputs, and the absorption of high-entropy waste matter-energy outputs. These contributions from nature have no costs of production, only a cost of extraction or disposal, which is paid and enters the cancelling stream of accounts. But we do not pump any money down into a well as we pump oil out nor do we dump dollars into the sea along with our chemical and radioactive wastes. If service is an "uncancelled fringe," then so is throughput. In other words, if we consolidate the accounts of all firms and households, everything cancels out except service and throughput.

In the SSE a different behavior mode is adopted with respect to each of the three basic magnitudes. (1) *Stock* is to be *"satisficed,"* that is, maintained at a level that is sufficient for an abundant life for the present generation, and ecologically sustainable for a long (but not infinite) future. (2) *Service* is to be *maximized,* given the constant stock. (3) *Throughput* is to be *minimized,* given the constant stock. In terms of the two ratios on the right hand side of the identity, this means that the ratio service/stock is to be maximized by maximizing the numerator, with denominator constant, while the ratio stock/throughput is maximized by minimizing the denominator with numerator constant. These two ratios measure two kinds of efficiency: service efficiency and maintenance efficiency.

Service efficiency (service/stock) depends on allocative efficiency (does the stock consist of artifacts that people most want, and are they allocated to the most important uses), and on distributive efficiency (is the distribution of the stock among alternative people such that the trivial wants of some people do not take precedence over the basic needs of others). Standard economics has much of value to say about allocative efficiency, but treats distribution under the heading of social justice rather than efficiency, thus putting it on the sidelines of disciplinary concern. Although neoclassical economists carefully distinguish allocation from distribution in static analysis, they seem not to insist on any analogous distinction between intertemporal allocation (one person allocating over different stages of his lifetime) and intertemporal distribution (distribution between different people, that is, present people and future people). Intertemporal distribution is a question of ethics, not a function of the interest rate. The notion of optimal allocation over time must be confined to a single lifetime, unless we are willing to let ethics and distributional issues into the definition of optimum. Neoclassical economics seems inconsistent, or at least ambiguous on this point.

Maintenance efficiency (stock/throughput) depends on durability (how long an individual artifact lasts), and on replaceability (how easily the artifact can be replaced when it finally does wear out). Maintenance efficiency measures the number of units of time over which a population of artifacts yields its service, while service efficiency measures the intensity of that service per unit of time. Maintenance efficiency is limited by the entropy law (nothing lasts forever, everything wears out). Service efficiency may conceivably increase for a very long time, since the growing "magnitude," service, is nonphysical. There may, however, be physical limits to the capacity of human beings to experience service. But the definition of the SSE is in terms of physical stocks and throughput, and is not affected by whether or not service could increase indefinitely.

Conceptually it is easier to think of stock as the operational policy variable to be directly controlled. Practically, however, as will be seen below, it would be easier to control or limit throughput directly, and allow the stock to reach the maximum level sustainable by the fixed throughput. This presents no problems.

The above concepts allow us to make an important distinction between growth and development. *Growth* refers to an increase in service that results from an increase in stock and throughput, with the two efficiency ratios constant. *Development* refers to an increase in the efficiency ratios, with stock constant (or alternatively, an increase in service with throughput constant). Using these definitions, we may say that a SSE develops but does not grow, just as the planet earth, of which it is a subsystem, develops without growing.

How do these concepts relate to GNP, the more conventional index of "growth"? GNP makes no distinction among the three basic magnitudes. It simply adds up value estimates of some services (the service of those assets that are rented rather than purchased, including human bodies, and omitting the services of all owned assets not rented during the current year, with the exception of owner-occupied houses), plus the value of the throughput flow (maintenance and replacement expenditures required to maintain the total stock intact), plus the value of current additions to stock (net investment). What sense does it make to add up benefits, costs, and change in inventory? Services of the natural ecosystem are not counted, and more important, services sacrificed are not subtracted. In fact, defensive attempts to repair the loss of ecosystem services are added to GNP. The concept of an SSE is independent of GNP, and what happens to GNP in the SSE simply does not matter. The best thing to do with GNP is to forget it. The next best thing is to try to replace it with two separate social accounts, one measuring the value of service (benefit), and the other measuring the value of throughput (cost). In this way costs and benefits could be compared, although this aggregate macro level comparison is not at all essential, since regardless of how it turns out, the behavior modes remain the same with respect to each of the three basic magnitudes. If we really could get operational cost and benefit accounts, then we might optimize the level of stocks by letting it grow to the point where the marginal cost of an addition to stock just equals the marginal benefit. But that is so far beyond our ability to measure that for a long time satisficing will remain a better strategy than optimizing. Aggregate economic indexes should be treated with caution, since there are always some kinds of stupid behavior that would raise the index, and thus become "justified."

Neither the concept nor the reality of an SSE is new. John Stuart Mill [8] discussed the concept in his famous chapter "on the stationary state." Historically, man has lived for 99 percent of his tenure on earth in conditions very closely approximating a steady state. Economic growth is essentially a phenomenon of the past 200 years, and only in the past fifty years has it become the dominant goal of nations. Growth is an aberration, not the norm. Development can continue without growth, and is in fact more likely under an SSE than a growth economy.

Even "cornucopians" like Weinberg and Goeller [16] evidently consider an SSE to be a precondition for achieving their Age of Substitutability, in which "society will settle into a steady state of substitution and recycling . . . assuming, of course, a stable population." But why postpone the SSE to some hypothetical future age? Why not seek to come to terms with the SSE now, before we use up the remaining easily available resources that could help in making the transition? Why continue to fan the fires of growth up to the point where the flame's appetite is so voracious that even maintaining it in a steady state would require technologies and social institutions that are so demanding and unforgiving as to reduce the quality of life to that of a regimented community of social insects?

VI
Policies for a Steady-State Economy

How can we achieve an SSE without enormous disruption? The difficult part is mustering the moral resources and political will to do it. The technical problems are small by comparison. People often overestimate the technical problems because they mistakenly identify an SSE with a failed growth economy. A situation of nongrowth can come about in two ways: as a result of the success of steady-state policies or the failure of growth policies. Nongrowth resulting from the failure to grow is chaotic beyond repair. This is precisely why we need an SSE—because it is so much better than a failed growth economy.

In an effort to stimulate discussion on policies for attaining an SSE, I have suggested three institutions [17] which seem to me to provide the necessary social control with a minimum sacrifice of individual freedom. They build on the existing bases of private property and the price system, and are thus fundamentally conservative, though they will appear radical to some. The kinds of institutions needed follow straight from the definition of an SSE: "constant stocks of people and artifacts maintained at chosen levels that are sufficient for a good life and sustainable for a long future, by the lowest feasible rate of throughput." We need an institution for limiting population, one for limiting stocks of artifacts, and one for limiting inequality in the distribution of artifacts among the population.

Let us leave population issues to one side. Of all the population control schemes now being debated, I prefer the *transferrable birth license plan,* first advocated by Kenneth Boulding (Boulding [18]; Daly [17]; Heer [19]), but for purposes of this discussion will invite the reader to substitute his own favorite population control scheme, if he does not like that one.

A constant aggregate stock of artifacts will result from holding the throughput flow constant by means of a *depletion quota auction,* to be discussed below. Since aggregate growth can no longer be appealed to as the "solution" to poverty, we must face the distribution issue directly by setting up a *distributist institution* which would limit the range of inequality to some justifiable and functional degree. This could be accomplished by setting a minimum income limit, maximum income and wealth limits for individuals and families, and a maximum size for corporations. The maximum and minimum would define a range within which inequality is legitimate and beyond which it is not. The exact numbers are of secondary importance, but just suppose a minimum of $7,000 and a maximum of $70,000 on family income. The idea of a minimum income is familiar, but the notion of a maximum is not, because in the growth paradigm it is not necessary. But in the steady-state paradigm the total stock is constant and this implicitly sets a maximum on individual wealth and income. Some limits on inequality are essential, though we may debate just how much inequality is legitimate.

The key institution would be the *depletion quota auction* by which the annual amount extracted of each basic resource would be set, and through which the quota rights would be auctioned by the government in conveniently divisible units. The resource market would become two-tiered. First, the government, as monopolist, would auction the limited quota rights to many resource buyers, who, having purchased their quota rights, would enter the second tier of the market where they would confront many resource producers in a competitive market. Buyers would pay the resource producers the market price and surrender the requisite quota rights to the producer at the time of purchase. The firms in the extractive industry would be audited to make sure that sales balanced with quota certificates collected.

Figure 3-2 illustrates more clearly how things would work.

DD' is the market demand curve for the resource in question, and SS' is the industry supply curve. A depletion quota in the aggregate amount Q is imposed, shown by the vertical line QQ'. The total price paid per unit of the resource (unit price paid to resource producer plus unit price of the quota right paid to the government) is OC. Of the total price OC the amount OB is the price paid to resource producers, and BC is the price paid to the government for the quota right. Of the total amount paid, $OQAC$, the amount $OSEQ$ is cost, reflecting necessary sup-

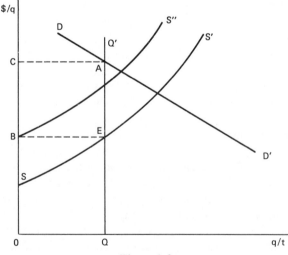

Figure 3-2.

ply price (extraction costs). The remainder, *SEAC,* is surplus or rent. Rent is defined as payment in excess of supply price. Of the total rent area, the amount *BES* is differential rent and accrues to the resource producers as profit. The remainder, the amount *CAEB,* is pure scarcity rent and accrues to the government. As a monopolist in the sale of quota rights (the first tier of the resource market which controls entry into the second tier), the government is able to extract the full amount of pure scarcity rent that results from the restricted quantity.

Let us review what is achieved by the depletion quota auction. First, the throughput of basic resources is physically limited, and with it the rate of depletion and pollution associated with those resource flows. Allocation of the fixed aggregate resource flow among competing uses and firms is done by the market. The price of the resource increases, inducing greater efficiency of use, both in production and in consumption. Resource-saving technical improvement is induced, and so is recycling. Dependence is gradually shifted away from scarce terrestrial sources and toward the abundant solar source of low entropy. The monopoly profits resulting from the higher resource prices are captured by the government, while resource producers earn normal competitive profits. The government revenues could be used to finance the minimum income part of the distributist institution. Efficiency is served by high resource prices, equity is served by redistributing the proceeds of the higher prices to the poor, and by a maximum limit on incomes of the rich. Rent is the optimal source of revenue for the government, and though one must stop short of proclaiming the realization of Henry George's dream of a single tax on rent, the depletion quota auction carries us about as far in that direction as is practical. Although ownership of resources remains in private hands, resource owners do suffer a capital loss when production is cut and their earnings are forced to the purely competitive level by the quota auction. Compensation for this one-time windfall loss could be given to the affected resource owners in the interest of fairness.

What criteria are there for setting the "proper" aggregate quota amounts for each resource? For renewable resources there is the fairly operational criterion of maximum sustainable yield. For nonrenewables there is, of course, no sustainable yield. But economist John Ise [20] suggested fifty years ago that, as a rule of thumb, nonrenewables should be priced equal to or more than their nearest renewable substitute. Thus virgin timber should be priced at least as much per board foot as replanted timber; petroleum should be priced at its Btu equivalent in terms of sugar or wood alcohol, assuming that is in fact the closest renewable substitute. For nonrenewables with no reasonably close renewable substitute, the matter is simply a question of how fast we should use it up, that is, an ethical weighing of the needs of present versus future people. One further criterion might be added: even if a resource is in no danger of depletion, its use may produce considerable pollution (e.g., coal), and depletion quotas may be imposed with the objective of limiting pollution, the other end of the throughput pipeline.

Over time, the supply curve for nonrenewable resources would shift upward as the more accessible sources become depleted, and previously marginal mines and wells have to be used. In the diagram, the higher supply curve is represented by BS'', which may be thought of as the "unused" segment of the original supply curve, ES', shifted in parallel fashion to the left until it touches the vertical axis. Assuming the same demand curve and quota, it is clear that the rising cost of production (area under the supply curve) will eventually eliminate the pure scarcity rent, leaving only differential rent. Quotas slow down the upward shift of the supply curve, relative to what it would have been with faster depletion, but of course cannot arrest the inevitable process. Probably the quota would have to be reduced as the supply curve shifted up in order to pass along the higher price signals to users, and to maintain some scarcity rent for public revenue.

For renewable resources with the quota set at maximum sustainable yield, there would be no upward shift in the supply curve. However, the demand curve for renewables would shift up as nonrenewable resource usage became restricted and more expensive. The quota on renewables would keep them from being exploited beyond their sustainable capacity, would ration access to the sustainable amount, and would divert the windfall profits into the public treasury. In sum, the depletion quota auction is an instrument for helping us make the transition from a nonrenewable to a renewable resource base in a gradual, efficient, and fair manner.

The combination of these three institutions presents a nice reconciliation of equity and efficiency, and provides the ecologically necessary macro control with the least sacrifice of micro freedom and variability. The market is relied upon to allocate resources and distribute incomes within imposed ecological and ethical boundaries. The market is not allowed to set its own boundaries, but is free within the boundaries imposed. The boundaries can be tightened with any degree of gradualism desired. It is necessary to set the boundaries externally. It is absurd to expect that market equilibria will automatically coincide with ecological or demographic equilibria, or with a reasonably just distribution of wealth and income. The very notions of "equilibrium" in economics and ecology are antithetical. In macroeconomics "equilibrium" refers not to physical magnitudes at all, but to a balance of desires between savers and investors. Macroeconomic equilibrium implies, under current conventions, a positive flow of net investment to offset positive savings. Net investment implies increasing stocks and a growing throughput, that is, a biophysical *dis*equilibrium. If a balance of desires between savers and investors is insufficient to ensure even full employment at a stable price level, as the Keynesians argue, then how much more remote is the likelihood that it will ensure ecological and demographic equilibria! Physical boundaries guaranteeing reasonable ecological equilibrium must be imposed on the market in quantitative terms. The orthodox economist's claim that economic and ecological equilibria would coincide, if only all external costs were internalized, is on a par with Archimedes' claim that he could move the earth if only he had a fulcrum and a long enough lever. A clever illustration of an abstract principle is not the same as an operational policy measure.

How do these proposals differ from the orthodox economists' prescription of "internalizing externalities via pollution taxes"? Pollution taxes are price controls on the output end of the throughput, while depletion quotas are quantitative controls on the input end. Depletion is spatially far more concentrated than pollution, and consequently much easier to monitor. Quantity rather than price should be the control variable because prices cannot limit aggregate throughput. Higher relative prices on resources would induce substitution and bring the resource content per unit of output down to some minimum. But prices cannot limit the number of units of output produced, and therefore cannot limit the total volume of resource throughput. Aggregate income is always sufficient to purchase the growing aggregate supply, regardless of prices. To paraphrase Say's law, "A growing supply creates its own growing demand." Taxes, by raising relative prices of basic resources, could provide a one-shot reduction in aggregate throughput by reducing throughput per dollar's worth of output to some feasible minimum, but the number of "dollar's worth" units of output could keep growing, unless the government ran an ever-growing budget surplus. Finally, it is quantity that affects the biosphere, not price. It is safer to set ecological limits in terms of fixed quantities, and let errors and unexpected events work themselves out in price changes, than to set prices and let errors and omissions cause quantity changes.

The "internalization of externalities" is a good strategy for fine tuning the allocation of resources by making relative prices better measures of relative social marginal costs. But it does not enable the market to set its own absolute physical boundaries within the larger ecosystem. To give an analogy: proper allocation arranges the weight in a boat optimally, so as to maximize the load that can be carried. But there is still an absolute limit to how much weight a boat can carry, even if optimally arranged. The price system can spread the weight evenly, but unless supplemented by an external absolute limit, it will just keep on spreading the increasing weight evenly until the evenly loaded boat sinks. No doubt the boat would sink evenly, *ceteris paribus, but* that is less comforting to the average citizen than to the neoclassical economist.

Two distinct questions must be asked about these proposed institutions for achieving an SSE. First, would they work if people accepted the need for an SSE and, say, voted these institutions into effect? Second, would people ever accept the goal of an SSE? I have argued that the answer to the first question is "yes." Although the answer to the second question would surely be "no" if a vote were held today, that is because the growth paradigm is still dominant. With time, the concepts and arguments sketched out here and the two critical traditions identified will look more appealing and will themselves be sharpened as the real facts of life push the growth paradigm into ever greater anomalies, contradictions, and practical failures.

References

1. Frederick Soddy, *Wealth, Virtual Wealth, and Debt* (London, Allen and Unwin, 1926).
2. John Ruskin, *Unto This Last: Four Essays on the First Principles of Political Economy,* edited by Lloyd J. Hubenka (Lincoln, University of Nebraska Press, 1967).
3. Nicholas Georgescu-Roegen, *The Entropy Law and the Economic Process* (Cambridge, Mass., Harvard University Press, 1971).
4. Anthony C. Fisher and Frederick M. Peterson, "The Environment in Economics: A Survey," *Journal of Economic Literature* vol. XIV, no. 1 (March 1976) pp. 1–33.
5. Robert Solow, "The Economics of Resources or the Resources of Economics," *American Economic Review* vol. LXIV (May 1974) pp. 1–14.
6. Frederick Soddy, *Cartesian Economics: The Bearing of Physical Science upon State Stewardship* (London, Hendersons, 1922).
7. Harold Barnett and Chandler Morse, *Scarcity and Growth: The Economics of Natural Resource Availability* (Baltimore, Johns Hopkins University Press for Resources for the Future, 1963).
8. John Stuart Mill, *Principles of Political Economy* (New York, Appleton-Century-Crofts, 1881).
9. Irving Fisher, *The Nature of Capital and Income* (London, Macmillan, 1906).
10. Kenneth Boulding, "The Economics of the Coming Spaceship Earth," in Henry Jarrett, ed., *Environmental Quality in a Growing Economy* (Balti-

more, Johns Hopkins University Press for Resources for the Future, 1966).

11. Nicholas Georgescu-Roegen, *Analytical Economics* (Cambridge, Mass., Harvard University Press, 1966).

12. Amory Lovins, "Energy Strategy: The Road Not Taken?", *Foreign Affairs* vol. LV (October 1976) pp. 65–96.

13. E. J. Mishan, "Growth and Anti-Growth: What Are the Issues?", *Challenge* (May/June 1973).

14. Herman E. Daly, "On Economics as a Life Science," *Journal of Political Economy* vol. LXXVI (May/June 1968) pp. 392–406.

15. Herman E. Daly, "The Economics of the Steady State," *American Economic Review* vol. LXIV (May 1974) pp. 15–21.

16. Alvin M. Weinberg and H. E. Goeller, "The Age of Substitutability," *Science* (February 20, 1976) pp. 683–688.

17. Herman E. Daly, ed., *Toward a Steady-State Economy* (San Francisco, W. H. Freeman, 1973). See reading number seven.

18. Kenneth Boulding, *The Meaning of the Twentieth Century* (New York, Harper and Row, 1964).

19. David Heer, "Marketable Licenses for Babies: Boulding's Proposal Revisited," *Social Biology* (Spring 1975).

20. John Ise, "The Theory of Value as Applied to Natural Resources," *American Economic Review* vol. XV (June 1925) pp. 284–291.

Bibliography

Abrahamson, Dean E. *The Energy Crisis: Some Policy Alternatives* (Los Alamos Scientific Laboratory of the University of California, 1972).

Belloc, Hilaire. *The Servile State* (Boston, LeRoy Phillips, 1912).

Bent, Henry A. "Haste Makes Waste: Pollution and Entropy," *Chemistry* vol. 44 (October 1971) pp. 6–15.

————. *The Second Law: An Introduction to Classical and Statistical Thermodynamics* (New York, Oxford University Press, 1965).

Boulding, Kenneth E. "Environment and Economics," in William W. Murdoch, ed., *Environment* (Stamford, Conn., Sinauer Associates, 1971).

————. "The Economics of the Coming Spaceship Earth," in Henry Jarrett, ed., *Environmental Quality in a Growing Economy* (Baltimore, Johns Hopkins University Press for Resources for the Future, 1966).

Brower, David R. *The de facto Wilderness: What is its Place?* (San Francisco, Sierra Club, 1962).

Brown, Harrison S. *Population: Perspective* (San Francisco, Freeman, 1971).

————, ed. *Are Our Descendants Doomed?* (New York, Viking Press, 1972).

Brown, Lester R. *In the Human Interest: A Strategy to Stabilize World Population* (New York, W. W. Norton, 1974).

————. "The Environmental Consequences of Man's Quest for Food," in Peter Albertson and Margery Barnett, eds., *Managing the Planet* (Englewood Cliffs, N.J., Prentice-Hall, 1972).

Caldwell, Lynton Keith. *Man and His Environment: Policy and Administration* (New York, Harper and Row, 1975).

———. *In Defense of Earth: International Protection of the Biosphere* (Bloomington, Ind., Indiana University Press, 1972).

Carlyle, Thomas. *Past and Present* (London, J. M. Dent, 1947).

Carson, Rachel L. *Silent Spring* (Boston, Houghton Mifflin, 1962).

Chesterton, G. K. *The Outline of Sanity* (London, Library Press).

Cloud, Preston. "Mineral Resources in Fact and Fancy," in William W. Murdoch, ed., *Environment: Resources, Pollution and Society* (Stamford, Conn., Sineaur Associates, 1971).

———, ed. *Resources and Man* (San Francisco, Freeman, 1969).

Cobb, John. "Ecology, Ethics, and Theology," in H. E. Daly, ed., *Toward a Steady-State Economy* (San Francisco, Freeman, 1973) pp. 307–332.

Commoner, Barry. *The Closing Circle: Nature, Man and Technology* (New York, Knopf, 1974).

———. *Environment* (New York, Knopf, 1971).

———. "Technology and the Natural Environment," *Architectural Forum* vol. 130 (1969) pp. 68–73.

Cook, Earl. "Energy Sources for the Future," *The Futurist* vol. 6 (1972) pp. 142–150.

Culbertson, John M. *Economic Development: An Ecological Approach* (New York, Knopf, 1971).

Daly, Herman E. *Steady-State Economics: The Economics of Biophysical Equilibrium and Moral Growth* (San Francisco, Freeman, 1977).

Davis, Kingsley. "Population," *Scientific American* vol. 209 (1963) pp. 62–71.

———. "Colin Clark and the Benefits of an Increase in Population," *Scientific American* vol. 218 (1968) pp. 133–138.

———. "The Urbanization of the Human Population," *Scientific American* vol. 213 (1965) pp. 40–53.

Derr, Thomas S. *Ecology and Human Need* (Philadelphia, Westminister, 1975).

Ehrlich, Paul R. *The Population Bomb* (New York, Ballantine Books, 1968).

——— and Anne H. Ehrlich. *Population, Resources Environment: Issues in Human Ecology* (San Francisco, Freeman, 1970).

——— and John Holdren. "Impact of Population Growth," *Science* vol. 171 (1971) pp. 1212–1217.

Elder, Frederick. *Crisis in Eden: A Religious Study of Man and Environment* (Nashville, Abingdon Press, 1970). Argues for an environmental theology against those who would exclude nature from theological concerns.

Ellul, Jacques. *The Technological Society.* Translated by John Wilkinson (New York, Vintage Books, 1967).

———. "Technique, Institutions, and Awareness," *American Behavioral Scientist* vol. 2 (1968) pp. 38–42.

Faulk, Richard. *This Endangered Planet: Prospects and Proposals for Human Survival* (New York, Random House, 1971).

Forrester, Jay. "Counterintuitive Behavior of Social Systems," *Technology Review* vol. 73 (January 1971) pp. 52–68.

———. *World Dynamics* (Cambridge, Mass., Wright-Allen, 1971).

Georgescu-Roegen, Nicholas. *The Entropy Law and the Economic Process* (Cambridge, Mass., Harvard University Press, 1971).

Goulet, Denis. *The Cruel Choice: A New Concept in the Theory of Development* (Cambridge, Mass., Atheneum, 1971).

———. "Voluntary Austerity: The Necessary Art," *Christian Century* vol. 83 (June 1966) pp. 748–752.

Hannon, Bruce. "Energy, Growth, and Altruism," (Mimeographed) (Center for Advanced Computation, University of Illinois, 1975).

Hardin, Garrett. "The Tragedy of the Commons," *Science* vol. 162 (1968) pp. 1243–1248. Reprinted in H. E. Daly, ed., *Toward a Steady-State Economy* (San Francisco, Freeman, 1973) pp. 133–149.

———. *Exploring New Ethics for Survival: The Voyage of the Spaceship Beagle* (New York, Viking, 1972).

Hayes, Denis. *Energy: The Case for Conservation,* Worldwatch Paper No. 4 (Washington, D.C., Worldwatch Institute, 1976).

Holdren, John, and P. Herrera. *Energy* (New York, Sierra Club, 1971).

Hubbert, Marion K. *U.S. Energy Resources, a Review as of 1972* (Washington, GPO, 1974).

———. "Energy Resources," in William W. Murdoch, ed., *Environment: Resources, Pollution, and Society* (Stamford, Conn., Sinauer Associates, 1971).

Illich, Ivan. *Energy and Equity* (New York, Harper and Row, 1974).

———. *Tools for Conviviality* (New York, Harper and Row, 1973).

Ise, John. "Theory of Value as Applied to Natural Resources," *American Economic Review* vol. XV (June 1925) pp. 284–291.

———. *Our National Park Policy: A Critical History* (Baltimore, Johns Hopkins Press for Resources for the Future, 1961).

———. *The United States Oil Policy* (New Haven, Conn., Yale University Press, 1926).

Keyfitz, Nathan. *Introduction to Mathematics of Population* (Reading, Mass., Addison-Wesley, 1968).

———. "World Resources and the World Middle Class," *Scientific American* vol. 235 no. 1 (July 1976) pp. 28–35.

Lotka, Alfred J. *Elements of Physical Biology* (Baltimore, Williams & Wilkins, 1925).

———. "The Law of Evolution as a Maximal Principle," *Human Biology* vol. XVIII (1945) pp. 180–191.

———. "Related Branches of Society," *Proceedings of the American Philosophical Society* vol. 90 (1951) pp. 601–626.

Lovins, Amory B. "Energy Strategy: The Road Not Taken," *Foreign Affairs* vol. 55 (1976) pp. 65–97.

Malthus, Thomas Robert. *Population: The First Essay* (London, MacMillan, 1926).

Marsh, George Perkins. *The Earth as Modified by Human Action* (New York, Arno, 1970).

Meadows, Dennis. "The Predicament of Mankind," *The Futurist* vol. 5 (1971) pp. 137–144.

Meadows, Donella, Dennis L. Meadows, Jørgen Randers, and William W. Behrens, III. *The Limits to Growth,* A Report for the Club of Rome's Project on the Predicament of Mankind (New York, Universe Books, 1972).

Mesarovic, Mihajlo, and Edward Pestel. *Mankind at the Turning Point* (New York, Dutton, 1975).

Mill, John Stuart. *Principles of Political Economy, with Some of Their Applications to Social Philosophy* (London, Longmans, 1929).

Mishan, E. J. *The Costs of Economic Growth* (London, Staples, 1967).

———. *Technology and Growth: The Price We Pay* (New York, Praeger, 1970).

Mumford, Lewis. *Techniques and Civilization* (New York, Harcourt, Brace & World, 1934).

Odum, Eugene. *Fundamentals of Ecology* (Philadelphia, Saunders, 1971).

———. "The Strategy of Ecosystem Development," *Science* vol. 164 (1969) pp. 262–270.

Odum, Howard T. *Environment, Power, and Society* (New York, Wiley–Interscience, 1970).

———. "Energy, Ecology, and Economics," *AMBIO* vol. 2, no. 6 (1973).

——— and Elisabeth C. Odum. *Energy Basis for Man and Nature* (New York, McGraw-Hill, 1976).

Ophuls, William. "Leviathan or Oblivion?" in H. E. Daly, ed., *Toward a Steady-State Economy* (San Francisco, Freeman, 1973) pp. 215–231.

Roszak, Theodore. *Where the Wasteland Ends: Politics and Transcendence in Post-Industrial Society* (Garden City, N.Y., Anchor Books, 1973).

———. *The Making of a Counter Culture: Reflections on the Technocratic Society and Its Youthful Opposition* (New York, Doubleday, 1969).

Ruskin, John. *Unto This Last* (New York, Merrill, 1862).

———. *Essays on Political Economy* (Westport, Conn., Greenwood).

Schumacher, E. F. *Small Is Beautiful: Economics As If People Mattered* (New York, Harper & Row, 1973).

———. *The Age of Plenty: A Christian View* (Edinburgh, St. Andrew Press, 1974).

4

Comments on the Papers by Daly and Stiglitz

Nicholas Georgescu-Roegen

The two papers presented at this session are so opposed in outlook that a commentator could not possibly find himself in sympathy, even partially, with both of them. Given my own stand on the crucial role played by natural resources in the economic process, it may be superfluous to say with which of the two papers I am in substantial agreement. Yet I deem it necessary to state from the outset that I am entirely out of sympathy with the manner in which J. E. Stiglitz dealt with his topic.

True, his task could hardly be more thankless. But he has chosen to set up a line of multifarious but ineffective fires in defense of a position to which many standard economists still cling with the tenacity of original sin. This position is that the analytical models designed by standard economics are completely fit to deal with the issue of optimal allocation of natural resources among successive generations, an issue that affects the survival of the human species. It is my contention, expounded in several of my writings, that this position is dangerously false.[1] Neoclassical economics—or standard economics, as I prefer to call the discipline as practiced for the past fifty years—has paid practically no attention to natural resources. To be sure, legions of production functions in the neoclassical literature contain the factor land, by which is meant, however, only Ricardian land. But Ricardian land raises no issue for the intergenerational allocation of resources. This is *the* problem of natural resources.[2]

Stiglitz avoids the admission, embarrassing nowadays, that the main body of standard economists has paid no attention to this vital problem. For the defense that economists have long since recognized the seriousness of the limitations of resources, Stiglitz has little choice other than

The author held an Earhart Fellowship during the preparation of this paper.
[1] See especially Georgescu-Roegen [1].
[2] And since we cannot possibly control the flow of solar energy reaching the earth, the problem of natural resources is reduced to that of *mineral* resources.

mentioning, not a neoclassical economist, but Malthus. Curiously, even that defense witness has no glory, because Malthus's forebodings "have not been borne out—at least not yet." This bare assertion is to be expected. Standard economists, having paid no attention to the problems raised by the size of population, cannot recognize now any valid point in Malthus's position. In this connection, one may cite Blaug's glaring verdict: "The Malthusian theory of population is a perfect example of metaphysics masquerading as science" [2].

Before disposing of Malthus in such expedient fashions, one should take account of the fact that millions of humans are half-alive in abject misery, dying slowly of squalor and starvation. Above all, one should (if one can) imagine a United States populated as thickly as Bangladesh: it would contain not less than 5 billion people, more by one quarter than today's population of the whole earth. Actually, Malthus—we can say it now—was not Malthusian enough; he allowed for population to increase indefinitely provided it would not grow too fast.

By now it is fashionable among standard economists to say high and loud that one does not need to invoke thermodynamic laws in order to realize that exponential growth must eventually run into physical barriers.[3] Stiglitz does not want to be an exception. Like all the others, he also ignores the question that now cries for an answer: Why have we then labored for years to fabricate and sell a theory of economic development based on exponential growth?

The claim that standard economics is not concerned "with very long-run projections, but rather with the more immediate future," is another means of avoiding the main issue that would incriminate the standard position. The problem of resources is not confined to the "foreseeable future," as many other writers also insist, but concerns the entire future. Obviously, if one takes the foreseeable future to be just 24 hours, then, as Wilfred Beckerman assured us, we all could go to bed tonight without worrying in the least about what growth may do to those of us who will be alive the day after tomorrow. If the standard position concerns only what will happen to natural resources "in the immediate future" of this moment of the twentieth century, then all the din about how the market mechanism (especially that moulded on standard assumptions) can save us from ecological catastrophes is utterly idle. But if the claim is that exponential growth can prevail not only in our immediate future but also in any "immediate future" in the future, then the claim acquires a factual, nonparochial significance. The opposite position

---

[3] See, for example, Landsberg [3]. But, sadly, these writers ignore the fact that thermodynamics tells us some fundamental things about the economics of resources that are not as obvious.

is that exponential growth has been only one historical interlude caused by a unique mineralogical bonanza of the past hundred years.

I am the first to agree with Stiglitz that a specific policy geared for the future should ideally be based upon some solid projections. Since any *quantitative* projection whatsoever is ultimately based on some time-invariant matrix, Stiglitz is right in searching for some constant element. I further agree with him on the indescribable predicament of the econometrician trying to discover a *historical* law on the basis of past observations. Concerning parameterization, years ago I pointed out that the situation of the econometrician is analogous to that of a deft sculptor who can prove to you that there is a beautifully carved Madonna inside almost any log.[4] How can one then tell what is really inside a log?

Let me also make another of Stiglitz's points stronger. If we are able to predict that after a certain age people are likely to develop arteriosclerosis, it is only because we have been able to observe millions of humans growing old. Unfortunately, we have not observed and will never observe another people struggling to survive on a planet such as ours. This is why we cannot say for sure what is in the cards for us as a species. By observing a single human until he reaches the age of, say, thirty, we may very well conclude that he will never develop arteriosclerosis. It is legitimate to expect, therefore, that data pertaining to the period of minerological bonanza mentioned above—such as those so ably used by Harold Barnett and Chandler Morse in support of their famous thesis—should support any hypothesis of continuous growth.

It is therefore curious that after insisting on such difficulties, Stiglitz claims that the burden of proof is on "the resource pessimists," such as me, to convince the resource optimists that some elasticities are low. This sort of argument would be in order only if the optimists had already offered some acceptable proofs that those elasticities are high. Worse still, the issue does not even concern elasticities at all. It concerns the physical finitude and the irrevocable exhaustibility of natural resources.

Stiglitz, however, even raises the question of "how essential" natural resources are. Apparently, like Robert M. Solow (whom he cites in this respect), Stiglitz believes that physical production can be maintained at the same level if capital (or some other factor) is continually substituted for natural resources.

This conjuring trick devised by Solow is easily shown up. Exclusive preoccupation with paper-and-pencil (PAP) exercises habit has led to accepting these exercises without any concern for their relation to facts. On paper, one can write a production function any way one likes, without

4 See Georgescu-Roegen [1, chapters 10 and 12].

regard to dimensions or to other physical constraints.[5] A good example is the famous Cobb–Douglas function, but the Solow–Stiglitz variant adds the sin of mixing flow elements with fund elements, namely,

$$Q = K^{\alpha_1} R^{\alpha_2} L^{\alpha_3} \tag{1}$$

where Q is output, K is the stock of capital, R is the flow of natural resources used in production, L is the labor supply, and $\alpha_1 + \alpha_2 + \alpha_3 = 1$ and, of course, $\alpha_i > 0$.[6]

From this formula it follows that with a constant labor power, L_0, one could obtain any given Q_0, if the flow of natural resources satisfies the condition

$$R^{\alpha_2} = \frac{Q_0}{K^{\alpha_1} L_0^{\alpha_3}} \tag{2}$$

This shows that R may be as small as we wish, provided K is sufficiently large. *Ergo,* we can obtain a constant annual product indefinitely even from a very small stock of resources $R > 0$, if we decompose R into an infinite series $R = \Sigma R_i$, with $R_i \to 0$, use R_i in the year i, and increase the stock of capital each year as required by (2). But this *ergo* is not valid in actuality. In actuality, the increase of capital implies an additional depletion of resources. And if $K_i \to \infty$, the R will rapidly be exhausted by the production of capital. Solow and Stiglitz could not have come out with their conjuring trick had they borne in mind, first, that any material process consists in the transformation of some materials into others (the flow elements) by some agents (the fund elements),[7] and second, that natural resources are the very sap of the economic process. They are *not* just like any other production factor. A change in capital and labor can only diminish the amount of waste in the production of a commodity; no agent can create the material on which it works. Nor can capital create the stuff out of which it is made. In some cases, it may also be that the same service can be provided by a design that requires less matter or energy. But even in this direction there exists a limit, unless we believe that the ultimate fate of the economic process is an earthly Garden of Eden.

The question that confronts us today is whether we are going to discover *new* sources of energy that can be safely used. No elasticities of some Cobb–Douglas function can help us to answer it. As to the scarcity

[5] More on this point in Georgescu-Roegen [4, chapter 9] and [1, chapters 2, 4, 5].

[6] The slipshod manner in which the factors are defined is another consequence of the infatuation with PAP exercises.

[7] See Georgescu-Roegen [4, chapter 9] and [1, chapters 2, 4, 5].

of matter in a closed system, such as the earth, the issue may, in my opinion, prove in the end more critical than that of energy [1, chapters 1; 5].

No one could possibly argue with some of the statements of section II of Stiglitz's paper; if they are taken with a grain of salt they may give some useful indication of the direction in which a market may move because of government intervention or changes in the industrial structure. But this does not settle the great issue at stake, namely, whether the market mechanism can be an instrument for the intergenerational distribution of natural resources. In view of Stiglitz's insistence that the market is fit for this role, I can hardly overemphasize my reasons for its denial.

To be sure, those who share Stiglitz's position also argue that although markets admittedly have serious failures, if prices were right everything else—depletion and pollution—would also be right.[8] But no one has yet defined "right" prices. (I assume that by "right prices" they do not mean the "just prices" of the Scholastics.) The rub is that market prices depend on many factors: income distribution, taxation systems, industrial structures, taste spectrums, etc.[9] To wit, the price of gasoline would certainly be different if the geographical distribution of oil deposits were different from what it actually is. I cannot see how we could say which conditions would bring about the right prices. Were the prices right or wrong when large tracts of land were deforested? Were the prices of crude oil until the establishment of the OPEC right or wrong? What kind of perfect market would have prevented the squandering of crude oil over the past forty years?

From another approach, we may note that in order to arrive at the "true" cost of any material commodity, we must know the true values of natural resources *in situ,* which constitute the first cost item. Some economists trained in the neoclassical tradition have occasionally spoken of the "true scarcity value" of natural resources *in situ.*[10] Yet, to my knowledge, the determination of these values is a problem totally ignored by all tints of economic theory. For perhaps the only reasonable solution we may turn to a general, albeit rarely used, economic principle, which is that the value of an irreproducible good—whether Leonardo's Mona Lisa or some crude oil in its earthly pouch—is its auction price. However, the ordinary formulation of this principle omits to add the *sine qua non* condition that all those having a possible interest in the

[8] See references in [1, p. 13].
[9] I naturally exclude the thought that the economic process works over time, even in some acceptable approximation according to the simplified assumptions of the Leontief system.
[10] For example, Amouzegar [6].

commodity must be allowed to bid. Otherwise, if only my neighbor and I were to bid on the Mona Lisa, for example, I may obtain it for a few dollars, since my neighbor hates Renaissance paintings.

The moral is obvious. To arrive at the true scarcity value of any mineral resource, all users of the resource must bid, that is, all users in this generation as well as future ones.[11] Unfortunately, the future generations cannot be present to bid now. The current generation must therefore take into account their needs. Devising a way by which this can be done is admittedly a difficult but not impossible problem. Suffice it to say here that the solution lies in the domain of ethics rather than that of economics.

Stiglitz asserts that the foregoing argument about the independence of the present market from the demand of future generations is fallacious. His point is that since each owner sells to a future owner, who sells to another, and so on, the algorithm will take care of the interests of all future owners *now*. I submit that, on the contrary, it is his argument that is fallacious, the usual fascination with formalism being again responsible for the misinterpretation of the **PAP** algorithm. It is beyond doubt that each individual's actions are geared to the future. But his decisions are based only on whatever evidence the individual has at *that* moment and, moreover, they concern only the probable events within his time horizon. That is, his evidence does not encompass the whole future, nor is his time horizon unlimited (optimistically, it may be taken to cover about thirty years only). Hence, nothing beyond that time horizon bears upon the usual decisions of any individual. It would be preposterous to maintain that, even in a businesslike society such as the United States, the earlier owners of oil fields acted on the thought that one day this country might experience a dangerous shortage of fuels. Had they done so, the shortage would have probably not come so early.[12]

With one important exception (to be considered presently), Stiglitz never instructs us about the criterion of optimality served by the market mechanism and instead speaks only of "efficiency" and "efficient market" without explaining the meaning of these terms. This fact might be taken as an unintentional admission that, whatever the markets may do, they cannot be relied on for a reasonable intergenerational allocation of natural resources. But there is that exception, a mathematical model in which there is a criterion of optimality to be satisfied under the constraint of a given (finite) amount of resources.

---

[11] I must hasten to add that even this *Gedankenexperiment* is not completely satisfactory. The auction price still depends on the income distribution. But this seems to be the best we can do even in the abstract.

[12] The above argument can be easily supported by a graphical analysis, for which see Georgescu-Roegen [1, pp. 30–32].

The model goes back to the famous 1931 article of Harold Hotelling [7]. Beautiful mathematical piece though that article is, it set a fallacious pattern of approach to the economics of exhaustible resources. As Stiglitz and every other writer who has been stirred by the recent events argue,[13] resources must be distributed so that *the sum of discounted future utilities*

$$\int_0^\infty U(c_t)e^{-\rho t}dt \tag{3}$$

must be a maximum, where $U(c_t)$ is the *utility intensity* of c_t, and ρ is the constant discount rate of the future.[14]

As we all know, the idea that future pleasures and pains do not appear to an individual as vivid as present ones constituted a main point of Jeremy Bentham's hedonistic calculus. W. Stanley Jevons introduced it in economics with some very careful considerations [9]. He separated the discount factor into a probability coefficient that the event will actually occur and a coefficient to represent the underestimation of the future experience. But Jevons, while recognizing that the individual's decisions are influenced by both factors, argued that the underestimation of the future is an irrational trait. When tomorrow comes we will be as hungry and as thirsty as we are today. Hence, we should not fail to put aside equal amounts for future satisfactions.[15] However, the reduction resulting from the uncertainty of the future must be retained because of its statistical validity. For a most elementary illustration, let us consider a population of three individuals, one of whom will die each day. If they possess among them six daily rations, they should distribute them in time by discounting the future only according to the probability of survival. This yields the distribution 3, 2, 1, not 2, 2, 2. As we see, the saying "let's eat, drink, and be merry today because tomorrow we may die" makes sense, *but only because humans are mortals.*

For quasi-immortal entities—such as a nation and especially mankind—discounting the future is wrong from any viewpoint. There is no specific reason why such an entity will not experience the same needs at all times. Nor is it subject to a mortality table. The upshot is that equation (3) may apply to a single individual in managing his narrow affairs myopically, but when we come to ask how to distribute resources among generations, we must not in any way discount the future.

To be sure, if all future utilities are treated alike, the beautiful solution reached by Hotelling is of no use anymore. The focus of the problem

---

[13] For example, Koopmans [8].

[14] For my argument I need not preserve the factor corresponding to the population growth in St glitz's formula.

[15] The point has been taken up in greater detail by Strotz [10].

is entirely shifted. The *analytical* solution is to spread resources evenly in time, which in the case of an infinite time horizon yields the paradoxical result that each year a null amount of resources should be consumed. The analytical impasse is eliminated by noting that what we may, for example, seek now is the maximum "amount of life," measured in man $\times$ years, which is tantamount to obtaining the longest life span for the human species [4, p. 304; 1, p. 23]. This solution presupposes that we know the standard level at which mankind must live as well as the future movement of population. Stiglitz's observation that resource planning requires a tremendous amount of information, most of which cannot possibly be available, is very welcome at this point. This is why whenever we may try to prescribe a quantitative policy for the economy of resources we can only play the tune by ear. Besides, instead of basing our recommendations on the ultrafamiliar principle of maximizing "utility," we should try *to minimize future regrets*. This seems to be the only reasonable (I do not think that we could call it rational) recipe for dealing with the most uncertain of all uncertainties—historical uncertainty. We should thus slow down the depletion of fossil fuels so as not to put ourselves in the impossible position of not having enough support for the search for other sources of energy, regardless of whether such a possibility is at present real or not. Had we tried to minimize regrets, we would not be so pressed today by the alarming dwindling away of crude oil resources.

Admittedly, all these considerations take us far away from the teachings of standard economics. But this is precisely the point that needed to be brought home at last.

Turning now to Herman Daly's paper, I do not think I am wrong in judging that by now he has associated his name with a steady-state economy, just as other economists have associated their names with the position "come what may, we will find a way, provided prices are right." For this reason I think that Daly's name should appear in the group "Humanist Economists" in his table of growth critics.[16]

This paper represents an improvement on Daly's earlier pleas. One new point deserves special attention. It is the map in which the hierarchy of ends and means is correlated with the categories of disciplines that keep the human mind continuously on the run. To have a single element by which everything is in the last analysis guided or judged has been a need felt by all truly philosophical schools. All great philosophers have imagined, if not a religious God, at least a philosophical one as the ulti-

---

[16] I have a few other ideas about that table but they are not important enough to mention here, save one: Agrarians in general, not only American Agrarians, deserve great credit for having opposed excessive economic growth.

mate criterion, not for what ought to be, but for what must be. There is an indisputable need for an ultimate end by which we can judge which of our actions are "good" and which are "bad." We always need a criterion of some sort or other. To take a simple but appropriate example: If the price ratio of coffee and meat is, say, 5 to 2, and I spend my budget at a point where my marginal rate of substitution between those commodities is 7 to 4, that is "bad." The criterion of maximum utility for my preference structure tells me so. But why should we not also ask the further question: Are my preferences good or bad? Daly's point is that for this question we must turn to the ultimate end. This paper thus strengthens the impression emerging from his previous writings that the essence of Daly's conception is not economic or demographic, but, rather, ethical—a great merit in a period in which economics has been reduced to a timeless kinematics. As a befitting commandment for the ultimate end of a religion that should help mankind to survive and lead a decent life, I would suggest "Love thy species as thyself" [5]. Such a religion would certainly bring about the amiable community for which Daly fights untiringly. But as intimated earlier, the most challenging enterprise is to establish any religious faith, any faith in an ultimate end.

This is perhaps why Daly does not limit his logistics at this point. He offers other reasons for his blueprint, and it is with respect to these reasons that I entertain some still unshakable doubts.

To begin with, I take exception to Daly's tenet (which actually is inherited from John Stuart Mill) that stationariness alone suffices to clear away all substantial conflicts between individuals or, especially, social classes. Quasi-stationary societies of the past proved that they were as vulnerable from this standpoint as the growing ones of recent times.

Second, there is nothing in Daly's setup to help us determine even in broad strokes the proper standard of living—"the good life"—and, worse still, the proper size of the population. In this last regard, I have suggested that at all times population must remain near the level at which it can be maintained biologically by organic agriculture (which does not necessarily imply a stationary population) [1, p. 34]. I do not know whether Daly subscribes to this necessary measure or not.

Third, a point in great need of clarification is his basic concept of a capital stock that remains constant in amount but may nevertheless undergo qualitative changes.[17] Currently, we measure the amount of capital over the years by values at some basic year. Is such a concessive practice sufficient for a blueprint that is meant to cover not only decades or even centuries, but millennia?

[17] The same difficulty does not arise in regard to constant population, not in any stringent sense.

While still hoping that mankind will ultimately and before it is too late progress toward an amiable congregation as envisioned by Daly and Mill, I have outlined elsewhere some basic reasons why I believe that a steady-state society is an unrealizable blueprint [5]. One of the proposals made in Daly's paper offers me an occasion for supporting my position from a different, more homely angle.

Figure 4-1 contains all the elements (with the same notations) of the diagram by which Daly explains how government may allocate natural resources optimally in a steady state. I take it that the curve *SS'* in his diagram represents only the average extraction cost for each successive unit of the resource in question. The natural resources *in situ* are free goods in the sense that they simply exist for us to mine at some cost whenever we wish. But let us consider now what will happen in the *next* period, after the amount *OQ* has been auctioned off and mined. The new extraction cost will be *BS''*, a curve obtained from *ES'* by horizontal translation to the left. For the same quantity *OQ,* the next generation will have to work much harder, and the government will receive a much smaller scarcity rent (represented by *CAB'E'*). The same mutation will take place for each successive period. How can we then think that such an economy may be in a steady state? To assume that technological progress will just bring the new cost curve *BS''* to the level of *SS'* would be utterly preposterous. It would mean joining the club of the believers in exponential progress.

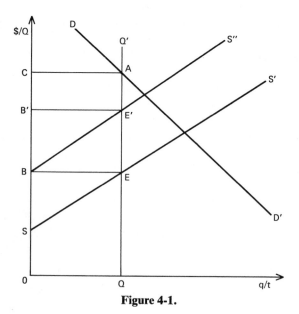

Figure 4-1.

The rub comes from the fact that we always mine "the highest grade and most accessible resources first," as Daly emphasizes. But from my foregoing observations it follows that to do so is not an economic imperative of a general validity. The practice is only one aspect of what I have called the dictatorship of the present over the future.

Conceivably, we could do away with it, too. The government should auction each year an identical representative sample of the entire mineralogical distribution of each kind of resource. But how can one know that distribution and how can the proposed sample be mined? There seems to be no way to do away with the dictatorship of the present over the future, although we may aim at making it as bearable as possible. Mankind's entropic problem will remain forever beyond the reach of any arithmomorphic manipulating model.

References

1. Nicholas Georgescu-Roegen, *Energy and Economic Myths* (New York, Pergamon, 1976).
2. Mark Blaug, "Malthus, Thomas Robert," *International Encyclopedia of the Social Sciences* (New York, Macmillan and Free Press, 1968) vol. 9, p. 551.
3. Hans H. Landsberg, "Growth and Resources," in National Academy of Sciences, *Mineral Resources and the Environment,* appendix to section I (Washington, D.C. NAS, 1975) p. A31.
4. Nicholas Georgescu-Roegen, *The Entropy Law and the Economic Process* (Cambridge, Mass., Harvard University Press, 1971).
5. Nicholas Georgescu-Roegen, "The Steady State and Ecological Salvation: A Thermodynamic Analysis," *Bioscience* vol. 27 (April 1977) pp. 266–270.
6. Jahangir Amouzegar, "The Oil Story: Facts, Fiction and Fair Play," *Petroleum Intelligence Weekly* Supplement, July 2, 1973, pp. 1–6. (Reprinted from *Foreign Affairs,* July 1973).
7. Harold Hotelling, "The Economics of Exhaustible Resources," *Journal of Political Economy* vol. 39 (April 1931) pp. 137–175.
8. Tjalling C. Koopmans, "Some Observations on 'Optimal' Economic Growth and Exhaustible Resources," in H. C. Bos, ed., *Economic Structure and Development: Essays in Honor of Jan Tinbergen* (Amsterdam, North-Holland, 1973) pp. 237–256.
9. W. Stanley Jevons, *The Theory of Political Economy* (London, Macmillan, 1871).
10. Robert H. Strotz, "Myopia and Inconsistency in Dynamic Utility Maximization," *Review of Economic Studies* vol. 23 (1956) pp. 165–180.

5

Fundamental Concepts for the Analysis of Resource Availability

Donald A. Brobst

I
Introduction

Analysis of the future availability of mineral and energy resources in the economy generally is made by examining the records of past production and probing the anticipated availability of these resources under given sets of events and conditions. Through the years, analysts have drawn an assortment of different conclusions from their efforts.

After studying the history of European mining, the geologist D. F. Hewett [1] suggested that the production of metals in a nation endowed with fuels will advance through successive cycles characterized by rises followed by declines in exports of metallic ores; in amount of domestic mining, smelting, and production of metal; and in imports of metallic ores (figure 5-1). Hewett suggested nearly fifty years ago that the position of the United States in such a system was already advanced well beyond the youth indicated by the early cycles.

Varying degrees of concern about the future availability of resources have been expressed in the reports of the President's Materials Policy Commission [2] and the National Commission on Materials Policy [3]. Extreme concern about the future availability of oil and gas was voiced by Hubbert [4] after a study of petroleum discovery and production records. Park [5, 6] questioned the world's ability to provide a universally high level of affluence through continued exponential growth. Meadows and others [7] sounded an alarm about possibilities for the collapse of civilization as we know it from a computerized analysis of factors related to population, industrialization, pollution, food production, and resource depletion. Brooks and Andrews [8] concluded that long before resources were depleted, pollution and social disorders would reduce current complexities to an overwhelming mass of unsolvable problems.

Many other authors, including Barnett and Morse [9] and Goeller and Weinberg [10], have reached more optimistic conclusions that relatively few resource problems loom ahead which cannot be overcome by economic adjustments and technological advancement.

The wide diversity of conclusions drawn from studies of resource availability has caused debate and confusion. The stage is set for controversy about resource use and policy between the extremes of the catastrophists, who foresee the death of our industrial society because of resource shortages, and the cornucopians, who foresee virtually no problems with resources that technology cannot overcome.

Events of the past few years are bringing the controversy over resources into the public arena. The importance of energy to the world economy now has become quite clear to many, although it is doubtful that the public has yet grasped the magnitude of the implications of possible restrictions on the future availability of energy materials. The world's economic life now consists of a system whose parts are interdependent, and tampering with any part may cause disruptions at many places. This latter point has been well demonstrated by such events as the sharp increase in petroleum prices, the nationalization of mineral- and energy-producing companies, and the attempts of mineral-producing nations to raise prices individually or through the formation of cartels. The results of social pressures here and abroad for more stringent environmental standards, especially with respect to mining and manufacturing activities, might reduce the ability of the world to meet its anticipated increase in demand for mineral and energy materials.

More and more the components of the economic system are being examined in detail to establish a better understanding of the relation of the parts to the whole system. This systems approach has been discussed by Churchman [11], who defined the method as simply a way of thinking about total systems and their components. The conclusions of a study

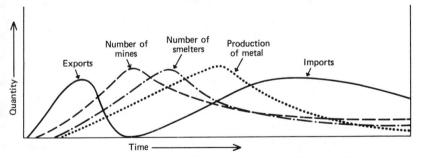

Figure 5-1. Cycles in metal production. (From D. F. Hewett, "Cycles in Metal Production," *Transactions of the American Institute of Mining and Metallurgical Engineers*, 1929, p. 89.)

done by a systems approach, however, will reflect the background of the analyst.

The study of mineral and energy resources brings together many disciplines, but especially economics, engineering, and geology, the latter itself a combination of physical sciences. Practitioners of each discipline will bring their own perspectives to the conclusions of a study. Economists generally have been most interested in the flow of resources from the mine portal and wellhead through the economic system. Engineers, depending on their specialty, have been most interested in how to mine, beneficiate, and use mineral and energy resources. Economists and engineers indicate a primary concern for the economic availability of resources. Geologists generally have been most interested in the scientific aspects of the occurrence of rocks, minerals, and energy materials and the application of geologic information to the search for deposits that will assure the availability of commercial supplies at the mine portals and wellheads. Geologists indicate a primary interest in the geologic availability of resources. There is overlap of interest, to be sure, but fundamental concepts as understood and applied by each analyst are bound to affect the conclusions drawn. I should like, therefore, to discuss from a geologist's perspective some concepts that are fundamental to making and evaluating analyses of resource availability.

The significance of the role of minerals and fuels in the U.S. economy can be overlooked easily in the gross national product (GNP). Table 5-1 shows the value of U.S. production and imports of fuels, nonmetals, and metals in wellhead and mine portal condition for 1972 and 1975. These years were chosen for comparison because 1972 was the last of the "normal" years prior to the oil embargo of 1973. The values for 1972 indicate the peak of economic growth at the last upward cycle. By 1975, the value of domestic production had nearly doubled to more than 62 billion dollars, whereas the value of imports had risen more than fivefold. In both 1972 and 1975, the largest values shown are for fuel materials, but notice the greatly increased value for both domestic and imported fuels in 1975. Another point that needs to be emphasized from these data is that the value of the nonmetals produced domestically in both 1972 and 1975 was nearly twice that of the metals. These relative values of materials are virtually unknown to the public, and perhaps unknown as well as to a large segment of those involved in certain aspects of business, economics, and government. The domestic production of these materials in 1975 had a value of 62.3 billion dollars in a 1.5 trillion dollar economy; only 4.1 percent of the GNP, but the basis of it all.

The statistical summary of the world's mining activity published annually in September by the *Mining Magazine* [12] offers some insights

Table 5-1. Mineral Materials in the United States Economy
(billions of dollars)

	1972	1975
U.S. production		
Fuels	22.1	47.9
Nonmetals	6.5	9.5
Metals (from U.S. ores)	3.6	4.9
Total	32.2	62.3
Gross national product (GNP)	1,152	1,516
U.S. production of fuels, nonmetals, and		
metals as percent of GNP	2.8	4.1
Imports		
Fuels	2.8	19.7
Nonmetals and metals	1.6	2.0
Total	4.4	21.7

Source: U.S. Bureau of Mines.

into the geographic distribution and current availability of twenty-three metals and minerals traded in world markets. The commodities are asbestos, bauxite (aluminum), boron, diamonds, fluorspar, phosphate, potash, iron, manganese, chromium, nickel, molybdenum, tungsten, titanium, copper, lead, zinc, tin, mercury, silver, gold, platinum, and uranium. The annual production of these twenty-three materials from only about 1,100 mines accounts for 90 percent of all mining output other than coal. Data from the Soviet Union, some nations in Eastern Europe, and the Peoples' Republic of China, however, are not included in the survey. The minimum annual production of mines on the list is 150,000 tons and the highest category of production includes those whose yield exceeds 3 million metric tons of ore annually. In this latter group are really the giant mines of the world, 191 of them with an average annual production of 7 million tons of ore. The United States has 185 (17 percent) of the 1,116 mines listed and 51 (27 percent) of 191 giant mines, but including some only for copper, iron, molybdenum, boron, potash, and phosphate.

The information in table 5-2 is a recapitulation of data about the 1,116 mines, their distribution by principal product, size of production, and location. The important considerations of coproducts and by-products in many metal mines, especially those of base and precious metals, had to be omitted from the table, but that does not greatly affect its usefulness. Some metals, such as iron, copper, lead, and zinc, are widespread and produced in many mines of all sizes. Other commodities, such as nickel, titanium, mercury, and fluorspar, are less widespread and come from the smaller size categories of mines. Some commodities are produced in highly restricted areas, such as molybdenum (North Amer-

Table 5-2. Summary of the Products, Distribution, and Annual Production of the World's Major Mines

	Iron	Man-ga-nese	Chro-mium	Nickel	Mo-lyb-de-num	Tung-sten	Alum-inum	Tita-nium
Mines—Size A[a]								
North America	15	—	—	1	3	—	—	—
Central & South America	7	—	—	—	—	—	2	—
Australasia	8	—	—	1	—	—	2	—
Europe	10	—	—	—	—	—	—	—
Africa	7	—	—	—	—	—	1	—
Asia	2	—	—	1	—	—	—	—
Total	49	—	—	3	3	—	5	—
Mines—Size B[b]								
North America	26	—	—	16	—	—	—	—
Central & South America	11	1	—	3	—	—	11	—
Australasia	5	1	—	4	—	—	1	—
Europe	33	—	—	2	—	—	2	—
Africa	10	1	—	—	—	—	2	—
Asia	10	—	—	—	—	—	1	—
Total	95	3	—	25	—	—	17	—
Mines—Size C[c]								
North America	21	—	—	11	2	3	2	5
Central & South America	11	1	—	2	—	—	6	—
Australasia	—	—	—	10	—	2	—	12
Europe	39	—	1	3	—	3	7	1
Africa	15	8	5	5	—	—	2	—
Asia	14	7	3	1	—	1	6	1
Total	100	16	9	32	2	9	23	19
World total: Mines	245	19	9	60	5	9	45	19

Source: Mining Magazine
[a] Production greater than 3 million tons per year.
[b] Production 1 to 3 million tons per year.
[c] Production 150,000 to 1 million tons per year.

ica), chromium (chiefly Africa), manganese (Africa and Asia), boron (United States and Turkey), tin (predominantly Asia), platinum (almost exclusively southern Africa), and asbestos (Canada and southern Africa).

Compilations, such as those in table 5-2, which are based principally on records of mine production, only indicate where mining is in progress, what is produced, and provide an idea of current capacity of production by mine and commodity. These data also reflect something about the past success of the search for needed materials. The mine may or may not be located close to its markets, depending in part on economics and or mineral commodity

Tin	Mercury	Silver	Gold	Platinum group	Uranium	Boron	Potash	Fluorspar	Phosphate	Diamonds	Asbestos	Total mines
—	—	—	—	—	1	1	2	—	14	—	2	75
—	—	—	—	—	—	—	—	—	—	—	—	17
—	—	—	—	—	—	—	—	—	—	—	—	13
—	—	—	—	—	—	—	5	—	—	—	—	18
1	—	—	6	3	—	—	—	—	5	9	—	40
15	—	—	—	—	—	—	—	—	0	—	1	28
16	—	—	6	3	1	1	7	—	19	9	3	191
—	—	—	2	—	1	—	14	—	9	—	9	102
2	—	—	1	—	—	—	—	—	—	—	—	33
—	—	—	—	—	—	—	—	—	2	—	1	18
—	—	—	—	—	—	—	10	—	2	—	1	55
3	—	—	27	1	1	—	—	1	7	3	4	73
6	—	—	1	—	—	—	1	—	4	—	—	30
11	—	—	31	1	2	—	25	1	24	3	15	311
—	2	5	17	—	18	—	1	—	9	—	2	161
7	—	4	2	—	—	—	—	4	—	—	1	81
4	—	—	4	—	1	—	—	—	2	—	—	45
3	1	1	3	—	2	—	7	2	1	—	—	127
12	—	—	15	1	—	—	—	2	11	3	9	116
2	1	1	5	—	1	2	—	1	2	—	—	88
28	4	11	46	1	22	2	8	9	25	3	12	618
55	4	11	83	5	25	3	40	10	68	15	30	1120

in part on the geology of the commodity and its ore deposits and the ease of discovery of such deposits. The richest and easiest-to-find deposits of workable ores generally are mined first. The analysis of production data is informative and valuable, but it faces the past, and not the future. These data indicate little or nothing about the economic health of the mine under anticipated conditions or about the geologic features that do or do not assure the future productivity of the mine. The most useful analysis of the future availability of mineral materials, therefore, should include an examination of related economic and geologic factors. Some important and specific characteristics of mineral and energy resources must be more widely recognized, as well as better understood, before the controversy about resource issues can be reduced.

II
Characteristics of Resources

This discussion will be concerned only with the nonrenewable resources, the minerals and rocks of commercial value, including the fossil fuels—coal, oil, and gas. A mineral resource is a concentration of a naturally occurring solid, liquid, or gaseous material in or on the earth's crust in such form that economic extraction of a commodity is currently or potentially feasible. That word "potentially" is very important, but the definition and application is still highly subjective despite the generation of much new data about supply and demand and changes in economics that may favorably or adversely affect profitable extraction.

The definition of resources involves geologic and economic factors. To be available on the market, a mineral material must have both geologic and economic availability. Geologic availability concerns the very existence, mode of occurrence, and distribution of these materials in our planet. The earth is abundantly endowed with useful mineral and fuel materials, but the concept of geologic availability must not be taken for granted. Today's knowledge of the geologic occurrence and the distribution of minerals and fossil fuels suggests that most of these materials will not be available into the infinite future without improved technology and significant changes in the availability of energy and water. Economic availability involves the well-known, broad considerations of the availability of capital for exploration and development, the costs of production, and the expected market price of the material through time, as well as many other critical technological, environmental, social, legal, and political factors. All of these geologic and economic factors must be in favorable balance to allow the production of the minerals and fuels at a profit, and profit is a key word in the description of a free-enterprise, market economy. Industry cannot, however, supply materials that are geologically unavailable or technologically unrecoverable, irrespective of continued price rise.

Figure 5-2 shows a scheme for the classification of resources and the relation between the geologic and the economic factors of resources. The general features of this resource classification were proposed by V. E. McKelvey [13] and, with modifications, the classification was used in U.S. Geological Survey Professional Paper 820, "United States Mineral Resources" in 1973. After further modification in association with the

U.S. Bureau of Mines, this classification was jointly adopted by both bureaus as as a basis for discussing mineral resources (U.S. Geological Survey [14]).

Total resources consist of those materials that have already been identified and those that are as yet undiscovered, but which at some time might be discovered and used. Considering the identified materials, there are those that are currently of economic value and those of sub-economic value that cannot be brought to market now. The special name for the identified resources of economic value is reserves. They are that portion of the identified resource from which a usable mineral and energy commodity can be economically and legally extracted at the time of determination. The term ore is often used for reserves of some minerals. There are two categories of undiscovered resources. The hypothetical resources are those yet to be discovered in known mining districts or oil and gas fields. Speculative resources are those undiscovered deposits that still lie in undiscovered mining districts and oil and gas fields. Careful examination of figure 5-2 shows undiscovered resources of economic value as well as undiscovered resources of subeconomic value. The arrow along the bottom of the diagram indicates an increasing degree from right to left of geologic assurance of the existence of the deposit. The arrow on the right side of the diagram indicates an increasing degree from the

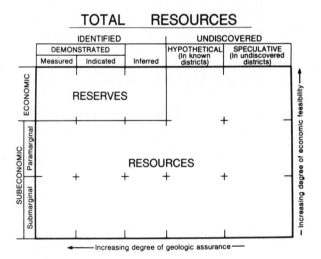

Figure 5-2. The classification of mineral resources as adopted by the U.S. Geological Survey, and the U.S. Bureau of Mines. (From "Principles of the Mineral Resource Classification System of the U.S. Bureau of Mines and the U.S. Geological Survey," Geological Survey Bulletin 1450-A, 1976.)

bottom to the top of the diagram of economic feasibility of recovering the material.

This scheme for the classification of mineral resources is not the only one available, but it can serve as a basis for further discussion. For those who wish to pursue further the philosophy and development of the terminology of resource classification, this and other suggested systems have been discussed critically by Schanz [15].

New reserves are sought from extensions of known deposits, through economic and technical changes that permit the conversion of identified subeconomic resources to reserves, or by the discovery of new deposits of economic value. These steps must be taken as old mines and old mining districts become geologically exhausted for lack of material or become economically exhausted by reaching their economic limits of production. In the short term, reserves of many commodities may likely be increased by concentrating effort on the search for undiscovered, now mostly hidden, deposits geologically similar to those now technically usable.

Geologic exhaustion is not imaginary. It happens. Many types of ore deposits have sharp physical boundaries. When mining reaches those boundaries in the three dimensions, the deposit is geologically, or physically, exhausted. In such cases, geologic and economic exhaustion are simultaneous.

Other geological types of deposits have gradational boundaries, commonly characterized by outward decreases in the content of the valuable material. In these types of deposits, therefore, geologic exhaustion commonly does not occur at the same time as economic exhaustion. The mine may cease to be profitable and operations cease, not necessarily for want of material, but because it has met an economic limit. Should economics change favorably, however, such a mine might have its identified subeconomic resources converted to reserves and mining operations might be resumed. Resumption of profitable operations requires that costs of rehabilitating the mine also be amortized. In some underground mines these costs can be especially high, perhaps too high to support the rehabilitation, in which case the mine remains in a state of economic exhaustion.

Deposits of petroleum are special cases in economic exhaustion. Primary recovery methods generally obtain only about 30 percent of the resource that occurs in the ground. Thus, an oil field generally is economically exhausted long before it is geologically exhausted. Secondary recovery methods may increase the recovery rate somewhat, but unless technology and other economic factors improve considerably, more of the identified resources may continue to remain beneath the surface than can be recovered.

Although geologic exhaustion is final, economic exhaustion may or may not be final, and only the changes of economic conditions through time provide the answers. In either case of exhaustion, wanted mineral and fuel materials cannot enter the supply system. It is necessary to understand the difference between the two kinds of exhaustion and how they relate to estimates of resource availability. Tilton [16] has recently discussed these concepts in detail.

The reserves of many mineral materials have been increased during past years despite increased production. It must be recognized, however, that should economic conditions change for what might be termed "the worse," materials also may easily drop out of the reserves and again become part of the identified subeconomic resources. Any change that reduces the value of material below the level of profitable production reduces the size of the reserve. For example, the sudden massive rise of energy costs and other increased production costs combined with depressed prices has reduced the reserves at many mines. How great is the reduction? This requires complete recalculations for each mine and commodity involved for every major change in conditions. The overall effect of changes may be slight or great, but constant checks are required. A reserve is calculated from a given set of conditions and it is necessary to know what conditions form the basis of the calculation. Without this information, it is virtually impossible to evaluate the meaning of a reserve figure. It is possible, however, to make a series of calculations for many varying sets of conditions and estimate what amounts of material might be available under many circumstances. All of these calculations for each deposit should take into consideration the basic geologic information about the tonnage, content (grade), spatial distribution, and mineralogical characteristics of the mineral materials in the ground.

Reserves are but a small part of the resources of any given commodity. Reserves and resources are part of a dynamic system and they cannot be inventoried like cans of tomatoes on a grocer's shelf. New scientific discoveries, new technology, and new commercial demands or restrictions are constantly affecting amounts of reserves and resources. Reserves and resources do not exist until commercial demand puts a value on a material in the market. Over the years, materials containing about 80 of the 92 naturally occurring elements have come into commercial use.

The diagram in figure 5-2 can be used to summarize the knowledge of the reserves and resources of any commodity. Resources are best treated on a commodity-by-commodity basis. The data may be summarized in a semiquantitative or a quantitative way, although filling in all the resource categories with accurate tonnages is currently impossible and is not likely ever to be possible. In the meantime, some information is needed to make value judgments. Quantitative reserve information can be assembled from the mining or petroleum companies for a given commodity. Companies in the United States are obliged neither to publish such data nor give it to government agencies, except in cases involving operations on public lands, but most companies cooperate with those agencies whose work involves a need to know about current and future availability of nonrenewable resources. It is understood, of course, that agencies receiving data considered confidential by a company will release such information to the public only in a composite way, so that records from individual companies are not specifically identifiable.

There are differences in virtually every resource and reserve estimate made because each is made for a specific purpose from the data available to the compiler. Each is biased somehow because of different approaches to analysis through the use of incomplete data that are not uniformly reported. There is little chance of escaping some subjectivity even when the compiler tries to be as objective as possible. If a geologist makes a resource estimate, it likely will be cast first in terms of material in place in the ground based on his best knowledge of the shape of the deposit and its grade and tonnage to a certain depth. Mining engineers are likely to think more in terms of how much of the commodity can be recovered through a period of time at today's or a future price. Estimates are likely to be in terms of ore of a certain grade or tons of the commodity or metal contained in the ore. The petroleum engineers will think in terms of oil or gas recoverable by primary and secondary methods. It is important to know what geologic and economic characteristics were used in making the estimate. All too often in the past a reader was left to decide for himself how the estimates were made by the author.

When the quantification of undiscovered resources is considered, one question looms over all others: How is the undiscovered resource quantified? Obviously the precision is low and much lower than estimates of the identified resources. Most of the estimates of undiscovered resources are based on geologic extrapolation. In the absence of better techniques, it seems reasonable that the earth scientists should be accorded the dubious honor of assisting in the assessment of these undiscovered resources through their best interpretation of the data available at the time. Better techniques to assess resources definitely are needed and they have a priority in the work of economic geologists, who are but a part of a relatively small profession. Although the need to assess the mineral resources of local areas, regions, and nations of the world has only recently been more widely recognized, scientists grappling with these problems through the years have produced some useful methods and thought-provoking papers.

More than twenty-five years ago, Lasky [17] discussed national mineral resource appraisal and Nolan [18] discussed the search for new ore deposits from a geological perspective. Lasky [19] also discussed cumulative resources of porphyry copper deposits as related to ore grade. The grade and tonnage relations among copper deposits were reexamined by Singer, Cox, and Drew [20]. Allais [21] brought a new approach to his study of resources in the Algerian Sahara. Harris [22] applied multivariate statistical analysis to mineral exploration and his ideas, developed in subsequent years, are reviewed in a later paper [23] that includes a pertinent bibliography of his own and other works. The state of the art of modeling mineral material systems has been surveyed and summarized in a report prepared for Resources for the Future by Vogely [24]. The evolution of techniques for assessing oil and gas resources was reviewed by Miller and coauthors [25], who also provided an extensive bibliography. A comprehensive posting of the literature on this subject is beyond the scope of this discussion, but the works cited can provide an entry into the complexities of estimating the availability of mineral resources.

Figure 5-3 can assist in clarifying several other points about the mineral resource diagram in figure 5-2, especially the nature of the right and bottom boundaries of the diagram. The right boundary of the diagram in figure 5-2 represents the limit of those undiscovered resources that occur in "conventional" ore deposits, those of types already known. Beyond the right boundary of this diagram lies an area of unconceived resources (in figure 5-3). This is the area in which lie those bodies of rocks and minerals that have not yet been recognized as types of deposits that may have potential commercial value. An example of such a deposit is the recent discovery of the mineral sphalerite, the sulfide of zinc, in fractures in coal in the Illinois Basin. These deposits were in years past not only undiscovered, but unconceived. When the deposits were discovered, however, they immediately became identified resources awaiting further evaluation to determine whether the sphalerite now constitutes a reserve, an economically recoverable resource, or a subeconomic resource.

In figure 5-3, the line labeled potential economic threshold coincides with the lower boundary of the resource diagram in figure 5-2. This threshold marks the lowest concentration of potential economic value of a desired material in a deposit. Below this concentration there is, at the time of determination, little or no expectation that the material will become commercially valuable. Thus, calculations of resources do have a lower limit based on economic considerations.

Geologic and technologic considerations have important effects on this economic boundary for each element or commodity sought. In some cases, the selection of this boundary varies for different types of deposits which contain the same, as well as different, materials from which the desired constituent is to be recovered. Many people in science and industry currently consider the value of this economic threshold for copper to be 0.1 percent. At this concentration, most of the copper still occurs in separate mineral particles that technologically can be separated from the rest of the associated minerals. The copper-bearing minerals referred to here are principally the various sulfides, sulfates, carbonates, and oxides, as well as native copper, which unlike many elements, does occur in its elemental form in nature. Any of these minerals may be abundant enough to be a major component of the copper ore in a deposit. The economic threshold of cobalt resources, however, was placed at 0.01 percent by Vhay and coauthors [26, p. 150], a value considerably below that of copper. Because of its geology and economics, cobalt rarely is the primary product of a mine, but has been, or might be, a by-product from some types of metallic ore deposits at home and abroad. Cobalt commonly occurs in many deposits, both in small amounts of minerals con-

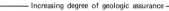

Figure 5-3. Diagram showing the relation of resources to noneconomic materials.

taining abundant cobalt and in more abundant minerals that contain little cobalt. Barite, the sulfate of barium, occurs in three major geologic types of deposits, each with its own economic threshold for purposes of calculating resources [27, pp. 81–82].

Figure 5-3 also shows two other boundaries, the mineralogical threshold, which lies in the field of noneconomic materials, and crustal abundance, which forms the base of the field of noneconomic materials. The mineralogical threshold in this context refers to the minimum natural conditions that will permit the formation of separate particles of specific minerals of the type that, if abundant enough, could be mined and processed by current methods as ores, commercial sources of a wanted material. This statement also implies that the mineralogical threshold might or might not coincide with the economic threshold, depending on the material under discussion and length of time being considered for potential development. Under the constraints of current technology, the economic threshold for most elements is not likely soon to fall below the mineralogical threshold. As the concentration of chemical elements decreases to levels below that which allows the formation of separate particles of ore minerals, the elements are dispersed in the crystal structures of the other kinds of minerals that comprise the noneconomic, ordinary rocks constituting the bulk of the earth's crust. At these low levels of concentration elements are said to occur at their crustal abundance.

The materials in the field bounded by the mineralogic threshold and crustal abundance have geologic characteristics so different from those in all of the fields above the mineralogical threshold that some examination of the composition of the earth's crust and the distribution of its chemical elements is necessary in order to recognize current limitations on resources. This information is especially pertinent to the frequently touted idea that the ultimate answer to man's resource problems lies in the mining of vast tonnages of rock to recover the many elements available only in the low concentration ranges of crustal abundance. Geologic reasons suggest that such a vision is not likely to be fulfilled in the foreseeable future without at least the availability of cheap energy in virtually unlimited quantities.

III
Crustal Abundance and Resources

Four of the many estimates of the composition of the earth's crust found in the literature are shown in table 5-3. Two recent estimates of the average composition of the earth's crust are given, along with two esti-

Table 5-3. Average Composition of the Earth's Crust and the Continental Crust in Weight Percent

	Earth's crust		Continental crust	
	Mason[a]	Vinogradov[b]	Skinner[c]	Taylor[d]
Oxygen	46.60	47.00	45.20	46.40
Silicon	27.72	29.50	27.20	28.15
Aluminum	8.13	8.05	8.00	8.23
Iron	5.00	4.65	5.80	5.63
Calcium	3.63	2.96	5.06	4.15
Sodium	2.83	2.50	2.32	2.36
Potassium	2.59	2.50	1.68	2.09
Magnesium	2.09	1.87	2.77	2.33
Titanium	0.44	0.45	0.86	0.57
Hydrogen	0.14	NG	0.14	NG
Total	99.17	99.48	99.03	99.91
All other elements	0.83	0.52	0.97	0.09

NG, Not given.

[a] From Brian Mason, *Principles of Geochemistry* (New York, Wiley, 1958).
[b] From A. P. Vinogradov, "Average Contents of Chemical Elements in the Principal Types of Igneous Rocks of the Earth's Crust," translated from the Russian in *Geochemistry*, no. 7 (1962), pp. 641–664.
[c] From B. J. Skinner, "A Second Iron Age Ahead," *American Scientist*, vol. 64 (1976), pp. 258–269.
[d] From S. R. Taylor, "The Abundance of the Chemical Elements in the Continental Crust—A New Table," *Geochemica et Cosmochemica Acta*, vol. 28 (1964), pp. 1273–1285.

mates of the composition of the crust underlying the continents, which now provides our useful mineral materials. The values for each of the ten most abundant elements are of the same order of magnitude. The data also make it quite clear that the ten most abundant elements comprise the bulk of the crust, more than 99 percent. Only a glance at table 5-2 is necessary to see that many of the elements most useful in industry do not appear in table 5-3. In fact, the remaining 82 naturally occurring elements comprise less than 1 percent of the crust. Consider, then, that these scarce elements, if evenly distributed throughout the crust, rarely would occur in amounts in excess of a few grams per metric ton. Conventional ore deposits currently of commercial value for given elements contain concentrations that are about 5 to more than 2,000 times greater than the estimated crustal abundance of the element. The occurrence of any of the scarce elements in concentrations sufficient for mining is exceptionally rare and of great importance to us, so much so that large amounts of time and money are devoted to their study in order to discover and use them.

Recently Parker [28] and Vokes [29] have discussed, summarized, and cited much pertinent information about the chemical composition of the crust. These chemical data about the abundant and scarce elements are the basis for calculations of the apparently astronomically large amounts of metallic and nonmetallic resources in the earth. There are virtually as many sets of data as there are estimators because each selects data and a method of approach to prepare for interpretation. Many chemical analyses are available from surface samples, but few are available from samples recovered from the depths of the earth. The accuracy and precision of the methods used to determine the concentration of each element, not only the scarce, but also the plentiful ones, in rock samples have been discussed in considerable detail in many reports. One of the most recent of these reports [30] contains a great deal of discussion and many bibliographic citations. Few samples are analyzed for every element. Analytical methods to determine some elements are complex and difficult. Defining accurately and precisely the chemical composition of the earth's crust becomes difficult at best, considering the problems of inadequate sampling and the variety of analytical and computational methods available. The interpretation of data used to estimate the composition of the earth's crust was discussed by Miesch [31], who suggested several ways to minimize inadequacies inherent in such an undertaking. In a discussion of the theory of error in geochemical data, Miesch [32, p. A16] warned that the effects of overall bias in geochemical errors are usually not severe, unless the purpose of the investigation is to estimate absolute mean concentrations of constituents to several significant figures.

Notice in table 5-3 that the estimates by Skinner and Taylor of the scarce elements in the continental crust vary by a factor of about ten. It is truly perilous to try to characterize the average composition of large volumes of rock because even small differences in the estimated abundance of the scarce elements will greatly affect the amount of the element anticipated to be available. The chemical composition of many minerals has some limited variation. Different minerals form rocks that have a wider range in composition, and the abundance of rock types varies in different parts of the crust. The problems compound quickly.

Despite these problems, some useful general and specific information is available. Ore minerals of many abundant elements are about as small a group as that of some scarce elements. Although iron, aluminum, and magnesium are among the more abundant elements in the earth's crust, their presence in many common minerals does not mean that any combination of minerals constitutes ore. The most desirable ores of iron and aluminum are oxides, but most of these two elements are bound with other elements in common and abundant silicate minerals of relatively little or no economic value as sources of the two metals. Much magnesium also is fixed in refractory silicate minerals, so much so that sea water and natural brines are its major ores.

The scarce elements are found concentrated many times more than their crustal abundance in various commercially valuable ore minerals that commonly, but not exclusively, are oxides, sulfides, sulfates, carbonates, and, in some cases, native elements. The mineralogical threshold, like the economic threshold, generally occurs at concentrations of 0.01 to 0.1 percent. Concentrations greater than 0.1 percent of a scarce element in a chemical analysis generally indicate that the sample might contain ore-type minerals of the element. Gold and uranium are two exceptions to this generalization, in that they may form separate minerals at concentrations well below 0.1 percent. In concentrations below the value of the mineralogical threshold, however, most scarce elements are dispersed in the crystal structure of other minerals according to physical laws that allow substitution of some elements for others under certain conditions. In many cases of such substitution, these small amounts of an element are not economically recoverable because of the manner in which the elements are bound tightly together in the crystal structure. This is especially true of small amounts of metals dispersed in silicate minerals, minerals that make up most of the earth's crust.

Mineralogy and chemistry are highly important in determining the occurrence of chemical elements in ore-type minerals or as substitutes for other elements in the structure of other minerals, especially silicate minerals. For example, as much as several tenths of 1 percent barium could occur in a rock where it could all be replacing some of the potassium in feldspar, a complex aluminum silicate mineral. In order to recover such barium, the feldspar would have to be recovered and then the barium from the feldspar. The same could be true for small amounts of lead. The removal of metals from silicate structures will require much more energy than the recovery of a similar amount of material from the minerals of a conventional ore deposit, not only because of the larger amount of material that must be processed, but also the greater difficulty of separating the metal from the atomic structure of the silicate.

Table 5-4 is a compilation of some industrially useful nonferrous and ferrous metals and their concentration in grams per metric ton of the average continental crust according to the estimate of Lee and Yao [33]. In this list only iron, aluminum, and titanium are among the most abundant elements; the others are among those scarce elements that are less than 1 percent of the earth's crust. The table also presents a calculation of the number of metric tons of average crust that would have to be processed at the unlikely recovery rate of 100 percent to obtain 1 ton of the desired element. The calculations indicate that if crust of this

Table 5-4.   Crustal Abundance and Minimum Grades of Ore of Selected Metallic Elements

	Grams per metric ton in continental crust[a]	Metric tons of average crustal rock required to produce 1 metric ton of element[b]	Metric tons of minimum grade ore required in 1977 per metric ton of element[c]
Aluminum	83,000	12	7
Titanium	5,300	188	180
Zinc	81	12,000	40
Copper	50	20,000	200
Lead	13	77,000	50
Tin	1.6	625,000	10,000
Silver	0.065	15,000,000	1,300
Platinum group	0.028	36,000,000	100,000
Gold	0.0035	285,000,000	100,000
Iron	48,000	20	4
Manganese	1,000	1,000	5
Vanadium	120	8,300	100
Chromium	77	13,000	14
Nickel	61	16,000	100
Niobium	20	50,000	1,200
Cobalt	18	55,000	200
Tungsten	1.2	830,000	200
Molybdenum	1.1	910,000	400

[a] Data from Tan Lee and Chi-lung Yao, "Abundance of Chemical Elements in the Earth's Crust and Its Major Tectonic Units," *International Geology Review*, vol. 12, no. 7 (1970) pp. 778–786.
[b] Assuming 100 percent recovery, which is not likely.
[c] Based on data in D. A. Brobst and W. P. Pratt, eds., *United States Mineral Resources*, U.S. Geological Survey Professional Paper 820, 1973.

composition were available, the number of tons to be processed per ton of some metals recovered would be staggering. The right column of table 5-4 presents for comparison the number of tons of ores of minimum grade mined in 1977 from some typical kinds of commercial deposits to yield 1 ton of the element. Notice that titanium, one of the abundant elements, is the only one listed whose current grade of ore closely approaches its estimated abundance in the crust.

IV
Distribution of Abundant and Scarce Elements

All of these geochemical considerations lead to several additional aspects of the resource system. Skinner [34] recently discussed two significant concepts on the distribution of the elements. The distribution of the most geochemically abundant metals such as iron, aluminum, and titanium can be illustrated by the unimodal curve shown in figure 5-4.

For these materials, mining has been carried on in the types of materials of the highest grade that would lie on the right side of the figure. For these elements, Skinner [34, p. 262] suggested that the same kinds of ore-type minerals occur in the rocks of the crust, regardless of the degree of concentration of that element. The concentrating techniques used in current beneficiation and refining processes to extract metal from high grade ores also can be used in the future with less rich material and even

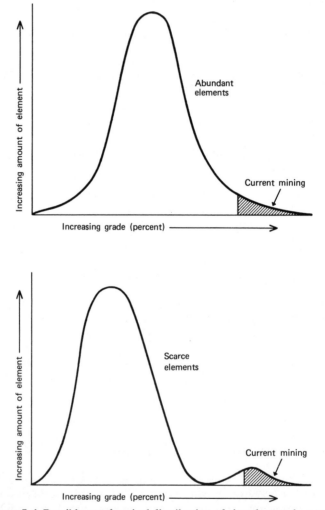

Figure 5-4. Possible geochemical distribution of abundant and scarce elements. (From B. J. Skinner, "A Second Iron Age Ahead?" *American Scientist* vol. 64, 1976, p. 263.)

common rock, but at increasing cost, especially in energy. As the grade or percent of metal in an ore declines arithmetically, the curve suggests that the amount of metal available at a given grade will increase geometrically down to a grade corresponding to the peak of the curve and then decline in both grade and tonnage.

Skinner's suggested distribution for the geochemically scarce elements in the earth's crust also is shown in figure 5-4. This is a bimodal distribution, with the large peak showing the distribution of these elements in common rocks, where they are trapped as atomic substitutes for more abundant metals in the crystal structure of minerals. The small peak represents that part of the scarce elements in the earth's crust that has been freed from such atomic substitution and is recombined as separate minerals. Material under the small hump may be considered the part of the scarce element that is concentrated by the geologic processes which form ore deposits.

If the bimodal distribution of the scarce elements is correct, then the richest grades of ore, represented by the area under the small hump, have been tapped first. There will be an early period during which mining of declining grades will yield larger and larger tonnages of ore. This is the condition that miners seem to have had for most of this century. Eventually, however, the distribution curve turns down again and further reductions in grade also bring declining tonnages of ore at a given grade. There are indications that this might already be happening in the mining of several metals, such as mercury, gold, and silver. The second feature of the bimodal distribution is the indication that a point will eventually be reached where reduction in grade reaches the mineralogical threshold, that point beyond which a scarce element occurs only in positions of substitution and is, therefore, no longer easily amenable to concentration. In figure 5-4, the mineralogical threshold for scarce elements lies somewhere between the humps of the bimodal curve.

Some indirect lines of reasoning suggest that the order of magnitude of the amount of metal concentrated in commercially valuable ore deposits might at least be estimated. Many geologists believe that some of the mass properties of ore deposits, such as size of the largest known deposits, the number of deposits that contain a million or more tons of a given metal, are features that seem to be related to the crustal abundance of the element. V. E. McKelvey [35] was the first to suggest that the discovered reserves of the scarce metals are proportional to their crustal abundance. Skinner [34, p. 266] went on to say that if the conclusion about the size of the hump (figure 5-4) representing the ore deposits of the scarce elements is acceptable, then the size of the humps for other scarce elements can be estimated. The report by the Committee on Mineral Resources and the Environment (COMRATE) of the National Academy of Sciences [36, pp. 128–130] has shown how this might be done. It is estimated that the mineralogical threshold for copper is reached at a grade of 0.1 percent. It also is estimated that no more than 0.01 percent of the total copper in the continental crust will be found concentrated in ore bodies with grades of 0.1 percent copper or more. The reasoning was based on the volume percent of mineralized rock in the most intensely mineralized regions so far discovered and on the distribution frequency of copper deposits in the crust. This value of 0.01 percent must be taken as the maximum possible yield, but it is not likely to be too large by more than a factor of 10. Thus, the size of the ore deposit hump may possibly fall between 0.001 and 0.01 percent of the amount of any scarce metal in the crust.

An important feature of the hypothesis of bimodal distribution for the scarce elements is the mineralogical threshold, or barrier as Skinner [34] called it. But even a recognized mineralogical threshold does not necessarily mean that chemical data from samples that cross such a threshold will produce a bimodal distribution. Analyses that detect amounts of an element contributed by the minutest amount of an ore-type mineral, and that resulting from an abundant substitution are indistinguishable. Even careful microscopic study might fail to detect a few minute grains of an ore mineral. The number and size of the samples selected for chemical study from different environments could well make a difference in the trends indicated by the analytical results. My colleague D. A. Singer [37] has suggested that the greater the variety of geological environments in which an element occurs, the more likely that the distribution of its concentration will be unimodal. This may be a reason for the unimodal distribution of the abundant elements proposed by Skinner [34, p. 263] as shown in figure 5-4.

Bimodal distribution is not evident in the histograms of analytical values for the content of various elements given in many geochemical studies reported in the literature. Few studies are extensive enough to be cited as definite proof because they examine only a suite of a few elements, generally in a restricted or specific environment. Among the larger studies, the histograms for 30 elements analyzed in an examination of 863 samples of surficial materials in the conterminous United States [38] offered no evidence of bimodal distribution of those elements. Histograms of the logarithms of the values suggest that the scarce elements are either log normally distributed or form a log normal distribution censored by analytical limits of their detection. Singer [37] also has pointed out that individual studies in specific geological environments do not prove the lack of a bimodal distribution, but they do suggest that if the distribution is bimodal, the high grade peak might be so small that many tens of thousands of carefully selected samples would be needed to identify it.

Proof for both the bimodal and log normal distributions is lacking, mostly because analytical sampling of the earth's crust is still in its most rudimentary stages, a point strongly made by Skinner [34, p. 265]. Only considerably more sampling will ultimately indicate what the distribution of the scarce elements is. Obtaining this information is important because it bears directly on how successful mineral exploration can, but not necessarily will, be in the next century in finding deposits of needed metals, nonmetals, and fuels that can be used commercially. This knowledge can be used to assign priorities to the types of deposits sought, to estimate the location, size, and grade of deposits remaining to be found and the chances of finding them at reasonable cost of time and money, and to estimate the amount of labor needed to develop new methods to search for hidden ore deposits of conventional and new types. Failure to maintain a satisfactory rate of success in the discovery of mineral and fuel deposits of sufficient size to permit production to meet anticipated future demands would be a devastating constraint upon the continuous economic growth desired and expected by many people.

V
Energy, Technology, and Minerals

These discussions about the geologic occurrence and availability of elements suggest that a steady rise in the amount of energy will be needed to mine larger volumes of lower and lower grade ores and to process their larger volumes by crushing and concentration. Page and Creasey [39] discussed the energy consumption for the utilization of lower and lower grade ores. They concluded that the energy required to produce a unit of metal can be used to determine a lower limit on the grade of ores used to calculate potentially economic resources. This lower limit of grade can be evaluated and that figure can be used as a limiting factor in the search for low-grade minerals that might be mined in the foreseeable future.

The energy requirements for the recovery of the scarcer elements might be very different from those for the abundant metals, as shown qualitatively in figure 5-5. The two curves are parallel until the conventional ores of scarce elements have been worked out. Once a mineralogical threshold is reached, however, a tremendous jump in energy consumption will take place to recover the scarce elements because traditional mineral concentration processes can no longer be used. The scarce metals will have to be sought in silicate minerals that will have to be broken down in order to release these tightly bound metals. The magnitude of energy increase will naturally vary with the kind of host minerals; but for most silicates, the energy demand will jump by a factor of 100 to 1,000. Few data are available pertaining to these energy needs, but they will no doubt be much higher than the needs for processing a conventional ore deposit. It seems unlikely that the mineralogical threshold will be exceeded simply because costs might become unbearable if only the current and traditional sources of energy are available.

To emphasize further the relationship of energy and concentration of elements in ore deposits, look at a set of examples for copper. If the concentration of copper in the continental crust is correctly estimated to be 50 grams per metric ton, 20,000 tons of rock would have to be processed to recover 1 metric ton of copper from silicate minerals. Consider the possibility that 0.1 percent copper will be the lower limit of grade of the ore (the mineralogical threshold), then 1,000 tons of rock will have to be processed to obtain 1 ton of copper from disseminated sulfide minerals. At a grade of 0.5 percent copper, as in a typical porphyry-type deposit mined today, only 200 tons of rock will have to be processed to obtain 1 metric ton of copper from sulfide minerals. Thus, the copper in the sulfide ore of porphyry deposits is concentrated 100 times more than that in crustal abundance.

Granting the point that a mineralogical threshold does not exist for ore-type minerals of abundant elements, it seems quite probable that the recovery of these minerals well may be constrained under certain condi-

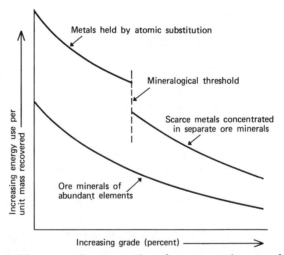

† ·**Figure 5-5.** Diagrammatic presentation of energy requirements for recovering abundant and scarce elements. (Modified from B. J. Skinner, "A Second Iron Age Ahead?" *American Scientist* vol. 64, 1976, p. 267.)

tions by an economic threshold, especially when those minerals are simply too disseminated to be recovered economically. We must not forget that vast amounts of even the most abundant elements in the earth's crust also are fixed as constituents of the common silicate minerals and that they will be just as difficult and relatively expensive to separate and recover from the tight bonds of the silicate crystal structures as the lesser amounts of the scarce elements. Without the readily available large amounts of inexpensive energy heralded by Goeller and Weinberg [10], the mineral materials geologically and economically available to the consumers of the world are much more distinctly limited than many people realize.

It seems likely that lower grade materials from conventional ore deposits probably will continue to be used before unconventional or new types of deposits will be opened, even in times of rising prices, because the technology and plants are available. It is hard to resist using tried and true methods, even with rising energy costs.

The increasing use of even the most abundant metals will lead to increased use of energy, although a better performance in recycling some metals could help to reduce energy demands. Aluminum refining has a deserved reputation as a high energy consumer, twice as much as copper and six times as much as steel with the same tonnage of product. This certainly has to be considered when aluminum is suggested as a substitute for copper. It will, moreover, require more energy to extract and produce aluminum from possible alternative aluminum-bearing minerals, such as alunite, a hydrated sulfate of aluminum and potassium, or dawsonite, a hydrated sodium-aluminum carbonate, each with an aluminum content of about 15 percent, than it does to extract the 25 percent of metallic aluminum from bauxite, the currently used oxide ore. But collected aluminum scrap can be reprocessed at perhaps as little as 5 percent of the energy cost needed to produce primary aluminum. Titanium, whose abundance makes it a prospective substitute for scarce metals, currently requires twice as much energy per ton to manufacture as primary aluminum from current sources. After collection, the recycling of copper takes about 5 percent as much energy as the production of primary copper.

The trash piles of our consumption-oriented society contain resources which would be valued highly if discovered in their native state. There is almost as much heat value in a ton of municipal trash as there is in a ton of lignite. The trash lies generally within a few miles of the point of potential use. Currently junked automobiles weigh about 4,000 pounds (1,800 kg) and contain about 80 percent iron and steel. Certainly the discovery of a deposit of iron ore in our nation yielding half that value in metallic iron would be welcomed. Instead, taconite containing 30 percent or less iron is mined and beneficiated. These ores, moreover, require five times as much energy to make a ton of molten steel than to make a ton of steel from collected scrap. The reuse of such materials helps to solve not one problem but three. Our needs for scarce materials are satisfied, energy is saved, and some much needed clean-up work is done at the same time.

More intensive recycling of mineral materials is possible. A system for recycling many materials has not been developed because of past conditions, when recycling was considered uneconomic, that is, unnecessary. Changes in economic conditions could bring about a rapid reappraisal of the value of recycling mineral materials.

The success of the long- and short-term search for ore deposits and energy resources will have to depend in good measure on the development of new technology. Starr and Rudman [40] of the Electric Power Research Institute recently pointed out in *Science* magazine that the application of technology is generally ten years behind the drawing boards in research departments. This backlog is a reservoir of information which will have to be utilized more fully and at faster rates in the future than in the past. There is no time for lag in the development of resource-related technology.

New and better techniques to search for and find hidden deposits of minerals and oil and gas will be required if increased supplies of resources are expected to reach the market in the future. Explorationists currently are using some sophisticated-looking geochemical and geophysical techniques, but they are mostly tools that produce information that must be interpreted "correctly" to obtain the desired results. These tools are still quite limited in their application. Looking to copper, for example, in the search for porphyry deposits, geologists can quite easily find those that crop out. It is generally possible to identify those with an exposed geochemical halo (figure 5-6), a sort of crown of other elements that commonly occurs at the outer margins of many types of metal deposits. Good geologic reasons indicate that other porphyry deposits, with or without these halos, are hidden beneath younger sedimentary or volcanic rocks. New techniques are needed to locate good sites for further detailed exploration and drilling. Oil and gas fields and hidden ore deposits are located by drilling, and increased success is, of course, desirable. As has been said many times about mineral and fossil fuel deposits, they are first found in the minds of men.

Undoubtedly the greatest requirement to assure a supply of raw materials where and when they are wanted is to develop an abundant supply of cheap energy. Without this energy, the task of supplying a growing population with abundant material becomes difficult, if not impossible. The development of these abundant sources of energy will take work and capital investment over time. Some of the material requirements for these energy systems are tremendous. Before abundant, cheap energy arrives, more of our conventional energy sources will have to be tapped in greater quantity. This will require not only more technology, but more mineral materials to develop the coal mines, drill new oil and gas wells, build the power plants and the distribution systems. These little-heralded requirements will put extra demands on the mineral suppliers.

The magnitude of the demands and supply of nonfuel mineral materials for the U.S. energy industry through the years 1975 to 1990 has been estimated by Albers and coauthors [41] and Goudarzi and coauthors [42], respectively, for the option to pursue business-as-usual as presented in Project Independence [43]. The reports contain basic information compiled from industry and government sources in order to estimate the physical quantities of minerals needed for the production of energy from various types of fuels. The anticipated needs are compared with the identified resources (reserves plus subeconomic resources, see figure 5-2).

The Federal Energy Administration (FEA) report in 1974 urged doubling domestic coal production by 1990 to 1.3 billion short tons per

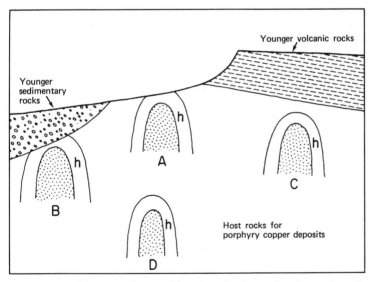

Figure 5-6. Hidden porphyry copper deposits. Deposits of type A can be found with current technology. The discovery of deposit types B-C, and D will require assistance from more advanced technology. The symbol "h" refers to the geochemical halos. The copper deposits are shown in the stippled areas.

132   DONALD A. BROBST

Table 5-5.   World and U.S. Barite Production, and U.S. Imports, 1850–1975
(millions of tons)

| | Production | | U.S. Imports |
	World	U.S.	
1850–1914	6.5	1.2	0.2
1915–1918	1.2	.7	.0
1919–1944	16.7	7.1	.9
1945–1975	86.2	27.6	15.2
Total	110.6	36.6	16.3
Percent of total since 1945	78	75	94

year. The increase was expected to require the development of seventy-four open-pit facilities, each capable of producing 4.5 million short tons of coal per year and eighty-two additional underground mines producing 2.7 million short tons of coal per year. The needs for nineteen metals in this task are summarized by Albers and coauthors [41, table 7, p. A6].

It is estimated that 2.6 billion feet of oil and gas wells will be drilled between 1977 and 1988 [41, table 11, p. A8]. The equipment involved will require 81 million metric tons of iron, about equal to the iron content of two years' domestic production of iron ore at current rates, 39 million metric tons of concrete, 33 million metric tons of solid ingredients for drilling mud, and lesser amounts of many more metals; and so the recital goes for refineries, power plants, pipelines, and nuclear facilities. The total mineral needs climb quickly and all are presumably in addition to normal needs, which also are expected to grow.

These increasing mineral needs can be put into a comprehensible frame of reference by surveying barite production (table 5-5). Barite is used as a weighting agent in drilling mud for oil and gas wells. About 85 percent of the world's supply goes to this use. The American Petroleum Institute estimates that barite needs in the United States during the next eleven years (1977–88) will be 23 million metric tons (25.3 million short tons). This is not just an indifferent, shoulder-shrugging number. Table 5-5 shows my estimate of the world barite production since 1850 based on a survey of the literature and data from the U.S. Bureau of Mines. Seventy-five percent of the total domestic barite production amounted to 27.6 million short tons in the past thirty years, and that just barely exceeds the expected domestic demand for the next eleven years. World demand is also rising because of increased well drilling. Continued import of at least 30 percent of our current needs may be more costly and less practical in the future due to world competition for supplies. There is good geological reason, however, to believe that world supplies can meet the demands, but not without work. A look at the statistics for most other commodities and oil and gas would reveal the same trends of growth, but the chances for meeting demands for all commodities are not equally good.

VI
Exponential Growth

Many trends of increased demand are indicators of exponential growth. Exponential growth is dangerous, especially when it takes people off their guard. If we were to start with what appeared to be a 1-billion-year supply of any commodity, based on current rates of consumption, and used it in increasingly large amounts, say at the rate of 3 percent growth annually, which has been the rate of economic growth in the United States in the not too recent past, that billion-year supply would be consumed in just under 600 years. A 2-billion-year supply would last only another 23½ years, because that is the time interval required for the last doubling, at which point the supply has vanished. That, of course, is not the way mineral resources are exhausted, but the example shows the importance of giving careful consideration not only to the size of the supply, but to the rate at which it is consumed. The rate at which things are consumed of course depends on the ability to produce through time.

A study currently under way by Dennis Cox and Nancy Wright of the U.S. Geological Survey and George Coakley of the U.S. Bureau of Mines (written communication) indicates that the demand for copper in the U.S. might exceed mine capacity by about 1981 and exceed total capacity from known and drilled deposits by 1987. After that time, a widening gap could occur between the demand and the minimum annual production curves. Although the magnitude of this gap cannot be precisely determined because of incomplete information, discovery and development of the new deposits possibly might provide sufficient production to fill the widening gap. By the year 2000, the gap between domestic production capacity and the anticipated primary demand might equal about 2 million short tons of annual production, which is about equal to current U.S. production capacity. Such needs could be met by the discovery and development of eight giant copper deposits or thirty to forty average-size deposits. To put it another way, current production is provided by thirty-eight deposits containing 68 million tons of copper. Another thirty-eight deposits or the same amount of ore must be found and developed within twenty-four years. Because of the ten- to fifteen-year lead time between discovery and first production of many mineral deposits, most of these new deposits must be identified by 1985.

The factor of lead time, that time between discovery and production, is invisible to many people. The lead time is lengthening because of many geological and economic factors, some of which have already been discussed. Exploration is time consuming and costly, as is development. Ultimate success is elusive. Investments of time, money, and labor through several to many years may be lost at any stage of the exploration and development process because any one or a combination of factors could force a halt to an individual project. The successful company scores enough success to cover the costs of its failures. Paul Bailly [44] of Occidental Minerals Corporation has presented a detailed summary with examples of some of these problems.

Success ratios for industries are not generally available, but under the federal government's Strategic Mineral Development Program from 1939 to 1949, about 10,000 prospects were examined [45, p. 8]; of these, 1,342 deposits were investigated in detail, but only 1,053 contained enough tonnage to be of commercial interest. The Defense Minerals Exploration Act authorized a similar program of support for exploration between 1951 and 1958. Requests were received for financial assistance from 3,888 applicants who wanted to explore for strategic and critical minerals. Assistance was granted for 1,159 projects, of which 399 resulted in certification of discovery of valuable minerals. In 1959 only forty-five of these were still in production. Historically, only about 1 percent of the "new field wildcat wells" drilled discovered a field estimated to have ultimate reserves of more than 1 million barrels of oil or 6 billion cubic feet of gas. In 1975, this discovery rate increased to about 1.8 percent. However, all the fields discovered in 1975 are small, and only one field is reported to have ultimate reserves of 25 to 50 million barrels of oil. In the face of rising need, a favorable discovery rate is not enough; the discoveries should preferably be economically significant. Not all discoveries are of economic value to the discoverer. Unless subsequent development is possible, a discovery adds nothing to the supply.

Some statistics on Canadian successes are available. In 1951, one in 100 prospects led to a mine development and by 1969 the ratio had been reduced to one in 1,000 [46, p. 134].

VII
Other Factors Bearing on the Resource System

A few other factors bearing on the resource system should be noticed. Political factors are becoming more evident, and these, too, have their geologic aspects. The world's energy and mineral resources are not evenly scattered around the world. Virtually every nation has some resource problems and varying degrees of resource potential. The United States has done well and has been blessed with good potential in many commodities, but not in all. Domestic reserves of many ferroalloy and several other elements are small or nonexistent. In 1974, there were no domestic reserves of chromium, manganese, niobium, and only small reserves of tin, cobalt, nickel, and bauxite for aluminum [47]. It is beyond the scope of this paper to delve into the details of the availability of all these elements, but the sources of these elements should be carefully considered in policy options if our domestic industry is to stay supplied satisfactorily. Stability in national governments is an integral part in the arrival of minerals in world markets. When deposits of a material are localized, and the commodity is important, supply problems may be critical. For example, nearly 97 percent of the world's identified resources of chromium lie in Rhodesia and the Republic of South Africa. The United States and the rest of the world look to those deposits for their supplies.

Problems with land use and environmental standards are adding as much as an estimated five years to many mineral projects and forcing the abandonment of others. Everyone is in favor of clean air and water, but some tradeoffs probably will have to be made. Rules that curb efforts to find, develop, and use fuels and minerals will have repercussions in the market. If oil and gas become unavailable soon, coal or nuclear sources will have to supply more energy, or we will have to do without it. Well-intended laws preventing open-pit coal mining remove some geologically available coal from use, because very shallow coal beds can be mined only by open-pit methods. Tight standards for sulfur content in coal may require costly long hauls of cleaner burning coal to areas whose coal may fail standards by a small degree. Removal of public land from mineral entry will reduce the potential for development of domestic mineral and energy resources, not only of those already known, but those yet to be discovered [48, pp. 81–93]. The nation might be forced into importing some materials at increasingly higher cost as competition grows for supplies in the world market. These are but the tip of an iceberg of rising social issues that now influence world industrial activity and that will do so increasingly in the future. It is no longer possible to consider geologically available supplies of resources as automatically available, even if the economics are favorable. This is a difficult part of the system to assess. How are the political and social problems to be ameliorated or overcome?

The availability of water is vital to the production and use of mineral and energy materials. This subject is much too complex to discuss in detail here, but the importance of water should be neither ignored nor minimized. Water is not available in sufficient amounts in many parts of the world to support either a mining or a manufacturing industry. Large-scale desalinization of salt water also likely must await the arrival of abundant, cheap energy.

VIII
Keeping the Resource System Functional

Geoscientists will be expected to press the search successfully for new supplies of mineral and fuel materials so that they will be available in time at reasonable prices to fill the needs and desires of a growing population. The task of keeping the resource system functional in the coming decades will be more difficult than ever, especially with rising energy costs and the need to recover more products from conventional deposits of minerals which are progressively becoming harder to find, develop, and use. The burden may be lightened when energy becomes abundant and cheap, but that day cannot be expected to arrive soon.

In the meantime, creative thought from many disciplines will have to be translated into action to meet the economic challenges ahead. Geoscientists can offer much assistance in the solution of resource problems. The earth is bountiful, but all of its treasures are not available to us. There is time to think and take action. Recognition of the following issues and research on them could well assist in successfully meeting the coming challenges.

IX
Issues for Study and Research

1. Geologic reasons discussed in this paper suggest that exponential growth at the anticipated rates in the world use of mineral and fossil fuel materials cannot continue indefinitely, although the national governments of the world appear committed to domestic and international policies that look forward to growth on a business-as-usual basis in the years ahead. Much of the reasoning for these policies of an expanding economy is founded on the premise that the past is the key to the future. The fact that we have done extremely well in attaining the goals of an affluent society by these policies in the past is, however, no guarantee that they will be just as completely successful in the future. Perhaps we should not overlook the possibility that the principles of economics do not tell us all that we need to know about mineral resources. Alternatives to the ever-expanding economy might well be examined before geologic and/or economic exhaustion of some materials forces the issue, at which time it might no longer be possible to avoid unwanted economic, social, and political upheavals. The words of Churchman [11, p. 8] seem appropriate

to this issue, "When you postpone thinking about something too long, then it may not be possible to think about it adequately at all."

2. New sources of abundant, inexpensive energy must be developed to enable the recovery of needed minerals from lower grade ores in conventional types of deposits and from new types of deposits yet to be discovered and found usable, and then to process these materials into useful goods. Without such sources of energy and major advances in technology, there is now little hope of successfully exceeding the limitations of the current economic thresholds in ore deposits by a large factor. There is even less hope of exceeding the mineralogical threshold, and no hope of using ordinary "average" crust of the earth as an ore. It is a snare and a delusion to maintain a blind faith in the near-term, abundant, economic availability of metals at the grade of crustal abundance in the silicate minerals of ordinary rocks.

3. Effort should be expended to use what is available in the best possible ways.

a. The recycling of many materials is well below the levels possible. Recycling has been called uneconomic for many reasons, mostly those left over from days when such activity was not done or little fostered because it was not deemed necessary. Only small volumes were involved in the past. As time has moved on, the volumes available for recycling have grown, but the necessary infrastructure has not yet really been instituted to make recycling economically attractive for most metals.

b. Substitutions are possible in which more abundant materials may be used for those that are scarce. Basic information about the geologic occurrence of the elements and minerals of the earth's crust and their physical and chemical properties must be examined carefully, case by case, and related to technical requirements and costs when considering various substitutions. Consideration of such aspects as geologic occurrence, ease of handling, and differences in energy requirements for recovery and fabrication might make some substitutions vastly more or less desirable than first thoughts would indicate.

c. Conservation is an important method of extending the available supplies of energy and minerals, but it is not a substitute for new supplies. An important aspect of conservation involves influencing the attitudes, tastes, and desires of the public.

d. It is necessary to foster a more ready availability and acceptance of coproducts as a regular source of supply for many minerals, such as fluorspar, barite, cobalt-bearing materials, and many minor metals (see Brooks [49]).

e. In the past, technology has been developed which required that explorationists set up crash programs to seek special minerals and make them more readily available, even if they are quite restricted in their geologic availability. An emphasis in technical development should include use of the most geologically available and least energy-intensive materials whenever possible.

4. Problems in mineral assessment and exploration must be solved more rapidly and efficiently in the coming years than in the past. New and better methods of expressing mineral assessments are needed. Values given for reserves and those given for undiscovered resources do not embody the same limits of confidence. To assume the potential economic availability of astronomical amounts of elements based on levels of crustal abundance can only lead to a complacency that is fraught with peril. How is the unknown quantified? We must learn to live with incomplete data while better use is made of available information from a reservoir that is growing constantly. Although much of the earth's crust remains to be explored at depth, most of the easy-to-find deposits of fossil fuels and minerals already have been identified. Geologic extrapolation suggests that more reserves and resources of useful mineral substances remain to be found. Without new tools to find the hidden deposits, the work of finding them will be costlier and take longer than in the past. The results of the search for some commodities may not lead to increasing the supplies necessary to accommodate exponential increases in use.

5. The need for prudent and reasonable tradeoffs of ecological and land-use factors for a domestic, or even a world, ability to produce what circumstances of the times may require must be better understood. Everyone wants clean air and water, but at what sacrifice? Nobody wants to live next to the stone quarry or the copper mine. Nobody will want to live next to those potential enormous open pits. But everyone wants the benefits of the products of resource operations at lower cost. Some adjustment of public values and sentiments may occur as the cost is recognized. The consumer pays, and we are the consumers!

6. Public understanding is absolutely essential to assure the best rate of success in meeting the challenges of discovering and using wisely mineral and energy resources in the years ahead. An informed public will be able to understand the options available to an industrial society. The public and its policy makers must understand that although the earth is not going to run out of mineral resources on a given day, the physical constraints of geologic and economic availability do place limits upon which of them can be useful to our needs in the foreseeable future. The effort to develop new energy sources and new technology for more efficient use of energy and minerals likely will be long and expensive. That effort should begin now. The next few decades are critical. Unless the problems of the short to middle term are bridged, an industrial society

may not survive to reach that longed-for utopian period of cheap, abundant energy.

The public must have some understanding of the options, and their consequences, related to such issues as:

a. Living with growth rates in consumption that will strain the limits of the world's mineral and energy resources;
b. Permanently withdrawing land from exploration for and development of minerals and energy materials;
c. Excessive dependence on foreign sources of mineral and fuel materials and, perhaps, even capital;
d. Trying to maintain an independence of choice in policy when there is no longer sufficient economic independence to support such an option;
e. Making foreign policies that might not recognize the necessity for access to sources of materials that will be needed in the future.

The facts of mineral and energy resources as they relate to maintaining the style of life in the United States, and improving it in many other parts of the world, must be brought out as soon as possible. The public and its elected representatives formulate public policy. Success in the future will require tremendous cooperation between the public, industry, academia, and all levels of government. Each will have to make its unique contribution in order for us not only to succeed in solving our problems, but to survive. Make no mistake about it, an industrial society lives on energy and mineral resources. We shall have to make intelligent choices, because there are no simple solutions for these problems.

References

1. D. F. Hewett, "Cycles in Metal Production," *Transactions of the American Institute of Mining and Metallurgical Engineers* (1929) pp. 65–98.
2. President's Materials Policy Commission, W. S. Paley, chairman, *Resources for Freedom* (Washington, GPO, 1952, 5 vols.).
3. National Commission on Materials Policy, *Material Needs and the Environment Today and Tomorrow* (Washington, GPO, 1973).
4. M. K. Hubbert, "Degree of Advancement of Petroleum Exploration in the United States," *American Association of Petroleum Geologists Bulletin* vol. 51, no. 11 (1967) pp. 2207–2227.
5. C. F. Park, Jr., *Affluence in Jeopardy* (San Francisco, Freeman Cooper, 1968).
6. C. F. Park, Jr., *Earthbound Minerals, Energy and Man's Future* (San Francisco, Freeman Cooper, 1975).
7. D. H. Meadows, D. L. Meadows, Jørgen Randers, and W. W. Behrens, III, *The Limits to Growth* (New York, Universe Books, 1972).

8. D. B. Brooks and P. W. Andrews, "Mineral Resources, Economic Growth, and World Population," *Science* vol. 185, no. 4145 (1974) pp. 13–19.

9. H. J. Barnett and C. Morse, *Scarcity and Growth: The Economics of Natural Resource Availability* (Baltimore, Johns Hopkins University Press for Resources for the Future, 1963).

10. H. E. Goeller and A. M. Weinberg, "The Age of Substitutability," *Science* vol. 191, no. 4428 (1976) pp. 683–689.

11. C. W. Churchman, *The Systems Approach* (New York, Delta Books, Dell Publishing, 1968).

12. *Mining Magazine*, "International Mining Survey," September issue (London) 1976, pp. 233–245.

13. V. E. McKelvey, "Mineral Resource Estimates and Public Policy," *American Scientist* vol. 60, no. 1 (1972) pp. 32–40.

14. U.S. Geological Survey, *Principles of the Mineral Resource Classification System of the U.S. Bureau of Mines and the U.S. Geological Survey,* Geological Survey Bulletin 1450-A, 1976.

15. J. L. Schanz, *Resource Terminology: An Examination of Concepts and Terms and Recommendations for Improvement,* EPRI Report 336 (Palo Alto, Calif., Electric Power Research Institute, 1975).

16. J. E. Tilton, "The Continuing Debate over the Exhaustion of Nonfuel Mineral Resources," *Natural Resources Forum* vol. 1, no. 3 (1977) pp. 167–173.

17. S. G. Lasky, "National Mineral Resource Appraisal," *Mining Congress Journal* vol. 35, no. 1 (1949) pp. 35–37.

18. T. B. Nolan, "The Search for New Mining Districts," *Economic Geology* vol. 45 (1950) pp. 601–608.

19. S. G. Lasky, "How Tonnage and Grade Relations Help Predict Ore Reserves," *Engineering and Mining Journal* vol. 151, no. 4 (1950) pp. 81–85.

20. D. A. Singer, D. P. Cox, and L. J. Drew, *Grade and Tonnage Relationships Among Copper Deposits,* U.S. Geological Survey Professional Paper 907-A, 1975.

21. M. Allais, "Method of Appraising Economic Prospects of Mining Exploration over Large Territories: Algerian Sahara Case Study," *Management Science* vol. 3, no. 4 (1957) pp. 285–347.

22. D. P. Harris, "An Application of Multivariate Statistical Analysis to Mineral Exploration," (Ph.D. dissertation, The Pennsylvania State University, 1965).

23. D. P. Harris, "Geostatistics in the Appraisal of Metal Resources," in W. A. Vogely, ed., *Mineral Materials Modeling,* Resources for the Future Working Paper EN-5 (Baltimore, Johns Hopkins University Press for Resources for the Future, 1975).

24. W. A. Vogely, ed., *Mineral Materials Modeling,* Working Paper EN-5 (Baltimore, Johns Hopkins University Press for Resources for the Future, 1975).

25. B. M. Miller, H. L. Thomsen, G. L. Dolton, A. B. Coury, T. A. Hendricks, F. E. Lennartz, R. B. Powers, E. G. Sable, and K. L. Varnes, *Geological Estimates of Undiscovered Recoverable Oil and Gas Resources in the United States*, U.S. Geological Survey Circular 725, 1975.

26. J. S. Vhay, D. A. Brobst, and A. V. Heyl, "Cobalt," in D. A. Brobst and W. P. Pratt, eds., *United States Mineral Resources*, U.S. Geological Survey Professional Paper 820, 1973, pp. 143–156.

27. D. A. Brobst, "Barite," in D. A. Brobst and W. P. Pratt, eds., *United States Mineral Resources*, U.S. Geological Survey Professional Paper 820, 1973, pp. 75–84.

28. R. F. Parker, *Composition of the Earth's Crust*, U.S. Geological Survey Professional Paper 440-D, 1967.

29. F. M. Vokes, "The Abundance and Availability of Mineral Resources," in G. J. S. Govett and M. H. Govett, eds., *World Mineral Supplies: Assessment and Perspective* (New York, Elsevier, 1976) pp. 65–98.

30. F. J. Flanagan, ed., *Descriptions and Analyses of Eight New USGS Rock Standards*, U.S. Geological Survey Professional Paper 840, 1976.

31. A. T. Miesch, *Methods of Computation for Estimating Geochemical Abundance*, U.S. Geological Survey Professional Paper 574-B, 1967.

32. A. T. Miesch, *Theory of Error in Geochemical Data*, U.S. Geological Survey Professional Paper 574-A, 1967.

33. Tan Lee and Chi-lung Yao, "Abundance of Chemical Elements in the Earth's Crust and Its Major Tectonic Units," *International Geology Review* vol. 12, no. 7 (1970) pp. 778–786.

34. B. J. Skinner, "A Second Iron Age Ahead?", *American Scientist* vol. 64 (1976) pp. 258–269.

35. V. E. McKelvey, "Relation of Reserves of the Elements to Their Crustal Abundances," *American Journal of Science* vol. 258-A (1960) pp. 234–241.

36. National Academy of Sciences, *Mineral Resources and the Environment*, Report by the Committee on Mineral Resources and the Environment (COMRATE), Commission on Natural Resources, National Research Council, National Academy of Sciences, 1975.

37. D. A. Singer, "Long-Term Adequacy of Metal Resources," *Resources Policy* vol. 3, no. 2 (June 1977).

38. H. T. Schacklette, J. C. Hamilton, J. G. Boerngen, and J. M. Bowles, *Elemental Composition of Surficial Materials in the Conterminous United States*, U.S. Geological Survey Professional Paper 574-D, 1971.

39. N. J. Page and S. C. Creasey, "Ore Grade, Metal Production and Energy," *U.S. Geological Survey Journal of Research* vol. 3, no. 1 (1975) pp. 9–13.

40. Chauncey Starr and Richard Rudman, "Parameters of Technologic Growth," *Science* vol. 182, no. 4110 (1974) pp. 358–364.

41. J. P. Albers, W. J. Bawiec, and L. F. Rooney, *Demand for Nonfuel Minerals and Materials by the United States Energy Industry, 1975–90*, U.S. Geological Survey Professional Paper 1006-A, 1976.

42. G. H. Goudarzi, L. F. Rooney, and G. L. Schaffer, *Supply of Nonfuel Energy Minerals and Materials for the United States Energy Industry, 1975–90,* U.S. Geological Survey Professional Paper 1006-B, 1976.

43. U.S. Federal Energy Administration, Project Independence Report— Project Independence Blueprint, Final Task Force Report (Washington, GPO, 1974).

44. P. A. Bailly, "The Problems of Converting Resources to Reserves," *Mining Engineering* vol. 21, no. 1 (1976) pp. 27–37.

45. U.S. Geological Survey, *Mineral Resource Perspectives, 1975,* U.S. Geological Survey Professional Paper 940, 1975.

46. W. E. Roscoe, "Probability of an Exploration Discovery in Canada," *Canadian Mining and Metallurgical Bulletin* vol. 64, no. 707 (1971) pp. 134–137.

47. W. P. Pratt and D. A. Brobst, *Mineral Resources: Potentials and Problems,* U.S. Geological Survey Circular 698, 1974.

48. U.S. Department of Interior, *Mining and Minerals Policy,* Annual Report of the Secretary of the Interior under the Mining and Mineral Policy Act of 1970 (Washington, GPO, 1976).

49. D. B. Brooks, *Supply and Competition in Minor Metals* (Baltimore, Johns Hopkins University Press for Resources for the Future, 1965).

6

The Age of Substitutability: A Scientific Appraisal of Natural Resource Adequacy

H. E. Goeller

As the twentieth century has progressed, life, society, and technology have become ever more complex compared with the relative simplicity of earlier times. Institutional, economic, societal, environmental, and technological problems have increased to the point where one wonders whether the twenty-first century, let alone the more distant future, can be safely attained in any sort of civilized form.

In a recent paper entitled the "Age of Substitutability," A. M. Weinberg and I inquired into some of these problems [1]. Because of our backgrounds we addressed mainly the technological and to a lesser extent some of the economic problems of the future, and alluded only peripherally to societal problems, which we regard as the most difficult of all. Our general conclusion has been that, at least technologically, even the far distant future can be bright, and that the material aspects of life do not have to be drastically different from today's. However, if social disruption is to be avoided, this state, we are sure, can only be achieved through unprecedented foresight and planning. We regard "business as usual" and "muddling through," particularly in the short term, to be increasingly inadequate and even dangerous options. Our outlook places us, technologically at least, among the more avid Cornucopians, provided extremely good planning is done.

The great debate on the future of society came to a head with the publications of the Club of Rome—first, *Limits to Growth* [2] in 1972 and later a more toned down, disaggregated, and detailed analysis, *Mankind at the Turning Point* [3] in 1974—both of which provided very pessimistic outlooks for mankind's future. The strongest reply to the Club of Rome thesis is *The Next 200 Years* by Herman Kahn [4]. Although we do not feel capable of judging all of his results, we do agree wholeheartedly with his arguments on the future of physical resources, energy, and materials.

Many futurists now concede that many economies must break away from their historic exponential growth patterns and that some areas, such as world population and even economic growth itself, will ultimately arrive at zero growth positions. Modern western society tends to forget that growth is the unusual rather than the usual state of most civilizations and that nongrowth does not necessarily imply sterile and static utopias with no change and no progress.

Weinberg and I envisioned our ultimate Age of Substitutability as that time in the future when the material requirements of society would be provided almost exclusively from unlimited nonrenewable resources, renewable resources, and through recycled rarer materials used nondissipatively. We also assumed that by that time the world's population would have leveled off at about 10 billion persons.

There appear to be three stages on the road to the ultimate Age of Substitutability. The first is a short-term period—perhaps thirty to fifty years—of initial transition. This is a period during which the existing investments of industry run through their amortization, but it is also a period of rapid technological change for new plants and facilities based on the best long-term schemes for conserving limited material and energy resources. As is shown later, this is the period during which all petroleum and natural gas is depleted and decisions are made on the development and deployment of transient (coal, oil shale, and nuclear burners) and ultimate energy systems. The second stage—encompassing perhaps a century—would be the final transition period during which coal and economic oil shale would be completely used up, when large in-use pools of elements used nondissipatively (generally metals) would be built up to reduce dependence on high-cost, low-grade virgin materials, and when the search for substitutes, particularly for elements in limited supply and used dissipatively, would reach its zenith—in short, the final transition period into stage 3, the true, nearly closed system for limited materials, the Age of Substitutability.

It is very unlikely that any futurists, including ourselves, can see so far ahead with any degree of precision. Thus much of what is said here is highly speculative at the least. However, in certain ways such long-term speculation, done above the turmoil of short-term commodity markets and the purchasing agents' anguish, may have more validity than at first seems plausible.

Certain basic resource facts are undeniable. For example, at least twenty chemical elements in the air, seas, and/or lithosphere, including several metals (iron, aluminum, magnesium, and possibly titanium), already exist in essentially infinite supply. This list may increase in the future with new technology, that is, nickel may be obtained from peridotites, manganese, and perhaps other metals from sea-floor nodules. Some futurists even envision obtaining everything we need from dirt or country rock, particularly if many products are recovered simultaneously [5]. Such a possibility seems unlikely for the near term, but given centuries for technological development, even this option may ultimately become economically feasible.

Table 6-1 compares the percentages of 1974 demands for such non-renewable materials in terms of quantity and value used in the United States and the world at large. Percentages are used because they change more slowly with time than quantities or prices. It is perhaps surprising that fossil fuels; sand, stone, and related products; iron, aluminum, and magnesium; and eight of the other most widely used elements (seven of which have near infinite resources) constitute more than 99.5 percent of all nonrenewable materials currently used by society. The remaining sixty or so elements (mostly with limited resources) account for only 0.35 percent of the nonrenewable materials used in the United States and 0.38 percent used throughout the world. As shown in table 6-1, however, the monetary value of the sixty rarer elements is considerably higher: 10.7 and 9.1 percent respectively.

Table 6-1 also lists the ultimate resource bases for all of the most used materials which are not based on all types of rock, but only on the more suitable "ores," such as salt or limestone, and seawater or air. Certainly those with resource to demand (R/D) ratios of a million or more may be considered infinite for all intents and purposes.

The outstanding fact to be drawn from table 6-1 is that by far the greatest resource scarcity is the impending scarcity of fossil fuels or CH_x,[1] particularly since the seemingly secure R/D ratio of 2,500 dwindles to a mere 100 years or so when future world growth in fossil fuel demand is taken into consideration. Admittedly there exists an additional 200 times as much reduced carbon in shales as in conventional fossil fuels,[2] but only a tiny part of this exists as economic oil shale; it is not enough to appreciably change the R/D ratio noted. On the other hand, the amount of oxidized carbon, principally in limestone, is enormous (R/D is 4×10^6).

Since about 90 percent of fossil fuels currently consumed is used to provide energy and since about 90 percent of the world's total energy is presently obtained by burning fossil fuels, the scarcity of extractable CH_x is synonymous with the limited long-term availability of the major present

---

[1] Oil that can be obtained from shale now or in the future at costs competitive with petroleum or synthetic oil from coal.

[2] Fossil fuels are a chemical combination of carbon and hydrogen, thus the symbol CH_x where $x = \sim1$ for coal, ~2 for petroleum and 4 for natural gas.

Table 6-1. A Comparison of U.S. and World Demand for Nonrenewable Materials With Their Respective World Resource Bases, 1974

Material	Demand United States % of total quantity	United States % of total value	World total % of total quantity	World total % of total value	World "usable" resources Resource base	Quantity (tonnes)	Resource to demand ratio (years)
Fossil fuels (CH_x)							
Coal and peat	13.05	8.12	17.02	11.37	Coal		
Petroleum	21.33	42.06	14.56	40.41	Oil	10^{13}	2500
Natural gas	11.14	5.99	4.87	2.75	Gas		
Subtotal	45.52	56.17	36.45	54.53			
Sand and gravel (SiO_2)	23.03	1.34	32.28	1.98	Limestone	2×10^{15}	4×10^6
Crushed stone ($CaCO_3$)	24.52	1.93	23.58	1.95	Sand, sandstone	1.2×10^{16}	5×10^6
Clay, gypsum, pumice	1.93	0.44	2.94	0.75	Limestone	5×10^{15}	4×10^6
Subtotal	49.48	3.71	58.80	4.68			
Iron	2.14	18.97	2.63	24.44	Basalt, laterite	1.8×10^{15}	4.5×10^6
Aluminum and magnesium	0.14	3.82	0.08	2.31	Clay/seawater	3.7×10^{15}	$\sim 3 \times 10^8$
Subtotal	2.28	22.79	2.71	26.75			
Other major							
Chlorine	0.26	1.17	0.14	0.66	Rock salt, seawater	2.9×10^{16}	4×10^8
Sodium	0.53	0.68	0.36	0.49	Rock salt, seawater	1.6×10^{16}	3×10^8
Nitrogen	0.51	2.08	0.37	1.91	Air	4.5×10^{15}	1×10^8
Sulfur	0.29	0.29	0.26	0.27	Gypsum, seawater	1.1×10^{15}	3×10^7
Oxygen	0.38	0.23	0.26	0.16	Air	1.1×10^{15}	3.5×10^7
Hydrogen	0.17	1.59	0.10	0.98	Water	1.7×10^{17}	$\sim 10^{10}$
Potassium	0.12	0.26	0.10	0.23	Sylvite, seawater	5.7×10^{14}	4×10^7
(Phosphorus)	0.11	0.36	0.07	0.24	Phosphate rock	1.6×10^{10}	1300
Subtotal	2.37	6.66	1.66	4.94			
All other	0.35	10.67	0.38	9.10	Limited resources		

Source: Calculated from data in U.S. Bureau of Mines, *Commodity Data Summaries, 1976* and *Mineral Trends and Forecasts; October 1976.*

sources of energy. For the interim, coal can be used either in direct combustion or as a source of synthetic oil and gas. Thus we have about a century to develop and totally deploy the ultimate energy-providing substitutes for fossil fuels. Natural steam geothermal and tidal energy systems can provide only miniscule amounts of energy; hydroelectric projects, particularly in developing countries, and nuclear burner reactors generally, are considerably more important, but only solar, fusion, nuclear breeders, and possibly dry hot rock geothermal systems can be capable of providing the world with limitless energy.

The remaining 10 percent of fossil fuels now consumed in the world is used as the basic raw material for producing a wide range of modern petrochemical products from oil and gas and as metallurgical coke derived from coal and used principally in producing iron and steel. In the Age of Substitutability, when practically all economic supplies of fossil fuels have been consumed, it will be necessary to produce essential petrochemicals from CO_2 obtained from calcined limestone, followed by conversion to methane (CH_4), and from there to more complex organic compounds. At that time hydrogen obtained by electrolysis of water will become the main reductant for metal ores. Both of these ultimate "substitutes" will require large amounts of cheap energy from nonfossil fuel sources.

The only other element listed in table 6-1 that has a limited R/D ratio is phosphorus. Phosphorus is extremely important because it is the only one of the three major plant foods or fertilizers (nitrogen, potassium, and phosphorus) that is not in near-infinite supply. However, it is generally conceded that speculative resources of phosphate rock are very large and that a shortage of economic phosphatic fertilizer may occur only in the very, very far term. At this point we may, as H. G. Wells noted, have to return all bones to the soil [6].

In all probability, shortages in the supply of some trace elements (Cu, Zn, Co, etc.) necessary for agriculture will occur before a shortage of phosphorus. This possibility certainly deserves a great deal of study, particularly since agricultural use dissipates a number of metals that could be currently recycled. Of all the activities of society, none looms larger in importance than an agriculture that provides sufficient food for the world's people.

As already stated, one of the chief attributes of the Age of Substitutability will be the absence or near absence of economically extractable fossil fuels. Table 6-2 is a revision of the demand data in table 6-1, with fossil fuels omitted. Thus, if all nonfossil fuel resources are used in the same proportion as now, the same sixty elements with limited resources would account for 0.65 percent of all nonrenewable materials used in the

Table 6-2. U.S. and World Demands for Nonfossil Fuel Nonrenewable Resources, 1974

Material	United States		World total	
	% of total quantity	% of total value	% of total quantity	% of total value
Sand and gravel (SiO₂)	42.28	3.08	50.86	4.37
Crushed stone (CaCO₃)	45.00	4.43	37.15	4.31
Clay, gypsum, pumice	3.54	1.01	4.64	1.65
Subtotal	90.82	8.52	92.65	10.33
Iron	3.93	43.48	4.15	53.97
Aluminum and magnesium	0.26	8.87	0.13	5.09
Subtotal	4.19	52.35	4.28	59.06
Other major				
Chlorine	0.48	2.68	0.22	1.47
Sodium	0.96	1.56	0.57	1.09
Nitrogen	0.93	5.09	0.59	4.22
Sulfur	0.53	0.67	0.40	0.60
Oxygen	0.70	0.52	0.40	0.35
Hydrogen	0.31	3.65	0.16	2.16
Potassium	0.22	0.60	0.16	0.51
(Phosphorus)	0.21	0.82	0.11	0.52
Subtotal	4.34	15.59	2.61	10.92
All other	0.65	23.54	0.46	19.69

Source: Calculated from data in U.S. Bureau of Mines, *Commodity Data Summaries, 1976* and *Mineral Trends and Forecasts, October 1976.*

United States and 0.46 percent in the world. We consider these percentages an upper bound for use of limited materials in the Age of Substitutability since appropriate substitutions, and to a lesser extent recycling, will tend to decrease these percentages.

At first glance, substitution is generally thought of as the use of an alternate material, normally but not always a more more plentiful one, for a more expensive and generally scarcer one. Often, however, it involves the substitution of a better performing material (for example, oil and gas for coal), even if it is scarcer or more expensive, or both. One must always take into account the difference between best performance and adequate performance since the latter is all that is normally necessary. Substitution in a broader sense often involves the functions provided by materials, since in many instances an alternative *way* of doing things may greatly reduce and occasionally eliminate the use of a material altogether. Thus, large-scale use of mass transport in lieu of private automobiles would provide a large savings in materials and the energy needed to make and use them. Similarly, use of radio and microwaves for communications saves large quantities of copper, and to a lesser extent, aluminum. One aspect of substitution that is chiefly societal and highly

Table 6-3. Distribution of U.S. and World Demand for Materials with Limited Resources that Constitute <1 percent of all Nonrenewable Materials Used by Society, 1974

	United States		World total	
	% of total quantity	% of total value	% of total quantity	% of total value
Other ferrous metals	17.59	14.39	24.49	12.86
Other nonferrous metals	33.47	70.25	30.74	73.09
Total other metals	51.06	84.64	55.23	85.95
Other refractory elements	12.25	9.69	12.86	6.98
Other elements	4.20	2.48	2.13	1.25
Other silicates	32.49	3.19	29.78	5.82
Total	100.00	100.00	100.00	100.00
Percent of all nonrenewable materials				
Including fossil fuels[a]	0.35	10.67	0.38	9.10
Excluding fossil fuels[b]	0.65	23.54	0.46	19.69

Source: Calculated from data in U.S. Bureau of Mines, *Commodity Data Summaries,* *1976* and *Mineral Trends and Forecasts, October 1976.*
[a] From Table 6-1.
[b] From Table 6-2.

subjective lies in the area of aesthetics. For example, about 90 percent of titanium goes for titania pigment, but as far as metals protection goes, red iron oxide is every bit as good as brilliant titania white.

Since the discovery of phosphorus in 1669 about sixty "new" chemical elements have been discovered, most of them with relatively limited resources [7]. Following the discovery of each new element—an act of basic science—applied scientists and businessmen have rapidly sought ways to produce the element cheaply and evolve practical uses for it. In some cases the new uses were, at least temporarily, uniquely essential to an evolving materialistic society; in other cases, however, they were not, although the new materials may have been marginally better and cheaper than older substances. In a few cases, such as arsenic and thallium, new uses have been hard to find. As long as resources are large compared with demand, any use, no matter how frivolous, can be tolerated; but as demand presses supplies ever harder, the contest between frivolity and need must yield to uses that conserve supply. In most cases, but not all, price in the marketplace is a trustworthy arbiter.

Of the sixty or so elements derived from nonrenewable resources in limited supply (the "all other" category of tables 6-1 and 6-2), the structural metals, so important to modern technology, are dominant in both quantity and monetary value. As shown in table 6-3, these metals account for about half the total quantity of limited materials used by society and

Table 6-4. U.S. and World Demand for Virgin Metals, 1974

	United States		World total	
	% of total quantity	% of total value	% of total quantity	% of total value
Ferrous metals				
Iron	87.06	60.39	91.79	71.14
Manganese	1.43	0.44	1.66	0.57
Chromium	0.54	0.25	0.44	0.23
(Silicon)	0.66	1.43	0.32	0.78
Nickel	0.21	2.29	0.13	1.54
Other	0.07	1.37	0.04	0.84
Subtotal	89.97	66.17	94.38	75.10
Nonferrous metals				
Aluminum	5.62	11.89	2.76	6.50
Magnesium	0.12	0.42	0.05	0.20
Titanium	0.02	0.28	0.01	0.15
Copper	1.87	8.93	1.17	7.53
Zinc	1.40	3.11	1.04	4.01
Lead	0.89	1.24	0.55	1.02
Tin	0.05	1.20	0.04	1.07
Other	0.05	6.76	0.03	4.42
Subtotal	10.03	33.83	5.62	24.90
Fe, Si, Al, Mg & Ti	93.48	74.20	94.93	78.77

Source: Calculated from data in U.S. Bureau of Mines, *Commodity Data Summaries, 1976* and *Mineral Trends and Forecasts, October 1976.*

about 85 percent of their monetary value. Further, the amount of energy needed to obtain and reduce metal ores is much greater than that needed to process most of the remaining materials with limited resources. Iron, aluminum, and magnesium are omitted from the above analysis because they all occur in near-infinite supply.

Table 6-4 gives further data on the structural metals for both the United States and the world. Silicon, a nonmetal, is also included because of its extensive use in steelmaking. Iron accounts for about 90 percent of the quantity and about two-thirds of the value of all metals and is one of the main metals used by society. It is reassuring that the metals derived from near-infinite resources—iron, silicon, aluminum, magnesium, and probably titanium—account for nearly 95 percent of the quantity and three-quarters of the value of all metals consumed.

As will be shown later, even when society is forced to use low-grade resources of these plentiful metals, energy and other costs will not increase by a factor of more than about two because near-infinite resources are not too different in either quality or concentration from presently used ores.

As Frasché [8] and others have pointed out, society never physically runs out of any nonrenewable resource; however, all of the elements are so mixed in rocks and seawater that as we go to ever leaner ores, the costs per unit of product in dollars, energy, and environmental degradation continually increase, with occasional respites when new technology, better suited for the leaner ores, is developed and adopted. Further, considerable attention is now being given to determining whether there are grade cutoffs from very low grade ore to near natural abundance [9]. In any event, the limited materials become more and more expensive and are gradually replaced by cheaper substitutes wherever possible. In a few cases, however, as with phosphatic fertilizers and trace metals for agriculture, there is no possible substitute and even extreme measures toward finding substitutes must certainly fail. Thus, we never run out; instead, certain materials become too expensive, compared with substitutes, for any except the most exotic uses, and for those few cases where there are no substitutes for an absolutely essential use, society just has to pay the price.

In a relatively recent study involving thirty-two-year predictions of future demands for all nonrenewable resources—admittedly made before the general alarm was sounded for conservation of energy and scarcer materials—only two materials were given negative growth rates over the prediction period [10]. This prediction, as most, was certainly "business as usual" for another third of a century—stage 1 of the Age of Substitutability. It is unfortunate that such predictions may become self-fulfilling prophecies when a diminishing use of scarce substances, particularly those with nonsubstitutable uses, appears a more appropriate forecast for long-range planning.

In assessing future demands for materials derived from limited resources, one must be careful not to simplify issues. First, one must set down the various uses of an element or material in decreasing order of quantity. Then he must determine for each use its ultimate importance to society: is it a frivolous or purely aesthetic use or is it an important basic one? Then it is necessary to determine whether it is a dissipative use or one which permits recycling so that the same material can be used again. Finally, he must determine whether adequate substitutes exist or appear likely to be developed.

Thus, basically adequate stainless steel flatware can be substituted for more aesthetic sterling silver, thereby making silver available for its more essential use in photography. On the other hand, although silver used in works of art is recyclable, it tends to be hoarded as heirlooms, thereby denying its more dissipative use in photography.

Similarly, mercury, a relatively scarce metal, has many uses. Over the long term, probably 95 percent of present uses can be satisfactorily replaced by alternative substances or functions. For example, a third of U.S. mercury consumption is in caustic-chlorine production cells; this use could be totally eliminated by returning to the adequate but somewhat less satisfactory diaphragm cells. A quarter of the mercury is used in special batteries; there are many other types. And so on. Such arguments do not imply that industry could immediately get along with only 5 percent of the present mercury supply; but, conversely, delaying presently feasible substitutions, even if they are slightly more costly, is inappropriate in the long-term interest of society.

To be thorough, one must then examine all the uses or at least the major uses of the other sixty or so scarce elements to determine for each the present possibilities and future likelihoods of more plentiful substitutes or unique new functional alternatives. A NATO research group has recently made such a study for eleven scarce metals [11].

In the thirty-two-year U.S. and world demand projections mentioned earlier, the average price increase for the sixty limited elements was about 50 percent by the year 2000. Thus, in table 6-2, the 23.5 percent monetary value contribution of these elements in the United States would increase by the year 2000 to about 31 percent, assuming that the percentages of limited materials and the price of plentiful materials remain fixed. If the limited elements continue to be used as extensively as now into the long term, their eventual contribution to the total value of all nonrenewable materials could easily become dominant.

The game for the future, then, is to discourage unnecessary uses of scarce elements by appropriate and early substitution in order to minimize increases in absolute monetary value. In many cases this will be done by normal pricing mechanisms.

Naturally this game can never be played perfectly; however, thorough and continuing study of these problems should be carried on to minimize unpleasant surprises. It is unpleasant to find too late that the price of some irreplaceable material affecting a key industry has skyrocketed to the point that an entire economy is seriously affected. The net effect of a well-planned regimen of substitution is that even though the cost of widely used plentiful materials will rise slightly because we must go to somewhat lower grade ores to obtain them, the continually decreasing requirements for high-priced limited materials will result in an overall cost increase for the aggregate nonrenewable resource base of a factor of only two or three.

But what about energy requirements in the Age of Substitutability for mining and converting ores into materials useful to society? Again, we resort to a comparison based on metals, rather than on all materials, because the production of metals is more energy intensive than most

Table 6-5. Energy Requirements for the Production of Abundant Metals and Copper

Metal	Source	Gross energy[a] (kWh/ton of metal)	E_L/E_H[b]
Magnesium ingot	Seawater	100,000	1
Aluminum ingot	Bauxite	56,000	1
	Clay	72,600	1.28
Raw steel	Magnetic taconites	10,100	1
	Iron laterites	11,900	1.17 (with carbon)
			~2 (with electrolytic hydrogen)
Titanium ingot	Rutile	138,900	1
	Ilmenite	164,700	1.18
	Titanium rich soils	227,000	1.63
Refined copper	Porphyry ore, 1 percent Cu	14,000	1
	Porphyry ore, 0.3 percent Cu	27,300	1.95

Source: J. C. Brevard, H. B. Flora II, and C. Portal, *Energy Expenditures Associated with the Production and Recycle of Metals* (Oak Ridge, Tenn., Oak Ridge National Laboratory, 1972) ORNL-NSF-CP-24.
[a] At 40 percent thermal efficiency for generation of electricity.
[b] Energy required for low grade ore/energy required for high grade ore.

other materials. Now and in the future iron is destined to be the preeminently used metal. Use of aluminum has grown rapidly all through this century and the metal is now in second place. Use of magnesium found in near-infinite supply in brines and seawater and titanium use since midcentury have been disappointing to producers, but both appear to have high potential for growth as the limited metals become scarcer and more expensive.

We believe the problem is well portrayed in table 6-5 taken from a study by Brevard, Flora, and Portal [12]. This table indicates how much of an energy increase can be expected in the future as society is forced to turn to lower grade ores. No change is envisioned for magnesium since its ore—seawater—is essentially infinite and homogeneous. For the near-infinite terrestrial ores of iron and aluminum, a 28 percent increase is projected for aluminum from clay rather than bauxite and a 17 percent increase for iron from laterites rather than magnetic taconites. But for copper, a relatively limited element, a 95 percent increase in energy use is anticipated, probably by the year 2000 for U.S. ores.

A second important point is that the energy increase given for iron is for a continuing use of coal coke as the ore reductant. When all economic fossil fuels are exhausted in the Age of Substitutability, hydrogen rather than coke must be used as the metal ore reductant (incidentally, a technology already exists), a process that will probably double the present energy demand [13]. In any event, because of the dominance of iron and aluminum metals, it is hard to see how the energy requirements for producing all metals can increase by much more than a factor of two, particularly since in the long run it is expected that scarcer metals (Cu, Zn, Pb, Sn, etc.) will be replaced to a large extent by more plentiful substances.

One dichotomy exists between aluminum and copper at the present time which is a good illustration of short-term advantages made at the expense of long-term good. Production of aluminum is considerably more energy intensive than production of copper; yet aluminum resources are vastly greater than those of copper. Because of the high rise in energy costs over the past few years, however, the tendency is now to produce copper more extensively than aluminum.

In the recent NATO report on the problems of future supply for the eleven scarce metals noted earlier, a major conclusion was to seek methods to reduce the dissipative uses of these metals so that more would be available for recycling, thereby extending the resource base further into the future.

The recycling of materials derived from near-infinite resources, such as iron and aluminum, is not required in order to conserve resources, as it is for copper, zinc, and lead, but to conserve energy and minimize disposal problems.

Although environmental problems are beyond the scope of this paper, a few comments on mine spoils and land disruption seem in order. Probably the major problems of land defacement still lie ahead of us, but not in the ultimate Age of Substitutability. It is highly likely that the most serious period of land defacement will occur in the late stage 1 and early stage 2 periods when the surface mining of coal reaches its greatest extent, particularly when the ratio of overburden to coal that can be economically mined may be on the order of 50 to 1, and when much more coal is needed to replace diminishing or exhausted supplies of oil and natural gas. The quantities of material so disrupted seem certain to be as great or greater than the mining of all other materials later on, even with greatly increased demand for nonfuel substances, and particularly as we place greater dependence on the use of near-infinite resources as substitutes for limited elements.

Disposal of mine spoils is only one of many environmental problems that must be faced and solved in the future. Appropriate and adequate solutions to these problems will certainly require great ingenuity from physical and biological scientists and engineers for a long time to come.

In the Age of Substitutability, with a population of possibly 10 billion persons (2.5 times the present world population) and with very good planning, it is quite likely that the world's people can be provided with the requisite quantities of nonrenewable resources for a comfortable life, and that an increase in average world social equity to about half that presently being experienced in the United States seems achievable. The amounts of energy and materials needed to reach such a goal will be much greater than those now consumed, but given several centuries to make the transition, this goal does not appear impossible. It will require an additional 2 kilowatts of installed energy-generating capacity per person in the United States and about 3 kilowatts per person elsewhere to provide everyone in the world with about half the nonrenewable materials per capita now being consumed in the United States alone plus the desalination of sea water for the increased agricultural requirements. An additional amount of energy for both the United States and the rest of the world would also be needed for other purposes. Thus, energy demand in the United States would increase from the present 11 kilowatts to 15 kilowatts of capacity per person, and in the world from 1.5 to 7.5 kilowatts per person. For 10 billion persons, this would require an installed energy capacity of 75×10^9 kilowatts, about 12 times the present capacity. This large increase would require an enormous endeavor but would not, in our opinion, be impossible, given a century or more in which to accomplish it.[3] In addition, it appears to be environmentally feasible since this much energy is still only 0.1 percent of the total solar energy absorbed and reradiated by the earth. The physical crux of the problem will certainly be based on our ability to develop and deploy one or more economic and essentially infinite nonfossil fuel energy systems before all economic supplies of fossil fuels are consumed. Since there are at least four contenders—solar, fusion, nuclear breeders, and possibly dry hot rock geothermal—the probability that at least one of these can be developed successfully seems extremely good; however, it is important that all possibilities be pursued for a considerable time in order to determine which can produce future energy needs most safely and cheaply.

One of the chief concerns in analyzing the future supply of nonrenewable resources is a politico-economic one; whether or not the free market system as it now operates, with its high discount rates, is always an adequate institution for formulating and implementing the most rational long-term resource policies. With high discount rates, decisions are almost always made in the interest of short-term advantages; the copper/aluminum argument previously given is such an example. Thus, unless lower rates soon prevail or tax and other incentives are established, the road to the Age of Substitutability may be filled with short-term road-

[3] A twelvefold increase in 150 years represents an average annual growth rate of only 1.7 percent.

blocks, making the journey far more arduous. Whether industry will be able to discipline itself in taking a longer term view of resource management in the interest of future generations is a moot question. If it cannot, then it seems necessary for governments to intervene; however, governments also suffer from a short-term outlook and are generally slow to take action. Only the most superb leadership, foresight, and planning seem capable of adequately and rapidly facing and solving such issues head on.

In this paper "rational" long-range materials policy implies, insofar as it is currently possible, development of plans for management of resources and their uses in a manner in which future generations are not penalized by today's economic and political actions. Until recently, it was a tenet held by most economists that future generations would always be better off and that therefore they could adequately take care of their economic needs despite present policies; this tenet now seems less certain with dwindling energy and limited materials resources.

Another example illustrates some of the problems involved. Helium is a rare commodity obtained exclusively from certain natural gas deposits; failure to recover it before the gas is burned releases it to the atmosphere where it is diluted from 10 to 1000-fold, depending on its content in a given natural gas. It has been an important material in the U.S. space program and may have large and important uses in certain future nuclear reactors and in the cryogenic (very low temperature) transmission of electricity under superconducting conditions, with great savings of transmission materials.

Until recently the U.S. government operated a helium stockpile program and amassed about a twenty-year supply at mid-1960 demand levels (around 5,000 tons/year). This program has now ceased and industry now separates only enough helium to meet current demands at prices which are well below the government price of $30/1000 ft^3. U.S. natural gas from conventional sources will be exhausted in twenty to thirty years and world supplies probably a decade later, at which time all the contained helium will have been vented to the atmosphere. If large needs then develop, it will be necessary to recover it from air at a few parts per million. At such low concentrations enormous facilities and expenditures of 50 to 100 times the current amount would be necessary to recover helium from air. The general argument against recovery now is that with high discount rates, the cost of today's smaller facilities is *more* than the cost of much larger facilities later discounted to today's value of money. Although such an argument may be sound under the rules of classical economics and a free market system, it does not sufficiently address the fact that recovery of helium from air would require expenditures of vastly larger amounts of energy and construction materials later on than would present recovery from natural gas. Further, the amounts of co-separated oxygen, nitrogen, and argon made available would be far in excess of demand so that the cost would have to be borne almost exclusively by the helium product. Although this example is an extreme one, it points out some of the problems which may ultimately be faced in maintaining a supply of those limited elements that are unrecyclable and have no known substitutes for essential uses.

As mentioned earlier, it may be important in some cases to depend on government intervention in normal free market operations to safeguard future supplies of certain key materials. It was also stated that government action is often slow to be instituted and is generally oriented toward short-term results. However, whereas industry is driven by short-term profit motives, whether or not it is in the best long-term interests of society, government has at least some responsibility for the well-being of posterity. Thus, although free market mechanisms are adequate, except in environmental matters, to control production of materials derived from near-infinite resources, they are increasingly less so in the control of rarer materials with present or future essential uses such as trace elements for agriculture and perhaps ultimately for the essential plant food phosphorus. The U.S. government has shown considerable wisdom in this decade in addressing environmental woes, but has not yet developed a fully coherent or adequate energy policy. It is important to continue to study materials policies and to reach conclusions before acute shortages in necessary materials can develop. Individually, such crises are certain to be less severe than the energy crisis, but collectively they could be even more severe. Only governments have the right to enact controls, regulations and tax incentives, and penalties to achieve public good.

As has been stated several times, it seems unlikely that the final Age of Substitutability will be achieved without extremely good planning which must include both technological research and development and studies in economics, environmental problems, and social and political issues. Technical efforts should include development of processes for the longer term which have high yields and are environmentally satisfactory, and development of products which have longer lives, are energy efficient, and are readily recyclable. These efforts go beyond the near-term research of industry and should not, therefore, compete unduly with their short-term goals. Economic studies should investigate in greater depth the adequacy of the free market and high discount rates in achieving long-term good as, for example, in the helium example given above. Economic/energy studies should be combined to see whether saving money or saving energy in the future is more important, particularly over the next twenty-five to thirty years until energy systems based on near-infinite resources are operable. Many social studies should also be made; for example, determination of the best methods to educate the public on energy and resource issues and investigations on how advertising might be modified to achive this end seem very pertinent now.

In summary, our conclusions on the future availability and management of nonrenewable resources are as follows:

1. By far, the greatest resource problem is the increasing shortage and ultimate depletion of fossil fuels or CH_x which is used both as the current primary basis for production of energy, and as the sole raw material for petrochemicals and metal reductants. Thus, an enormous effort is required to rapidly develop and deploy one or more "infinite" nonfossil fuel energy systems. Ultimately CO_2 must become the source for petrochemicals and hydrogen from water electrolysis the chief reductant for metals ores. Both are highly energy intensive. A corollary is that unless nuclear breeders are developed, the nuclear burner age will be shorter than the petroleum and natural gas age.

2. Use of twenty or so elements with near-infinite resources as substitutes for those with limited resources must be vigorously promoted. The greatest need here is the early substitution of iron, aluminum, magnesium, concrete, glass, and possibly titanium for nonferrous metals and some steel alloying agents. If this is appropriately accomplished, the unit monetary and energy "bill" for all nonrenewable resources (except fossil fuels) should not increase by more than a factor of two or three over the next several centuries.

3. Probably the single most important long-term problem is perpetual assurance that supplies of the elements necessary for modern agriculture are always available. We would envision shortages of certain trace elements as a first "crisis" in this area and possibly a shortage of phosphorus in the very long term, but could recycle bones in the latter case.

4. The production of metals is highly energy-intensive compared with other nonrenewable resources. However, because iron and aluminum now constitute 94 percent of the metals used world-wide, greater substitution of these metals plus magnesium and titanium should assure that our unit "energy bill" for all metals will be less than twice the present need.

5. Recycling, applicable only to elements used nondissipatively, is an admirable goal, but should not be overemphasized as a materials conservation measure because unless it is very efficient (say greater than 90 percent recovery) it is relatively ineffective over many recycles. However, for metals it is a large energy-saving expedient.

6. With regard to land spoilage, especially by strip mining, the most environmentally damaging era will probably be the next fifty years, the period when near-surface coal is depleted.

All of the above solutions are principally technological. Little progress seems likely to be made in any of them, however, if we continue to pursue standard production practices, including many of our present economic concepts which stress so strongly short-term advantages. Physical scientists and engineers can provide the requisite new technologies, environmentalists and sociologists will provide more than enough conscience, but the final decision in our modern civilization must be made by the economists and politicians. Let us hope that in order to achieve a smooth road to a not-physically impossible Age of Substitutability they can rise to new heights of success in planning and action.

References

1. H. E. Goeller and A. M. Weinberg, "The Age of Substitutability," *Science*, vol. 191 (February 20, 1976) pp. 683–689.
2. D. H. Meadows, D. L. Meadows, Jørgen Randers, and W. W. Behrens III, *The Limits to Growth* (Universe Books, New York, 1972).
3. M. Mesarovic and E. Pestel, *Mankind at the Turning Point* (New York, Dutton, 1974).
4. Herman Kahn, W. Brown, and L. Martel, *The Next 200 Years* (New York, William Morrow, 1976).
5. Harrison Brown, *The Next Ninety Years* (Pasadena, California Institute of Technology, 1967) p. 17.
6. H. G. Wells, J. S. Huxley, and G. P. Wells, *The Science of Life* vol. 3 (Garden City, N.Y., Doubleday, 1931) pp. 1031, 1032.
7. N. A. Lange, *Handbook of Chemistry* (3rd ed., Sandusky, Ohio, Handbook Publishers, 1939) p. 34.
8. D . F. Frasché, (Washington, D.C., National Academy of Sciences-National Research Council, 1963) Pub. 1000-C, p. 18.
9. B. J. Skinner, "A Second Iron Age Ahead," *American Scientist,* vol. 64 (May/June 1976) pp. 258–269.
10. U. S. Bureau of Mines, *Mineral Facts and Problems, 1970,* Bulletin 650 (Washington, GPO, 1970).
11. NATO Scientific Affairs Division, *Rational Use of Potentially Scarce Metals,* (Brussels, Belgium, May 1976).
12. J. C. Brevard, H. B. Flora II, and C. Portal, *Energy Expenditures Associated with the Production and Recycle of Metals* (Oak Ridge, Tenn., Oak Ridge National Laboratory, 1972) ORNL-NSF-EP-24.
13. R. A. Labine, "New: Making Iron in a Fluidized Bed," *Chemical Engineering* vol. 67 (February 8, 1960) pp. 96–99.

7

Comments on the Papers by Brobst and Goeller

Bruce M. Hannon

Each author is so expert in his field and these fields are so foreign to me that I can only comment on what I perceive to be their omissions.

Basically, Brobst writes of resource availability. He believes that the cost of accelerating the discovery rates of larger and larger supplies of critical resources, particularly those for new electric energy supplies, is very high.[1] He is consequently rather pessimistic about our abilities to meet the resource demands of growth. Goeller is more optimistic. He argues that substitutability of resources can allow continued aggregate economic growth.

Both authors work entirely in physical units and avoid reference to changing dollar resource prices as resources become scarce. Neither author emphasizes the difference between energy and nonenergy resources. While short-run substitution of one of these for the other is possible, in the long run there is no substitute for energy resources. This fact, I believe, provides a reason for the unique position of energy resources in economic production functions, as distinct from other resources.

The inclusion of the rapidly rising direct (Brobst's paper) and indirect resource inputs into resource price trends (see Barnett's paper) should surprise resource economists who believe these trends change gently. Neither speaker discussed the effects that continued or accelerated resource use would have on land use.

Both authors only touched on recycling as a means of extending a resource life. They were pessimistic about the ability of recycling to significantly extend resource availability, however. The importance of recycling increases only as economic growth rates slow.

In deciding on the amount of effort which should be devoted to

---

[1] Note that the average heat rate for average U.S. electric power plants has declined over the past several years. This is a signal that the energy inputs to electrical power plants are becoming less effective in meeting demand patterns for electricity. This is a physical measure of declining resource utility.

recycling, or to resource substitution, it seems to me that the objective should be to minimize the physical resource costs among the alternative ways of obtaining a desired good or service. Of particular interest to the resource engineer would be the relative direct and indirect energy costs of competing alternatives. An economist would wish to minimize the dollar cost. The effectiveness of recycling depends on a complex array of factors little understood by today's policy makers. Basically, we should act to minimize the entropy or disorder created in performing economic services. This prescription implies using materials for as long as possible and then dismantling, sorting, and returning them to their original point of manufacture. Inevitably, foreign materials degrade recycled materials or they suffer structural breakdown and are diverted into downgraded secondary markets. These markets tend to become saturated as a result of the independence of the demands for the original and the secondary products. This concept of saturation points defines the physical limit of the utility of recycling. Market defects which are detrimental to recycling, such as inaccurate freight rates for virgin and recycled materials, inadvertent tax subsidies favoring virgin material use, and the vertical integration of virgin sources with final production, also ought to be remedied.

A major need of special importance to geologists is the present and predicted costs (direct and indirect, in physical units) of use of a particular resource, including the effects of recycling. Input–output models are probably an effective tool for this determination. The next step would be to establish the ranked and quantified importance of physical resources by analyzing economic final demand scenarios.

Alternatively, one could rank the types of resources on the basis of the demands of a subsistence economy, yielding the absolute minimum nature of the demand. With such a ranking, one can compare the demands with the known remaining amount of these resources. Goeller has done this for a single period, but, of course, without knowledge of the relative demand for these resources in a dynamic economy and without detailed knowledge of the ability to substitute among these resources. To gain this latter knowledge, we would need large and expensive modeling efforts, at the very least.

One of the principal economic concerns is the effect of resource shortages on labor productivity. Increases in capital and labor inputs have historically explained only 10 to 20 percent of the change in rising labor productivity [1]. Changes in resource inputs, particularly energy, may have accounted for the bulk of the change, with "technological change" playing a much smaller role than usually believed. If resources, particularly energy, are now becoming scarce, at least in the United States, then other factors of production, capital and labor, will be substituted for the resources. In the past, technological change may well have been the strategy by which the resources were substituted for capital and labor, making the latter more productive. But we must remember that a unit of technology itself can have significant, perhaps even increasing demands for resources, labor, and capital. If technology is not able to counteract declining capital and labor productivity (and capital and labor depreciation) in the face of declining resources, the returns to capital or/and labor would decline. This is the basic flaw in the paper by Stiglitz. Further, it is not at all clear that technology can reverse its major direction, the substitution of resources for labor and capital, and overcome its own costs plus the increasing inputs of capital, in order to guarantee future income levels. The present direction of technology produces a return on investment in the technology itself. Can the same be true in a resource-short economy?

If technology does not achieve the above goal, then income of capital holders and labor will decline, although employment may increase. Besides the distinct possibility for inequitable income distribution, this decline would produce a reduction in long-run aggregate demand. This decrease in final demand would mean a decline in the aggregate resource demand. It also means, perhaps more importantly, that the composition of the reduced demand would change. Consequently, the composition of the resource demand would also change, possibly even exacerbating the supply shortage of certain critical resources. Taxes on those resources, especially on energy, could be used to reduce the demand for critically short resources on an individual basis. In addition, direct demand controls, some of which are already being seriously considered (e.g., container deposits, peak load pricing of electricity) could specifically redirect demand away from critical resources.

In general, too much of this conference was dedicated to conditions of resource supply, addressing the question: Can we have economic growth? A full examination of the issues surrounding economic growth requires that consideration be given to the possible mechanisms, natural and policy induced, for influencing society's pattern of final demands. Once such an investigation is recognized as an integral component of any evaluation of economic growth, then growth strategies can be appraised, based on the answers they imply for the questions: What are the real economic and social benefits and costs of growth in material use rates? Is such growth necessary or indeed desirable?

References

1. Kuznets, Simon, *Modern Economic Growth Rate, Structure and Spread,* (New Haven, Conn., Yale University Press, 1966).

8

Scarcity and Growth Revisited

Harold J. Barnett

I
Background for the Scarcity and Growth Analysis

A. Introduction. *Scarcity and Growth: The Economics of Natural Availability* (hereafter *S and G*) was one of several publications by members of Resources for the Future (RFF) that were prepared during RFF's first five-year term (approximately 1955–60) in response to the implicit mandates of the President's Commission on Materials Policy. While several articles by Barnett and Morse preceded its publication in 1963, this volume summarizes their overall evaluation of natural resource adequacy.

In this paper, "Scarcity and Growth Revisited," I seek to review and supplement that analysis with the benefit of fifteen to twenty years' hindsight. While this paper is a modest effort, and incomplete, I do hope to offer some perspective on the earlier analysis and to present some evidence on the intervening period.

This section reviews the findings of *Scarcity and Growth*. In section II we discuss the evidence on the adequacy of natural resources for the United States that has become available since 1957. Section III considers the movements in various measures of real unit costs and relative prices of resources for a selected sample of countries throughout the world.

I am grateful to several organizations: Washington University, for sabbatical leave; the International Institute for Applied Systems Analysis, Laxenburg, Austria, where a substantial portion of the paper was prepared in very congenial conditions; and Resources for the Future, for arranging this conference and requesting the paper.

In addition, I have personal obligations for help and friendly cooperation to Professor Chandler Morse, coauthor of *Scarcity and Growth;* Professor V. Kerry Smith, who arranged the Conference and very generously edited and improved my paper; Dr. Morris Norman, who most kindly computer programmed my untidy data on European and world productivity, which appears in section III; and Messrs. Loeser, Popper, and their IIASA library colleagues, for helping me to find these basic European and world data.

After summarizing the nature of these results, I reconsider the environmental effects of meeting the need for natural resources.

B. Brief Summary. I begin with a summary concerning one central element from the original *S and G* volume—the doctrine of increasing economic scarcity of natural resources. There are many and diverse views on the social aspects of natural resources. Among these, a major interest resides in the concept of a natural resource scarcity and its economic effects. The belief seems to be that natural resources are economically scarce; that economic scarcity increases with passage of time; and that this impairs levels of living and economic growth. These views have been widely held for a long time in western societies. Professor Morse and I found them present in the conservation movement and among the classical economists and others. Moreover, the concerns arising from these beliefs are also present among many economists, policy makers, and a segment of the general populace today.

The analysis in *Scarcity and Growth* suggested that the classical theory of increasing economic scarcity of natural resources was invalid except in highly constrained, unrealistic models. For real economies, theory cannot answer whether or not there is increasing economic scarcity of natural resources. The question must be answered factually, on the evidence.

For the United States in the period from the Civil War to 1957, the evidence denies the doctrine of increasing economic scarcity in agriculture, minerals, and the aggregate of extractive industries. The principal reasons for this were: (1) substitutions of economically more plentiful resources for less plentiful ones; (2) increased discoveries and availability of domestic mineral resources; (3) increased imports of selected metallic minerals; and (4) a marked increase in the acquisition of knowledge and sociotechnical improvements relevant to the economics of resource discovery, development, conversion, transportation, and production. These factors have made it possible for the economy to produce larger and larger volumes of extractive goods at declining real marginal costs.

While these observations were among the major findings of *Scarcity and Growth,* we also discussed problems associated with use of natural resources and the attendant implications for intergenerational equity. We found that, in U.S. history, each generation has passed to the next improved conditions of natural resource availability and economic productivity. Moreover, the phenomena of accumulated knowledge, scientific advances, and self-generating technological change have more than overcome tendencies of increasing costs for utilization and exhaustion of specific resources. It is not by chance that advances in knowledge, market processes, and government policies provide solutions to actual and prospective natural resource cost problems. The motivations, mechanisms, and choice of solutions appear to be endogenous in modern efficiency-seeking economies.

Finally, *Scarcity and Growth* discussed the implications of these patterns of technical change and growth for a broad class of social and environmental factors which we grouped under the heading "quality of life" effects. We noted that while society had been very successful in avoiding increased economic scarcity of natural resources in terms of cost of extractive goods, other problems relating to natural resources were appearing.

We identify several such cases of impact which have emerged during the past generation: urban agglomeration; waste disposal and pollution; changes in income distribution, particularly in relation to distressed areas; water supply; land use; international relations with underdeveloped nations. [1, pp. 253–254]

Moreover, sometime earlier I concluded:

I am greatly impressed by a "new" form of resource scarcity—the problem of space, privacy, and nature preservation. . . . This category of doctrine already includes a quality scarcity concern over fouling streams, disfiguring land, and air pollution. And I guess it should also include concern over atmospheric and land contamination by radioactivity. [2]

In *S and G* we chose to identify and describe these problems but did not integrate them into our analysis.

C. Statistical Measures and Tests. *Scarcity and Growth* defined increasing resource scarcity as increasing real cost of extractive products. The hypothesis of increasing resource scarcity (hereafter simply resource scarcity) can be tested by examining time series of the real cost of these products. The resource scarcity hypothesis was defined in a strong and in a weak form.

The Strong Hypothesis of Increasing Economic Scarcity. The strong hypothesis states that the real cost of extractive products per unit will increase through time due to limitations in the available quantities and qualities of natural resources. For the strong hypothesis, we measure real cost in terms of labor (man-days, man-hours, or man-years) or labor plus capital (depreciated investments adjusted for price level) per unit of extractive output. This formulation offered the traditional form of the hypothesis. In it, increasing scarcity is visible in an increasing

Table 8-1. Summary of Movements in Real Unit Costs
(1929 = 100)

Years	Total extractive	Agriculture	Minerals	Forestry
1870–1900	134	132	210	59
1919	122	114	164	106
1957	60	61	47	90

trend of L_E/O_E or $L_E + C_E/O_E$.[1] In the classical economies described by Smith, Malthus, and Ricardo, it was not necessary to attach the "E" subscripts. The extractive sectors—agriculture, forestry, fishing, mining—and the total economy were nearly equivalent in quantitative terms, with the extractive sector bulking very large in the full economy.

The strong or traditional form of the hypothesis has been rediscovered by a number of contemporary movements. These include ecological, environmental, no-growth, ZEG, ZPG, Crisis of Mankind, and steady-state movements led variously by the Club of Rome, Forrester–Meadows, Hardin, Ehrlich, Daly, and others. These popular no-growth movements of the day must subscribe to the strong hypothesis—to increasing real cost defined as above—because only such increasing cost trends, in association with growing population, could significantly restrain and ultimately stop economic growth in modern economies.

The U.S. output in extractive sectors increased markedly from the Civil War to 1957. The increase in agriculture, following Engel's law, was slower than the increase in real gross national product (GNP). Minerals output, on the other hand, increased roughly as fast as real GNP. The stage was clearly set in extractive products for operation of the classical economic doctrine of increasing cost or diminishing returns. The extensive frontier of the nation is believed to have disappeared by the end of the nineteenth century. Given a substantial expansion in population and economic activity, the strong hypothesis proposes increasing labor and labor plus capital costs per unit of output of extractive goods.

The statistical record fails to support, and in fact is contradictory to, the classical hypothesis. Real costs per unit of extractive goods, measured in units of labor plus capital, did not rise. They fell, except in forestry (which is less than 10 percent of extraction). Table 8-1 briefly summarizes the evidence. Interestingly, the pace of decline in real costs accelerates following World War I, compared with the preceding period. The classical scarcity hypotheses would suggest that the tendency to increase

[1] Editor's note: The unit costs defined as $(L_E + C_E)/O_E$ have been adjusted to resolve the units of measurement problem. Thus this formulation corresponds to Brown and Field's definition on page 220 of this paper. The exact procedure in the original Barnett–Morse study is described in their appendix B.

in real costs becomes greater as size of the economy increases. These results are opposite to this view, with the appearance of a more favorable record in the later period.

The foregoing observations are important historical evidence or events, not statistical artifacts. We tested whether different weighting systems could affect the aggregate unit cost indexes which we presented. Figure 8-1 shows the index of labor plus capital cost per unit of output in extraction, based on three different sets of weights for output. In each case, every individual commodity's output in the extractive cost index is weighted by the price of that commodity relative to other prices in the extractive sector, the prices being those of the widely separated years, 1902, 1929, and 1954.

The comparisons in figure 8-1 show that the weighting system for the output indexes has not been primarily responsible for the declining trend in cost of extractive products. The extractive cost index declines at simi-

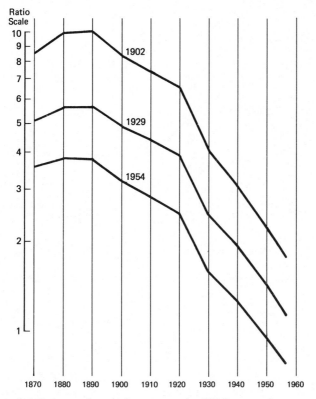

Figure 8-1. Labor and capital cost per unit of U.S. extractive output, 1902, 1929, and 1954 weights.

lar rates irrespective of the weighting system. In the 1902 price weighted index (of gross output), the unit cost of the extractive goods index has an average decline of 1.32 percent per annum since 1890; this compares with 1.25 percent for the 1954 index, and an intermediate figure for the 1929 index. We obtained similar results in both agriculture and minerals by varying the weight of output of individual commodities according to their prices in 1902, 1929, or 1954. The 1954 weighting system which we have used does not primarily account for the fact of declining unit cost in total agriculture. The situation is similar in minerals as an aggregate. All three weighting systems show substantial and similar declining unit costs.

Figures 8-2 through 8-7 show that the contradiction of the strong scarcity hypothesis holds for the great majority of extractive commodi-

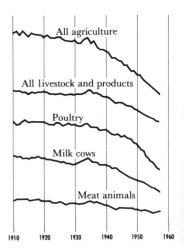

Figure 8-2. U.S. agriculture: labor cost per unit of output in all crops and nine major commodities, 1910–57.

Figure 8-3. U.S. agriculture: labor cost per unit of total output and of output of livestock and products, 1910–57.

Figure 8-5. U.S. mineral fuels: labor cost per unit of output, 1870–1957. Solid lines connect points in annual series; dashed lines connect points over a year apart.

Figure 8-4. U.S. minerals: labor cost per unit of output, 1870–1957. Note: Solid lines connect points in annual series; dashed lines connect points over a year apart.

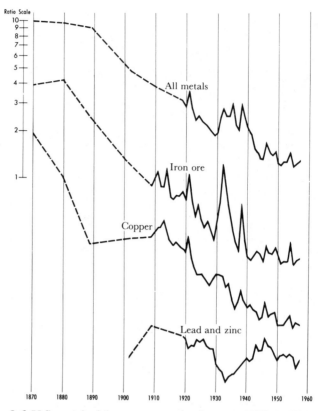

Figure 8-6. U.S. metals: labor cost per unit of output, 1870–1957. Solid lines connect points in annual series; dashed lines connect points over a year apart.

ties, excluding forestry. In these charts, only labor costs and gross outputs can be used, since neither capital input data nor net output figures are available for individual commodities. (For reference, we show the comparable labor cost per unit of gross output in the corresponding aggregate categories.)

The Weak Hypothesis of Increasing Economic Scarcity. The weak hypothesis suggests that while increasing resource scarcity does tend to increase real cost (L_E/O_E or $L_E + C_E/O_E$), this increase is more than offset by sociotechnical progress or other favorable, economy-wide changes. While the tendency for real costs of extractive outputs to rise as a result of increasing scarcity is more than offset by the dynamic forces in the economy, nonetheless, the resulting rate of decline in real costs of

Figure 8-7. U.S. nonmetals: labor cost per unit of output, 1880–1957. Solid lines connect points in annual series; dashed lines connect points over a year apart.

extractive goods may be less than in the rest of the economy. We can test this hypothesis by assuming that these favorable dynamic forces (the progress of civilization, to use Mill's term) are operating equally in both extractive and nonextractive sectors. In this case we can test for increasing scarcity by examining the trend of $(L_E/O_E) \div (L_N/O_N)$, or the equivalent with labor plus capital. (The subscript N represents the nonextractive sector of the economy.) If the weak scarcity hypothesis is valid, then

Table 8-2.   Real Unit Costs in Relative Terms
(1929 = 100)

Years	All extractive goods	Agriculture	Minerals	Forestry
1870–1900	99	97	154	37
1919	103	97	139	84
1957	87	89	68	130

the unit cost of extractive goods *relative* to nonextractive will rise, even though the absolute unit cost is declining. With certain other assumptions, the weak scarcity hypothesis can also be tested by examining the trend of P_E/P_N or P_E/P, that is, the trend of relative price of extractive products. If the weak scarcity hypothesis is true, the price of extractive goods will rise relative to the price index of all goods (P).

The weak hypothesis can be interpreted as a more sophisticated measure of real cost than the traditional one. Modern economists would say it is a better measure than that of classical economics. In the weak hypothesis, real cost is measured as "opportunity cost," that is by reflecting the goods and services which are forgone in order to produce a unit of extractive product, where L is valued at its productivity in the overall economy at each respective date. Similarly, in defining real costs as P_E/P, we consider the extractive product relative to the value of goods and services forgone to obtain it. These two real cost measures for the weak scarcity hypothesis—relative cost and relative price—are equivalent to each other as indicators, under certain assumptions.[2]

These "opportunity cost" measures of real cost are quite different from the cost measures which are relevant to the strong hypothesis of classical economics or the present-day alarmists—Meadows [4], Erlich [5], Hardin [6]—mentioned earlier. Only the strong form of natural resource scarcity, in which the costs of extractive goods rise absolutely and eventually dominate the expenditures comprising GNP, can halt and reverse economic progress. The weak form, in which the costs of extractive goods decline in absolute terms although they rise relative to the costs of other goods, offers, at worst, a slow rate of economic progress, but could never halt it, let alone bring about the decline which the alarmists say has been occurring or will occur soon.

Table 8-2 shows the historical trends of unit costs in the United States for the weak scarcity hypothesis. The figures are indexes (1929 = 100) of labor plus capital cost in extractive sectors *relative to the non-extractive sector of the economy:*

[2] The assumptions and alternative measures are discussed in *S and G,* pp. 202–16, and in Barnett [3].

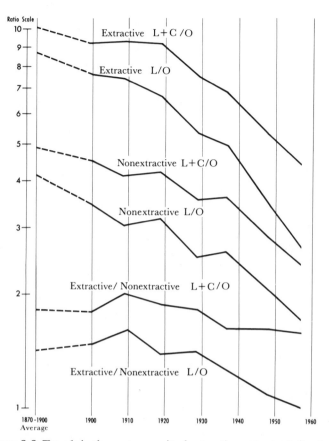

Figure 8-8. Trends in the cost per unit of extractive output relative to nonextractive output in the United States, 1870–1957.

The weak scarcity hypothesis fails in all extraction, agricultural, and mineral sectors. Costs per unit of output in these sectors decline no less rapidly than in the economy at large. Only in forestry is the weak scarcity hypothesis supported.

Figure 8-8 presents the absolute and relative unit cost data (both labor plus capital and labor alone) for the aggregate extractive and nonextractive sectors. The weak scarcity hypothesis fails for all extraction. The relative price data are shown in figure 8-9. These show that over the whole period relative prices did not rise in the full extractive sector, agriculture, or minerals, but did in forestry. These data tend to confirm the relative cost data. The weak scarcity hypothesis fails for extraction, agriculture, and minerals, but is supported in forestry.

Figure 8-9. Trends in unit prices of forest products relative to nonextractive products in the United States, 1890–1957. Solid lines connect points in annual series; dashed lines connect points over a year apart.

II
Extension of U.S. Statistical Tests to 1970

Based on the evidence in section I, the hypothesis of increasing resource scarcity in the United States, 1870–1957 is not supported by the data. The findings fail to support increasing resource scarcity for the United States over the period involved. However, it now becomes relevant, fifteen years later, to reconsider the statistical analysis. In this section, we examine U.S. real cost data since 1957. In the next section, we compile and analyze data for other countries of the world since World War II, to offer further support for these findings.

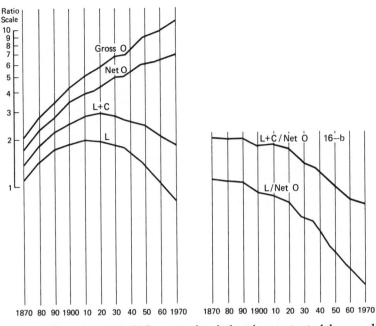

Figures 8-10 and 8-11. U.S. extractive industries: output, labor, and capital inputs, and cost per unit of output, 1870–1970.

Manley Johnson and Frederick W. Bell, of Florida State University, have updated certain of the original labor, capital, and output data in *Scarcity and Growth* to 1970. Their extensions have been graphed in a manner consistent with the earlier analysis (in *S and G*) and are given in figures 8-10 and 8-11.[3]

These results indicate that, in general, the record of declining real cost, measured as L_E/O_E or $(L_E + C_E) O_E$, observed in the 1870–1957 period, continues. The rapid rates of decline in labor costs per unit of extractive, agricultural, and mineral output appear to persist unabated, but the rates of decline for $L + C$ per unit of net output seem to have slowed in the 1960–70 decade. There is no sign of upturn to support the strong scarcity hypothesis.

With respect to the weak scarcity hypothesis, Robert R. Manthy of Michigan State University has extended the relative price data in *S and G* to 1973. V. Kerry Smith's analysis [7] of their trends suggests that the erratic relative price trends in Barnett and Morse continue (see figure

---

[3] Reproduced from R. R. Wilson and D. A. Samuelson, "America's Natural Resources: Boom or Doom," paper presented to Southern Economic Association Meetings, 1976. The citation is to Johnson's unpublished Ph.D. dissertation, 1976.

8-9). There is *no* increase, and the weak scarcity hypothesis fails to be supported.

Smith has analyzed the 1900–73 data intensively, using statistical techniques beyond simple observation, plotting of the observed values, and fitting of moving averages and trends. His view appears to be that the relative price data are so volatile as to cause him to question our ability to draw any conclusions from the data. He explains this at length in his paper. However, it seems the interpretation of these findings is not at variance with the *S and G* conclusions. That is, we can observe 100 years of extractive and nonextractive prices, and long-term segments within the period; relate them to national events; and interpret the economic trends in extractive and other prices. These movements can, in turn, be related to long-term trends in real costs, and we can further interpret all of these relative to economic scarcity hypotheses. It may be that Smith's agnosticism results from emphasis on short-term and second-order fluctuations (and possibly statistical niceties) not related to the economic history and scarcity concepts.

III
Labor Cost of Minerals and Agricultural Products in World Regions and Various Countries

The findings reported in this section should be regarded as a preliminary appraisal of the evidence on resource scarcity in various nations of the world.[4] It is an exploratory effort, but nonetheless suggestive of the movements in real resource costs elsewhere.

A. Strong Hypothesis of Increasing Economic Scarcity. *Labor Cost of Mineral Production in Major World Regions.* One of the more interesting of the data sets which are used in testing the increasing scarcity hypotheses is published by the United Nations. These statistics report, for major regions of the world, labor productivity (reciprocal of labor cost) in each of four mineral categories: coal mining (CO), petroleum and gas extraction (PG), mining of metallic minerals (MM), and all minerals extraction (MI). The data begin with a "world" region (W), then are broken into types of economies: market (M), centrally planned (CP), developed market (DM), and developing market (GM), and then into continental groupings. The 1974 Year Book presents data for a sixteen-year period, 1958 through 1973, but omits 1959, 1961, 1962, 1964–67, and 1970.

---

[4] I am most grateful to my colleagues in the IIASA (Laxenburg, Austria) library—to Messrs. Loesser, Popper, and their associates for help.

These data have been evaluated for the world region and for each of the four "market types." With four mineral classes and five regions, there are twenty individual time series. The trends and parameters estimates are shown in appendix B. The series are numbered 11 through 35.[5]

All of the time series fail to support the strong hypothesis of increasing scarcity for minerals. Indeed, all are consistent with an opposite hypothesis, that of increasing resource availability. Productivity in minerals production not only does not decline, but increases rather strongly and somewhat persistently in all five of the regions for all four of the mineral classes. This is equivalent to decline in real labor cost, measured in conventional man-hour or man-day units.

The trends of labor productivity increase are not uniform among the series. A simple trend model of the form: $y = ae^{bt}$ was estimated with ordinary least squares. The following observations summarize the statistical evidence:

(1) The rates of increase in labor productivities per year can be tabulated as:

Rate	Number of cases
2.00–2.99%	3
3.00–4.99%	14
> 5%	3

(2) All but one of the R^2 (coefficient of determination) for these relations exceed 0.9; all of the coefficients are statistically significant.

(3) Finally, there may be a deceleration in the rates for the *linear* trend lines in the following nine cases:

Identification number	Series	R^2
14	Metals mining, W	0.967
21	Minerals, M	0.987
22	Coal, M	0.941
24	Metals mining, M	0.942
27	Coal, DM	0.909
29	Metals mining, DM	0.963
32	Coal, GM	0.951
33	Petroleum and gas, GM	0.977
34	Metals mining, GM	0.844

Labor Cost of Coal Production in Selected Countries. The U.S. Bituminous Coal Association, a trade association of coal mining compa-

---

[5] A labor cost in manufacturing series appears also in each region, with the symbol MA. This is used later in examining labor productivity in minerals relative to manufacturing.

Table 8-3.   Productivity Movements for Coal

Data source	Productivity change in last four years, to 1973
U.S., underground	Down
U.S., strip	Level
U.S., auger	Erratic level
U.S., overall	Down
Belgium	Level

nies, has published comparative productivity figures in coal mines in the United States and six European countries over the period 1944–73. The figures for U.S. mines are in four series— underground, strip, auger, and total. These time series are identified as numbers 1 through 10 in the statistical appendix (B). In addition, there are two other productivity series in appendix B—one for the European Coal Community (no. 36, 1960 to 1966) and one for Great Britain (no. 212, 1964–73).

Least squares trend lines using the same model as that given above were fitted to all of these series. In all cases there were strong upward trends in labor productivity. The *t* statistics ranged from 5 to 31, and the R^2 statistics ranged from 0.70 to 0.97. The annual rates of increase in productivity ranged from 2 to more than 8 percent, with the majority falling in the 3 to 5 percent range. These data all deny the strong scarcity hypothesis.

In addition, these series have been plotted against *linear* trend lines. In the U.S. and Belgium series, labor productivity turns down or levels off in the late 1960s or 1970 and this continues to 1973. If one were to fit these past several years instead of the whole period, the story is somewhat altered as shown in table 8-3. The earlier findings for Great Britain, France, the Netherlands, Germany, Poland, and the European Coal Community remain unchanged. In order to evaluate the significance of the U.S. and Belgium productivity data, more information is needed. We have to ask, "What may have changed each of these series?" One possibility is resource scarcity. Other possibilities are environmental constraints, changes in safety regulations, stage of the business cycle, and so on.

Labor Cost of Agricultural and Mineral Products in West Germany. The analysis for West Germany is based on labor productivity series for agriculture and minerals. The agriculture series is in two parts, one component (designated 242) from 1956–62 and a second (number 243) from 1962–71. The minerals series (number 245) is from 1957–71. Agricultural productivity rises at 8½ percent a year in the first part of the period ($t = 10.4$; $R^2 = 0.78$) and 6 percent in the second ($t = 10.4$; $R^2 = 0.92$). The improvement in productivity is persistent and rather regular. Moreover, output was rising during the period.

The results for labor productivity in the minerals sector are quite similar. It increases at 4.3 percent; $t = 20.7$ and $R^2 = 0.97$. Output was rising in the early years and became erratic without apparent trend in the later ones. Thus there is no support for the strong scarcity hypothesis in the productivity movements for agriculture and minerals sectors in West Germany.

B. Relative Cost Measures to Test the Weak Scarcity Hypothesis.
Relative Labor Costs of Minerals Output in Major World Regions. In this section results for *relative* labor productivity measures across regions will be related to the *weak hypothesis* concerning increasing natural resource scarcity. We test the weak scarcity hypothesis by examining *relative* labor cost of minerals or its reciprocal, *relative* labor productivity in minerals.

Each of the mineral productivity series previously discussed has been divided by the manufacturing (MA) productivity series in the same year and region. These data were compiled from the same sources. The results of regressing these series on time are also shown in appendix B. Table 8-4 summarizes these results. From this evidence, we are unable to accept the weak scarcity hypothesis. The only exception to this conclusion comes with the cases of coal and possibly minerals in centrally planned economies, and coal in developing market economies.

Examination of the graphs of linear trends and the actual observations of these relative productivity data reveal some evidence which would be favorable to the weak scarcity hypothesis beginning to emerge for some of the minerals. That is, although the series for 1958–72/73 generally provide evidence against the weak hypothesis, the last two years or so of some of the series are more favorable to the weak hypothesis. Table 8-5 summarizes the relative productivity series showing declines to 1972 or 1973 for two or more years.

These results may be a signal of impending weak scarcity. However, two years of divergence are too brief a period to be taken seriously in this type of analysis. The change in relative productivity can be due to many things other than scarcity, as mentioned earlier.

Relative Agricultural Prices in Selected Countries of the World. Two basic series measuring relative agricultural prices have been used for the weak scarcity hypothesis. The first is the ratio of agricultural prices to

Table 8-4. Relative Labor Cost in Major Regions of the World[a]

	Outcome
Statistically significant support for increasing scarcity hypothesis[b]	
Support ($R^2 > 0.5, b > 0.01$)	Coal in centrally planned economies (219).[c]
Support ($R^2 < 0.5, b < 0.01$ or both)	Minerals in centrally planned economies (218) and coal in developing market economies (229).
Statistically significant evidence adverse to increasing scarcity hypothesis	
Adverse ($R^2 > 0.5, b > 0.01$)	Petroleum and gas in each of world (215), market (225), developed market, (230), developing market (235), and centrally planned economies (220). Minerals in market (223) and developing market economies (233). Coal in developing market economies (234). Metallic minerals in centrally planned economies (221).
Adverse ($R^2 < 0.5$ or $b < 0.01$)	Minerals in world (213).
Statistically insignificant results;[b] no support $t < 2.0$.	Coal in world (214) and market (224) economies. Metallic minerals in world (216), market (226), developed market (231), and developing market economies (236). Minerals in developed market economies (228).

[a] The above regression parameters were taken from ordinary least squares estimates of the model $y = ae^{bt}$.
[b] In all cases "statistically insignificant" means $t < 2.0$.
[c] Numbers in parentheses indicate series.

Table 8-5. Summary of Declines in Relative Productivity

Extractive output	Region[a]	Length of period
213 Minerals	W	2 years
214 Coal	W	2 years
216 Metallics	W	2 years
218 Minerals	CP	(see table 8-4)
219 Coal	CP	(see table 8-4)
223 Minerals	M	2 years
224 Coal	M	2 years
226 Metallics	M	2 years
228 Minerals	DM	2 years
229 Coal	DM	(see table 8-4)
230 Petro + Gas	DM	2 years
231 Metallics	DM	4 years
236 Metallics	GM	2 years

[a] W—world; CP—centrally planned; M—market; DM—developing market.

prices of other goods. If increasing resource scarcity is present in the agricultural sector, we would expect agricultural prices to rise compared with the prices of all other goods, where price movements of resources will play a much smaller role.

Each of the two relative agricultural price series is in two parts, for selected countries:

(1) Ratio of prices received by farmers to prices paid (RP)
   • Series 143–164 from approximately 1950 to 1963, 15 countries
   • Series 165–191 from approximately 1963 to 1972, 25 countries
(2) Ratio of agricultural prices to the general wholesale price index of the country (AGW)
   • Series 264–285 from approximately 1950 to 1962, 22 countries
   • Series 286–316 from approximately 1961 to 1972, 31 countries.

It seems reasonable that the "prices received/prices paid" (series 143–191) should be ignored. While these data would be strongly adverse to the weak scarcity hypothesis, they are not directly relevant to it. There are two reasons underlying this judgment. First, the "prices paid" figure can include "wages," which makes this relative price series inappropriate for a test of the weak scarcity hypothesis. Second, the "prices paid" data may emphasize goods which use natural resources intensively, such as fuels, fertilizers, and seed. This property tends to make the deflator in the "prices received/prices paid" less representative of *non* resource-intensive goods.

The second series consists of prices of agricultural products relative to the general wholesale price index for the country. Table 8-6 is a summary list for the 53 identified cases. Thirty of these cases offer no support for the weak hypothesis, but 23 do. Table 8-7 indicates that support for the scarcity hypothesis is more concentrated in the later period, 1961–72, and its rejection is somewhat more in the former. This time sequence is itself a piece of supporting evidence for the weak, increasing scarcity hypothesis.

In table 8-8 the countries and periods for the "support" cases discussed above are identified specifically. In addition, the table reports the regression parameters for each of the eight countries which experienced relatively rising agricultural prices in the first period. Several overall observations can be made:

1. All eight countries are advanced in development. However, *most* of the developed countries are *not* in this list of countries providing evidence for the weak scarcity case.
2. Five of the countries are European. Four of them do not repeat their scarcity evidence in the second period, and the fifth (Spain) exhibits

Table 8-6. Test of Scarcity Hypothesis: Trends of Ratios of Agricultural Prices to General Wholesale Prices, Series 264–316

Statistically adverse to scarcity hypothesis		Statistically support scarcity hypothesis
Statistically insignificant	Sign is opposite to hypothesis	
264	267	266
265	269	268
270	274	271
275	277	272
280	279	273
282	281	276
283		278
284	287	285
	296	
286	304	288
290	316	289
291		293
292		295
294		297
299		298
303		300
307		301
309		302
310		305
312		306
314		308
		311
		313
		315
(20 cases)	(10 cases)	(23 cases)

Table 8-7. Summary of the Evidence for Relative Prices of Agricultural Products by Time Period

Type of evidence	Number of cases		
	1950–62	1961–72	1950–72
Adverse evidence	14	16	30
Support evidence	8	15	23
Total	22	31	53

rather weak evidence with low b, t, and R^2. How should we interpret evidence which appears in 1950–62 and disappears in 1961–72 relative to a long-term scarcity hypothesis? One possibility is that evidence of resource scarcity is a transient phenomenon in market economies because its appearance induces economic forces, that is, technical change, substitution, and so on, which tend to mitigate the long-term effects.

Table 8-8. Identification of Support Cases

Country	(Series No.) First period	(Series No.) Second period	Parameters[a] b	Parameters[a] t	Parameters[a] R^2
Germany (D)	266	—	0.008	3.3	0.55
Italy (I)	268	—	0.006	2.0	0.25
Spain (E)	271		0.007	2.3	0.64
		313	0.004	2.1	0.23
Sweden (S)	272	—	0.012	0.45	0.64
Yugoslavia (YU)	273	—	0.037	2.7	0.57
Mexico (MX)	276		0.007	3.4	0.46
		289	0.007	5.4	0.72
Argentina (AR)	278	—	0.014	2.9	0.55
Japan (JP)	285		0.018	3.4	0.51
		300	0.032	8.4	0.86
Costa Rica (CR)	—	288			
Chile (CE)	—	293			
Ecuador (EC)	—	295			
India (IN)	—	297			
Iran (IR)	—	298			
Korea (KR)	—	301			
Philippines (PP)	—	302			
Belgium (B)	—	305			
France (F)	—	306			
Greece (GR)	—	308			
Netherlands (NL)	—	311			
United Kingdom (GB)	—	315			

[a] The model used is of the form $y = ae^{bt}$

3. One of the countries, Japan, is generally viewed as a classic agricultural scarcity case. Thus it is not surprising to find it repeats evidence in the second period. By contrast, Mexico is usually viewed as agriculturally strong, and so scarcity evidence here seems surprising.

Finally, with respect to the other twelve cases which provide evidence of scarcity in the second, but not in the first period, five are European and developed. It is difficult to evaluate these results without further in-depth analysis. There may well be particular circumstances relative to some of these countries in this period which explain the apparent support for the scarcity hypothesis and which are not directly related to the question of the adequacy of the natural resource base.

Relative Labor Cost of Agriculture and Minerals Output in Germany. Two alternative series for agricultural productivity relative to industrial productivity, 1956–62 (numbers 247 and 248), another series for 1962–71 (number 249), and one for productivity in the minerals sector in Germany have been analyzed to test the weak scarcity hypothesis. Table 8-9 presents the results. In the agricultural series none of the series

Table 8-9. Relative Labor Productivity in Germany

Definition of time series	Slope coefficient[a]	t	R^2
Agriculture			
No. 247	0.04	1.80	0.27
No. 248	0.04	2.00	0.35
No. 249	0.008	1.20	0.04
Minerals			
No. 250	−0.0067	−3.20	0.40

[a] The model used to estimate the trend in labor productivity in the extractive sector relative to nonextractive is $y = ae^{bt}$.

supports the scarcity hypothesis. The correlations and t values are not only too low to be useful, but the signs on the b coefficient estimates fail to support the hypothesis. The data on relative minerals productivity (1957–71) offer weak support for the weak scarcity hypothesis.

$$\text{No. 250 } R^2 = 0.40, b, = -0.0067, t = -3.2$$

Plots of the component series comprising the relative productivity measure in minerals have been examined. Both minerals productivity (245) and industrial productivity (200) observations are regular and persistent, including the later years. The *relative* productivity series (250) is erratic. It falls sharply from high above its trend line to far below, 1957–60; rises sharply above the line in 1961–63; falls sharply below the line in 1964–68; and rises sharply above it in 1970–71. Thus it is difficult to offer an explanation for these results.

Relative Prices of Raw Materials and Minerals in Germany. Raw materials (RM) are not all identical with agricultural, forestry, and mineral products, but they may be closely related. In an effort to provide supplemental information for the weak scarcity hypothesis, I have examined some of the relative price data for raw materials (RM), as well as minerals (MI). These are each deflated by prices of manufactured goods (MA), wholesale prices (W), or retail trade prices (RT) in the even numbered series 252–262. Two of the series are 1960–71, the other four are 1949 or 1950 to 1971. The findings are given in table 8-10.

It seems that raw material products and prices account for a substantial fraction of the total costs of manufactured and wholesale goods and therefore influence their price movements. Deflation using the manufacturing price series apparently leaves only noise. Thus it seems reasonable to ignore series 252–256.

Series 258–262 offer mild support for the proposition that minerals

Table 8-10. Relative Price Movements for Extractive Outputs in Germany

Time series[a]	b	t	R^2
252 RM/MA	0.0007	0.61	0.03
254 RM/W	−0.0022	−1.35	0.07
256 RM/RT	−0.0051	−2.62	0.22
258 MI/MA	0.0189	6.57	0.66
260 MI/W	0.0110	3.80	0.55
262 MI/RT	0.0149	3.83	0.38

[a] RM—raw materials; MA—manufactured goods; W—wholesale prices; RT—retail trade prices; MI—minerals.

prices have moved up relative to nonextractive prices. This may reflect scarcity, according to the weak hypothesis.

C. Summary. I have examined world-wide agricultural and minerals data in the post-World War II period relative to the hypothesis of increasing scarcity. The findings may be summarized as follows:

	Support of strong hypothesis
Labor cost of several classes of mineral production in all world regions.	No in 20 cases.
Labor cost of coal production in major producing countries.	No in 10 cases.
Labor cost of agricultural and mineral products in West Germany.	No in 2 cases.
	Support of weak hypothesis
Relative labor cost of several classes of minerals output in all world regions.	No in 17 cases. Yes in 3 cases.
Prices of agricultural goods relative to general wholesale price index.	No in 30 cases. Yes in 23 cases.
Relative labor cost of agricultural and minerals output in West Germany.	No in 3 cases. Yes in 1 case.
Relative prices of raw materials and minerals in Germany.	No in 3 cases. Yes in 3 cases.

I commented on the foregoing findings when I presented them and I refer the reader to the trend estimates in the statistical appendix. It is also desirable to repeat the earlier warning. These results should be regarded as preliminary since the series involved are available for short periods and in several of the cases are of uncertain quality. Nonetheless, pending an in-depth analysis of the recent evidence, it seems we can tentatively accept three general insights which emerge: (a) the strong scarcity hypothesis is contradicted; (b) the weak hypothesis is not supported in most cases; and (c) in several selected cases the most recent data appear to offer limited support for the weak hypothesis.

IV
Environmental Pollution

As I noted at the outset of this paper, the Barnett–Morse *Scarcity and Growth* volume identified environmental pollution and abatement as a significant social problem. Using the term "quality of life" to describe these factors, we argued that these concerns were more genuine and pressing than alleged Malthusian–Ricardian dilemmas of increasing resource scarcity and the cost of extractive products. It seems useful at this point to update these views in two respects. First, I present some estimates of present and future costs of pollution abatement. Second, I discuss the nature of the social function for pollution abatement over time.

On the first question we have a number of estimates, including data from the Council on Environmental Quality and the Environmental Protection Agency, studies done at Resources for the Future by Ridker [8], and others. In 1970, annualized costs of pollution abatement, both public and private, were about $10 billion. At this level of outlay the public believed it had unsatisfactory levels of water, air, and land quality. Moreover, if the policies and technology of the 1960s continued to the year 2000, air and stream pollution would become very much worse as the economy grew. The increased pollution would be quite unacceptable to most of us.

Prompted by this outlook, remedial measures have been taken. These were officially put forward in the standards of the early 1970s and in the 1973 water and 1975 air emission standards of the Environmental Protection Agency. They are all technologically feasible. They relate to presently known techniques, without any dramatic technical breakthroughs. But, of course, they entail substantial costs.

In annual terms such policies would raise abatement costs from the $10 billion in 1970 and $26 billion in 1974 to about $55 billion (1974 prices) in 1983. Annual costs would then rise perhaps to $100–120 billion (1974 prices) in the year 2000, depending on the rate of population growth. Put another way, annual pollution abatement costs would rise from 1 percent of the nation's output in 1970 to 2 percent in 1974, to 3 percent by the end of the century. Large though these figures are, they are quite small relative to our income and economic growth. We would have to give up less than a tenth of one percentage point in annual growth of national output to pay for this active abatement policy.

What would we get—what are we getting—for this large absolute but small relative payment? The data in the annual reports of the Council on Environmental Quality show that already environmental quality is significantly improving, and further gains are a prospect. For example, from 1970 to 1974, the national ambient levels of the major air pollutants —particulates, sulfur dioxide, and carbon monoxide—declined significantly (Sixth Annual Report, figure 4, page 311). From 1961 to 1974, river quality—including the protection of aquatic life and suitable drinking water—in the nation increased significantly (Sixth Annual Report, figure 19, p. 352). The data on air, stream, and land pollution are generally favorable, but not uniformly so over every pollutant and region. As some problems are solved, others become more apparent and need to be addressed. We have now become aware of problems of fine particulates, synergistic reactions, and trace chemical and metal contaminants. In some quarters there is concern that the pace of improvement is not rapid enough, and that public support for the costs of environmental clean-up may be waning. For our purposes here, however, we observe that increases in environmental pollution levels can be avoided and, in fact, reduced in our growing economy. The expenditure levels are well within our means and need not appreciably affect rates of growth in income and output per capita. Indeed, the probable situation may be more favorable than I have described. Some technical breakthroughs in pollution control will in fact occur, some cost reductions will occur, and improved policies can be adopted as necessary.

In summary, large improvements in environmental quality of air, streams, and land are fully compatible with economic growth in the United States. This may be seen in table 8-11 in which we show real national GNP and environmental maintenance and improvement costs in the years 1974 and 2000. It seems reasonable to conclude that growth in per capita income and improvement in technology provide the economic and technical means to seek improvement in the environment.

It is also necessary to consider the nature of social cost functions for pollution abatement. The "doomsday sayers" are pessimistic about pollution abatement. They have stated that environmental clean-up cannot run a winning race against pollution from economic growth. The argument goes as follows. The atmosphere or waters have a limited capacity to be self-cleaning, dictated by their natural characteristics. Abatement efforts must remove all pollution emissions above this rate of discharge. Pollution emissions, however, are proportionate to economic activity and increase in proportion to real GNP. Therefore, abatement efforts must

Table 8-11. An Analysis of Annual Costs of Environmental
Inprovement Relative to Real GNP
(in billions)

	1974	2000	Comments
Real GNP before deducting environ- mental costs	$1,407	$3,900	$(1.04)^{26} = 277\%$
Less environmental improvement costs	28	120	Based on CEQ data
Real GNP remaining after paying en- vironmental improvement costs	$1,379	$3,780	Increase to 274%

remove larger and larger percentages of the pollutants in gross emissions, in order to keep the net emissions below the percentage which the atmosphere and waters can cleanse by nature's processes. The cost function, these people allege, is exponential with respect to percentage of pollutants to be cleaned from emissions:

Cost rises asymptotically to infinity at 100 percent cleansing.

The argument is essentially the same as Malthusian-type limits on natural resources for agriculture, forestry, or minerals production.[6] In conventional Malthusian-type models, the natural resource and sociotechnical parameters are viewed as fixed, there is only one other factor (labor or "doses" of labor plus capital), and the production function exhibits constant returns to scale with constant quality factors. Thus, after a point, output does not rise proportionate to the increase in the variable input. In this pollution model, gross emissions are of constant quality in parts per million pollutants relative to pure air or water. But they have to be "cultivated" or "mined" more and more intensively to remove more of the impurities, in order that the total pollutant discharges to air and water should not exceed the fixed limit of nature's capacity to clean itself. Inevitably, given the Malthusian assumptions, costs eventually rise.

If it is viewed as a Malthusian model, the argument of increasing pollution costs is subject to all the deficiencies of the Malthusian model when applied to agriculture, forestry, and minerals. These have been discussed at great length in parts 2 and 3 of *Scarcity and Growth*. Actually, Malthusian pollution models may be even more defective than other

[6] *Scarcity and Growth* discussed these same issues.

Malthusian models. One aspect of their limitations concerns their accounting of space. Some of the manmade enterprises which emit pollution can be concentrated, or their emissions concentrated, so that pollutants become concentrated in sewers or area sectors. Thus, particular water courses can be made sewers, with the sludge eventually extracted for chemical processing. Other enterprises, such as power plants, can be concentrated in regions where the ambient air is still capable of self-cleaning very large discharges. Or tall smokestacks can disperse dilute pollutant discharge over large areas, not exceeding the satisfactory self-cleaning level. The oceans, except at some coastal points, have enormously greater self-cleansing capacity than is being used. Concentrations of population and production in urban places aggravate pollution problems initially. But then, when substantial abatement efforts are undertaken, they may provide important economies of scale or conjuncture for remedy.

Another error in the allegations of Malthusian pollution cost functions is the omission of technological changes and innovations. Here the opportunities are much wider than in, say, Malthusian agriculture models. Our chief air pollution offenders are four-cycle private automobile engines and coal power plants. The increasing cost argument assumes that we must make stack and car pipe discharges cleaner and cleaner by afterburners, catalysts, and filters. But, of course, we need not have gasoline engines in cars, nor even private cars, and the fuel that goes into power plants need not be high sulfur coal. The chief offenders for water pollution are electric power thermal discharge and chemical plant and municipal sewer discharges. Cooling towers, settling tanks, and secondary sewage treatment are not subject to increasing costs under constant technology, and actually would be subject to declining costs per unit of economic activity as a result of technological change.

The complete substitution of new products and processes denies that it is necessary to traverse an increasing cost curve. Nonetheless, even if for some commodities and processes the cost curve does increase, there is no reason to assume a priori that the product is a large proportion of the social bill of goods. Unless it is large, cannot be substituted for, and cannot be made more efficient, it need not be troublesome. The air and water pollutants from conventional power plants, autos, and sewers are merely social costs to be taken care of from the growing GNP, in the many ways which we know.

In summary, an advancing economy can select among the services or functions it wants from its GNP; among the products to provide the services; among numerous processes and branches to provide products; among basic resources; among locations for each of many stages of economic activity; and among innumerable pathways through time. Assuming constant ratios of pollutants to GNP and increasing cost functions for pollution abatement is an excessively simple-minded form of economic analysis.

Nuclear dangers are sometimes lumped with other environmental quality or pollution problems. I do not think nuclear hazards should be viewed so, anymore than Idi Amin or DNA manipulations should be viewed so—it is not sensible. In origins, kinds, and magnitudes of problems and solutions, nuclear hazards differ from environmental pollution caused by automobiles, fossil fuels, and sewage. There are tens of thousands of nuclear weapons and related nuclear minerals, facilities, and wastes in half a dozen countries. The nuclear nightmare is rooted in military and political affairs and violence, not in economic growth. The dangers, no matter whether the source of nuclear materials is weapons, power plants, research reactors, or other, are societal terrorism, violence, mass destruction, and related political problems. The solutions are not the cleansing of air and stream pollutants or the benefit–cost analysis of economics textbooks. The solutions for environmental pollution are relatively simple and at hand, even though expensive. This cannot be said of nuclear dangers.

Appendix A: Notes on Concepts

Cartel Scarcity.   The ratios

$$\frac{L_E + C_E}{O_E} \div \frac{L_N + C_N}{O_N}$$

and P_E/P_N are alternative indicators of scarcity, relevant for the weak scarcity hypothesis. But they are not equivalent or equal in magnitudes. Rather, they are substitute indicators. Each incorporates special assumptions which affect magnitude. These relate to whether the output measure is net or gross (treatment of intermediate goods used in the production), governmental tax and subsidy treatment of the industry, inflation, foreign trade, degree of competitiveness of the market, as well as other elements. One of these additional considerations relates to the fact that prices tend to indicate cost of marginal producers or supply, whereas $L + C$ tends to measure average cost over the whole product sector.

Of great importance today is the fact that prices of energy resources will immediately tend to reflect the influence of oligopoly and cartels, but the cost measure will do so less quickly, fully, and directly. The striking case is the OPEC cartel, which has imposed an international market price of about $14 a barrel on crude oil, while in the Middle East average cost measured in $L + C$ may have risen little from the pre-fall 1973 figure of much less than $1 a barrel. Even before the fall of 1973, price and cost in international markets differed because of monopoly profits and governmental levies, although the differences were far smaller than they are today.

To what extent should we let monopoly market scarcity enter into our consideration of the question of increasing scarcity? Originally, I thought it should not enter at all, but I am no longer sure of this. In the case of many minerals and even in agriculture and forestry, natural resources may be concentrated in space. They may be much more vulnerable than other sectors to monopoly action because of their concentration. The relative price measure may tend to indicate increasing scarcity resulting from monopoly markets, while an average $L + C$ cost measure would not. If the cause of a relative price rise is a condition of concentration of natural resources in specific space and limitations of resources elsewhere, we might say that monopoly of resource products should be viewed as part of the increasing scarcity question. To the extent, however, that another necessary condition was cartelization, we might hold this fact responsible for price rises and exclude such monopolies.

The consequences of monopoly market scarcity are similar to, but possibly less onerous than, "natural" scarcity. Both prompt economic, technological, and other efforts at substitution and relief from scarcity, because of higher prices. As the efforts are successful and the supply and demand curves made more elastic, the monopoly price solution will shift toward the competitive one. This can be expected in petroleum. Indeed, it is already happening, with the Middle East oil price remaining steady or increasing slightly, but being eroded by inflation since 1973.

In the United States at the national level, we have recently experienced increasing scarcity of petroleum resources. The phenomenon has been much more complicated than Malthusian and Ricardian propositions. The nation discovered and developed petroleum resources at *declining* cost in foreign places. It and other countries permitted themselves to become highly dependent on these sources. When this situation was well developed and locked in, the cartel struck. It remains to be seen, over the longer run, what will be the outcome, now that more economic resources are being devoted to energy resources, conservation, and technology development at home and elsewhere, rather than primarily to oil and gas development in the OPEC nations. Meanwhile P_E/P_N movements correctly indicate that there has been a severe and abrupt increase in petroleum scarcity, even though the U.S. government has moderated the increase with price ceilings.

$$\frac{L_E + C_E}{O_E} \div \frac{L_N + C_N}{O_N}$$

movements in the nation correctly indicate that petroleum scarcity has developed. But these are average costs and the indicator has risen less for the industry than for, say, stripper wells.

We must consider seriously whether cartel monopolization of foreign supplies should, in some circumstances, be viewed as part of a modernized Ricardian phenomenon of natural resource scarcity (see *S and G,* chapters 1 and 11). The cost burden on the nation is real. One major element in cartelization was concentration of the lowest cost petroleum resources and developed supplies in one area, that is, in the Middle East. Another major element was neglect and failure by almost all economists in the 1950s and 1960s to warn of the prospect of enormously successful OPEC cartelization, with world scarcity effects far exceeding $100 billion a year and U.S. scarcity effects in excess of $30 billion a year.

The Marginal Supplier.   We should give thought to compiling $L + C$ data on marginal suppliers of extractive products. This information could supplement price data, which already tend to reflect costs of marginal suppliers, but which are subject to aberration and noise of various kinds. Also, price data cannot be used to test the strong scarcity hypothesis. The marginal supplier $L + C$ data would be a more sensitive indicator of resource scarcity than average $L + C$. Such marginal data would also reveal some of the reasons for price movements and tendencies in resource scarcity.

A difficulty, however, is that the marginal supplier is frequently a short-term supplier, bringing in idle, high-cost capacity in response to short-term market imbalances. Indeed, most short-term suppliers are of this nature. Our concern is with the marginal suppliers on a *long-run* supply curve.

In minerals, it may be possible in some cases to distinguish marginal suppliers on the long-run supply curves. In iron ore, taconite has been in marginal supply for a long time and will be in the future. Compilation of taconite $L + C$ data might be possible. In copper, perhaps the porphorys are the marginal suppliers in the long run. In aluminum, until further development of the enormous reserves of years of highest grade bauxite resources in West Africa, Brazil, and other places, perhaps Australia's lower grade bauxite is the world's marginal supply. Within our own country, various nonbauxitic ores would become the marginal supply if world supply were cut off, but none of these are presently in commercial use.

In petroleum, the present marginal supply in the United States is secondary and tertiary recovery. Such production should be viewed as marginal supply short run and also on the long-run curve. If 30 percent of an oil field is viewed as recoverable at a price of $3 a barrel, then clearly the percentage might be greatly expanded at $14 or more a barrel. Increased recovery percentages from oil pools certainly will be in the long-run supply curve, but at present prices such recovery will be planned in the development of the resource, rather than tacked on as a go-back activity. Possibly, marginal supply could be viewed as costs from fields just coming in, such as Alaska or the Atlantic Coast.

The concept of long-term marginal supply is very well known in natural gas, from the Permian Basin case and subsequent multiprice regulation activities of the U.S. Federal Power Commission. Earlier, in World War II and the Korean War, marginal supply at higher prices was used in price incentive schemes for metallic minerals; frequently short-term marginal supply was induced more than long term.

In theory, changes in long-term marginal supply cost would be a fine measure for testing both the strong and weak hypotheses of increasing resource scarcity. In practice, in a dynamic, rapidly changing world, the data problems are very great and may be insuperable. The practical difficulty may be compared with the use of economic rent as a scarcity indicator, to which the marginal supply concept is related.

Increases in Economic Rent.   It is frequently proposed that we test for increasing resource scarcity by observing changes in economic rent. The sources of the concept are Malthusian or Ricardian long-run, static theory for agricultural land, thus:

In the Malthusian case, land is of constant quality but at E_1 it is fully utilized, and beyond that point must be cultivated more and more intensively, at rising unit cost. In a Ricardian case, more land is available beyond E_1, but it is of monotonically declining economic quality, and cultivation beyond that point is at a rising unit cost for the product. (For convenience we have given the same rising cost curve to both Malthus and Ricardo; in fact they would be different. See *S and G,* chapters 3 and 5.)

At time 1 rent is zero. At time 2, demand has grown to D_2 and rent is the shaded area $p_2E_2p_1$, which measures scarcity effect. At time 3, rent has grown to $p_3E_2p_1$; the increase from time 2 is the increased scarcity effect.

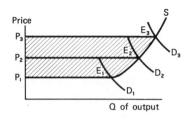

If the world conformed to the specifications of these parametrically invariant, no-depletion models, increases in economic rent would reflect increasing resource scarcity, and nothing else. Assume for example, the Ricardian model where unhomogeneous resources are free goods until productive [9]. Assume standard resources to be the highest quality ever available historically. Then their rent would always equal the marginal resource conversion cost for unhomogeneous resources of marginal quality, and would be a precise index of the increase in scarcity that had occurred from the beginning of man's economic history.

By now, however, we have recognized that there will be many types of standard resources; therefore, there will be many different figures for standard rent; and, for institutional reasons, unhomogeneous resources (including those at the margin) command a reservation price in private enterprise societies. Rent will now contain a pecuniary element that reflects, but does not measure, increasing scarcity; and there will be no single figure for rent—it will be different for each type of resource. As scarcity increases, rents will increase, and rents will also change as the result of changes in general price levels, interest rates, relative demands, and expectations concerning future resource availability. Under these conditions, advances in rent on unhomogeneous resources are an ambiguous indicator of increases in scarcity.

The inappropriateness of economic rent as an indicator of increasing scarcity is also compelling in the case of depletable mineral resources. As the best resources are used up, they disappear from the left-hand portion of the supply curves, and so do the economic rent areas. At the time that Mesabi range hematite ore is exhausted and Mesabi taconite is used, the only visible rent could be the differences among taconites.

Rent would be a useful indicator of increasing scarcity in a Ricardian no-depletion world where the resource conversion path for employment of declining quality resources stayed put, and the process of growth involved nothing more complicated than a systematic traversal of the path. But in a world of depletion, of variable reservation prices and degrees of reservation, and especially of sociotechnical change, this is no longer so. The conversion path changes shape and position, with the result that quality differences among resources, their rank in the quality spectrum, and, therefore, the rents that they earn, vary irregularly over time. Rents on different resources will disappear, decrease, or increase as a result of the depletion and economic reordering of resources, of changes in resource economizing behavior, or of changes in the technical or social parameters that determine the rank of resources in order of quality. Because of these changes in the resource quality spectrum which are induced by sociotechnical change, depletion, and so on, economic rent is a nonoperational concept in the modern world. The changes cause capital gains and losses and a variety of income elements to be blended with economic rent and make its determination impossible.

Urban land has anti-Ricardian elements of particular interest. Let us assume that rent per unit of urban land is high and increasing in the United States, even if income earned on the cost of improvements is deducted. Does this signify increasing natural resource scarcity? We think not. The emergence of urban rent does not reflect declining productivity from use at the extensive margin or inefficiencies from more intensive use in the United States. Increasing urban rent does not reflect a declining absolute quality (increasing resource conversion cost) of marginal land under the impact of growth. It reflects, on the contrary, the absolute *increase* in economic quality of intramarginal urban land due to its advancing productivity. Man's propensity to build where he has already built—his liking for crowds, together with the existence of economies of concentration—has raised the price of land in metropolitan areas. What advances the value of urban land is the fact that it offers new economies which the combination of sociotechnical advance and agglomeration create. Urban rents thus reflect the economic advantages of agglomeration, not disadvantages imposed by nature. The rents result from a *decline* in the intramarginal portion of the cost curve.

As demand rises as a result of growth and technical advance, the labor plus capital efficiency in production of the urban product increases and is supplied at a declining unit cost. The marginal productivity of strategically located blocks of land increases under these conditions, and rents rise. Urban rents have risen primarily because labor plus capital cost per unit of urban product has fallen. Thus, urban rent is not an indicator of natural resource scarcity in the classical sense. The increase in urban rent accompanies a declining cost trend for urban product that is opposite to that postulated by the classical growth doctrine of increasing resource scarcity and increasing rent. Economic rent would not be an indicator of increasing resource scarcity in our sense, even if it could be measured. Specifically, increases in urban land rent do not signify an imminent cost-increasing shortage of either land or natural resources in general.

We conclude as follows. First, Ricardian (or Malthusian) economic rent is a fine static theory. It is not a dynamic one, in a society with technical change, depletion, inflation, and great varieties of resources. Second, in general it is not practical to measure economic rent changes in order to measure or test the increasing scarcity hypotheses for various resources. Practically speaking, it is much better to measure changes in costs and prices.

Appendix B: Foreign Country and Region Time Series on Productivity, Relative Productivity, and Relative Price Regressions

CODES FOR PRODUCTS, VARIABLES,

AND COUNTRIES/REGIONS
(8 place code)

PRODUCTS (Places 1 and 2)	CODES
Agriculture	AG
Agriculture, alternative	A2
Coal	CO
Coal, Auger	CA
Coal, Ship	CS
Coal, Underground	CU
Economy	E
Economy, Alternative	E2
Industry	I
Iron Ore	IR
Iron Ore & Coal	IC
Manufacturing	MA
Metallic Minerals	MM
Minerals	MI
Mining, Energy, & Water	N
Petroleum & Gas	PG
Retail	RT
Wholesale Trade	W

VARIABLES (Places 4 and 5)	
Labor Input	L
% Labor Input of Force	LP
Output	O
Price	P
Price received ÷ Price paid	RP
Productivity	PY
Relative Productivity	RY

COUNTRY/REGION (places 7 and 8)		COUNTRY/REGION cont.	CODES
Algeria	AL	India (West Bengal)	IB
Argentina	AR	Iran	IR
Australia	AA	Iraq	IQ
Austria	A	Ireland	IL
Belgium	B	Israel	IS
Brazil	BR	Italy	I
Canada	CN	Japan	JP
Centrally Planned Economy	CP	Korea	KR
Chile	CE	Market Economies	M
Columbia	CO	Mexico	MX
Costa Rica	CR	Netherlands	NL
Czechoslovakia	CS	New Zealand	NZ
Denmark	DK	Norway	N
Developed Market Economies	DM	Phillipines	PP
Developing Market Economies	GM	Poland	P
Ecuador	EC	Portugal	PO
ECC	EE	Spain	E
Federal Republic of Germany	D	Sweden	S
Finland	SU	Switzerland	CH
France	F	Thailand	TH
Greece	GR	United Kingdom	GB
Hungary	H	United States	US
India	IN	Venezuela	VE
India (Assam)	IA	World	W
India (Punjab)	IP	Yugoslavia	YU
India (Uttar Pradest)	IU		

log time trends

1 cu-py-us	time44=1	const	r/se	dw/df
ols	0.041356	1.572144	0.864646	0.000000
log tred	13.647477	29.223665	0.143660	28.000000

2 cs-py-us	time44=1	const	r/se	dw/df
ols	0.036176	2.584150	0.953441	0.000000
log tred	24.389854	98.138855	0.070316	28.000000

3 ca-py-us	time44=1	const	r/se	dw/df
ols	0.034578	2.829618	0.744595	0.000000
log tred	7.888243	31.479095	0.130442	20.000000

4 co-py-us	time44=1	const	r/se	dw/df
ols	0.048680	1.668265	0.940536	0.000000
log tred	21.440306	41.388245	0.107639	28.000000

5 co-py-gb	time44=1	const	r/se	dw/df
ols	0.034129	0.258354	0.897274	0.000000
log tred	15.946941	6.799798	0.101461	28.000000

6 co-py-b-	time44=1	const	r/se	dw/df
ols	0.045858	-0.277905	0.971725	0.000000
log tred	31.585577	-10.781933	0.068830	28.000000

7 co-py-f-	time44=1	const	r/se	dw/df
ols	0.041679	-0.040677	0.962628	0.000000
log tred	27.349289	-1.503521	0.072247	28.000000

8 co-py-nl	time44=1	const	r/se	dw/df
ols	0.025868	0.351459	0.744314	0.000000
log tred	9.242305	7.073358	0.132687	28.000000

9 co-py-d-	time44=1	const	r/se	dw/df
ols	0.051594	-0.013058	0.965301	0.000000
log tred	26.912653	-0.364247	0.077589	25.000000

10 co-py-p-	time44=1	const	r/se	dw/df
ols	0.020716	0.433913	0.706689	0.000000
log tred	7.511003	8.431286	0.103934	22.000000

11 mi-py-w-	time44=1	const	r/se	dw/df
ols	0.044261	-1.198902	0.993539	0.000000
log tred	30.391232	-35.147858	0.019694	5.000000

12 co-py-w-	time44=1	const	r/se	dw/df
ols	0.037325	-1.021738	0.981183	0.000000
log tred	17.716257	-20.705931	0.028489	5.000000

13 pg-py-w-	time44=1	const	r/se	dw/df
ols	0.059213	-1.614774	0.993935	0.000000
log tred	31.373508	-36.529228	0.025522	5.000000

14 mm-py-w-	time44=1	const	r/se	dw/df
ols	0.041358	-1.121608	0.950970	0.000000
log tred	10.833899	-12.544446	0.051621	5.000000

continued-log time trends

```
15 ma-py-w-   time44=1      const        r/se      dw/df
ols           0.037885    -1.021943    0.996345    0.000000
log tred     40.455555   -46.592659    0.012663    5.000000

16 mi-py-cp   time44=1      const        r/se      dw/df
ols           0.044540    -1.193449    0.991702    0.000000
log tred     28.940407   -31.857979    0.023213    6.000000

17 co-py-cp   time44=1      const        r/se      dw/df
ols           0.036279    -0.978449    0.988019    0.000000
log tred     24.046745   -26.643608    0.022756    6.000000

18 pg-py-cp   time44=1      const        r/se      dw/df
ols           0.067557    -1.824031    0.982308    0.000000
log tred     19.739670   -21.895712    0.051620    6.000000

19 mm-py-cp   time44=1      const        r/se      dw/df
ols           0.065963    -1.768069    0.997614    0.000000
log tred     54.107224   -59.581596    0.018388    6.000000

20 ma-py-cp   time44=1      const        r/se      dw/df
ols           0.052146    -1.399343    0.994349    0.000000
log tred     35.110645   -38.707981    0.022401    6.000000

21 mi-py-m-   time44=1      const        r/se      dw/df
ols           0.044938    -1.218694    0.977205    0.000000
log tred     16.069048   -18.606010    0.037816    5.000000

22 co-py-m-   time44=1      const        r/se      dw/df
ols           0.037508    -1.040128    0.931637    0.000000
log tred      9.097634   -10.771440    0.055751    5.000000

23 pg-py-m-   time44=1      const        r/se      dw/df
ols           0.063597    -1.737559    0.981229    0.000000
log tred     17.737984   -20.691511    0.048483    5.000000

24 mm-py-m-   time44=1      const        r/se      dw/df
ols           0.037892    -1.030951    0.927648    0.000000
log tred      8.827659   -10.254536    0.058045    5.000000

25 ma-py-m-   time44=1      const        r/se      dw/df
ols           0.034302    -0.925322    0.997700    0.000000
log tred     51.021683   -58.764652    0.009091    5.000000

26 mi-py-dm   time44=1      const        r/se      dw/df
ols           0.045133    -1.257720    0.981112    0.000000
log tred     19.094748   -21.860647    0.035651    6.000000

27 co-py-dm   time44=1      const        r/se      dw/df
ols           0.032394    -0.932738    0.897997    0.000000
log tred      7.913613    -9.361102    0.061742    6.000000

28 pg-py-dm   time44=1      const        r/se      dw/df
ols           0.055844    -1.542553    0.995873    0.000000
log tred     41.113274   -46.655052    0.020487    6.000000
```

```
         log time trends

 29 mm-py-dm   time44=1        const         r/se          dw/df
   ols          0.041999    -1.178717     0.948386      0.000000
   log tred    11.385123   -13.126996     0.055641      6.000000

 30 ma-py-dm   time44=1        const         r/se          dw/df
   ols          0.041832    -1.120172     0.996113      0.000000
   log tred    42.367138   -46.608089     0.014893      6.000000

 31 mi-py-gm   time44=1        const         r/se          dw/df
   ols          0.044325    -1.169400     0.960901      0.000000
   log tred    12.184214   -13.724585     0.049193      5.000000

 32 co-py-gm   time44=1        const         r/se          dw/df
   ols          0.046783    -1.270374     0.943644      0.000000
   log tred    10.073006   -11.678428     0.062804      5.000000

 33 pg-py-gm   time44=1        const         r/se          dw/df
   ols          0.079246    -2.149493     0.950459      0.000000
   log tred    10.775532   -12.478989     0.099448      5.000000

 34 mm-py-gm   time44=1        const         r/se          dw/df
   ols          0.032277    -0.867715     0.831203      0.000000
   log tred     5.526822    -6.343762     0.078971      5.000000

 35 ma-py-gm   time44=1        const         r/se          dw/df
   ols          0.022833    -0.630921     0.984610      0.000000
   log tred    19.617771   -23.144156     0.015739      5.000000

 36 co-py-ee   time44=1        const         r/se          dw/df
   ols          0.087790    -0.692818     0.865198      0.000000
   log tred     6.285708    -2.467947     0.073905      5.000000

143 ag-rp-aa   time44=1        const         r/se          dw/df
   ols         -0.037299     0.394641     0.713697      0.000000
   log tred    -5.779826     4.340480     0.097336     12.000000

144 ag-rp-a-   time44=1        const         r/se          dw/df
   ols         -0.010587     0.145832     0.630319      0.000000
   log tred    -4.444706     4.107432     0.028485     10.000000

145 ag-rp-b-   time44=1        const         r/se          dw/df
   ols         -0.026772     0.183012     0.886423      0.000000
   log tred   -10.122259     4.911243     0.039893     12.000000

147 ag-rp-cn   time44=1        const         r/se          dw/df
   ols         -0.023774     0.383495     0.718453      0.000000
   log tred    -5.845803     6.693031     0.061341     12.000000

148 ag-rp-ct   time44=1        const         r/se          dw/df
   ols          0.008933    -0.118951     0.760874      0.000000
   log tred     6.000068    -6.161269     0.017803     10.000000

151 ag-rp-d-   time44=1        const         r/se          dw/df
   ols         -0.004658     0.053609     0.148857      0.000000
   log tred    -1.604374     1.188775     0.033467      8.000000
```

continued-log time trends

```
152 ag-rp-gr   time44=1      const         r/se          dw/df
    ols        0.005652     -0.092059      0.104288      0.000000
    log tred   1.303296     -1.240157      0.022948      5.000000

153 ag-rp-ia   time44=1      const         r/se          dw/df
    ols        0.003941     -0.011498     -0.046304      0.000000
    log tred   0.651676     -0.134938      0.091220     12.000000

154 ag-rp-ip   time44=1      const         r/se          dw/df
    ols       -0.005581      0.016785      0.054112      0.000000
    log tred  -1.320491      0.281872      0.063750     12.000000

155 ag-rp-ib   time44=1      const         r/se          dw/df
    ols        0.019588     -0.087005      0.228040      0.000000
    log tred   1.833908     -0.535187      0.082733      7.000000

158 ag-rp-jp   time44=1      const         r/se          dw/df
    ols        0.007611     -0.071033      0.211555      0.000000
    log tred   2.054223     -1.322979      0.049984     11.000000

159 ag-rp-nl   time44=1      const         r/se          dw/df
    ols       -0.039894      0.332979      0.966214      0.000000
    log tred -19.307499     11.438099      0.031165     12.000000

160 ag-rp-n-   time44=1      const         r/se          dw/df
    ols       -0.006082      0.054456      0.195021      0.000000
    log tred  -1.850049      1.080507      0.034481      9.000000

163 ag-rp-ch   time44=1      const         r/se          dw/df
    ols       -0.009628      0.026867      0.806804      0.000000
    log tred  -7.435678      1.472754      0.019530     12.000000

164 ag-rp-us   time44=1      const         r/se          dw/df
    ols       -0.022631      0.316638      0.813191      0.000000
    log tred  -7.588789      7.536225      0.044980     12.000000

165 ag-rp-cn   time44=1      const         r/se          dw/df
    ols       -0.008819      4.746822      0.337977      0.000000
    log tred  -2.364023     51.580559      0.033885      8.000000

166 ag-rp-us   time44=1      const         r/se          dw/df
    ols       -0.010055      4.559631      0.523947      0.000000
    log tred  -3.298093     60.631462      0.027690      8.000000

167 ag-rp-ia   time44=1      const         r/se          dw/df
    ols        0.031898      4.024894      0.727560      0.000000
    log tred   4.729650     24.723330      0.052241      7.000000

168 ag-rp-ip   time44=1      const         r/se          dw/df
    ols       -0.032330      5.454360      0.490970      0.000000
    log tred  -2.413751     16.581160      0.056031      4.000000

169 ag-rp-iu   time44=1      const         r/se          dw/df
    ols        0.004793      4.612051     -0.221213      0.000000
    log tred   0.309084     13.181527      0.064866      4.000000
```

```
          log time trends

170 ag-rp-ib  time44=1       const        r/se       dw/df
   ols        -0.031960     5.408308    0.348371    0.000000
   log tred   -1.435156    11.556107    0.031493    1.000000

171 ag-rp-is  time44=1       const        r/se       dw/df
   ols         0.000424     4.532634   -0.153333    0.000000
   log tred    0.130957    59.312439    0.020975    6.000000

172 ag-rp-jp  time44=1       const        r/se       dw/df
   ols         0.013475     4.236064    0.479019    0.000000
   log tred    3.045040    38.806290    0.040194    8.000000

173 ag-rp-kr  time44=1       const        r/se       dw/df
   ols        -0.001494     4.661682   -0.120587    0.000000
   log tred   -0.171060    21.632227    0.079348    8.000000

174 ag-rp-pp  time44=1       const        r/se       dw/df
   ols        -0.013006     4.992368    0.560957    0.000000
   log tred   -3.536418    55.031330    0.033404    8.000000

175 ag-rp-a-  time44=1       const        r/se       dw/df
   ols        -0.006043     4.664383    0.248742    0.000000
   log tred   -1.992247    62.335293    0.027552    8.000000

176 ag-rp-b-  time44=1       const        r/se       dw/df
   ols        -0.013464     4.908550    0.663867    0.000000
   log tred   -4.331133    64.009789    0.028236    8.000000

177 ag-rp-cs  time44=1       const        r/se       dw/df
   ols         0.014178     4.251705    0.835526    0.000000
   log tred    5.132826    57.966038    0.011555    4.000000

178 ag-rp-dk  time44=1       const        r/se       dw/df
   ols         0.008012     4.415236    0.369318    0.000000
   log tred    2.500812    55.865509    0.029101    8.000000

179 ag-rp-su  time44=1       const        r/se       dw/df
   ols         0.001123     4.970140   -0.103155    0.000000
   log tred    0.424268    76.125237    0.024040    8.000000

181 ag-rp-d-  time44=1       const        r/se       dw/df
   ols        -0.014029     4.924053    0.498438    0.000000
   log tred   -3.153552    44.871151    0.040407    8.000000

182 ag-rp-h-  time44=1       const        r/se       dw/df
   ols        -0.002250     4.796964   -0.123084    0.000000
   log tred   -0.499576    41.600239    0.029188    6.000000

183 ag-rp-ir  time44=1       const        r/se       dw/df
   ols         0.013741     4.494890    0.377021    0.000000
   log tred    2.538894    33.667591    0.049159    8.000000

184 ag-rp-i-  time44=1       const        r/se       dw/df
   ols        -0.013628     5.004635    0.348734    0.000000
   log tred   -2.410138    35.879196    0.051360    8.000000
```

continued—log time trends

```
185 ag-rp-n-    time44=1        const        r/se         dw/df
     ols        -0.007994      4.784759     0.750000     0.000000
     log tred   -4.688795    109.620354     0.011049     6.000000

186 ag-rp-p-    time44=1        const        r/se         dw/df
     ols         0.020159      4.212204     0.795950     0.000000
     log tred    6.007713     50.889275     0.030478     8.000000

187 ag-rp-e-    time44=1        const        r/se         dw/df
     ols         0.015283      4.340639     0.473976     0.000000
     log tred    2.867272     32.401951     0.041287     7.000000

188 ag-rp-s-    time44=1        const        r/se         dw/df
     ols        -0.000551      4.595370    -0.200000     0.000000
     log tred   -0.106999     34.242546     0.027232     5.000000

189 ag-rp-ch    time44=1        const        r/se         dw/df
     ols        -0.022163      4.882158     0.928968     0.000000
     log tred  -10.894522     97.289658     0.018477     8.000000

191 ag-rp-aa    time44=1        const        r/se         dw/df
     ols        -0.026463      5.169402     0.396913     0.000000
     log tred   -2.630939     20.834494     0.091359     8.000000

192 ic-py-d     time44=1        const        r/se         dw/df
     ols         0.051635     -0.711510     0.964533     0.000000
     log tred   10.477617    -17.771471     0.015584     3.000000

193 co-py-d     time44=1        const        r/se         dw/df
     ols         0.031683     -0.655029     0.885094     0.000000
     log tred    5.640169    -14.353466     0.017764     3.000000

194 ir-py-d     time44=1        const        r/se         dw/df
     ols         0.082698     -0.640232     0.735031     0.000000
     log tred    3.477947     -3.314326     0.075192     3.000000

195 ma-py-d     time44=1        const        r/se         dw/df
     ols         0.078423     -0.604122     0.941753     0.000000
     log tred    8.103927     -7.684351     0.030602     3.000000

196 ag-o--d-    time44=1        const        r/se         dw/df
     ols         0.020235     -0.223351     0.770667     0.000000
     log tred    5.882573     -4.524014     0.036077     9.000000

197 ag-o--d-    time44=1        const        r/se         dw/df
     ols         0.015406     -0.279842     0.585873     0.000000
     log tred    4.069629     -2.987724     0.045270    10.000000

198 mi-o--d     time44=1        const        r/se         dw/df
     ols         0.007753      4.413868     0.366087     0.000000
     log tred    3.623535    110.816940     0.063673    20.000000

199 i--o--d     time44=1        const        r/se         dw/df
     ols         0.066204      3.289886     0.972737     0.000000
     log tred   27.391510     73.124619     0.071922    20.000000
```

```
                log time trends

200 i--py-d    time44=1        const         r/se        dw/df
   ols         0.045467     -0.841110     0.991859     0.000000
   log tred   50.591499    -50.278332     0.026743    20.000000

201 ag-1--d    time44=1        const         r/se        dw/df
   ols        -0.045788      0.911351     0.944733     0.000000
   log tred  -16.044062     15.197762     0.052624    14.000000

202 a2-1--d    time44=1        const         r/se        dw/df
   ols        -0.042206      0.827853     0.987149     0.000000
   log tred  -32.809040     30.015823     0.021526    13.000000

203 ag-1p-d    time44=1        const         r/se        dw/df
   ols        -0.050595      3.516257     0.909349     0.000000
   log tred  -12.307386     40.707188     0.075803    14.000000

204 n--1--d    time44=1        const         r/se        dw/df
   ols        -0.044222      0.847547     0.978719     0.000000
   log tred  -25.394140     22.700449     0.029140    13.000000

205 e--1--d    time44=1        const         r/se        dw/df
   ols         0.003969     -0.090430     0.259162     0.000000
   log tred    2.499471     -2.710137     0.029282    14.000000

206 e2-1--d    time44=1        const         r/se        dw/df
   ols         0.001483     -0.035322     0.122989     0.000000
   log tred    1.721429     -1.912748     0.014413    13.000000

207 rm-p-d     time44=1        const         r/se        dw/df
   ols         0.008355      4.450535     0.505882     0.000000
   log tred    4.743849    135.755844     0.052408    20.000000

208 mi-p-d     time44=1        const         r/se        dw/df
   ols         0.027190      4.066377     0.759351     0.000000
   log tred    8.391692     68.773643     0.103075    21.000000

209 ma-p-d     time44=1        const         r/se        dw/df
   ols         0.008330      4.445939     0.666102     0.000000
   log tred    6.701231    196.001816     0.039543    21.000000

210 w--p-d     time44=1        const         r/se        dw/df
   ols         0.006121      4.485813     0.354460     0.000000
   log tred    2.649790     85.315834     0.027621    10.000000

211 rt-p-d     time44=1        const         r/se        dw/df
   ols         0.012295      4.374485     0.862557     0.000000
   log tred   11.792424    229.922684     0.033168    21.000000

212 co-py-gb   time44=1        const         r/se        dw/df
   ols         0.027202      3.007384     0.728941     0.000000
   log tred    5.020041     21.628185     0.049217     8.000000

213 mimapy-w   time44=1        const         r/se        dw/df
   ols         0.006338     -0.176021     0.697765     0.000000
   log tred    3.853840     -4.569756     0.022239     5.000000
```

```
continued-log time trends

214 comapy-w  time44=1      const        r/se        dw/df
    ols       -0.000527   -0.000749   -0.189706   0.000000
    log tred  -0.208000   -0.012632    0.034234   5.000000

215 pgmapy-w  time44=1      const        r/se        dw/df
    ols        0.021340   -0.593080    0.937886   0.000000
    log tred   9.570629  -11.356465    0.030152   5.000000

216 mmmapy-w  time44=1      const        r/se        dw/df
    ols        0.003494   -0.100053   -0.035686   0.000000
    log tred   0.890651   -1.089060    0.053042   5.000000

218 mimapycp  time44=1      const        r/se        dw/df
    ols       -0.007620    0.206300    0.984668   0.000000
    log tred -21.226696   23.607830    0.005415   6.000000

219 comapycp  time44=1      const        r/se        dw/df
    ols       -0.015858    0.420807    0.985854   0.000000
    log tred -22.109550   24.103689    0.010818   6.000000

220 pgmapycp  time44=1      const        r/se        dw/df
    ols        0.015432   -0.425462    0.674146   0.000000
    log tred   3.934723   -4.456561    0.059157   6.000000

221 mmmapycp  time44=1      const        r/se        dw/df
    ols        0.013859   -0.369666    0.896206   0.000000
    log tred   7.838451   -8.589347    0.026668   6.000000

223 mimapy-m  time44=1      const        r/se        dw/df
    ols        0.010647   -0.293652    0.672382   0.000000
    log tred   3.648833   -4.296928    0.039456   5.000000

224 comapy-m  time44=1      const        r/se        dw/df
    ols        0.003188   -0.114292   -0.082796   0.000000
    log tred   0.735672   -1.126216    0.058591   5.000000

225 pgmapy-m  time44=1      const        r/se        dw/df
    ols        0.029284   -0.811999    0.901511   0.000000
    log tred   7.477985   -8.853021    0.052955   5.000000

226 mmmapy-m  time44=1      const        r/se        dw/df
    ols        0.003588   -0.105620   -0.052266   0.000000
    log tred   0.837842   -1.053003    0.057910   5.000000

228 mimapydm  time44=1      const        r/se        dw/df
    ols        0.003361   -0.138877    0.080576   0.000000
    log tred   1.270222   -2.156084    0.039913   6.000000

229 comapydm  time44=1      const        r/se        dw/df
    ols       -0.009445    0.187645    0.340651   0.000000
    log tred  -2.148613    1.753740    0.066301   6.000000

230 pgmapydm  time44=1      const        r/se        dw/df
    ols        0.014016   -0.422463    0.838672   0.000000
    log tred   6.114716   -7.571801    0.034573   6.000000
```

```
          log time trends

231 mmmapydm  time44=1       const        r/se        dw/df
   ols        0.000176    -0.058617    -0.166310    0.000000
   log tred   0.042841    -0.585683     0.062017    6.000000

233 mimapygm  time44=1       const        r/se        dw/df
   ols        0.021480    -0.538271     0.828723    0.000000
   log tred   5.480044    -5.863317     0.053003    5.000000

234 comapygm  time44=1       const        r/se        dw/df
   ols        0.023968    -0.639837     0.776074    0.000000
   log tred   4.668461    -5.321057     0.069424    5.000000

235 pgmapygm  time44=1       const        r/se        dw/df
   ols        0.056387    -1.517945     0.889287    0.000000
   log tred   7.013851    -8.061581     0.108711    5.000000

236 mmmapygm  time44=1       const        r/se        dw/df
   ols        0.009449    -0.236851     0.197914    0.000000
   log tred   1.574960    -1.685626     0.081125    5.000000

238 icmapy-d  time44=1       const        r/se        dw/df
   ols       -0.026771    -0.107409     0.846153    0.000000
   log tred  -4.795828    -2.368505     0.017652    3.000000

239 comapy-d  time44=1       const        r/se        dw/df
   ols       -0.046653    -0.051564     0.949660    0.000000
   log tred  -8.744099    -1.189620     0.016872    3.000000

240 irmapy-d  time44=1       const        r/se        dw/df
   ols        0.004244    -0.036057    -0.299148    0.000000
   log tred   0.280963    -0.293801     0.047771    3.000000

242 ag-py-d   time44=1       const        r/se        dw/df
   ols        0.086238    -1.455256     0.776050    0.000000
   log tred   4.668157    -4.885415     0.097753    5.000000

243 ag-py-d   time44=1       const        r/se        dw/df
   ols        0.060560    -1.169290     0.922263    0.000000
   log tred  10.381453    -8.466550     0.052985    8.000000

245 mi-py-d   time44=1       const        r/se        dw/df
   ols        0.042878     3.767149     0.968275    0.000000
   log tred  20.695358    84.807014     0.034669   13.000000

247 agi-py-d  time44=1       const        r/se        dw/df
   ols        0.043445    -5.254023     0.271288    0.000000
   log tred   1.798619   -13.489925     0.127813    5.000000

248 agi-py-d  time44=1       const        r/se        dw/df
   ols        0.041922    -0.614627     0.345650    0.000000
   log tred   2.041913    -1.856622     0.108637    5.000000

249 agi-py-d  time44=1       const        r/se        dw/df
   ols        0.008482    -0.173063     0.045545    0.000000
   log tred   1.195601    -1.030455     0.064434    8.000000
```

continued-log time trends

```
250 mii-py-d   time44=1       const         r/se          dw/df
    ols        -0.006734      4.702411      0.401709      0.000000
    log tred   -3.225191    105.044388      0.034939     13.000000

252 rmma-p-d   time44=1       const         r/se          dw/df
    ols         0.000745     -0.010600     -0.030751      0.000000
    log tred    0.611142     -0.467060      0.036281     20.000000

254 rmw-p-d    time44=1       const         r/se          dw/df
    ols        -0.002241      0.061244      0.070604      0.000000
    log tred   -1.354861      1.626908      0.019776     10.000000

256 rmrt-p-d   time44=1       const         r/se          dw/df
    ols        -0.005146      0.101270      0.219049      0.000000
    log tred   -2.624936      2.775120      0.058337     20.000000

258 mima-p-d   time44=1       const         r/se          dw/df
    ols         0.018862     -0.379550      0.656948      0.000000
    log tred    6.567353     -7.241822      0.091367     21.000000

260 miw-p-d    time44=1       const         r/se          dw/df
    ols         0.011057     -0.211062      0.550354      0.000000
    log tred    3.803112     -3.189260      0.034766     10.000000

262 mirt-p-d   time44=1       const         r/se          dw/df
    ols         0.014890     -0.308048      0.383731      0.000000
    log tred    3.833890     -4.346382      0.123554     21.000000

264 agw-p-b    time44=1       const         r/se          dw/df
    ols        -0.004550      0.067088      0.130474      0.000000
    log tred   -1.673506      1.823983      0.036680     11.000000

265 agw-p-f    time44=1       const         r/se          dw/df
    ols         0.004272     -0.115940      0.193694      0.000000
    log tred    1.970456     -3.953066      0.029249     11.000000

266 agw-p-d    time44=1       const         r/se          dw/df
    ols         0.008737     -0.133254      0.550177      0.000000
    log tred    3.284016     -3.290655      0.020608      7.000000

267 agw-p-ir   time44=1       const         r/se          dw/df
    ols        -0.018571      0.290347      0.839130      0.000000
    log tred   -6.924278      7.323632      0.024361      8.000000

268 agw-p-i    time44=1       const         r/se          dw/df
    ols         0.005759     -0.105450      0.250452      0.000000
    log tred    2.001810     -2.479642      0.026131      8.000000

269 agw-p-nl   time44=1       const         r/se          dw/df
    ols        -0.005974      0.114503      0.315830      0.000000
    log tred   -2.557245      3.623381      0.031515     11.000000

270 agw-p-po   time44=1       const         r/se          dw/df
    ols         0.000288      0.004019     -0.089659      0.000000
    log tred    0.112355      0.115836      0.034603     11.000000
```

```
          log time trends

271 agw-p-e    time44=1        const        r/se        dw/df
    ols        0.007075      -0.106284    0.633671    0.000000
    log tred   2.814097      -2.550146    0.013586    3.000000

272 agw-p-s    time44=1        const        r/se        dw/df
    ols        0.011505      -0.153560    0.636831    0.000000
    log tred   4.504324      -4.314540    0.030544   10.000000

273 agw-p-yu   time44=1        const        r/se        dw/df
    ols        0.037378      -0.526620    0.571274    0.000000
    log tred   2.768116      -2.500996    0.056487    4.000000

274 agw-p-cn   time44=1        const        r/se        dw/df
    ols       -0.010619       0.166949    0.401971    0.000000
    log tred  -3.010965       3.499194    0.047580   11.000000

275 agw-p-cr   time44=1        const        r/se        dw/df
    ols       -0.002941       0.046410    0.001349    0.000000
    log tred  -1.006060       1.074196    0.026548    8.000000

276 agw-p-mx   time44=1        const        r/se        dw/df
    ols        0.006792      -0.135851    0.462842    0.000000
    log tred   3.367463      -4.979258    0.027209   11.000000

277 agw-p-us   time44=1        const        r/se        dw/df
    ols       -0.025162       0.362218    0.853998    0.000000
    log tred  -8.437472       8.978766    0.040231   11.000000

278 agw-p-ar   time44=1        const        r/se        dw/df
    ols        0.013880      -0.195632    0.550235    0.000000
    log tred   2.887959      -2.524448    0.025431    5.000000

279 agw-p-br   time44=1        const        r/se        dw/df
    ols       -0.010162       0.184314    0.534254    0.000000
    log tred  -3.842540       5.151968    0.035678   11.000000

280 agw-p-ce   time44=1        const        r/se        dw/df
    ols       -0.014235       0.401283    0.198631    0.000000
    log tred  -1.993582       4.154287    0.096331   11.000000

281 agw-p-ec   time44=1        const        r/se        dw/df
    ols       -0.008270       0.121694    0.904319    0.000000
    log tred  -8.752765       8.461636    0.007319    7.000000

282 agw-p-pr   time44=1        const        r/se        dw/df
    ols        0.006477      -0.023816    0.053170    0.000000
    log tred   1.271893      -0.360621    0.060901   10.000000

283 agw-p-ve   time44=1        const        r/se        dw/df
    ols       -0.002424       0.032924   -0.040897    0.000000
    log tred  -0.726990       0.729835    0.044988   11.000000

284 agw-p-ir   time44=1        const        r/se        dw/df
    ols        0.002484      -0.027100    0.005250    0.000000
    log tred   1.031181      -0.831769    0.032492   11.000000
```

continued-log time trends

```
285 agw-p-jp  time44=1      const        r/se        dw/df
     ols       0.017516    -0.326239    0.513501    0.000000
     log tred  3.399270    -4.411177    0.054044    9.000000

286 agw-p-al  time44=1      const        r/se        dw/df
     ols      -0.008211     0.169698    0.399981    0.000000
     log tred -1.732007     1.662627    0.010601    2.000000

287 agw-p-cn  time44=1      const        r/se        dw/df
     ols      -0.006050     0.147397    0.370595    0.000000
     log tred -2.734379     2.804737    0.026458   10.000000

288 agw-p-cr  time44=1      const        r/se        dw/df
     ols       0.012837    -0.261464    0.723486    0.000000
     log tred  5.457200    -4.679581    0.028130   10.000000

289 agw-p-mx  time44=1      const        r/se        dw/df
     ols       0.007334    -0.128911    0.722846    0.000000
     log tred  5.448776    -4.032402    0.016095   10.000000

290 agw-p-us  time44=1      const        r/se        dw/df
     ols      -0.000393     0.012088   -0.093424    0.000000
     log tred -0.245233     0.317160    0.019188   10.000000

291 agw-p-ar  time44=1      const        r/se        dw/df
     ols       0.006687    -0.204800    0.059226    0.000000
     log tred  1.300963    -1.677529    0.061464   10.000000

292 agw-p-br  time44=1      const        r/se        dw/df
     ols       0.002662    -0.045842   -0.035721    0.000000
     log tred  0.787798    -0.571257    0.040402   10.000000

293 agw-p-ce  time44=1      const        r/se        dw/df
     ols       0.009262    -0.140263    0.326191    0.000000
     log tred  2.416813    -1.576532    0.040192    9.000000

294 agw-p-co  time44=1      const        r/se        dw/df
     ols      -0.000411     0.037285   -0.095147    0.000000
     log tred -0.210514     0.804245    0.023341   10.000000

295 agw-p-ec  time44=1      const        r/se        dw/df
     ols       0.007523    -0.142998    0.778409    0.000000
     log tred  5.394677    -4.629351    0.010802    7.000000

296 agw-p-ve  time44=1      const        r/se        dw/df
     ols      -0.010150     0.251273    0.641709    0.000000
     log tred -4.549865     4.741961    0.026678   10.000000

297 agw-p-in  time44=1      const        r/se        dw/df
     ols       0.012290    -0.217693    0.442642    0.000000
     log tred  3.120252    -2.326892    0.047101   10.000000

298 agw-p-ir  time44=1      const        r/se        dw/df
     ols       0.011206    -0.208064    0.533450    0.000000
     log tred  3.684742    -2.880275    0.036369   10.000000
```

log time trends

```
299 agw-p-iq   time44=1        const          r/se         dw/df
    ols        0.001454       -0.047374      -0.057063     0.000000
    log tred   0.678359       -0.912881       0.022484     9.000000

300 agw-p-jp   time44=1        const          r/se         dw/df
    ols        0.032899       -0.649446       0.862475     0.000000
    log tred   8.365743       -6.952824       0.047027    10.000000

301 agw-p-kr   time44=1        const          r/se         dw/df
    ols        0.035486       -0.881507       0.513151     0.000000
    log tred   3.071191       -3.046515       0.095902     7.000000

302 agw-p-pp   time44=1        const          r/se         dw/df
    ols        0.010766       -0.213938       0.677242     0.000000
    log tred   4.688603       -4.013283       0.024082     9.000000

303 agw-p-th   time44=1        const          r/se         dw/df
    ols        0.020363       -0.589875      -0.207097     0.000000
    log tred   0.696633       -0.760815       0.065364     2.000000

304 agw-p-a    time44=1        const          r/se         dw/df
    ols       -0.003774        0.092731       0.216680     0.000000
    log tred  -2.010669        2.079720       0.022448    10.000000

305 agw-p-b    time44=1        const          r/se         dw/df
    ols        0.006608       -0.156643       0.311503     0.000000
    log tred   2.444758       -2.439856       0.032323    10.000000

306 aga-p-f    time44=1        const          r/se         dw/df
    ols        0.006174       -0.141045       0.551731     0.000000
    log tred   3.293392       -3.396643       0.014521     7.000000

307 agw-p-d    time44=1        const          r/se         dw/df
    ols       -0.007505        0.153821       0.120173     0.000000
    log tred  -1.538141        1.357924       0.051173     9.000000

308 agw-p-gr   time44=1        const          r/se         dw/df
    ols        0.010231       -0.208961       0.715281     0.000000
    log tred   5.111006       -4.324562       0.022012     9.000000

309 agw-p-ir   time44=1        const          r/ se        dw/df
    ols        0.000369        0.009708      -0.096820     0.000000
    log tred   0.170284        0.188661       0.025906    10.000000

310 agw-p-i    time44=1        const          r/se         dw/df
    ols        0.002488       -0.065103       0.075634     0.000000
    log tred   1.317725       -1.397906       0.017148     8.000000

311 agw-p-nl   time44=1        const          r/se         dw/df
    ols        0.008394       -0.176855       0.428060     0.000000
    log tred   3.038552       -2.695397       0.033034    10.000000

312 agw-p-po   time44=1        const          r/se         dw/df
    ols        0.002212       -0.047557       0.040255     0.000000
    log tred   1.208873       -1.094171       0.021882    10.000000
```

```
continued-log time trends

313 agw-p-e    time44=1      const        r/se        dw/df
    ols        0.004019    -0.082755    0.230155     0.000000
    log tred   2.070890    -1.795274    0.023207    10.000000

314 agw-p-s    time44=1      const        r/se        dw/df
    ols        0.003387    -0.086435    0.130237     0.000000
    log tred   1.626999    -1.748179    0.024893    10.000000

315 agw-p-gb   time44=1      const        r/se        dw/df
    ols        0.066561    -1.274024    0.815910     0.000000
    log tred   7.053606    -5.684109    0.112844    10.000000

316 agw-p-nz   time44=1      const        r/se        dw/df
    ols       -0.019689     0.425144    0.684707     0.000000
    log tred  -4.286399     3.696080    0.038124     7.000000
%
```

riables in data ban

1 cu-py-us	56 w--p--yu	111 ag-p--kr	166 ag-rp-us
2 cs-py-us	57 ag-p--cn	112 w--p--kp	167 ag-rp-ia
3 ca-py-us	58 w--p--cn	113 ag-p--pp	168 ag-rp-ip
4 co-py-us	59 ag-p--cr	114 w--p--pp	169 ag-rp-iu
5 co-py-gb	60 w--p--cr	115 ag-p--th	170 ag-rp-ib
6 co-py-b-	61 ag-p--mx	116 w--p--th	171 ag-rp-is
7 co-py-f-	62 w--p--mx	117 ag-p--a-	172 ag-rp-jp
8 co-py-nl	63 ag-p--us	118 w--p--a-	173 ag-rp-kr
9 co-py-d-	64 w--p--us	119 ag-p--b-	174 ag-rp-pp
10 co-py-p-	65 ag-p--ar	120 w--p--b-	175 ag-rp-a-
11 mi-py-w-	66 w--p--ar	121 ag-p--f-	176 ag-rp-b-
12 co-py-w-	67 ag-p--br	122 w--p--f-	177 ag-rp-cs
13 pg-py-w-	68 w--p--br	123 ag-p--d-	178 ag-rp-dk
14 mm-py-w-	69 ag-p--ce	124 w--p--d-	179 ag-rp-su
15 ma-py-w-	70 w--p--ce	125 ag-p--gr	180 ag-rp-f-
16 mi-py-cp	71 ag-p--ec	126 w--p--gr	181 ag-rp-d-
17 co-py-cp	72 w--p--ec	127 ag-p--il	182 ag-rp-h-
18 pg-py-cp	73 ag-p--pr	128 w--p--il	183 ag-rp-ir
19 mm-py-cp	74 w--p--pr	129 ag-p--i-	184 ag-rp-i-
20 ma-py-cp	75 ag-p--ve	130 w--d--i-	185 ag-rp-n-
21 mi-py-m-	76 w--p--ve	131 ag-p--nl	186 ag-rp-p-
22 co-py-m-	77 ag-p--ir	132 w--p--nl	187 ag-rp-e-
23 pg-py-m-	78 w--p--ir	133 ag-p--po	188 ag-rp-s-
24 mm-py-m-	79 ag-p--jp	134 w--p--po	189 ag-rp-ch
25 ma-py-m-	80 w--p--jp	135 ag-p--e-	190 ag-rp-gb
26 mi-py-dm	81 ag-p--al	136 w--p--e-	191 ag-rp-aa
27 co-py-dm	82 w--p--al	137 ag-p--s-	192 ic-py-d
28 pg-py-dm	83 ag-p--cn	138 w--p--s-	193 co-py-d
29 mm-py-dm	84 w--p--cn	139 ag-p--gb	194 ir-py-d
30 ma-py-dm	85 ag-p--cr	140 w--p--gb	195 ma-py-d
31 mi-py-gm	86 w--p--cr	141 ag-p--nz	196 ag-o--d-
32 co-py-gm	87 ag-p--mx	142 w--p--nz	197 ag-o--d-
33 pg-py-gm	88 w--p--mx	143 ag-rp-aa	198 mi-o--d
34 mm-py-gm	89 ag-p--us	144 ag-rp-a-	199 i--o--d
35 ma-py-gm	90 w--p--us	145 ag-rp-b-	200 i--py-d
36 co-py-ee	91 ag-p--ar	146 ag-rp-br	201 ag-l--d
37 ag-p--b-	92 w--p--ar	147 ag-rp-cn	202 a2-l--d
38 w--p--b-	93 ag-p--br	148 ag-rp-ct	203 ag-lp-d
39 ag-p--f-	94 w--p--br	149 ag-rp-su	204 n--l--d
40 w--p--f-	95 ag-p--ce	150 ag-rp-f-	205 e--l--d
41 ag-p--d-	96 w--p--ce	151 ag-rp-d-	206 e2-l--d
42 w--p--d-	97 ag-p--co	152 ag-rp-gr	207 rm-p-d
43 ag-p--ir	98 w--p--co	153 ag-rp-ia	208 mi-p-d
44 w--p--ir	99 ag-p--ec	154 ag-rp-ip	209 ma-p-d
45 ag-p--i-	100 w--p--ec	155 ag-rp-ib	210 w--p-d
46 w--p--i-	101 ag-p--ve	156 ag-rp-ir	211 rt-p-d
47 ag-p--nl	102 w--p--ve	157 ag-rp-i-	212 co-py-gb
48 w--p--nl	103 ag-p--in	158 ag-rp-jp	213 mimapy-w
49 ag-p--po	104 w--p--in	159 ag-rp-nl	214 comapy-w
50 w--p--po	105 ag-p--ir	160 ag-rp-n-	215 pgmapy-w
51 ag-p--e-	106 w--p--ir	161 ag-rp-pr	216 mmmapy-w
52 w--p--e-	107 ag-p--iq	162 ag-rp-po	217 mamapy-w
53 ag-p--s-	108 w--p--iq	163 ag-rp-ch	218 mimapycp
54 w--p--s-	109 ag-p--jp	164 ag-rp-us	219 comapycp
55 ag-p--yu	110 w--p--jp	165 ag-rp-cn	220 pgmapycp

variables in data bank

221	mmmapycp	276	agw-p-mx
222	mamapycp	277	agw-p-us
223	mimapy-m	278	agw-p-ar
224	comapy-m	279	agw-p-br
225	pgmapy-m	280	agw-p-ce
226	mmmapy-m	281	agw-p-ec
227	mamapy-m	282	agw-p-pr
228	mimapydm	283	agw-p-ve
229	comapydm	284	agw-p-ir
230	pgmapydm	285	agw-p-jp
231	mmmapydm	286	agw-p-al
232	mamapydm	287	agw-p-cn
233	mimapygm	288	agw-p-cr
234	comapygm	289	agw-p-mx
235	pgmapygm	290	agw-p-us
236	mmmapygm	291	agw-p-ar
237	mamapygm	292	agw-p-br
238	icmapy-d	293	agw-p-ce
239	comapy-d	294	agw-p-co
240	irmapy-d	295	agw-p-ec
241	mamapy-d	296	agw-p-ve
242	ag-py-d	297	agw-p-in
243	ag-py-d	298	agw-p-ir
244	ag-ll-d	299	agw-p-iq
245	mi-py-d	300	agw-p-jp
246	n-ll-d	301	agw-p-kr
247	agi-py-d	302	agw-p-pp
248	agi-py-d	303	agw-p-th
249	agi-py-d	304	agw-p-a
250	mii-py-d	305	agw-p-b
251	ii--py-d	306	aga-p-f
252	rmma-p-d	307	agw-p-d
253	mama-p-d	308	agw-p-gr
254	rmw-p-d	309	agw-p-il
255	ww-p-d	310	agw-p-i
256	rmrt-p-d	311	agw-p-nl
257	rtrt-p-d	312	agw-p-po
258	mima-p-d	313	agw-p-e
259		314	agw-p-s
260	miw-p-d	315	agw-p-gb
261	ww-p-d	316	agw-p-nz
262	mirt-p-d		
263	rtrt-p-d		
264	agw-p-b		
265	agw-p-f		
266	agw-p-d		
267	agw-p-ir		
268	agw-p-i		
269	agw-p-nl		
270	agw-p-po		
271	agw-p-e		
272	agw-p-s		
273	agw-p-yu		
274	agw-p-cn		
275	agw-p-cr		

ables in data bank

259		63	ag-p--us	166	ag-rp-us	296	agw-p-ve
202	a2-1--d	89	ag-p--us	306	aga-p-f	273	agw-p-yu
201	ag-1--d	75	ag-p--ve	247	agi-py-d	3	ca-py-us
244	ag-11-d	101	ag-p--ve	248	agi-py-d	6	co-py-b-
203	ag-1p-d	55	ag-p--yu	249	agi-py-d	17	co-py-cp
196	ag-o--d-	242	ag-py-d	304	agw-p-a	193	co-py-d
197	ag-o--d-	243	ag-py-d	286	agw-p-al	9	co-py-d-
117	ag-p--a-	144	ag-rp-a-	278	agw-p-ar	27	co-py-dm
81	ag-p--al	175	ag-rp-a-	291	agw-p-ar	36	co-py-ee
65	ag-p--ar	143	ag-rp-aa	264	agw-p-b	7	co-py-f-
91	ag-p--ar	191	ag-rp-aa	305	agw-p-b	5	co-py-gb
37	ag-p--b-	145	ag-rp-b-	279	agw-p-br	212	co-py-gb
119	ag-p--b-	176	ag-rp-b-	292	agw-p-br	32	co-py-gm
67	ag-p--br	146	ag-rp-br	280	agw-p-ce	22	co-py-m-
93	ag-p--br	163	ag-rp-ch	293	agw-p-ce	8	co-py-nl
69	ag-p--ce	189	ag-rp-ch	274	agw-p-cn	10	co-py-p-
95	ag-p--ce	147	ag-rp-cn	287	agw-p-cn	4	co-py-us
57	ag-p--cn	165	ag-rp-cn	294	agw-p-co	12	co-py-w-
83	ag-p--cn	177	ag-rp-cs	275	agw-p-cr	239	comapy-d
97	ag-p--co	148	ag-rp-ct	288	agw-p-cr	224	comapy-m
59	ag-p--cr	151	ag-rp-d-	266	agw-p-d	214	comapy-w
85	ag-p--cr	181	ag-rp-d-	307	agw-p-d	219	comapycp
41	ag-p--d-	178	ag-rp-dk	271	agw-p-e	229	comapydm
123	ag-p--d-	187	ag-rp-e-	313	agw-p-e	234	comapygm
51	ag-p--e-	150	ag-rp-f-	281	agw-p-ec	2	cs-py-us
135	ag-p--e-	180	ag-rp-f-	295	agw-p-ec	1	cu-py-us
71	ag-p--ec	190	ag-rp-gb	265	agw-p-f	205	e--1--d
99	ag-p--ec	152	ag-rp-gr	315	agw-p-gb	206	e2-1--d
39	ag-p--f-	182	ag-rp-h-	308	agw-p-gr	199	i--o--d
121	ag-p--f-	157	ag-rp-i-	268	agw-p-i	200	i--py-d
139	ag-p--gb	184	ag-rp-i-	310	agw-p-i	192	ic-py-d
125	ag-p--gr	153	ag-rp-ia	309	agw-p-il	238	icmapy-d
45	ag-p--i-	167	ag-rp-ia	297	agw-p-in	251	ii--py-d
129	ag-p--i-	155	ag-rp-ib	299	agw-p-iq	194	ir-py-d
127	ag-p--il	170	ag-rp-ib	267	agw-p-ir	240	irmapy-d
103	ag-p--in	154	ag-rp-ip	284	agw-p-ir	209	ma-p-d
107	ag-p--iq	168	ag-rp-ip	298	agw-p-ir	20	ma-py-cp
43	ag-p--ir	156	ag-rp-ir	285	agw-p-jp	195	ma-py-d
77	ag-p--ir	183	ag-rp-ir	300	agw-p-jp	30	ma-py-dm
105	ag-p--ir	171	ag-rp-is	301	agw-p-kr	35	ma-py-gm
79	ag-p--jp	169	ag-rp-iu	276	agw-p-mx	25	ma-py-m-
109	ag-p--jp	158	ag-rp-jp	289	agw-p-mx	15	ma-py-w-
111	ag-p--kr	172	ag-rp-jp	269	agw-p-nl	253	mama-p-d
61	ag-p--mx	173	ag-rp-kr	311	agw-p-nl	241	mamapy-d
87	ag-p--mx	160	ag-rp-n-	316	agw-p-nz	227	mamapy-m
47	ag-p--nl	185	ag-rp-n-	270	agw-p-po	217	mamapy-w
131	ag-p--nl	159	ag-rp-nl	312	agw-p-po	222	mamapycp
141	ag-p--nz	186	ag-rp-p-	302	agw-p-pp	232	mamapydm
49	ag-p--po	162	ag-rp-po	282	agw-p-pr	237	mamapygm
133	ag-p--po	174	ag-rp-pp	272	agw-p-s	198	mi-o--d
113	ag-p--pp	161	ag-rp-pr	314	agw-p-s	208	mi-p-d
73	ag-p--pr	188	ag-rp-s-	303	agw-p-th	16	mi-py-cp
53	ag-p--s-	149	ag-rp-su	277	agw-p-us	245	mi-py-d
137	ag-p--s-	179	ag-rp-su	290	agw-p-us	26	mi-py-dm
115	ag-p--th	164	ag-rp-us	283	agw-p-ve	31	mi-py-gm

variables in data bank

21	mi-py-m-	86	w--p--cr
11	mi-py-w-	42	w--p--d-
250	mii-py-d	124	w--p--d-
258	mima-p-d	52	w--p--e-
223	mimapy-m	136	w--p--e-
213	mimapy-w	72	w--p--ec
218	mimapycp	100	w--p--ec
228	mimapydm	40	w--p--f-
233	mimapygm	122	w--p--f-
262	mirt-p-d	140	w--p--gb
260	miw-p-d	126	w--p--gr
19	mm-py-cp	46	w--p--i-
29	mm-py-dm	128	w--p--il
34	mm-py-gm	104	w--p--in
24	mm-py-m-	108	w--p--iq
14	mm-py-w-	44	w--p--ir
226	mmmapy-m	78	w--p--ir
216	mmmapy-w	106	w--p--ir
221	mmmapycp	80	w--p--jp
231	mmmapydm	110	w--p--jp
236	mmmapygm	112	w--p--kp
204	n--l--d	62	w--p--mx
246	n-ll-d	88	w--p--mx
18	pg-py-cp	48	w--p--nl
28	pg-py-dm	132	w--p--nl
33	pg-py-gm	142	w--p--nz
23	pg-py-m-	50	w--p--po
13	pg-py-w-	134	w--p--po
225	pgmapy-m	114	w--p--pp
215	pgmapy-w	74	w--p--pr
220	pgmapycp	54	w--p--s-
230	pgmapydm	138	w--p--s-
235	pgmapygm	116	w--p--th
207	rm-p-d	64	w--p--us
252	rmma-p-d	90	w--p--us
256	rmrt-p-d	76	w--p--ve
254	rmw-p-d	102	w--p--ve
211	rt-p-d	56	w--p--yu
257	rtrt-p-d	210	w--p-d
263	rtrt-p-d	255	ww-p-d
130	w--d--i-	261	ww-p-d
118	w--p--a-		
82	w--p--al		
66	w--p--ar		
92	w--p--ar		
38	w--p--b-		
120	w--p--b-		
68	w--p--br		
94	w--p--br		
70	w--p--ce		
96	w--p--ce		
58	w--p--cn		
84	w--p--cn		
98	w--p--co		
60	w--p--cr		

References

1. H. J. Barnett and Chandler Morse, *Scarcity and Growth: The Economics of Natural Resource Availability* (Baltimore, Johns Hopkins University Press for Resources for the Future, 1963).
2. ————, "Population Change and Resources: Malthusianism and Conservation," in *Demographic and Economic Change in Developed Countries.* Conference of the Universities—National Bureau Committee for Economic Research, 1958 (Princeton, N.J., Princeton University Press, 1960).
3. ————, "The Measurement of Change in Natural Resource Economic Scarcity," in *Output, Input, and Productivity Measurement,* 1958 NBER Conference on Income and Wealth (Princeton, N.J., Princeton University Press, 1961).
4. D. H. Meadows, D. L. Meadows, J. Randers, and W. W. Behrens III, *The Limits to Growth* (New York, Universe Books, 1972).
5. P. R. Ehrlich, *The Population Bomb* (New York, Ballantine, 1968).
6. Garrett Hardin, "The Tragedy of the Commons," *Science* vol. 162 (December 13, 1968) pp. 1243–1248.
7. V. Kerry Smith, "Measuring Natural Resource Scarcity: Theory and Practice," *Journal of Environmental Economics and Management* vol. 5 (June 1978) pp. 150–171.
8. R. G. Ridker, "Resource and Environmental Consequences of Population Growth in the United States: A Summary," in R. G. Ridker, ed., *Population, Resources and the Environment,* The Commission on Population Growth and the American Future Research Reports, vol. 3 (Washington, GPO, 1972).
9. David Ricardo, *Principles of Political Economy and Taxation* (London, 1926).

9

The Adequacy of Measures for Signaling
The Scarcity of Natural Resources

Gardner M. Brown, Jr. and Barry Field

I
Overview

Are natural resources, collectively or individually, growing more scarce in an economic sense? The answer to this question requires an index or indicator that will register scarcity accurately, when it occurs. There are several candidates for such an indicator and disagreement about which is best. We have concentrated on the three most common measures: unit cost, omitting the cost of natural resources, as developed by Barnettt and Morse in their widely referenced work; extractive natural resource product price; and natural resource rental rate. We conclude that each of these measures has flaws.

In the first part of the paper each index is defined and illustrations of its use are cited from the literature. In some cases the indexes have been updated, amended, and revised. Then the scarcity indicators are compared and evaluated.

The elasticity of substitution between natural resources and other inputs is discussed in the second part of the paper. The elasticity of substitution, while not a scarcity indicator itself, gives some feeling for the difficulty of adjusting for growing natural resource scarcity.

In the final section, a menu of topics for future research is provided. A summary of our conclusions follows.

1. The unit cost measure of Barnett and Morse, the most commonly cited index of scarcity among economists, is an ambiguous indicator of scarcity for the following reasons.

This paper is an outgrowth of a research project (SIA 75-15189) sponsored by National Science Foundation in 1975. A distilled version was presented at the American Economics Association Meetings in Atlantic City, N.J., September 1976. In addition to being a substantial embellishment, the present piece discusses future research directions. We would like to acknowledge the helpful contributions made by Charles Grebenstein, Richard Hartman, and Ron Johnson.

a. In a dynamic world the unit cost measure mistakes certain types of technological progress for growing natural resource scarcity.
b. Under all conditions the unit cost measure mistakes ease of adjustment to increasing scarcity (which we should welcome) for increasing scarcity itself (which is not desired).
c. The unit cost measure is a lagging, not a leading, indicator. Expected future costs of extraction are not contained in this measure.
d. The unit cost measure does not warn us of impending physical exhaustion.
e. Unit cost is a difficult index to measure precisely.

2. The real price of natural resource-intensive products is relatively superior to unit cost as an indicator of scarcity.

a. The real price of the resource-intensive product is forward looking insofar as it reflects the expected future cost of exploration, discovery, and extraction.
b. Technical progress distorts the scarcity signal provided by real price. Timber became more scarce in the late nineteenth century but technological progress was responsible for maintaining stable product prices.
c. Real price does not presage impending exhaustion for resources which have close substitutes. The passenger pigeon became extinct with hardly a ripple in its commercial price.
d. The real price of a resource can rise or fall, indicating increasing or decreasing scarcity, depending upon which particular price deflator is used to adjust the nominal resource price. Therefore, this measure gives mixed scarcity signals.

3. The rental rate of natural resources, or the value of resources *in situ,* is a third measure of scarcity. Rental rates may indicate scarcity while the other indexes do not. The rental rate on timber generally rose during the past sixty years; the unit cost generally fell during this period while the product price (lumber) fell relative to the rental rate.

a. So little data are available, however, that often the rental rate is not a practical measure in the short run.
b. The rental rate anticipates growing scarcity in an economic sense, but impending physical exhaustion is compatible with any prior path and level of the rental rate.

All of the above indexes may be biased because futures markets don't really exist and because they fail to reflect the pressure of non-market demands associated with environmental quality. For these reasons the search for exact measures of scarcity may be frustrated. Nevertheless, we feel that continued effort is yet justified. There appear to be a few opportunities to study rental rates, as in the case of public oil leases, and rather more options for looking at the paths of discovery costs as a proxy for rental rates. Applied research incorporating the effect of uncertainty on rates of extraction is overdue.

Efforts should be directed at devising new measures of scarcity. One of these would be to focus on the extent of economic disruption that would result from scarcities of particular natural resources. The elasticity of substitution is a measure that takes this perspective, since it indicates the ease with which other inputs may be substituted for scarce natural resources. It is feasible to apply modern techniques to estimate the elasticity of substitution between conventional inputs (labor and capital) and individual natural resources. This is especially true for such widely used resources as steel, aluminum, copper, and pulp and paper; we sketch our preliminary results for these resources. We also propose further studies; however, small sample size may lead to poor estimates of substitutability when it comes to such resources as zinc, lead, mercury, silver, tin, and uranium, whose physical supplies, some believe, are inadequate.

Finally, we suggest that it would be very useful to investigate how responsive and extensive institutional change has been to changing availability of natural resources.

II
Unit Costs of Extractive Output

Probably the most common source of empirical conclusions about natural resources scarcity cited by economists is the work of Barnett and Morse [1]. Their principal measure of scarcity is the "unit cost of extractive output," defined as $(\alpha L + \beta K)/Q$ where L is labor, K is reproducible capital, and Q is the output of extractive industries. The factors α and β are weights for aggregating inputs. Data on L and Q were derived from Potter and Christy [2] while Barnett and Morse obtained estimates of K, α, and β directly from Kendrick [3]. It needs to be stressed that the capital measure includes only reproducible capital, and does not include the value of natural resources.

Unit cost, as Barnett and Morse define it, is not the common garden variety unit cost one would construct to include the cost of all inputs per unit of output. Nevertheless, the Barnett and Morse measure is the empirically relevant one. It is the one cited in many references, including [4–8], whereas the all-inclusive measure of unit cost has not, to our knowledge, been referenced at all in the professional literature.[1]

---

[1] Note that the inclusive measure of unit cost is simply product price in a competitive environment and where economists customarily limit production functions to be homogeneous of degree one.

Table 9-1. Indexes of Labor-Capital Input per Unit of Extractive Output, as Given in *Scarcity and Growth*

	Total extractive		Agriculture		Minerals		Forestry		Fishing
	A	B	A	B	A	B	A	B	A
1870–1900	134	99	132	97	210	154	59	37	200
1919	122	103	114	97	164	139	106	84	100
1957	60	87	61	89	47	68	90	130	18

Source: H. J. Barnett and C. Morse, *Scarcity and Growth: The Economics of Natural Resource Availability* (Baltimore, Johns Hopkins University Press for Resources for the Future, 1963) pp. 8, 9, 172.
Key: A, indexes of direct unit extraction costs.
  B, indexes of unit extraction costs relative to nonextractive goods.

Barnett and Morse reasoned in support of their unit cost measure as follows. Imagine that a dose of constant quality capital and labor combine with a dose of constant quality natural resources to produce a given amount of output. As natural resources grow more scarce, lower quality resources are drawn into the production process; it takes more than a dose of capital and labor to produce the same output as previously. Thus the unit cost of extractive output must rise through time. Barnett and Morse's empirical results are summarized in table 9-1. In most industries the unit cost of extractive output generally fell at an increasing rate from 1870 to 1950, thus signifying that natural resources were growing more plentiful, not more scarce. Forestry in the United States was a major exception.

The advantages claimed for unit cost are summed up as follows: it is the only measure "capable of reflecting and netting out the effects of (a) all resource constraints, (b) all offsets to (and reversals of) these constraints, and (c) the real costs of developing and effectuating these offsets and reversals" [9, p. 127]. In other words, the primary advantage of unit extraction cost is that it includes the effects of technological changes in the extractive sector, which are conceived of as serving to relax natural resource constraints. This approach to the problem may create more difficulties than it solves, for technological progress in extraction may be only one, and not even the most important, source of the escape from scarcity. Clearly, under static conditions it can be shown that an increase in unit extraction cost as defined by Barnett and Morse is associated with a decrease in aggregate per capita output, hence a decline in measured consumption (welfare) per capita. But in a world enriched throughout by technical progress, this could be an ambiguous scarcity indicator, as Barnett and Morse see: "the unit cost of aggregate social output, therefore, may . . . decrease (social welfare is improving) even if the unit cost of extractive output rises continuously." They conclude that it therefore is "virtually impossible to postulate a realistic set of conditions that would yield either generally increasing natural resource scarcity or diminishing returns in the social production process" [7, p. 7]. If unit extraction cost may go up without implying diminishing returns, it is also true that it may stay steady or decline without implying reduced scarcity of a natural resource.

We are concerned with economic scarcity, not physical scarcity—the actual reduction of the number of units left of a particular natural resource. In some sense physical exhaustion may be considered the terminal phenomenon in a course of rising economic scarcity. At any rate, there seems to be implicit faith that Barnett and Morse's unit extraction costs will signal imminent exhaustion. Herfindahl [10, p. 1] says that long before exhaustion occurs "difficulties will arise in the form of persistently increasing cost because new deposits are becoming harder to find or because the quality of the new deposits found is deteriorating." But as exhaustion is approached, there is every reason to expect the search for, discovery, and introduction of various technological developments in extraction that will lower unit cost. The path of unit cost would be related to these changes in technique and could show almost any pattern. Since unit cost reflects current resource costs associated with extraction, it says nothing about costs of future extraction. A vivid example recently has been uncovered by Norgaard [11]. He found that technological change in oil well drilling has been sufficiently strong to offset a substantial part of the large decline in resource quality. As a result, unit costs have increased far less than they would have had technology been constant.

There is another important conceptual problem with using unit cost, so defined, as a scarcity measure. Suppose that the price (rental rate) of a natural resource increases and induces producers of extractive output to substitute out of natural resources and into relatively lower cost factors. This substitution clearly increases the unit cost of extractive output as defined by Barnett and Morse, but the magnitude of increase depends on the ease of substituting capital and labor for natural resources. Assume for example, that the extractive sector is characterized by the CES production function:

$$Q = (aL^{-\beta} + bR^{-\beta})^{-1/\beta}, \qquad \frac{1}{1 + \beta} = \sigma; \qquad \beta > -1 \qquad (1)$$

where L is a composite labor-capital input, R is a natural resource input, and σ is the elasticity of substitution. In competitive factor markets the ratio of the marginal product of each factor equals the factor price ratio.

Letting w be the price of the labor-capital input and λ that of the natural resource, we have

$$\frac{aL^{-\beta-1}}{bR^{-\beta-1}} = \frac{w}{\lambda} \tag{2}$$

or

$$\frac{R}{L} = \left(\frac{wb}{\lambda a}\right)^{\sigma} \tag{3}$$

Since (1) is constant returns to scale, (3) can be substituted into (1) after expressing (1) as labor/capital per unit of output, giving

$$\frac{L}{Q} = \left[a + b\left(\frac{\lambda a}{wb}\right)^{\beta\sigma}\right]^{1/\beta} \tag{4}$$

Relationship (4) has its most dramatic interpretation if, eschewing subscripts, we imagine instead that it describes production relations for two separate outputs. All parameters are alike except that the elasticity of substitution differs in the two hypothesized cases. Suppose the price of the natural resource input (λ) common to both outputs rises relative to w. Then (5) says that unit cost registers the greatest increase in the case where substitution is easiest! That is,

$$\frac{\partial(L/Q)}{\partial\lambda} > 0 \quad \text{and} \quad \frac{\partial^2(L/Q)}{\partial\lambda\partial\sigma} > 0$$

This is perverse.[2] The unit cost of extractive output alarms us with signs of dramatically increasing scarcity when, in fact, technology has made it easy to decrease the use of natural resources. As steamships became better substitutes for sailing craft, followers of the unit cost measure of scarcity would have grown even more strident in their demand to preserve the tall pole timber for masts.

Unit extraction costs have important practical difficulties as well. There is the problem of measuring the inputs, particularly capital, and combining them into a meaningful aggregate. Because of a poor data base, Barnett and Morse were forced to draw statistics from different stages of the total manufacturing process. Whereas the metals output series appears to be at the extractive level [2, p. 368ff.], the metals employment data include some undetermined fractions of workers in the separate processing sectors. There is the further problem of developing a valid index of aggregate inputs, particularly capital. Usually a substantial proportion of capital investment is devoted to finding new deposits of

---

[2] We are grateful to John Moroney for pointing out an error in an earlier formulation of this argument.

minerals and ought not to be, but frequently is, attributed to the cost of producing current output [10, pp. 5–6].

III
Real Price of Natural Resource Products

The most readily computed measure of natural resource scarcity in economics is the real price of extractive products. This is the price of a natural resource *after* it has been extracted and perhaps also after some amount of processing or fabrication. Clearly, a complete natural resource-using cycle could be subdivided into many steps. Perhaps the simplest is a breakdown of the following sort:

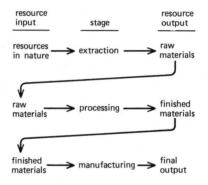

In terms of the schema, our reference to the "real price of natural re-source products" relates to the price of "raw materials," the output of the extractive sector, or sometimes "finished materials," the output of the processing sector.

Barnett and Morse calculated extractive output prices relative to a GNP deflator, concluding that "where the trend of relative price is upward—certainly forestry and possibly in fishing—there is support for . . . the natural resource scarcity hypothesis. Where the trend is approxi-mately horizontal—in agriculture, minerals and total extraction—the scarcity hypothesis fails" [1, p. 211].

V. Kerry Smith [12], analyzing the updated time paths of natural resources prices, finds that the rate of decline has diminished in the real prices of metals and fuels, two resources untouched by any scarcity effects in the Barnett and Morse analysis. Smith concludes that this implies the presence of persistent, though disguised, scarcity effects. However, in agriculture and forestry the rate of price increase has been diminishing.

Herfindahl [4] appraised the scarcity of copper in terms of the price

Table 9-2. Relative Price of Minerals to Labor
(1900 = 100)

	1900	1920	1940	1950	1960	1970
Coal	459	451	189	208	111	100
Copper	785	226	121	99	82	100
Iron	620	287	144	112	120	100
Phosphorus	—	—	—	130	120	100
Molybdenum	—	—	—	142	108	100
Lead	788	388	204	228	114	100
Zinc	794	400	272	256	125	100
Sulfur	—	—	—	215	145	100
Aluminum	3,150	859	287	166	134	100
Gold	—	—	595	258	143	100
Crude petroleum	1,034	726	198	213	135	100

Source: From W. D. Nordhaus, "The Allocation of Energy Resources," *Brookings Papers on Economic Activity*, no. 3 (1973) pp. 529–570.
Note: Values are price per ton of mineral divided by hourly wage rate in manufacturing.

of refined copper relative to the wholesale price index of the Bureau of Labor Statistics. His main results indicate a decline until about the 1920s but relative stability from then until 1957. On this basis Herfindahl concludes that there is no evidence for increasing scarcity in copper.

Ruttan and Callahan [13] follow Herfindahl's approach in their study of scarcity in forestry and agriculture, as does Irland [14] in his study of forestry. Irland concludes that on the whole, "the statistical record of real prices for lumber and plywood sheds considerable doubt on the hypothesis that sawtimber is a scarce resource" [14, p. 23]. He finds general support for this conclusion in the real prices of major paper products.

Real prices were also used by Nordhaus [15]. For eleven minerals he took the price of refined output relative to manufacturing wage rate for selected years during the period 1900–70. The results are presented in table 9-2. In all eleven cases the trend of this index was downward, but with a few temporary reversals.

Real prices are meant to reflect relative costs. All users agree that the sectors being studied and compared have to exhibit the same degree of competition in product and factor markets. Changes in the degree of monopoly, level of unionization, and in taxes and subsidies between the extractive and nonextractive sectors could drive up the relative price of extractive output. This would erroneously indicate increasing natural resource scarcity, according to many authors. Accordingly, they must believe that changes in market structure and government policies should be thought to be fundamentally different from other causes of price increase.

Table 9-3. Real Price of Selected Minerals Using Price of Capital as Numeraire, Selected Years, 1920–50

	1920	1940	1950
Coal	340	195	413
Copper	170	125	129
Iron	216	149	146
Phosphorus	—	141	170
Molybdenum	—	—	186
Lead	292	211	298
Zinc	301	281	335
Sulfur	—	—	281
Aluminum	647	297	217
Gold	—	615	337
Crude petroleum	547	205	278

Source: Taken from D. Jorgenson and Z. Griliches, "The Explanation of Productivity Change," *Review of Economic Studies*, vol. 34 (July 1967) pp. 250–282; U.S. Bureau of Census, *Historical Statistics of the United States, 1789–1945* (Washington, GPO, 1949); U.S. Bureau of Census, *Long-Term Economic Growth 1860–1965* (Washington, GPO, 1966); and U.S. Bureau of Census, *Statistical Abstracts of the United States, 1974* (Washington, GPO, 1974).

There is agreement that *relative* prices are the appropriate measures of scarcity because changes in natural resource product prices by themselves mean nothing. There is less agreement on what natural resources product prices should be compared with. We think there is no one correct answer. A consumer probably should be interested in the price of resource products relative to other products he purchases and would therefore use a retail price index or the equivalent. A firm using a resource product as an input should be interested in the price of other inputs, such as labor or capital, or an index of other factor prices.

The choice of the numeraire point of reference is crucial. For example, if one computes for the minerals selected by Nordhaus, the prices of minerals relative to the price of capital, as measured by Jorgenson and Griliches [16], four of the indexes show increasing scarcity of minerals (see table 9-3), even though the mineral price relative to wage rate fell for all eleven minerals, according to Nordhaus. The other seven mineral prices fall relatively more slowly when the price of capital replaces the wage rate as the numeraire.

There is a less dramatic comparison when Denison's [17, 18] quality adjusted wage rate is used. As shown in figures 9-1 to 9-4 the minerals exhibit a fall in relative price from 1920 to 1970, but using the quality adjusted wage dampens the price decrease by roughly 25 percent.[3] The constant quality wage rate is the proper wage rate to use because the

[3] Denison's index is used because it is available for more years, making it particularly useful for the comparison in trends for Douglas fir below.

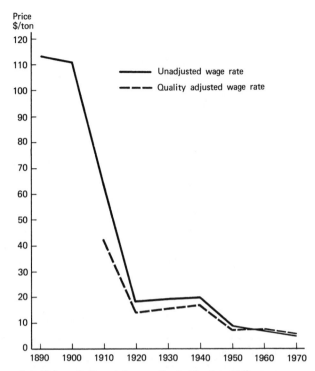

Figure 9-1. Price of all metals, as adjusted by two difference numeraires. (Figures 9-1 through 9-4 derived from E. F. Denison, *The Sources of Economic Growth in the United States and the Alternatives Before Us,* Supplementary paper 13, Committee for Economic Development, 1962; *Accounting for U.S. Economic Growth, 1929–1969,* Washington, D.C. Brookings Institution, 1974; and R. S. Manthy, *Natural Resource Commodities, 1870–1973: Prices, Output, Consumption, and Employment,* Baltimore, Johns Hopkins University Press for Resources for the Future, 1978.)

numerator is the price of a mineral whose quality has been held constant at a given concentrate over the time period in question. The price of a natural resource product is clearly an ambiguous indicator of the scarcity of the underlying natural resources.

IV
Rental Rates on Natural Resources

The conceptually ideal measure of economic scarcity is price. If something is not scarce, it has an exchange value of zero. When more is wanted than is available at a zero price, the exchange value ultimately

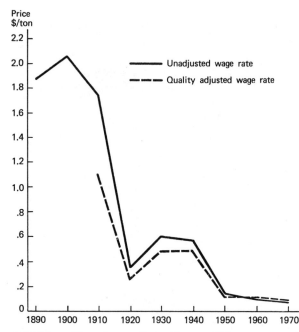

Figure 9-2. Price of bauxite as adjusted by two different numeraires. (See figure 9-1 for sources.)

must become positive. And if something is more scarce in one place than in another, or at one time compared with another, we would know this because its price is greater in the more scarce circumstance. This argument, so fundamental to economics, applies to natural resources. Natural resources are said to be growing more scarce if their relative price is rising over time.

By relative resource price, or rental rate, we refer to the price of the resource in nature. There has been a fair amount of confusion in the past over the proper relationship of natural resources rents, royalties, user costs, net prices, and the like.[4] We do not propose here to sift through this literature, except to say that what we have in mind is the price that a rational individual would pay to have available today one more unit of the natural resource in question. This is applicable to both renewable and nonrenewable resources.

Not everyone agrees that rents are useful scarcity measures. Barnett and Morse argue that rent is not a useful measure of scarcity "in a world of depletion, . . . [or] of sociotechnological change" [1, pp. 225–226]. An increasing rent will reflect increasing scarcity, but increases in rent

---

[4] For a discussion of some of these concepts see [19].

Figure 9-4. Price of iron ore, as adjusted by two different numeraires. (See figure 9-1 for sources.)

Figure 9-3. Price of copper ore as adjusted by two different numeraires. (See figure 9-1 for sources.)

may also be due to "changes in interest rates, relative demand, and expectations concerning future resource availability. Under these conditions, advances in rent on unhomogeneous resources are an ambiguous indicator of increases in scarcity" [1, p. 225].[5] But it is important that a scarcity indicator *does* pick up the influence of these factors. Whether a resource is becoming more scarce or not, for example, ought to depend in part on "expectations about future supplies." We see no economic reason for ranking sources of changes in rental rates, rejecting some and accepting others.[6] It may be that some of the changes are more readily countermanded by public policy than others. This is a quite separate issue. But even if these influences on rental rates are thought to bias this index of scarcity, critics still must show that a fall in interest rates or a rise in tax rates or a change in the structure of competition due to corporate, labor union, or public sector activity, imparts a smaller bias to the index of their choosing. We know of no suggestive evidence, much less substantive research results, to support such a view.

Some question arises over the relation of resource rental rates as defined above and Ricardian rents as measures of scarcity. There is reluctance to view Ricardian rents, such as rents on location or input quality, as valid measures of scarcity. According to Barnett and Morse, for example, the price of urban land may rise, not because of "intrinsic" physical and locational qualities which advance the value of urban land, but because of the fact that man has a "propensity to build where he has already built. . . . Urban rents thus reflect the economic advantages of agglomeration, not disadvantages imposed by nature" [1, p. 226].[7] But the scarcity of any resource is a reflection of the interacting effects of the physical supplies cast up by nature and the demands made on these supplies by man. If people choose to live in cities, then desirable location or accessibility will become a scarce resource. Thus there is no reason to discount changes in urban land rent as a scarcity index. Nevertheless, it is certainly true that the rental rates with which we primarily concern

[5] Barnett and Morse appear to believe that rent as a measure of scarcity requires an assumption of homogeneous land. Marshall argued that "all rents are scarcity rents" [20, p. 351].

[6] The distinguishing feature cannot be degree of permanence. Wars consume vast quantities of natural resources and are more irreversible than government policies in general. Changes in taste which shift demand are not decidedly more or less irrevocable than changes in market structure.

[7] Marshall [20] differentiated among the causes of urban land rent and further distinguished between public and private sources of increased rental values. The private part of land rent stems from the "work and outlay of its individual holders." The public value arises from such factors as the growth of an industrial population near it [21, p. 360]. This part of land rent Barnett and Morse say is unrelated to true scarcity. In contradistinction, Marshall argues that the industrial demand for land is *in all respects* parallel to the agricultural demand [20, p. 373].

ourselves in this paper refer to rents on conventional types of extractive natural resources.

V
Comparisons Among Rival Scarcity Measures

The different scarcity measures can be compared on both conceptual and empirical grounds. Owing to data problems, it is usually easier to do the former than the latter.

Unit Cost and Price. Price data are generally available for specific resources such as copper, bauxite, and the like. Unit cost data are not, however, nor can they be easily constructed from secondary information.

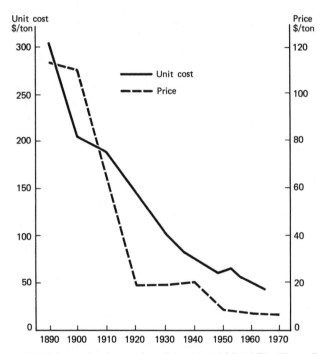

Figure 9-5. Price and unit cost for all metals, 1890–1970. (From L. C. Irland, "Is Timber Scarce? The Economics of a Renewable Resource," Bulletin 83, New Haven, Yale University School of Forestry and Environmental Studies, 1974; J. W. Kendrick, *Postwar Productivity Trends in the United States, 1948–1969,* Washington, D.C., National Bureau of Economic Research, 1973; and R. S. Manthy, *Natural Resource Commodities, 1870–1973: Prices, Output, Consumption, and Employment,* Baltimore, Johns Hopkins University Press for Resources for the Future, 1978.)

Unit cost data have been worked out by Kendrick [3, 22] for natural resource aggregates, "all metals," "all mining," "forestry," and the like, and these may be compared with updated price series for the same aggregates developed by Manthy [23]. Figure 9-5 shows a comparison of unit extraction cost and price for all metals over the past century.

The superiority of price over unit cost as a measure of scarcity is frequently stated in terms of its higher degree of inclusiveness: "The cost that is reflected in price movements over long periods . . . includes not only the cost of mining and processing copper ore, but also the cost of finding and developing deposits" [10, p. 7]. In a variety of circumstances relative price can give a different impression of scarcity than unit extraction costs. If, for example, the elements in price excluded by unit cost are changing over time, there will be a discrepancy. It very well could be the case, as observed by Solow [24] and Schulze [25], that the cost of labor and capital per unit of output is falling, owing to technological progress, but the cost of the natural resource is rising, with a result that product price is constant or falling.[8] The empirical point is made by Irland: "From the Civil War to about 1900, lumber prices were stable while timber prices rose. Prominent forces were the decline in real transport costs and improvements in milling" [14, p. 13]. It is this fact that technological change can intervene and present us with misleading trends in prices of natural resource products which makes this index so problematic. This phenomenon is very likely to happen in resources that are held in common and receive no rent. Then technological change need only keep up with the tendency for capital and labor costs to rise, in order for output price to remain constant. A particularly vivid example is the passenger pigeon, first harvested commercially in about 1840. Tober presents evidence suggesting that the market price for wild pigeons fluctuated, with little tendency to increase, right up until they became effectively extinct in the 1890s [26, p. 181ff.]. A major, though not the sole, reason for this was the development of improved methods for catching the birds.

Passenger pigeons probably had good substitutes in demand, and this illustrates another problem with using price as a scarcity indicator when resource values are observed at early stages of production. A highly elastic demand curve for the private good may permit no scope for substantial and obvious price increases to reflect the social value of preserving a species. Of course the presence of close substitutes casts doubt on the whole notion of what is meant by "scarcity" and "running

[8] The Barnett and Morse relative price test for agriculture shows little change in scarcity, while their unit cost test shows a marked decrease in agricultural scarcity.

out" of a particular resource, at least for those who believe that "running out" is not good.

Price and Rental Rate. The explicit relationship between the rental rate of the natural resources (R) and the natural resource extractive product price (P) is easy to establish. R is simply P weighted by the contribution of natural resources to extractive output (the marginal product of natural resources).

Suppose there are reserves of natural resources, S_t, which can be depleted by use, denoted by R_t, and augmented by a discovery process, denoted by $D(E, t)$ where E is some input. At all times,

$$S_t = S_{t-1} + D(E, t) - R_t \tag{5}$$

Production of final output is governed by a constant returns-to-scale production function,

$$Q = F(L, R, t) \tag{6}$$

where L represents labor or some composite input. Time subscripts are added only when necessary to avoid possible confusion. We have specified a very simple relationship between the natural resource (R) and final output Q. There is, however, no reason why (6) cannot represent a compact way of writing a production process which includes extractive, processing, . . . and final product production. L can then be thought of as a vector. The objective function for the owner of natural resources with profit-maximizing motives is

$$W(L, E, R) = \sum_t \{PQ - P_E E - WL + \lambda_t[-S_t + S_{t-1} \\ + D(E, t) - R_t]\}\theta^t \tag{7}$$

where the discount factor, $\theta^t = 1/(1 + r)^t$, λ_t is a Langrangian, and the cost of variable factors, W and P_E are parametric.

Anticipating only interior solutions, the necessary conditions for a maximization of $W(\cdot)$ yield[9]

$$PF_L = W \tag{8a}$$

$$PF_R = \lambda \text{ and} \tag{8b}$$

$$\lambda D_E = P_E \tag{8c}$$

Equation $(8a)$ says quite simply that in every period natural resources should be used in amounts which equalize the shadow price (λ)

---

[9] When discovery is not possible, our model, adjusted for a boundary value solution, readily yields the standard result that the price of natural resources rises at the rate of discount. From (7)

$$\frac{\partial W}{\partial S_t} = \theta^{t+1} \lambda_{t+1} + \theta^t \lambda_t = 0, \text{ whence } \lambda_{t+1} = \lambda_t \theta^{-1} = \lambda_t(1 + r)$$

or rental rate of the natural resource with the value of its marginal product. It shows clearly the relationship between product price and rental rate: these two measures of scarcity differ by the marginal product of natural resources, bearing a constant relationship to each other only in the unlikely case that F_R is constant through time.[10] Rearranging (8b) and differentiating with respect to time yields

$$\frac{\dot{P}}{P} = \frac{\dot{\lambda}}{\lambda} - \frac{\dot{F}_R}{F_R} \tag{9}$$

The last term in this expression can be put into more familiar terms, using the assumption of constant returns to scale and the standard expression for σ, the elasticity of substitution. Letting r be the resource-labor ratio, (9) becomes

$$\frac{\dot{P}}{P} = \frac{\dot{\lambda}}{\lambda} + \frac{\alpha}{\sigma}\left(\frac{\dot{r}}{r}\right) \tag{10}$$

where α is the share of nonresource inputs in total output.[11]

When substitution is possible, product price underestimates the seriousness of growing natural resource scarcity because price rises less rapidly than the rental rate of natural resources. Second, the magnitude of this bias varies directly with the share of output going to factors other than natural resources. This is a particularly serious criticism since it is widely believed, and there is supporting empirical evidence that the share of natural resources in production is small [28, 29]. Our research corroborates this finding with respect to pulp and paper, steel, aluminum, and copper. It is also true that neutral and capital- or labor-augmenting technological progress drives down the cost of production and product price, movements unrelated to changing natural resource prices.

The connection between these two measures of scarcity and the unit cost of extraction output is not drawn as easily. Still, these measures can be compared under a special case when substitution is not possible between natural resources and other inputs in the production of natural

---

[10] Suppose a more elaborate production process was specified

$Q = h(L, I)$

$I = g(L, E)$

$E = \psi(L, R)$

where I is intermediate product and E is extractive output. Then (8.2) becomes

$$p \frac{\partial Q}{\partial I} \frac{\partial I}{\partial E} \frac{\partial E}{\partial R} = \lambda$$

It is still true that product price and rental rate differ by the marginal product of natural resources, but its computation is just a bit more roundabout.

[11] This result is more general than that of Dasgupta and Heal [27, p. 11] which holds when $\dot{\lambda}/\lambda$ is rising at the rate of discount.

resource-intensive extractive products. In this case, the extractive product price will change by the absolute amount of any change in the rental rate, as long as the prices of other inputs aren't changing and output expands at the rate inputs increase. Under these conditions, the unit cost of extractive output remains constant, wrongly signifying no changes in scarcity, while the two other indexes are signaling increasing scarcity when the prices of natural resources are rising. The fixed coefficient assumption lets the natural resource cost component move separately from the unit cost element which, in turn, is changed by technological progress affecting capital, labor, and so forth. Thus, the *path* of the unit cost of extractive output will bear no necessary relationship to increasing natural resource scarcity or impending exhaustion. This may be an empirically uninteresting case because it is unlikely that fixed coefficients will occur in practice. But its consideration is useful because it shows us what is going on and helps us see an important point: owners of natural resources express their best guess about the future prospects for discovery and avoidance of exhaustion through changes in the rental rate. Such forward-looking adjustments occur quite independently of present changes in the unit cost of extractive output.

A rising rental rate always portends increasing scarcity and eventual exhaustion, unless there is a "backstop technology" [as in, e.g., 30]. A rising unit cost or price of extractive output gives an ambiguous signal. However, a rental rate increasing at a given rate provides no information about the date of resource exhaustion. On the other hand, the *price level* of the natural resource relative to correctly measured other prices is a measure of scarcity and an indication of the perceived consequence of exhaustion. The indicator is accurate insofar as the markets are competitive and those bearing the burden of exhaustion can express their preferences or, if they are future generations, have their preferences accurately expressed by present traders.

Rental rates have been rejected on practical grounds because they are not readily available. There is some truth in this. Rental rates for minerals are the prices of given deposits that hold, with some probabilities, prospective quantities and qualities of ore. Companies engaged in exploiting these deposits, or in looking for new deposits, are loath to make public the sort of price information that might put them at a competitive disadvantage. Given the fact that each deposit has its own unique characteristics, the motive of profit maximization is likely to be better served if full price information does not become widespread. To this must be coupled the fact that valuation of deposits usually has enormous tax implications for the people who own them.

There is one important exception to the paucity of data on rental

236

GARDNER M. BROWN, JR., AND BARRY FIELD

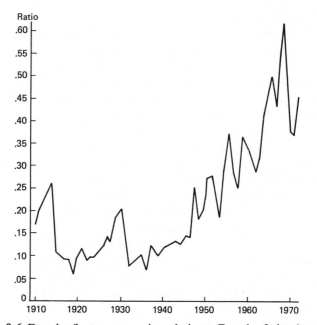

Figure 9-6. Douglas fir stumpage price relative to Douglas fir lumber price. (Taken from USDA Forest Service, "The Demand and Price Situation for Forest Prices, 1972," Washington, GPO, 1972; U.S. Bureau of Census, *Historical Statistics of the United States, 1789–1945,* Washington, GPO, 1949; *Long-Term Economic Growth, 1860–1945,* Washington, GPO, 1966; and *Statistical Abstracts of the United States 1974,* Washington, GPO, 1974.)

rates. The U.S. Forest Service manages a significant fraction of this nation's timber supply. The technical term for the rental value of standing timber is the stumpage price. It can be seen (figure 9-6) that the stumpage price of Douglas fir relative to Douglas fir lumber price has risen rather sharply through time, while the "unit cost of extractive output" has fallen (figure 9-7).[12] For the past fifty years, the "unit cost" halved but the stumpage price (relative to extractive product price) increased by about a factor of four. Note also that the two indexes move in opposite fashion. Whenever the stumpage prices increase within a decade, the unit cost falls, and vice versa. Figure 9-8 shows that the stumpage price of Douglas fir relative to the quality adjusted wage rate

[12] Douglas fir stumpage prices and lumber prices were obtained from the U.S. Forest Service [31]. Employment data came from Potter and Christy [2] and the U.S. Bureau of Census [32, 33, 34].

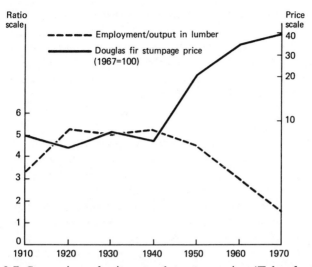

Figure 9-7. Comparison of unit cost and stumpage price. (Taken from
N. Potter and F. T. Christy Jr., *Trends in Natural Resource Commodities:
Statistics of Prices, Output, Consumption, Foreign Trade and Employment in the United States, 1860–1959,* Baltimore, Johns Hopkins University Press for Resources for the Future, 1962; see figure 9-6 for other
sources.)

has increased since about 1920. The increase is comparable to the rise
when the numeraire is the unadjusted wage rate.[13]

VI
When Conventional Scarcity Indicators May Fail

There are four reasons why rental rates and product price poorly
measure increasing natural resource scarcity. First, many valuable resources such as passenger pigeons, whales, salmon, and migratory water-
fowl are common property resources. No spot markets post daily or
annual prices for these resources. In the absence of public intervention,
harvesters will make decisions on the assumption that the stock has zero
value. Thus, actual rental rates are not good measures of scarcity in
this instance, and resources are depleted at too fast a rate.

[13] The conclusion of increasing scarcity from these data very likely is unaffected
by observations [35] that the private timber companies do not pay competitive
stumpage values. Even if the accusations are true, they bear on level of stumpage
values, not the path over time.

Second, in the absence of forward markets, traders in natural resources have to form their own expectations about future prices. Geoffrey Heal [36] has shown that the assumptions about how expectations are formed and the value economic parameters take on, can produce a full range of rates of extraction relative to an optimal rate. Therefore, formal analysis or intuition can lead reasonable men to become alarmed about the propriety of using current rental rates (or product price) as valid measures of scarcity.

Third, much has been written about the misallocation of resources which arises when there are no markets for contingent commodities. Heal's helpful discussion of the problem in the context of natural resources makes it unnecessary to dwell on the subject. It is sufficient to note that depletion proceeds too rapidly and consumption shifts to the more certain present if traders are risk averse on balance. Since simple and complex forward markets are virtually nonexistent, it is no wonder that prudent men doubt the accuracy of actual prices or rental rates as scarcity measures.

Finally, spot and futures markets may exist but their prices may fail to reflect the existence of aggregate demand for the public goods aspects of natural resources. Although it is difficult to quantify, a broad spectrum of people believe there is economic value in such nonexclusory services

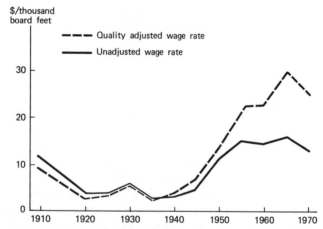

Figure 9-8. Douglas fir stumpage price relative to unadjusted wage rates. (Taken from E. F. Denison, *The Sources of Economic Growth in the United States and the Alternatives Before Us,* Supplementary paper 13, Committee for Economic Development, 1962; *Accounting for U.S. Economic Growth,* 1929–1969, Washington, D.C., Brookings Institution, 1974; for other sources see figure 9-7.)

as maintaining the gene pool, preserving species diversity, and knowing that a particularly wondrous natural setting will remain undeveloped. Yet it is difficult for these demands to find accurate expression in markets, most of which don't even exist. S. V. Ciriacy-Wantrup [37] spoke persuasively about this general point twenty-five years ago, recommending the adoption of a safe minimum standard which would prohibit extinction of species; and John Krutilla [38] a decade ago expressed his case for less depletion in terms of the potential contribution of a species or botanical specimen to scientific discovery in general and to modern medicine in particular. The passenger pigeon again provides an example. The path or rental rates did not rise because improved methods of harvest were developed. None of the scarcity measures was a harbinger of extinction. But even if the passenger pigeon was not a common property resource, it would have been extremely difficult to express future certain private demands and future certain and uncertain demands for nonconsumptive (public) uses in markets that did not exist.

VII
Other Scarcity Indicators

While work ought to continue on the comparative evaluation of conventional scarcity indicators, the search should also be pressed for appropriate modifications of these indexes and development of new indexes. In this section we discuss some new directions in natural resource scarcity measures.

Modification of Conventional Measures. With the rising interest in environmental quality, it has become common to point out that conventional scarcity indicators do not take environmental costs into account. Should these costs actually be going up through time, the conventional indexes may be giving us misleading signals regarding natural resources scarcity, broadly considered. We need to consider two things: (1) Of the three conventional indexes, unit cost, output price, and rent, is there any reason to suspect that one may be more sensitive than the others in terms of environmental impacts? (2) What feasible modifications might be made in the conventional indexes to heighten their environmental sensitivity?

Regarding question (1), the most interesting subquestion is whether rents might be more effective in picking up the effects of environmental scarcity than would unit extraction costs. It seems clear that unit extraction costs, defined so as to exclude the value of the natural resource, will never be able to pick up environmental costs unless regulations or taxes are instituted to cause these costs to be internalized. On the other hand, we think it barely possible that rental rates might be sensitive to entrepreneurial expectations regarding the likelihood of being forced to undertake environmental costs in the future. We know of nobody who has tried to model this phenomenon, and suggest that it might be worthwhile for someone to do so, at least on the strictly theoretical level.

The other part of this question concerns the possibility of developing something like environmental impact shadow prices that might be used to adjust conventional scarcity indexes. Take, for example, the unit cost of extracting copper ore as it has behaved through recent history. Might it be possible to adjust this cost to reflect the amount of environmental damage attributable to copper mining during this period?

Elasticities of Substitution. Perhaps the search for exact measures of natural resource scarcity is misguided owing both to conceptual and to empirical difficulties. Attention might better be redirected from trying to determine if we are running out of particular resources to the question of the ability of the economic system to adjust and accommodate to increasing resource scarcities if and when they occur.

The process of "running out" of a natural resource need not cause much alarm if it is easy to substitute conventional inputs or more plentiful natural resources for the scarce natural resource. A resource is not scarce, in this sense, as long as it is easy to find substitutes. This suggests that a useful scarcity index might be the elasticity of substitution, which depicts the responsiveness of changes in the use of natural resources and conventional inputs to changes in their prices. To our knowledge only two studies [28, 39] present estimates of elasticities of substitution involving natural resources. The resource commodity in the study by Humphrey and Moroney is an aggregate of nineteen resources.[14]

We have explored, on the other hand, the possibility of estimating elasticities of substitution for individual resources such as copper, aluminum, pulp and paper, and steel.[15] Our estimates indicate that technology

[14] There are several very recent studies dealing exclusively with energy and the substitutability of conventional inputs for energy inputs [see 40, 41, 42, 43].

[15] We used a translog production function specification, which does not require an assumption that the elasticity of substitution is constant over the full range of input combinations. The translog function has been discussed at length elsewhere [44, 45] so we need not go into details here. Briefly, for an n-input translog function, we have

$$\ln Q = \ln \alpha_0 + \sum_j \alpha_j \ln X_j + \tfrac{1}{2} \sum_j \sum_k \gamma_{jk} \ln X_j \ln X_k$$

$$j, k = 1, \ldots, n,$$

Table 9-4.   Measures of Responsiveness for Selected Natural Resources, 1967

Elasticity of substitution between:	Steel	Aluminum	Copper[a]	Pulp and paper
Labor and natural resources	4.5	3.0	15.1	1.9
Capital and labor	1.0	1.4	0.6	0.8
Capital and natural resources	3.0	3.4	9.4	6.0

Source: See footnote 14.
[a] Estimates are for 1963.

favors users of pulp and paper and that it is very easy to use capital and labor in place of pulp and paper in the production of goods using these services (table 9-4). It is only slightly more difficult to make substitutions between capital and labor in the pulp and paper-using sectors. A case in point has been the recent increase in the use of mechanical wood chippers for converting formerly nonusable logging residue into a readily usable form as an input into paper and building board manufacturing.

The conclusion that the natural resource input has good substitutes also holds for steel, copper, and aluminum. In the first two cases, however, labor is a more facile substitute for the resource than is capital, while for aluminum the opposite is the case.

VIII
Further Research Directions

We thought it would be useful to have a look at contemporary research on this topic to jog our imagination about future research directions. The results are hardly electrifying as judged by what the Smithsonian Science Information Exchange spewed forth under the subject of "The Economics of Natural Resources Scarcity." Of about fifty entries for the recent year, one-third were devoted to studies of energy resources; 15 percent pertained to increasing the efficiency of processes related to coal and oil development and use; three focused on geothermal

---

where Q is output and the X's are inputs. The coefficients are estimated by using the first-order conditions:

$$M_j = \alpha_j + \sum_k \gamma_{jk} \ln X_k$$

where M_j is the share of the jth input in total cost. Estimation was done by means of iterative Zellner-efficient estimation. After estimating the γ_{jk} we use these, together with the M_j, to construct estimates of the Allen partial elasticities of substitution. Data were gathered from publications of the departments of agriculture [31] and commerce [46–50]. For steel, aluminum, and copper the data refer to fabrication processes, in which processed metal is combined with other inputs to produce final output; for pulp and paper the data refer to all four-digit industries consuming pulp and paper in significant quantities.

resources; 20 percent were resource (or residuals) specific such as zinc, sand, and gravel, forests and water (four); about 20 percent seemed to have been misfiled or the grant jargon made them impenetrable ("explore and adopt new computational tools . . . for rapid processing"). Only about 10 percent of the projects (most of whose project investigators are at this conference) seemed interesting. Frankly, the compilation dulled our senses.

Obtaining Better Estimates of Elasticities of Substitution. Since elasticities of substitution warn us about how difficult it will be to substitute other inputs for natural resources if they grow more scarce, it makes sense to pursue this kind of research in a number of ways. First, studies should be expanded to cover more individual natural resources such as lumber, lead, zinc, and so forth.

Second, for some natural resources such as mercury (based on the information available for deliveries of resources to purchasing SIC sectors) there may be too few observations. Thus the statistical precision of the estimates using such data is questionable. Some of these resources having few entries also are in short physical supply. It would be productive to explore the possibility of estimating elasticities of substitution by using cross-section data across states.

Third, another way to expand sample size is to conduct the analysis using cross-section data obtained from different countries. Sufficient data are available to study ferrous and nonferrous metals in this fashion.

Fourth, it would be desirable to adduce empirical evidence to test the analytical proposition that changes in the Barnett and Morse measure of unit cost of extractive output, instead of signaling decreasing natural resource scarcity, may simply be revealing that substitution possibilities are diminishing over time. To test this hypothesis, investigations should be undertaken of the trend in elasticities of substitution through time and/or for different time periods.

The analytical and estimation procedures we used to estimate elasticities of substitution are so new that there remain many snags to be worked out. We are particularly concerned about the sensitivity of our results to changes in definitions of capital and labor; inclusion or exclusion of intermediate goods in the analysis; and related definitional matters. Some of our estimates do not seem completely reasonable and work ought to be carried out to develop more accurate measures in these cases.

The elasticity of substitution provides relative information about ease of substituting other inputs for natural resources. The analysis leaves out a major source of adjustment, the possibility of substituting away from natural resource-intensive products and into other goods. On the one hand, the concept of the price elasticity of demand for a natural resource captures explicity the two major adjustment possibilities resulting from increasing scarcity of natural resources: the adjustment from one natural resource-intensive product to another product and from one natural resource input to other inputs. On the other hand, the general unavailability of rental rates on natural resources has precluded estimation of the price elasticity of demand for natural resources by other investigators. Now, however, the price elasticity of demand for natural resources can be estimated by combining separate estimates of the elasticity of substitution which we have begun to obtain and estimates of output elasticities which remain to be done.

Analysis of Rental Rates. Rental rates for natural resources are not readily available. We have uncovered one important exception. Offshore or onshore oil leases periodically are auctioned off at public sales. Successful bid prices are published. The U.S. Geological Survey makes estimates of the oil and gas supplies on these properties and these data are available in field offices. It should be possible to construct an index of the price of oil *in situ* during the past two decades or so.

We are not optimistic that rental rates for various minerals can be obtained by searching through the trade journals and publications. One finds sales prices occasionally posted but mineral quantities rarely, if ever, are mentioned. On the other hand, earlier we showed the connection between rental rates and discovery costs. Discovery costs may be fairly good proxies for rental rates. In real life, the exploration and discovery processes are quite complicated, therefore more sophisticated models are appropriate before large-scale empirical work is undertaken. The fact that exploration is subject to uncertainty, for example, may drive a wedge between rents and marginal exploration costs, depending on such factors as prospectors' attitudes toward risk. It may also be necessary to adjust here, as always, for market structure effects that can lead to exploration becoming a tool for "market control, price maintenance, preclusive aggrandizement, perpetuation of management, premature acquisitiveness under conditions of imperfect tenure, etc." [19, p. 356]. Furthermore, information externalities may be an important distorting factor in the discovery process, as analyzed by Peterson [51]. Nevertheless, for those willing to make a perfectly competitive "leap of faith," comparing the trend in discovery costs over time (as a proxy for rental rates) with product price and unit cost may be a tractable exercise.

Special Studies of Renewable Resources. We are struck by public concern that we are running out of nonrenewable resources such as oil.

Yet the most famous cases of resource exhaustion or truly threatened exhaustion are all drawn from the renewable category. Instances of near exhaustion caused by commercial harvest are easy to find and include the beaver, buffalo, Alaskan fur seal, and most recently, the blue whale. Some people recently have gone so far as to conclude that many of our "nonrenewable" resources are, for all practical purposes, available without limit, as new technology becomes available to exploit lower quality stocks and as substitution phenomena continue. This implies that more of our attention ought to be devoted to "renewable" resources, particularly those that have run out, or nearly so. It would be very instructive to establish, for a number of these renewable resources, how the different scarcity indexes performed as the resources approached exhaustion. It would also be valuable to identify those social mechanisms through which exhaustion was averted (in those cases where it actually was). One of those mechanisms undoubtedly would be substitution in production, similar to the process covered in detail above for "nonrenewable" resources. But there may be more potent social processes at work and available for public policy. In the case of renewable resources, the most effective way of dealing with threatening exhaustion (extinction) may be changes in the social institutions which determine the rate at which particular natural resources are exploited. More needs to be done along the lines of careful case studies of renewable resources to identify how public policy and economic institutions changed (or did not change) in response to scarcity situations, and how these changes affected the resources in question.

Incorporating Uncertainty. We have mentioned that the lack of forward markets and markets for contingent commodities casts doubt on the accuracy of conventional natural resource scarcity indicators. It would be very useful to derive accurate indicators of natural resource scarcity given that these futures markets do not exist. There may even be some plausible adjustments to apply to one or more of the conventional measures. It seems reasonable to believe that the failure of the futures markets has tilted consumption of natural resources toward the more certain present. Is this bias most pronounced in those resources about which there is most uncertainty? Since there is so much uncertainty surrounding the available quantity of natural resources *in situ* and regarding future demand, it makes a good deal of sense to encourage applied research to stem from models in which the variables take on a stochastic character.

Thomas Tietenberg made a similar point at the Conference on the Political Economy of Depletable Resources [21]. A proceedings document with the same name contains useful ideas for future research. Some of them sounded nonoperational, a number were tied specifically to energy research, and others are not amenable to easy summarization. But a few should be mentioned: (1) ideal institutional and policy arrangements for dealing with depletion should be compared with the actual; (2) principles for evaluating resource management and using institutions should be formulated and tested; (3) the formation and behavior of cartels, particularly international ones, was thought to be an attractive subject, not surprisingly, in light of OPEC's evident ability to flex its profitable muscles.

Research about the optimal size of the genetic reservoir and the distribution of its components provides a fine opportunity for an interdisciplinary endeavor containing applied and empirical content as well as having a heavy component of uncertainty. Only a little work has been done (namely, Myers [52]) on this most basic natural resource of all.

IX
Concluding Remarks

Controversial issues are seldom resolved by one study or by one conference. Our more modest hope is that this paper increases the reluctance of investigators to conclude from trends in unit cost and product price that natural resources are growing more or less scarce through time. It may be too much to expect that vast sums of money now will be devoted to the estimation of time series data on natural resource rental rates, a superior measure of scarcity. But the identification of growing natural resource scarcity in an economic sense would be facilitated if public agencies began to assemble data on the costs of discovering selected natural resources over time. A time series begun this year soon would have merit for indicating where we are going, even if it is silent about historical scarcity.

References

1. H. J. Barnett and C. Morse, *Scarcity and Growth: The Economics of Natural Resource Availability* (Baltimore, Johns Hopkins University Press for Resources for the Future, 1963).

2. N. Potter and F. T. Christy, Jr., *Trends in Natural Resource Commodities: Statistics of Prices, Output, Consumption, Foreign Trade and Employment in the United States 1860–1957* (Baltimore, Johns Hopkins University Press for Resources for the Future, 1962).

3. J. W. Kendrick, *Productivity Trends in the United States* (Princeton, N. J., Princeton University Press, 1961).

4. P. Bradley, "Increasing Scarcity: The Case of Energy Resources," *American Economic Review* vol. 63 (May 1973) pp. 119–125.

5. A. C. Fisher, J. V. Krutilla, and C. Cicchetti, "The Economics of Environmental Preservation: A Theoretical and Empirical Analysis," *American Economic Review* vol. 62 (September 1972) pp. 605–619.

6. E. J. Mishan, "Ills, Bads, and Disamenities: The Wages of Growth," in M. Olson and H. Landsberg, eds., *The No-Growth Society* (New York Norton, 1973) pp. 63–87.

7. M. Roberts, "On Reforming Economic Growth," in M. Olson and H. Landsberg, eds., *The No-Growth Society* (New York, Norton, 1973) pp. 119–139.

8. V. Kerry Smith, "The Effect of Technological Change on Different Uses of Environmental Resources," in J. V. Krutilla, ed., *Natural Environments* (Baltimore, Johns Hopkins University Press for Resources for the Future, 1972).

9. C. Morse, "Discussion," *American Economic Review* vol. 63 (May 1973) pp. 126–128.

10. O. C. Herfindahl, *Copper Costs and Prices: 1870–1957* (Baltimore, Johns Hopkins University Press for Resources for the Future, 1959).

11. R. B. Norgaard, "Resource Scarcity and New Technology in U. S. Petroleum Development," *Natural Resources Journal* vol. 15 (April 1975) pp. 265–295.

12. V. Kerry Smith, "A Re-Evaluation of the Natural Resource Scarcity Hypothesis," Paper presented at the meetings of the Western Economic Association, June 25, 1975.

13. V. W. Ruttan and J. C. Callahan, "Resource Inputs and Output Growth: Comparison Between Agriculture and Forestry," *Forest Science* vol. 8 (March 1962) pp. 68–82.

14. L. C. Irland, *Is Timber Scarce: The Economics of a Renewable Resource.* Bulletin no. 83 (New Haven, Yale University School of Forestry and Environmental Studies, 1974).

15. W. D. Nordhaus, "Resources as a Constraint on Growth," *American Economic Review* vol. 64 (May 1974) pp. 22–26.

16. D. Jorgenson and Z. Griliches, "The Explanation of Productivity Change," *Review of Economic Studies* vol. 34 (July 1967) pp. 250–282.

17. E. F. Denison, *The Sources of Economic Growth in the United States and the Alternatives Before Us.* Supplementary Paper 13, Committee for Economic Development, 1962 (Reprinted 1973).

18. E. F. Denison, *Accounting for U. S. Economic Growth 1929–1969* (Washington, D.C., Brookings Institution, 1974).

19. M. Gaffney, ed., *Extractive Resources and Taxation* (Madison, University of Wisconsin Press, 1967).

20. A. Marshall, *Principles of Economics* (London, Macmillan, 1959).

21. A. C. Fisher (Conference Organizer), Conference on the Political Economy of Depletable Resources, sponsored by National Science Foundation at Brookings Institution, June 9–10, 1975.

22. J. W. Kendrick, *Postwar Productivity Trends in the United States 1948–1969* (Washington, D.C., National Bureau of Economic Research, 1973).

23. R. S. Manthy, *Natural Resource Commodities 1870–1973: Prices, Output, Consumption, and Employment* (Baltimore, Johns Hopkins University Press for Resources for the Future, 1978).

24. R. M. Solow, "Richard T. Ely Lecture: The Economics of Resources or the Resources of Economics," *American Economic Review* vol. 64 (May 1974) pp. 1–14.

25. W. D. Schulze, "The Optimal Use of Non-Renewable Resources: The Theory of Extraction," *Journal of Environmental Economics and Management* vol. 1 (May 1974) pp. 53–73.

26. James A. Tober, "The Allocation of Wildlife Resources in the United States, 1850–1900." Unpublished Ph.D. dissertation, Yale University, 1974.

27. P. Dasgupta and G. Heal, "The Optimal Depletion of Exhaustible Resources," *Review of Economic Studies* Symposium Issue (1974) pp. 3–28.

28. H. Binswanger, "The Measurement of Technical Change Biases with Many Factors of Production," *American Economic Review* vol. 64 (December 1974) pp. 964–976.

29. T. Schultz, *The Economic Organization of Agriculture* (New York, McGraw-Hill, 1953).

30. W. D. Nordhaus, "The Allocation of Energy Resources," *Brookings Papers on Economic Activity* no. 3 (Washington, D.C., Brookings Institution, 1973) pp. 529–570.

31. U.S. Department of Agriculture, Forest Service. *The Demand and Price Situation for Forest Products, 1972* (Washington, GPO, 1972).

32. U.S. Department of Commerce, Bureau of the Census, *Historical Statistics of the United States 1789–1945* (Washington, GPO, 1949).

33. U.S. Department of Commerce, Bureau of the Census, *Long-Term Economic Growth 1860–1965* (Washington, GPO, 1966).

34. U.S. Department of Commerce, Bureau of the Census, *Statistical Abstract of the United States 1974* (Washington, GPO, 1974).

35. W. J. Mead, "Natural Resources Disposal Policy—Oral Auction versus Sealed Bids," *Natural Resources Journal* vol. 7 (April 1967) pp. 194–224.

36. G. Heal, "Economic Aspects of Natural Resource Depletion," in D. W. Pearce and J. Rose, eds., *The Economics of Natural Resource Depletion* (New York, Wiley, 1975) pp. 118–139.

37. S. V. Ciriacy-Wantrup, *Resource Conservation* (Berkeley, University of California, 1952).

38. J. V. Krutilla, "Conservation Reconsidered," *American Economic Review* vol. 57 (September 1967) pp. 777–786.

39. D. B. Humphrey and J. R. Moroney, "Substitution Among Capital, Labor and Natural Resource Products in American Manufacturing," *Journal of Political Economy* vol. 83 (February 1975) pp. 57–82.

40. S. E. Atkinson and R. E. Halvorsen, "Interfuel Substitution in Steam

Electric Power Generation," *Journal of Political Economy* vol. 84 (October 1976) pp. 959–978.

41. E. R. Berndt and D. O. Wood, "Technology, Prices and the Derived Demand for Energy," *Review of Economic Statistics* vol. 57 (August 1975) pp. 259–268.

42. M. Fuss, "The Demand for Energy in Canadian Manufacturing: An Example of the Estimation of Production Structures with Many Inputs," *Journal of Econometrics* vol. 5 (January 1977) pp. 89–116.

43. J. M. Griffin and P. R. Gregory, "An Inter-Country Translog Model of Energy Substitution Responses," *American Economic Review* vol. 66 (December 1976) pp. 845–857.

44. E. R. Berndt and L. R. Christensen, "The Translog Function and the Substitution of Equipment, Structures and Labor in U.S. Manufacturing 1929–68," *Journal of Econometrics* vol. 1 (March 1973) pp. 81–114.

45. L. R. Christensen, D. W. Jorgenson, and L. J. Lau, "Transcendental Logarithmic Production Frontiers," *Review of Economic Statistics* vol. 60 (February 1973) pp. 28–45.

46. U.S. Department of Commerce, Bureau of the Census, *Census of Manufacturers, 1963,* vol. 1, *Summary and Subject Statistics* (Washington, GPO, 1966).

47. U.S. Department of Commerce, Bureau of the Census, *Annual Survey of Manufacturers, 1964 and 1965* (Washington, GPO, 1968).

48. U.S. Department of Commerce, Bureau of the Census, *Census of Manufacturers, 1967,* vol. 1, *Summary and Subject Statistics* (Washington, GPO, 1971).

49. U.S. Department of Commerce, Bureau of the Census. *Annual Survey of Manufacturers, 1968 and 1969* (Washington, GPO, 1973).

50. U.S. Department of Commerce, Office of Business Economics. *Input–Output Structure of the U.S. Economy, 1967,* 3 vols (Washington, GPO, 1974).

51. F. M. Peterson, "The Theory of Exhaustible Natural Resources: A Classical Variational Approach," Unpublished Ph.D. dissertation, Princeton University, 1972.

52. N. Myers, "An Expanded Approach to the Problem of Disappearing Species," *Science* vol. 193 (July 16, 1976) pp. 198–202.

10

Measures of Natural Resource Scarcity

Anthony C. Fisher

I
Introduction: Physical and Economic Scarcity

The widely publicized predictions of impending scarcity and even exhaustion of extractive natural resources such as metals and fuels, in the Club of Rome study *The Limits to Growth,* and the less widely publicized rebuttals (see, for example, Beckerman [1], Nordhaus [2], and Kay and Mirrlees [3]) suggest that a careful analysis of what is meant by resource scarcity, and of how it is measured or indicated, might be worthwhile. This paper is intended to provide such an analysis. Specifically, in this section I consider the meaning of scarcity, and in subsequent sections a number of proposed measures, their properties, and their behavior as a resource stock is depleted or augmented over time.

Perhaps the question, "What is scarcity?" is too simple for economists, or at any rate, too simple to be made explicit. We ordinarily say a good—or a resource—is scarce if the quantity demanded exceeds the quantity supplied at some benchmark price, such as the prevailing one, so that in a competitive market there is an upward pressure on the price. As a special case, goods are sometimes considered scarce, or "economic," as opposed to "free," if this excess demand is positive at a *zero* price. But much of the current debate about natural resource scarcity focuses on *physical* measures, such as the stock of reserves. To obtain some idea of the economic implications of an estimated reserve base, it is typically compared with another physical quantity, projected consumption, giving rise to conclusions on how many years' worth of coal, or iron, or whatever is left at current or projected rates of consumption.[1]

Now, a physical measure such as reserves makes no sense for a non-

I am grateful to Bengt Hansson, Geoffrey Heal, Alvin Klevorick, Harvey Lapan, and Karl-Göran Mäler for helpful discussions and comments on an earlier draft.

[1] One of the best examples of this type of analysis is *Population, Resources, and Environment,* a report of the (U.S.) Commission on Population Growth and the American Future [4].

extractive commodity, since we can, at a cost, produce as much as we want. Except in the very short run, "reserves" are not important. But looking more closely at extractive resources, the simple distinction begins to blur. That is, it is not clear that there really is a limited stock, at least one corresponding to reserves. Reserves are defined as the known amounts of a mineral that can be profitably recovered at current prices for the mineral and the inputs used in extracting and processing it.[2] Obviously, then, reserves can be expanded by, among other things, discoveries of new deposits or technical changes which convert formerly uneconomic materials, such as ores with low metal content, into "reserves." We might say that the stock of an extractive resource can be augmented by investing in information, just as the number of effective units of labor can be augmented by human capital formation—or for that matter, the supply of any nonextractive commodity. But if this is true, then the economic concept of scarcity, rising price, becomes significant for extractive natural resources as well as these other items. The point is that for most, if not all, resources it is difficult to speak precisely about physical scarcity, either because we are uncertain about the extent, location, and quality of deposits, or because of ambiguities in the definition of ultimately recoverable reserves. Coal deposits, for example, though subject to less uncertainty than those of oil and gas, and most metallic minerals, are (necessarily) rather arbitrarily reckoned as consisting only of a given thickness of seam, and at most a given overburden of soil.[3] The economic measure, price, then, is a kind of summary statistic, reflecting a precise outcome of conflicting influences on an unknown and perhaps unknowable physical magnitude.

The similarity of extractive and nonextractive resources may be a bit overdrawn. One could object that in the long run extraction is bound by the finite stocks of minerals in the earth's crust. Long before these limits are reached, it is likely that the incremental energy and environmental costs of extraction would become prohibitive. In the next section I shall set out a fairly traditional model of competitive extraction under certainty, that is, a model which does not explicitly include investment in augmenting the resource stock. But later on I consider, less formally, how results might be affected by such augmentation. In succeeding sections investment in creating reserves by exploration is made endogenous to the model.

The purpose of the model in the next section is to bring out the relationships between a number of different economic scarcity measures

---

[2] This is the generally accepted definition, as explained in greater detail by Schanz [5], drawing on U.S. Geological Survey publications and practice.

[3] For precise specifications, see Darmstadter [6].

that have been proposed for resources. I have referred to rising price as "the" measure of scarcity, but as we shall see, resources *are* different. There are at least two candidates for price measures: the ordinary market price, and something that might be called a pure scarcity rent, the value of a unit of the resource "in the ground." Further, in the most influential study to date, that by Barnett and Morse [7], still another measure, the unit cost of extractive output, is emphasized. This in fact derives from perhaps the earliest scarcity theorist, Malthus, who believed that increasing agricultural output would require ever-increasing "doses" of labor and capital, and also from Ricardo, who extended this conclusion to mineral output.[4] A simple model of optimal extraction by a competitive firm will not only bring out the relationships between these measures, but will shed some light on how each is affected by changes in the resource stock.

Broadly speaking, the conclusion is that each is well behaved, in the sense that it is generally (though not always, as we shall see) negatively related to the size of the stock. That is, the smaller the stock, the higher the price (rent, cost), and the larger the stock, the lower the price (rent, cost). But it does not follow that all three are equally sensitive or accurate measures of scarcity. This raises the question of what properties such a measure should have. In the remainder of this section I propose an answer that enables us to discriminate at least between cost, price, and rent. Also, I attempt to justify briefly the statement made at the outset that an inquiry into the meaning and measurement of scarcity may be worthwhile.

Perhaps the two key questions about natural resource use that have emerged in the recent theoretical literature are (1) whether the time pattern of extraction produced by a competitive market is socially efficient and (2) how various sources of market imperfection—monopoly, externalities, etc.—distort the competitive pattern.[5] Implicit in these questions is the possibility that market-determined rates of extraction could be too slow, as well as too rapid. So in a sense my concern with scarcity is a restricted one. It assumes that the underconsumption of resource stocks is less of a problem than overconsumption. Two things can be said about this. First, there is no presumption that (existing) markets do, on balance, overconsume; this has not been demonstrated in the literature.

---

[4] For a clear and informative discussion of the views of the classical economists, see Barnett and Morse [7, pp. 51–71].

[5] See the several studies in the *Review of Economic Studies Symposium on the Economics of Exhaustible Resources*. Resource market imperfections are also classified and analyzed by Sweeney [8], and Kay and Mirrlees [3]. Nordhaus [9], Solow [10], and Heal [11] consider in particular the problems caused by the lack of futures markets.

Second, however, it seems reasonable to worry more about the consequences of this possibility. As Common [12] has put it:

Depleting finite stocks of fossil fuels closes our future options in a way that
depreciating a capital stock does not, in that the former is irreversible while the
latter is not. Given labour and natural resources, capital equipment can be
created from scratch: if, today, the world's entire capital stock were destroyed,
it could be recreated. Given labour and capital equipment, natural resources
cannot be created: if, today, the world's entire stock of fossil fuels were
destroyed, it could not be recreated. [12, p. 8].

I have suggested that natural resource stocks can, in a sense, be augmented, but that does not really counter Common's point. It is precisely
the possibility of substituting producible capital, such as machines or
knowledge, for nonproducible materials, such as highly concentrated
ores, that allows us to effectively augment resource stocks. For some
types of resources, such as unique natural environments, even this may
not be possible. Once the redwood forests or the Grand Canyon are gone,
they are gone; they are irreplaceable.[6] The point is that a concern with
natural resource scarcity, which seems to be shared by a wide segment
of the general public, is not entirely irrational, however irrational some of
the arguments motivated by this concern appear to be. I need hardly add
that this does not imply that investigations into possible sources of over-
conservation should not be undertaken. But in this paper I am simply
trying to respond to the concern about impending exhaustion by indicating how it might be reflected in some alternative measures.

If it is agreed that a measure of scarcity may be of interest, what
properties should it have? Let me propose a very simple answer. A
measure of a resource's scarcity should have just one essential property:
it should summarize the sacrifices, direct *and indirect,* made to obtain a
unit of the resource. This appears to concentrate on the supply side, to
the exclusion of demand, but in fact it does not. First, note the operative
word, "made"; this implies a willingness to pay. Second, note the emphasis on indirect cost. In general, consumption of a unit of a resource today
will have a direct cost, the labor and capital (and other resource) inputs
required to extract and convert it, and an indirect cost, the value of future
consumption forgone. After describing the relationships between cost,
price, and rent with the aid of the model in the next section, I shall argue
that the unit cost of extractive output is, in *theory,* deficient as an indicator of scarcity because it does not capture this indirect component.
Price is the preferred measure, though there is something to be said for

---

[6] A substantial literature on the economics of natural environments, which
emphasizes the implications of the irreversibility of their consumption, has recently
emerged. For perhaps the most complete statement, see Krutilla and Fisher [13].

rent. Even unit cost comes back into the picture because, though it does not reflect the demand for, and value of, future output forgone, it typically moves in the right direction (increases) as a stock is depleted.

There is in fact, as I shall show in sections III and IV, an interesting duality between cost and rent. Where production conditions are such that cost increases with depletion, rent behaves erratically, and if cost increases sufficiently, rent ultimately falls to zero. On the other hand, where cost does not increase with depletion, rent rises smoothly. Once again, then, price is the preferred measure, since it is in both cases negatively related to stock size. This suggests one other desirable property, hinted at earlier, for an economic measure: that it be related to stock changes in an intuitively plausible way. The plan of the paper is as follows. In the next section, some elements of a model of optimal extraction are set out. Section III focuses on the much-discussed unit cost measure, noting its advantages and disadvantages. Section IV takes up the behavior of resource rents and prices over time, and their relationships to stock changes. Finally, in section V investment in stock-augmenting exploration is introduced into the model. This has the advantage of leading to a practical proposal for estimating rent, though it also raises some troubling questions of market failure.

II
Optimal Extraction and the Relationship Between Scarcity Measures

In order to discuss sensibly the advantages and disadvantages of the alternative cost, price, and rent measures of scarcity, we need a clear idea of how these measures are related to each other. A simple model of optimal extraction by a competitive firm can provide this.[7] Further, it can be extended to show how they behave as a resource stock is depleted— or augmented, as through exploration—and how rent, ordinarily very difficult to observe, might be estimated. Now, if we are interested in social scarcity, that is, scarcity to society, not just to a single firm, it might seem preferable to model extraction to maximize an (social) objective such as discounted aggregate consumers' plus producers' surplus from the resource. But as the necessary conditions which delineate the relations between cost, price, and rent are the same in either case, under standard assumptions, it will do just as well to analyze the slightly more convenient case of the firm.[8] On the other hand, when it becomes important to

---

[7] The model is based in part on one in Peterson and Fisher [14].

[8] The original proof of something like this proposition is in Hotelling [15]. More recently, it has been extended by Schulze [16] and Sweeney [8], among others.

broaden the focus to economy-wide depletion, I shall do this explicitly, as in parts of section IV.

A key construct in the model is an extraction production function,

$$Y = f(E, X, t) \tag{1}$$

where Y is extractive output, E is effort (an index of labor and capital) devoted to extraction, X is the resource stock, and t is time. The function is assumed to have the normal concavity in E, that is,

$$f_E > 0, \quad f_{EE} < 0$$

Also, and very importantly, I assume a positive "stock effect" on output, that is, $f_X > 0$ and $f_{EX} > 0$. In other words, with a larger stock, more output is obtained for a given effort and also for a given increment of effort. It is in fact this stock effect that drives costs up as a resource is depleted. It is possible to think of processes that do not exhibit the property—for example, the extraction of salts from sea water—but they are not typical. As John Stuart Mill observed, mineral extraction costs rise because "shafts must be sunk deeper, galleries driven further," and so on.[9] Similarly, for one of the most valuable resources, oil, the decrease in pressure as a well is depleted requires increasing inputs of effort. I emphasize all this because many, if not most, of the recent contributions to the theoretical literature on natural resource depletion assume, explicitly or otherwise, no such stock effect—in terms of our model, $f_X \equiv f_{EX} \equiv 0$. This in turn has, as we shall see, implications for the behavior of rents and prices, as well as costs, as a resource is depleted.

The firm's objective is to maximize the present discounted value of its profits from sales of the resource. It does this by choosing a path of extraction subject to nonnegativity restrictions on effort, $E \geq 0$, and to the finite stock constraint,

$$X(t) = X(0) - \int_0^t Y(\tau)\, d\tau, \quad X(t) \geq 0 \tag{2}$$

where $X(0)$ is the initial stock.[10] Differentiating equation (2) with respect to time, we obtain the system equation for the state variable X,

$$\frac{dX}{dt} = -Y(t) \tag{3}$$

The formal statement of the firm's problem is:

$$\max \int_0^\infty [Pf(E, X, t) - WE]e^{-rt}\, dt \tag{4}$$

[9] The quotation from Mill is taken from Barnett and Morse [7, p. 67].

[10] For the time being I assume a known, initial stock to be depleted, with no possibility of augmentation as through exploration.

subject to the nonnegativity restrictions and the system equation (3), where P is the price of the resource (a parameter to the competitive firm), W is the wage of effort, and r is the rate of discount.

The problem is now in a form suited to the application of the maximum principle of Pontryagin and coauthors [17]. The Hamiltonian equation is

$$H = [Pf(E, X, t) - WE - qY]e^{-rt} \qquad (5)$$

where q is the costate variable attached to the constraint on the state variable X. It may be interpreted, as in other constrained maximization problems, as the change in the optimal value of the objective function resulting from a small change in the constraint. *In particular in this problem $q(t)$ is the effect on (discounted) future profits of removing a unit of the resource from the stock at time t.*[11] The maximum principle states that the control variable E must be chosen to maximize H. Differentiating H with respect to E we obtain

$$H_E = PY_E - W - qY_E \qquad (6)$$

and, ignoring corner solutions and setting the result equal to zero,

$$P = \frac{W}{Y_E} + q \qquad (7)$$

This is an important result, but before I discuss it let me briefly say something about the technique used to obtain it.[12] The basic principle is that we solve a complicated problem—choosing an entire time path of a variable—by breaking it down into a series of simple ones—choosing, in each short interval of time, a desired level for the variable.

The net return or profit to the resource-extracting firm, in a short interval dt, is $(PY - WE)dt$. The choice of E in the interval should obviously be influenced by its impact on this quantity. But it should not be influenced *solely* by this, because it also has an impact, as seen from equations (1) and (3), on depletion of the stock. This is essentially what equation (5), the Hamiltonian, suggests. The right-hand side of equation (5), $(PY - WE - qY)e^{-rt}$ is just the (rate of) flow of profit due to current extraction $(PY - WE)$, plus the (negative) value, in terms of the objective function, of depletion of the stock due to current extraction, qY— all appropriately discounted back to $t = 0$. Central to this explanation is of course the interpretation of q as the effect on the objective

[11] For an interpretation of dual variables as shadow prices in nonlinear programming, see Balinski and Baumol [18].

[12] For further details, see the intuitive development of Dorfman [19] and the more rigorous one of Arrow and Kurz [20].

function of removing a unit of the resource from the stock, where Y represents the number of units removed.

Now let us return to equation (7). What it tells us is that, at all points along the firm's optimal extraction path, the market price P is equated to the sum of the *marginal cost of current extraction, W/Y_E*, and the marginal loss in profit from future extraction, q. Note that had we assumed the firm to choose E to maximize current return, the resulting necessary condition would have been the conventional $P = W/Y_E$, or price equals marginal cost. Note also that the divergence of price from marginal cost in a resource market does not arise from any market imperfection.

I have already given a couple of interpretations of the costate variable q. Now let me give another: q is the *rent* to a unit of the resource, the difference between what is received by the resource owner, P, and what is paid out to contractual inputs, W/Y_E.[13] So we have the following simple relationship between cost, price, and rent: price equals marginal cost plus rent, where q, the rent, is our desired measure of the indirect or opportunity cost of resource extraction.

This seems to settle the question of which measure of scarcity is "best." Price, which reflects both the direct and indirect sacrifices required to obtain a unit of the resource, would seem to fit the bill. But here I am going to get very slippery and suggest that it depends on what one means by "resource." Is a resource the raw material in the ground? Or is it the extracted, or extracted and converted, product? If the latter, then price is the appropriate measure of scarcity. But if the former, as Brown and Field (chapter 9) argue, the extraction cost component of price is not relevant and rent is the appropriate measure.[14]

However one views this matter, rent clearly has a role in any assessment of scarcity. But as I shall show in section IV, rent as an indicator of scarcity has the disturbing property of sometimes decreasing as the resource stock decreases. In section IV I spell out the circumstances in which this can occur. But first, I consider some problems with the unit cost measure.

III
Problems with the Unit Cost Measure

Before turning to the problems with unit cost, let me start on a positive note. This measure, as Morse has observed,[15] is suggested by the

---

[13] Still another term for q is marginal user cost, due to Scott [21]. It corresponds also to Nordhaus's [9] royalty, and Solow's [22] net price.

[14] This distinction is drawn also by Smith [24].

[15] Forum on the Economics of Natural Resource Scarcity, Resources for the Future, Washington, D.C., October 18–19, 1976.

classical economists' concern that the natural resource sector would draw ever-increasing amounts of labor and capital from other sectors, exerting a drag on growth. This seems to me a reasonable concern, and sufficient motivation for the cost calculations reported by Barnett and Morse [7] and Barnett (chapter 8, this volume). It is true, as Brown and Field (chapter 9) point out, that as richer deposits of a mineral are depleted, technical change in methods of extraction and conversion can offset the tendency to higher costs that would otherwise result from the movement to thinner deposits. The same sort of offsetting effect has probably also been produced by economies of scale in working the thinner deposits, which typically occur in larger concentrations. But in any event, it seems legitimate to try to sort out these several effects. *Ceteris paribus,* it should be true that depletion of higher grade ores leads to a rise in the unit cost of mineral production. The potential for technical change and economies of scale is not inconsistent with this proposition, and indeed is worth exploring, not only for the purpose of interpreting our cost data, but also for what it can tell us about these processes in the natural resource sector and in the economy generally.

I do, however, see a number of theoretical and empirical difficulties with the unit cost measure. One is that unit costs of production (or extraction) do not reflect anticipated future scarcity. It is perfectly possible, in theory, for unit costs to remain stable—and at a very low level— as a resource approaches exhaustion. Now it must be noted that this phenomenon is more a feature of highly simplified neoclassical models of optimal extraction than it is of extraction in the real world. There, as I have suggested earlier, following Mill, a positive stock effect ($f_X > 0$, $f_{EX} > 0$) means that costs will rise as the stock is depleted. To see how this works, recall that marginal extraction cost is given in our model by the expression W/f_E. Now, as X decreases, f_E decreases

$$\left[\frac{\partial\left(\frac{\partial f}{\partial E}\right)}{\partial X} > 0 \right]$$

so the marginal cost is driven up. Conversely, an increase in X caused, for example, by new information suggesting that a resource deposit is larger than originally believed, or by technical change that creates reserves out of formerly uneconomic materials, results in an increase in f_E and consequently a decrease in marginal cost W/f_E. But it must be acknowledged that future scarcity is not *explicitly* captured by any measure of current extraction costs. A positive stock effect merely pushes it in the right direction.

Another difficulty with unit cost, an empirical one, is that it is not readily observed. It must be constructed, as Barnett and Morse [7] have done, from series on labor and capital inputs and extractive outputs. This gives rise to problems of aggregation. One problem well known from investigations in another branch of economics is how heterogenous capital is to be aggregated into a single input series. Another, noted by Brown and Field (chapter 9), has to do with the aggregation of the various input series: "whereas the metals output series [in Barnett and Morse] appears to be at the extractive level, the metals employment data include some undetermined fractions of workers in the separate processing sectors" (p. 223). These are serious problems. The moral, I think, is not that we should abandon cost estimation, simply that we must recognize that it may not be a straightforward procedure.

Resource Scarcity and the Environment.   Perhaps the most serious difficulty with this measure, and one that was emphasized at the recent Resources for the Future Forum on the Economics of Natural Resource Scarcity,[15] is that it does not fully reflect the effects of resource use on the environment. This is not a new point. Barnett and Morse [7] in their pathbreaking study of trends in unit costs and prices observed that the effects of landscape disfigurement were not reflected in their calculations. If, as many people believe—though the time series evidence is scanty— such disruptions of the environment have been growing over time, then results like those of Barnett and Morse, which indicate a relative *decline* in the unit cost or price of extractive output, need to be reconsidered. That is, although the private cost has declined, the social cost may not have. Note, by the way, that failure to reflect environmental effects is a problem for any conventional measure of scarcity. I discuss it here because it has recently (at the RFF forum) received attention with respect to cost measures.

Barnett (chapter 8, this volume) has in fact reconsidered this question, and provides a partial answer to the concern about environmental cost. Recognizing the difficulty of estimating pollution damages, he looks at current and projected future costs of abatement implied by the recent clean air and water standards of the U.S. Environmental Protection Agency. Of course, even with these standards there will remain some pollution and other environmental disruption. But laying these aside for the moment, what can be said about the costs of achieving the standards? It turns out that, although these costs are growing both absolutely (in 1974 dollars) and relatively (to GNP), they are still quite small (3 percent of GNP) by the year 2000. Put another way, "we would have to

[15] Forum on the Economics of Natural Resource Scarcity, Resources for the Future, Washington, D.C., October 18–19, 1976.

give up less than a tenth of one percentage point in annual growth of national output to pay for this active abatement policy" (p. 187, this volume). This relatively complacent view can be challenged on a number of grounds. The basic problem, as it has been stated by Krutilla,[16] is that to use an extractive natural resource such as coal, say, it is generally also necessary to use a common property resource, such as air or water. Implicit in Barnett's calculations is the possibility of uncoupling these joint products. That is, the idea is that it should be possible to produce and consume increasing tonnage of coal without at the same time "consuming" increasing amounts of clean air. This seems plausible with respect to many conventional pollutants, such as, for example, large particulates from coal burning power plants. But if Krutilla's point has any force, it is precisely that there may be a rather rigid relationship between goods and *some* bads. Again taking coal as our our example, the buildup of carbon dioxide in the atmosphere that results from the combustion of coal (and other fossil fuels) may be a problem that cannot be dealt with by any conceivable abatement technology because it proceeds from the basic chemistry of combustion.[17] In fact, this is recognized by Barnett, along with radiation and nuclear waste storage, as a possible exception to his broad conclusion that pollution can be taken care of by a growing gross national product.

Mention of radiation and nuclear waste suggests a more general point. Technical change, which as documented by Barnett and Morse and others, has played such an important role in relaxing natural resource constraints, has in some ways put more of a burden on the environment. We are now becoming concerned, for example, about trace metals and other new and exotic chemical contaminants or carcinogens in drinking water and some agricultural products, as stressed by Page.[18] Some of these substances may be sufficiently toxic that virtually complete abatement, or prohibition of discharge, will be required. Complete abatement can of course be very costly. A closely related point has to do with threshold levels for various pollutants. As suggested by Mishan,[19] ozone depletion and oil spills in the oceans, to take two examples, may not register until critical accumulations have been reached. Neither the damages nor the costs of preventing them will be taken into account by calculations like those presented earlier in this section.

Barnett has suggested an answer to the concerns about increasing

[16] Ibid.
[17] For a discussion of relationships between fossil fuel combustion, carbon dioxide in the atmosphere, and global climate, see Nordhaus [25].
[18] Forum on the Economics of Natural Resource Scarcity, Resources for the Future, Washington, D.C., October 18–19, 1976.
[19] Ibid.

amounts of conventional pollution which may be applicable to the newer, more exotic forms as well. It is that just as substitution in production and consumption, and technical change, have prevented the unit costs of extractive output from rising, they may do the same for pollution abatement. In order to meet a given air quality standard, for example, it will not be necessary to remove an ever-increasing proportion of the sulfur from coal. Instead, cleaner sources of power may be substituted for coal over time, a less energy-intensive mix of goods may be consumed, or perhaps the sulfur can be removed cheaply from the coal with the aid of a new technology developed for the purpose.

A resource optimist would emphasize this line of reasoning, along with the relatively modest costs of achieving a substantial degree of cleanup even with currently known technologies. A resource pessimist, on the other hand, would perhaps be impressed by the difficulty in breaking the historical links between consumption of extractive and common property resources, and also with the dangers posed by some of the newer pollutants, which may be highly toxic even in minute quantities. It seems fair to say that in determining to what extent conventional measures of the cost of extractive output may need to be modified to reflect environmental concerns, we are confronted with a major research task. I think the key question—and it is an empirical one—is, to what extent processes generating the "new pollution" can be modified through substitution, technical change, or other methods.

IV
The Behavior of Rents and Prices over Time

Consider the equation for the evolution of the shadow price or rent, q, in the model.[20] The result that rent need not rise at the rate of interest, or even monotonically as a resource is depleted follows almost immediately:

$$\dot{q} = rq - \hat{H}_X \tag{8}$$

Substituting for $\hat{H}_X$, the partial derivative of $\hat{H}$ (where $\hat{H} = He^{rt}$) with respect to X, and rearranging terms, we obtain

$$\frac{\dot{q}}{q} = r + \left(1 - \frac{P}{q}\right)Y_X \tag{9}$$

In other words, the rate of change of rent, $\dot{q}/q$, is equal to the rate of interest, r, only if there is no stock effect, that is, only if $Y_X = 0$, or there is no marginal extraction cost, that is, $P = q$. In the general case in

---

[20] Again, see Arrow and Kurz [20] for a derivation of this equation.

which these conditions do not hold, what does equation (9) tell us about the behavior of rent over time? Assuming $Y_x > 0$, and since $P > q$, the right-hand side of equation (9) must be less than r. The pure return to holding a unit of the resource in the stock over a short interval of time, $\dot{q}/q$, is less than the return on an alternative investment, given by r, because there is value, in the form of reduced extraction costs, to holding a unit "in the ground." Note that not only is the rate of change of q not equal to r, in general, it may even become negative.

I think these results are worth emphasizing because they run counter to a fairly commonly held notion that in an optimal program, rent, or the shadow price of an exhaustible resource, rises over time as the resource is depleted, and moreover rises at precisely the rate of interest. As I have shown, the latter will occur only in the special case in which there is no stock effect. As for the possibility that rent as an indicator of scarcity is not well behaved, that is, does not rise as the stock shrinks, this can be demonstrated more strikingly with the aid of a slightly different model, and different definitions of resource and rent.

Let me start by recalling the classic concept of a resource rent as described by David Ricardo. Ricardo argued, in essence, that rent was just the difference between the payment to some resource input, such as a parcel of good agricultural land, and the (labor and capital) costs of producing from it. Rent could persist, even in a competitive equilibrium, if the good land was in limited supply relative to demand. That is, if demand were sufficient to call into production poor land as well, the cost of production and hence the price of the product would be above the cost of production from the good land, the difference constituting a rent to the land. Although agricultural land is generally used to illustrate this concept, Ricardo noted that it applied to mineral resources as well. These too vary in "fertility," some being richer or more accessible than others. But as Barnett and Morse [7, p. 64] also observe, the Ricardian rent to a mineral, or the land on which it is found, is *not* a payment for the exhaustion of the mineral. After all, even if it were replenishable, like agricultural land, Ricardian rent would arise as long as market demand in any period could not be met by production from the richest and most accessible units alone. Conversely, as we shall see, even where production in any period depends only on a single (large) deposit, with constant marginal and average costs of extraction, so that there is no Ricardian rent, a scarcity rent like q in our model will exist.

A couple of simple diagrams will bring out these distinctions more clearly. In figure 10-1, the equilibrium relationship $P = W/f_E + q$ is illustrated by the intersection of the price line (P) with the curve $(W/f_E + q)$. At the equilibrium output $Y = Y^*$, there is, in general, a

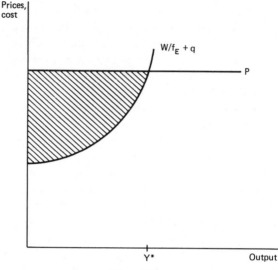

Figure 10-1.

positive scarcity rent q. But on all of the inframarginal units, there is also a Ricardian rent, the shaded difference between price and cost, where q is regarded as a part of the cost, which of course it is, whether paid by the producer to the owner of the resource rights, or simply imputed if producer and owner are one and the same. Now consider a somewhat different case, in which all of the economy's production of a resource, in any period, is at constant marginal and average costs, from a deposit or deposits of constant quality. The necessary conditions, namely

$$P = W/f_E + q \qquad (W/f_E = \text{constant}) \tag{i}$$

and

$$\frac{\dot{q}}{q} = r \qquad\qquad \text{(no stock effects)} \tag{ii}$$

continue to hold, though the demand price P is now $P = P(Y)$, where Y is total output in the period, so condition (i) describes the intersection of a downward sloping demand ($\partial P/\partial Y < 0$) with a horizontal line.[21] Just above I suggested that production at constant costs will entail no rent in the sense of Ricardo, but it will entail a scarcity rent like q. The

---

[21] In all of this I am abstracting from the problem of monopoly. If the deposit is privately owned, I assume the owner is a discriminating monopolist. If publicly owned, I assume optimization of something like producer's plus consumers' surplus. In either case, as I noted earlier, the necessary conditions are like (i) and (ii), and price does not include any element of monopoly rent.

proof of the first part of this proposition is obvious. But what is the nature of the scarcity rent? Suppose, following Nordhaus [9], there exists some substitute for the resource—a "backstop," such as nuclear fusion reactors for fossil fuels—which produces the same final services as the resource, but at higher cost. Then, as Nordhaus also shows, the resource is used first, and its shadow price or scarcity rent—or royalty, as he calls it—is just equal to the difference between the cost or price of producing from the backstop (P^B) and the cost of producing from the resource (C), at the switch date (T) from resource to backstop. At any time, t, $0 \leq t \leq T$, the royalty, equivalent to our q, is $(P^B - C)e^{-r(T-t)}$. That is, in the absence of stock effects, the royalty grows at the rate r as the resource is depleted. So far, so good; as the stock shrinks, the rent rises. Note, by the way, that this rent in fact looks rather Ricardian. That is, although there is no true Ricardian rent, all production in any period coming from a constant quality deposit, the rent does reflect a cost difference.

But now suppose there is a second quality of deposit, poorer than the first, but still more economical than the backstop. In this case, which is realistic certainly for most resources, it is easy to show that the rent or royalty does not rise monotonically as the resource is depleted. Starting from the switch date from the first, good quality deposit to the second, poor quality one, the analysis is exactly as above. The royalty on the second deposit is $(P^B - C_2)e^{-r(T_2-T_1)}$, where T_1 is the switch date from the first to the second deposit, T_2 is the switch date from the second to the backstop, and C_2 is the (constant) cost of producing from the second. The royalty rises at the rate r to $(P^B - C_2)$ at T_2. The price of the second deposit at T_1, when it enters production, is again the sum of marginal extraction cost and royalty, or $C_2 + (P^B - C_2)e^{-r(T_2-T_1)}$. This price, call it P_2, plays the same role, in turn, in the determination of the royalty on the first deposit as the price of the backstop plays in the determination of the royalty on the second. Thus the royalty on the first deposit is initially, at $t = 0$, $(P_2 - C_1)e^{-rT_1}$, where C_1 is the (constant) cost of producing from the first deposit, and it rises to $(P_2 - C_1)$ at $t = T_1$. At this point, where the resource price is P_2, and recalling that $C_1 < C_2$, the royalty must fall, to $(P_2 - C_2)$, on the second deposit. So the scarcity rent on the *resource* must fall.

Of course, one could take the view that the different quality deposits are different resources. In the absence of stock effects, the rent or royalty on each must rise—at the rate of interest. This is what I meant, earlier, in suggesting that whether rent rises monotonically as a resource stock is depleted depends on the definition of "resource." But my impression is that the same word—"copper," or "oil," or whatever, is commonly used to describe deposits of varying quality, so the result is not trivial. The

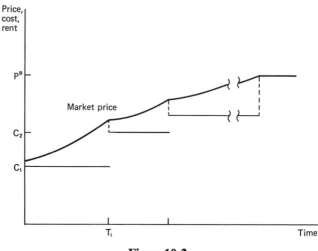

Figure 10-2.

analysis is easily extended from two to many different qualities of a resource, with each transition to a lower quality as the higher is depleted leading to a fall in the rent. Recalling the old distinction between intensive and extensive margins, as applied to agricultural land, we might say that the resource rent rises on the intensive margin and falls on the extensive. If and when resource extraction costs reach P^B, the price of the backstop, the rent falls to zero. All of this is represented in figure 10-2. Market price always rises as the resource is depleted, cost rises in discrete jumps, and rent rises and falls, ultimately falling to zero when the market price reaches P^B.[22] Another way of interpreting the result that rent vanishes is to consider the backstop as "average rock," instead of a new technology that substitutes for the resource. That is, ultimately all of the above-average concentrations of the resource are exhausted, and it is extracted from a virtually limitless supply of material in the earth's crust.[23] It is intuitively plausible that, in this situation, there will be no rent, Ricardian or other, accruing for any unit, since one is as good, or as bad, as another now and forever (almost).

Finally, note that we can approximate the continuous case described in the model of the preceding section, and equations (8) and (9), by letting the time between cost jumps approach zero. Although the analysis there was for a single firm, and we are now talking about the resource

[22] This diagram, and the related analysis, are essentially the same as in Herfindahl and Kneese [26], one difference being that there the ultimate price, P^B, is the price at which demand for the resource equals zero.

[23] A similar model is considered by Heal [27].

industry, the result is the same. Rent evolves smoothly over time, according to an equation like (9), either rising or falling, but ultimately falling to zero if stock effects push up extraction costs indefinitely.

What conclusions can we draw, then, about the behavior of rent as the stock of a resource is depleted? First, the statement in the introductory section, that rent generally rises as the stock falls, is too sweeping. Where the costs of extraction are not affected by depletion, it is correct. But where they are, either in a continuous fashion as in the original model, or in a discrete fashion as in the transition to different quality deposits in this section's model, there are conflicting tendencies, and if extraction costs rise all the way to the price of the backstop, the result is that rent falls to zero. Interestingly, there is a kind of duality between rent and cost as indicators of scarcity. Where cost is not a good indicator, rent is, and vice versa. That is, where there are no stock or quality effects, cost does not rise as a stock is depleted, but rent does. On the other hand, where these effects are present, cost is driven up, and rent rises along the intensive margin but falls along the extensive, ultimately to zero.

Thus far I have considered the evolution of rent as a stock is depleted over time. Another question is, what is the effect of a stock change on the *initial* value of the rent? In other words, instead of asking how rent behaves as a resource stock is depleted over time, I am now asking the comparative statics question of how the initial value is affected by a change on the initial stock. In symbols, what is the sign of $\partial q_0 / \partial X_0$, where X_0 refers to initial stock for the economy? Notice that this introduces uncertainty. X_0 will be affected, as suggested in the introduction, by information about new deposits, or methods of producing a resource product from lower grade materials. These would be positive effects, but one can also imagine better information leading to a downward revision of an estimated stock, as has recently occurred, for example, in the case of U.S. offshore oil deposits. In any event, it is clear that the sign of $\partial q_0 / \partial X_0$ is negative, as inspection of the expression for q in this section's model of economy-wide depletion suggests.

Taking the simplest case, sufficient for our purposes, of depletion of a single grade of the resource up to replacement by a backstop, $q_0 = (P^B - C)e^{-rT}$. The only thing affected by a stock change, dX_0 is the switch date T, since P^B and C are technologically determined and r is a parameter to the resource sector. For a given pattern of demand for the resource, then, we have $T = T(X_0)$, where $dT/dX_0 > 0$. From this we obtain

$$\frac{\partial q_0}{\partial X_0} = \frac{\partial q_0}{\partial T} \frac{dT}{dX_0} = (-r)(P^B - C)(e^{-rT})\left(\frac{dT}{dX_0}\right) \tag{10}$$

Since $(P^B - C) > 0$, $e^{-rt} > 0$, and $dT/dX_0 > 0$, for $r > 0$ we must have $\partial q_0/\partial X_0 < 0$. A slightly more complicated analysis yields a similar but qualified result for price, as I shall presently indicate.

Now, what can be said of the relationship between stock change and price? Price appears to be generally well behaved, as seen for example in figure 10-2. The equilibrium condition for both competitive firm and social planner, that price in any period equals marginal cost plus rent, ensures that price will always move in the right direction as a stock is depleted over time, pushed up either by rising cost or rising rent. The only remaining question is, how is the current market price affected by a change in the current estimate of the stock size?

In a world without a complete set of resource futures markets, the answer is not clear. But I think there is some presumption that price will continue to be well behaved. The crucial question is, how are price expectations formed? A number of theorists have recently considered this question, with interesting but not definitive results.[24] Here I just indicate the links, as I see them, in the chain connecting stock to price changes. This will enable us to identify the conditions under which current price increases (decreases) with a decrease (increase) in the estimated initial stock.

Suppose at $t = 0$ the reserve base for a mineral resource increases, due to a new process which makes profitable the extraction and conversion of a very thin ore. This lowers the price expected to prevail in the future, when the new material will come on line—or, what is the same thing, the current rent, as indicated by equation (10). This, in turn, should lead either the public resource agency or private resource owners to expand current production, resulting (for given demand) in a fall in the current price. So, through the links of negative relations between initial stock and rent $[(\partial q_0/\partial X_0) < 0]$, and current output and price $[(\partial P/\partial Y) < 0]$, a larger initial stock is associated with a lower current price.

The difficulty, or potential difficulty, lies in the effect that a change in the current price will have on the expected future price. Let us define the elasticity of expectations as

$$\epsilon = \frac{dP_t^e}{P_t^e} \bigg/ \frac{dP_0}{P_0}$$

where P_t^e is the price expected to prevail at time $t > 0$ in the future. If $\epsilon = 0$, then the story is ended. The expected future price is determined solely by estimates of future demand and technology, which are not

[24] See, for example, Nordhaus [9], Solow [22], Stiglitz [28], Heal [11], and Mishan [29].

speculatively related to current price changes. But it is conceivable, and quite plausible, that $\epsilon > 0$. In this case, the reduction in P_0 leads to a reduction in P_t, which leads in turn to a further expansion of current output and further reduction in P_0, and so on. Whether an equilibrium is reached should depend on the size of ϵ; if it is small enough, the current price changes should approach zero. But in any event, with these speculative effects we have perhaps too much of a good thing: current price overreacts to a change in the estimated initial stock. If, finally, $\epsilon < 0$, which is conceivable, though not very plausible, then current price could react perversely, increasing with an increase in the stock.[25]

Although the possibility of speculative effects can cause problems for price as an indicator of scarcity, I don't think too much should be made of this. In the first place, the really bad result of current price varying positively with current estimated stock could occur only if there were a sufficiently strong negative elasticity of expectations. But it is hard to tell a convincing story that would produce this result. In the second place, even the more realistic positive elasticity is not likely to persist. At some point beliefs about future demand and technology will call a halt to the round of speculative price decreases. Admittedly, the net result could be some deviation from an efficient extraction path, but this is of greater relevance to the question of whether the lack of a complete set of resource futures markets will lead to inefficiency than to the narrower question of whether price is likely to reflect scarcity.

V
Exploration and Externalities

I have spoken of the possibility of augmenting a resource stock through investment devoted to this purpose, as in the exploration for new deposits. In this section such exploration is introduced into the model of section II. This is not merely a formal exercise, however, as it leads to a new insight into resource rent and a practical proposal for estimating it. The basic idea is that, once we recognize that optimal depletion is not simply a matter of using up a known stock, but involves the allocation of effort to find new sources, we might conjecture that the rent, or indirect cost of a unit extracted today, will reflect not the loss in future income from that unit, but the cost of finding another to replace it. This is precisely the result we shall obtain, as do also Brown and Field (chapter 9). There does arise, however, an interesting problem involving externalities in exploration which they do not consider.

[25] For a detailed analysis of the implications for competitive extraction paths of different expectations elasticities, though not in the context of a discussion of scarcity, see Mishan [29].

Before proceeding it is important to recognize just how strong the assumption about exploration is, and how it changes the earlier model. It makes the exhaustible resource into something like a renewable one—only more so, since the growth of a renewable resource is usually constrained by nature. And as with a renewable resource, a steady state, in which stock size and rent (the shadow price of a unit in the stock) do not change, becomes possible. In any event, the earlier criterion for judging a measure of scarcity—how it behaves as a stock is physically depleted—is no longer relevant, as the stock is potentially without limit. But effort is in fact required to extend the limit at any time, and this brings us back to the desirable property for a measure of scarcity suggested in the introduction: that it reflect the sacrifices made to obtain the resource. As we shall see, rent can be considered a good indicator in this sense, in a model with exploration—at least if one is interested in the resource in the ground.

I don't intend to consider the dynamics any further here. Instead, I shall derive an expression that can be used to estimate the rent at any point in time. No doubt the associated view of exploration is too optimistic. On the other hand, section II's model, which allows no growth in the resource stock, is probably too pessimistic. In any event, let us here develop the implications of the optimistic view. The relevance of either is of course an empirical matter.

Formally, the new element in the model is an exploration or discovery production function, $f^d(E^d, t)$, where f^d represents new discoveries, measured in units of the resource, say tons, and E^d is effort devoted to exploration. The idea is that the stock can be augmented by exploration, as well as diminished by extraction. The system equation then becomes

$$\frac{dX}{dt} = f^d(E^d, t) - f^e(E^e, X, t) \tag{11}$$

where the extraction production function is now written $f^e(E^e, X, t)$, and effort devoted to extraction E^e.

The firm maximizes the discounted present value of profits

$$\int_0^\infty [Pf^e(E^e, X, t) - W^dE^d - W^eE^e]e^{-rt}\, dt \tag{12}$$

where W^d is the wage of effort E^d, and W^e the wage of effort E^e. The necessary condition (7) is replaced by a pair of conditions corresponding to the two control variables E^d and E^e:

$$-W^d + qf^d_{E^d} = 0 \tag{13}$$

$$Pf^e_{E^e} - W^e - qf^e_{E^e} = 0 \tag{14}$$

Equation (14) is just the same as equation (7), but from equation (13), we can substitute $W^d/f^d_{E^d}$ for q. This term, $W^d/f^d_{E^d}$, is clearly the marginal cost of exploration, as $W^e/f^e_{E^e}$ is the marginal cost of extraction.

Somewhat surprisingly, complicating the optimal extraction model by introducing exploration results in a simple suggestion for estimating rent. This also has implications for efficiency if, as suggested in the preceding section, we are worried about the way in which q is determined by the expectations of agents in resource markets. Of course, an exploration cost or production function must still be estimated, but this is less of a venture into the unknown than forming an expectation of an entire price path.

The results are misleading, however, in appearing to banish uncertainty from the process of deciding how to allocate effort to exploration and extraction over time. Uncertainty is important in particular in exploration, which might in fact be viewed as fundamentally an exercise in reducing uncertainty. Two interesting strains of analysis have emerged in this area. One, following Allais [30], considers exploration formally as a problem in sampling from an incompletely known size distribution of deposits. Another, more recent, and exemplified by the work of Gilbert [31], introduces uncertainty into relatively simple versions of optimal depletion models. Though further discussion is beyond the scope of this paper, these approaches are clearly central to a better understanding of the economics of exploration.[26] But I think it is fair to say that the deterministic production function approach taken above also has a role to play.

A fruitful way to proceed here might be to introduce a stochastic term into the exploration production function. Exploration in one period could then have several effects. It would locate deposits, as in the deterministic case, but it could also reduce the effort needed to locate deposits in future periods by developing information about the geology of a region. In other words, it could shift the exploration production function —and perhaps also the extraction production function. Exploration might also result in a reduction in the variance of the stochastic term. If the agent undertaking the exploration were risk averse, such a reduction would be valuable. But in any event, a first approximation to the marginal user cost measure of rent might be obtained by looking just at exploration costs, as suggested by equations (13) and (14).

There is just one other issue I want to touch on, and that, is externalities in exploration. It is easily introduced through extension of the basic model. This will also shed some light on the effects of uncertainty.

---

[26] An informative presentation of recent work in probabilistic assessment of mineral prospects is found in Grenon [32].

We keep the same objective function as in equation (12), but change the system equation (11) in order to reflect the influence of past discoveries on the relationship between current exploratory effort and output. We do this by putting another argument, D, for cumulative past discoveries, into the exploration production function. In symbols, this is

$$\frac{dX}{dt} = f^d(E^d, D, t) - f^e(E^e, X, t) \tag{15}$$

I shall consider the role of past discoveries presently, but first let us complete the structure of the problem and indicate the solution.

In addition to equation (15), there is a system equation describing the change in D over time, which we write as

$$\frac{dD}{dt} = f^d(E^d, D, t) \tag{16}$$

The Hamiltonian for this problem is

$$H = [(Pf^e - W^dE^d - W^eE^e) + q(f^d - f^e) + p(f^d)] e^{-rt} \tag{17}$$

where p is the costate variable attached to the system equation for D. Differentiating H with respect to the control variables E^d and E^e respectively, and setting the resulting partial derivatives equal to zero, we obtain

$$H_{E^d} = -W^d + qf^d_{E^d} + pf^d_{E^d} = 0 \tag{18}$$

and

$$H_{E^e} = Pf^e_{E^e} - W^e - qf^e_{E^e} = 0 \tag{19}$$

Equation (19) tells us, once again, that price should be set equal to the sum of marginal extraction cost and marginal user cost, or rent. But rearranging equation (18) we have a new expression for rent,

$$q = W^d/f^d_{E^d} - p \tag{18'}$$

The first term on the right-hand side of equation (18') is just the marginal discovery cost. The second term, p, represents the shadow price of a unit added to the stock of discovered resources, D. The sign of p will reflect the influence of D on the exploration production function, but a priori, the direction of the influence is not clear. It could be positive, in the sense that discovering another unit provides information that can reduce the effort involved in future discoveries. This is a possibility I hinted at just above in discussing a stochastic exploration production function. But it could also be negative. Suppose there is a finite number of discoverable deposits of a mineral in a region. Then one more discovered today means one less discovered tomorrow. Not only that, but to the extent that the better deposits are discovered soon, there could be a substantial opportunity loss in depleting the "stock of discoveries." The upshot of these remarks is that p could be positive or negative, and the marginal discovery cost accordingly adjusted up or down. This seems to be a question which could usefully be addressed in specific cases, depending on the geology of the mineral and region.

Where do the externalities come in? They come in with both of the effects just discussed, as noted first in a paper by Peterson [33]. Suppose a discovery does in fact provide information about where to look for further deposits and how. To the extent that this information is not kept within the firm making the discovery, it will benefit other firms, or even potential firms, searching for the mineral. The information spillover is an external economy, and if not appropriately compensated, will lead to a nonoptimal allocation of effort to exploration by decentralized decision makers. In particular, it seems likely that firms will explore too little, each sitting back and waiting for the other to provide information, as Peterson [33] and also Stiglitz [34] have suggested.

The other effect, depletion of a stock of discoveries, is a classic common property phenomenon. Clearly, it is not just the firm making the discovery whose future prospects are diminished. All others are the poorer as well—there is that much less for them to find, and it will be that much harder to find. This creates an incentive for each firm to over-explore, compared with what would be optimal if it enjoyed a secure tenure in all of the deposits of a mineral within a region. As is well known, one method of getting an individual economic agent to behave as if he were the sole owner in a common property setting, short of actually making him the owner, is to impose a tax that reflects the losses he imposes on others.

I conclude, then that the determination of p, the adjustment to the marginal cost of discovery, or something analogous to it in an appropriate multiparty setting, is still more complicated than it appeared when we were concerned only with the effects of discovery internal to the firm. This looks like a very promising area for future research—though calculations of the behavior of discovery costs as proxies for rents need not wait on its completion.

VI
Conclusions

The main point of this paper has been to examine the behavior of a number of proposed economic measures of a resource's scarcity as the resource is depleted or augmented (as through discovery of new sources) over time. A secondary point has been to examine the effect on the current value of each measure of a change in the current estimate of the resource stock. The proposed measures are price, cost, and rent. It turns out that price is preferred, always increasing (decreasing) as a stock is depleted (augmented) over time. Also, current price generally varies inversely with estimated stock at a moment in time—though this conclusion is subject to the condition that there not be a strong negative elasticity of expectations.

Cost and rent are sometimes well behaved as indicators of scarcity, sometimes not. It depends on the technology of extraction, and specifically on the strength of stock or quality effects on extraction costs. Where there are such effects, extraction cost rises as a stock or high quality deposit is depleted, but rent is erratic, rising and falling, in either discrete or continuous fashion, and ultimately falling to zero if extraction cost rises all the way to the price of the backstop for the resource. For a given quality deposit, and if there are no stock effects, cost does not rise as exhaustion nears, but rent does. So there is a kind of duality between cost and rent as measures of scarcity: where cost moves in the right direction, rent does not, and vice versa.

Another question considered in the paper is, to what extent must these conventional economic measures be adjusted to reflect the environmental effects of resource use? On the basis of currently available evidence, this remains an unresolved question. Calculations like those reported by Barnett (chapter 8), which show a very small fraction of gross national product required to attain fairly stringent air and water quality standards, suggest a modest adjustment, one that in most cases would not reverse the long-term decline in unit costs.

This finding is strengthened by theoretical arguments for substitution and technical change in pollution control, as in resource extraction. On the other hand, one cannot, it seems to me, reject the hypothesis that the costs of dealing with a variety of new and exotic pollutants may be quite high, particularly as unknown thresholds are reached. Substitution and technical change may be less effective where, as with the accumulation of carbon dioxide from the combustion of fossil fuels, the bad is difficult or impossible to separate from the good. The whole question of the adjustment of scarcity measures to reflect the consumption of common property environmental resources, and in particular of the possibilities for substitution away from these resources, seems to me deserving of further research effort.

A final question deals with behavior of rent—and one could extend the analysis to cost and price—when the resource stock can be indefinitely renewed by exploration. In this case, the relationship between rent and depletion is not particularly relevant. Complicating the formal model of optimal extraction by introducing the possibility of expanding the stock frees the economic measure from its tie to the physical. It turns out that rent on a mineral resource can be estimated, at least to a first approximation, by the marginal replacement cost, that is, the cost of discovering new deposits. This is not a bad measure of scarcity, at least of the resource "in the ground," in that it reflects the sacrifices required to obtain the resource. It also raises interesting possibilities for empirical investigation—and challenging theoretical issues—because uncertainty about the size and location of deposits, and externalities in their exploration, indicate adjustments to the discovery cost measure of rent. For example, the cost might be adjusted up or down, depending on whether a discovery carries a cost in that it depletes the "stock of discoveries" or a benefit in that it provides information about the prospects for future discoveries. Moreover, the question is complicated by the fact that neither effect is internal to the firm making the discovery.

References

1. W. Beckerman, "Economists, Scientists, and Environmental Catastrophe," *Oxford Economic Papers* vol. 24, no. 3 (November, 1972) pp. 237–244.
2. W. D. Nordhaus, "World Dynamics—Measurement Without Data," *Economic Journal* vol. 82, no. 332 (December 1973) pp. 1156–1183.
3. J. Kay and J. M. Mirrlees, "The Desirability of Natural Resource Depletion," in D. W. Pearce, ed., *Economic Aspects of Natural Resource Depletion* (London, MacMillan, 1975).
4. R. G. Ridker, ed., *Population, Resources, and the Environment*, U.S. Commission on Population Growth and the American Future (Washington, GPO, 1972).
5. J. J. Schanz, "Problems and Opportunities in Adapting USGS Terminology to Energy Resources," in M. Grenon, ed., *First IIASA Conference on Energy Resources*, International Institute for Applied Systems Analysis (Laxenburg, Austria, 1976).
6. Joel Darmstadter, *Energy in the World Economy* (Baltimore, Johns Hopkins University Press for Resources for the Future, 1971).
7. H. J. Barnett and C. Morse, *Scarcity and Growth: The Economics of Natural Resource Availability* (Baltimore, Johns Hopkins University Press for Resources for the Future, 1963).
8. J. L. Sweeney, *Economics of Depletable Resources: Market Forces and Intertemporal Bias* (Washington, D.C. Federal Energy Administration, 1976).
9. W. D. Nordhaus, "The Allocation of Energy Resources," *Brookings Papers on Economic Activity* vol. 3 (a) (1973) pp. 529–570.
10. R. M. Solow, "Intergenerational Equity and Exhaustible Resources," *Review of Economic Studies Symposium on the Economics of Exhaustible Resources* (b) (1974) pp. 29–45.

11. G. Heal, "Economic Aspects of Natural Resource Depletion," in D. W. Pearce, ed., *The Economics of Natural Resource Depletion* (London, MacMillan, 1975).

12. M. Common, "Comments on the Papers by Robinson, Surrey and Page," in D. W. Pearce, ed., *The Economics of Natural Resource Depletion* (London, MacMillan, 1975).

13. J. V. Krutilla and A. C. Fisher, *The Economics of Natural Environments: Studies in the Valuation of Commodity and Amenity Resources* (Baltimore, Johns Hopkins University Press for Resources for the Future, 1975).

14. F. M. Peterson and A. C. Fisher, "The Exploitation of Extractive Resources," *Economic Journal* vol. 87 (December 1977) pp. 681–721.

15. H. Hotelling, "The Economics of Exhaustible Resources," *Journal of Political Economy* vol. 39 (April 1931) pp. 137–175.

16. W. D. Schulze, "The Optimal Use of Non-Renewable Resources: The Theory of Extraction," *Journal of Environmental Economics and Management* vol. 1, no. 1 (May 1974) pp. 53–73.

17. L. S. Pontryagin, et al., *The Mathematical Theory of Optimal Processes,* translated by K. N. Trirogoff (New York, Wiley, 1962).

18. M. L. Balinski and W. J. Baumol, "The Dual in Nonlinear Programming and Its Economic Interpretation," *Review of Economic Studies* vol. 35, no. 3 (1968) pp. 237–256.

19. Robert Dorfman, "An Economic Interpretation of Optimal Control Theory," *American Economic Review* vol. 59, no. 5 (December 1969) pp. 817–831.

20. K. J. Arrow and M. Kurz, *Public Investment, the Rate of Return, and Optimal Fiscal Policy* (Baltimore, Johns Hopkins University Press for Resources for the Future, 1970).

21. A. D. Scott, "Notes on User Cost," *Economic Journal* vol. 63 (June 1953), pp. 368–384.

22. R. M. Solow, "The Economics of Resources or the Resources of Economics," *American Economic Review* vol. 64, no. 2a (May 1974) pp. 1–14.

23. G. M. Brown and B. Field, "The Adequacy of Measures for Signaling the Scarcity of Natural Resources," in V. Kerry Smith, ed., *Scarcity and Growth Revisited* (Baltimore, Johns Hopkins University Press, for Resources for the Future).

24. V. Kerry Smith, "Measuring Natural Resource Scarcity: Theory and Practice," *Journal of Environmental Economics and Management* vol. 5 (June 1978) pp. 150–171.

25. W. D. Nordhaus, "The Climatic Impact of Long Run Energy Growth," paper presented at American Economic Association Meetings, Atlantic City, August 16–18, 1976.

26. O. C. Herfindahl and A. V. Kneese, *Economic Theory of Natural Resources* (Columbus, Ohio, Charles E. Merrill, 1974).

27. G. Heal, "The Relationship Between Price and Extraction Cost for a

Resource with a Backstop Technology," *Bell Journal of Economics* vol. 7, no. 2 (Autumn, 1976) pp. 371–378.

28. J. E. Stiglitz, "Growth with Exhaustible Natural Resources: The Competitive Economy," *Review of Economic Studies Symposium on the Economics of Exhaustible Resources* 1974, pp. 139–152.

29. E. J. Mishan, "Does Perfect Competition in Mining Produce an Optimal Rate of Exploitation?" (London School of Economics, unpublished paper, 1977).

30. M. Allais, "A Method of Appraising Economic Prospects of Mining Exploration over Large Territories: Algerian Sahara Case Study," *Management Science* vol. 3 (July 1957) pp. 285–347.

31. R. Gilbert, "Optimal Depletion of an Uncertain Stock," Institute for Mathematical Studies in Social Sciences, Stanford University, 1976.

32. M. Grenon, ed., *First IIASA Conference on Energy Resources,* CP-76-4 International Institute for Applied Systems Analysis (Laxenburg, Austria, 1976).

33. F. M. Peterson, "Two Externalities in Petroleum Exploitation," in G. M. Brannon, ed., *Studies in Energy Tax Policy* (Cambridge, Mass., Ballinger, 1975).

34. J. E. Stiglitz, "The Efficiency of Market Prices in Long Run Allocations in the oil industry," in G. M. Brannon, ed., *Studies in Energy Tax Policy* (Cambridge, Mass., Ballinger, 1975).

11

Summary and Research Issues

V. Kerry Smith and John V. Krutilla

V. Kerry Smith and John V. Krutilla

I
Introduction

There is a diversity of opinion, popular and professional, today over the importance of natural resources for economic growth and the maintenance of society's well-being. The papers in this volume span the whole range of positions. Such diversity in the speculation on the adequacy of natural resources is not new. Adam Smith saw limits to the possible size of a nation's industrial production which would be set by the difficulty of obtaining an expanding supply of raw materials without dramatic increases in their prices. Economic historians, notably Wrigley [1], have more recently observed that Smith failed to realize the potential powers of the natural endowments when the transition from organic to inorganic raw materials is recognized.[1] With recognition of these possibilities, many economists felt the limits to size evaporate. However, Jevons [2] warned that new limits were forthcoming, because natural resources play an essential role in production. He observed that:

Coal, in truth, stands not beside but entirely above all other commodities. It is the material energy of the country—the universal aid—the factor in everything we do. With coal almost any feat is possible or easy; without it we are thrown back in the laborious poverty of early times. [2, p. viii]

Despite the many seemingly persuasive arguments, the same concerns over a materials limit to economic activity have arisen almost invariably in association with sharp increases in the materials consumed during a given period. Thus the Paley and Cooke commissions can be considered as responses to the concern over resource availability following the heavy materials demand of World War II. Since that time, however, the

V. Kerry Smith and John Krutilla are Senior Fellows in the quality of the environment division, Resources for the Future.

[1] In this case they were not referring to the scientific definitions, but the consideration of organic as having to do with living matter and inorganic nonliving sources of raw materials.

work of Barnett and Morse [3] has played an important role in buoying optimism regarding natural resource availability. Their arguments are intriguing, suggesting that the very factors giving rise to heavy materials demands also provide strong incentives, through the market, to meet them. Thus they concluded that there is no resource problem in a limitational sense. Rather, they argued that the issue is best viewed:

as one of continual adjustment to an ever changing economic resource quality spectrum. The physical properties of the natural resource base impose a series of initial constraints on the growth and progress of mankind, but the resource spectrum undergoes kaleidoscopic change through time. Continual enlargement of the scope of substitutability—the result of man's technological ingenuity and organizational wisdom—offers those who are nimble a multitude of opportunities for escape. [3, p. 244]

This perspective is appealing and has remained a widely accepted conceptualization of the natural resource problem. Nonetheless, as we argued in our introductory essay, it does not address all of the significant aspects of the natural resource problem. Natural resources include more than simply the raw material inputs to production and consumption activities. They should be considered as including all the original endowments of the earth whose services may bear directly or indirectly on our ability to produce and consume utility-yielding goods and services while maintaining ambient conditions supportive of life. With this more general definition of natural resources, it seemed appropriate to reconsider the issues first advanced comprehensively in *Scarcity and Growth*. Our reevaluation does not pretend to have been comprehensive. The Barnett–Morse volume commented on the intellectual concern over the availability of natural resources and the economic modeling of their role in production. It also evaluated the trends in scarcity indexes. It was impossible in our discussion to fully reflect all the diverse views on each element of the Barnett–Morse argument, and we have implicitly reserved many for further research. The papers in this volume have focused on the divergence in views in each of three general areas: (1) the appropriate modeling of the role of natural resources in economic activity; (2) the nature of the physical (primarily geological) constraints to providing natural resources as they have conventionally been defined; and (3) the measurement of the adequacy of our stocks of natural resources for maintaining economic well-being.

The last two of these issues relate to different sources of information on the availability of natural resources. When the definition of these resources is restricted to materials exchanged on commodity markets, we can rely on well-functioning markets to provide signals on competing needs relative to available supplies for the goods exchanged. They do not necessarily provide an absolute index of resource availability. How ever, Barnett and Morse, as we noted at the outset, adopted a classica view of economic processes. In this framework, long-run prices tend t "natural" values determined by the real resource costs of production While this perspective is not explicitly detailed in *Scarcity and Growth* it seems that this is what the authors had in mind. To fully understanc the framework and results, it is useful to consider Eagly's [4] recen explanation of the classical model. He observed that one must:

distinguish between the classical concepts of "market price," which is deter mined by cost of production. *Ricardian natural price is a cost-of-productio concept in which commodities exchange with one another according to th relative quantities of inputs used in the production of each.* . . . Marke price may diverge from natural price in the short run. When the two d diverge in a given industry, the profit rate in that industry diverges from the profit rate in the lead sector. In turn, it is this discrepancy in the profit rate that provides the basis for capital movements within the economy." [4, p. 51 emphasis added]

This view of the world was deemed desirable, for it was believed to pro vide an objective benchmark for evaluating resource availability—the natural price. While market prices would tend toward these natural levels, they could not be relied upon to accurately gauge availability in the short run. Thus in a genuine sense the philosophical issues we addressed on the meaning of scarcity and appropiate definition of society's ends did not have to be addressed within the classical model.

Unfortunately, these issues must be addressed. We recognize today that economic processes do not conform to the classical paradigm. There are no objective prices free of consumers' valuations. As a result, two difficult issues must be faced in resolving the problems associated with natural resource availability. The first of these concerns the definition of natural resources and the ability of markets to provide all of the informa tion necessary to signal resource scarcities. The Barnett–Morse descrip tion of the natural resource problem is based on the existence of perfect markets, natural tendencies for prices, and a specific (raw materials) definition of natural resources. Even if we accept initially the presump tion of perfect markets, for the sake of argument, the last two matters call for careful reconsideration. Taking the last first, the services of com mon property environmental resources are not exchanged or organized markets. One must ask how the information otherwise provided and transmitted by markets is to be conveyed. In order to address this issue, we explore briefly the role of other institutions in the allocation of re sources and the functions we might expect them to perform in dealing with common property resources.

The second difficulty is equally important and concerns the objective appraisal of scarcity. Once we deny the existence of natural or objective signals, then prices are recognized as indexes of the social interaction postulated to be taking place in a perfect market. Thus:

neither the marginal evaluation of the demanders nor the marginal costs of suppliers . . . can be employed as a basis for determining prices. . . . There is no "theory" of normal exchange rates with positive content here. The analysis provides an "explanation of results, a logic of interaction . . . [5, pp. 85–86]

Section II discusses the role of institutions in the allocation of resources, and considers the potential information available from non-market institutions to assist in the efficient allocation of common property environmental resources. The third section discusses the importance of the treatment of physical or natural endowment constraints to economic activity in evaluating the adequacy of natural resources. In the last section we consider the implications of these general issues for future research.

II
Institutions and the Allocation of Resources

As we noted in the introductory essay, four reasons for the Barnett–Morse [3] findings concerning the trends in real unit costs and relative prices for extractive outputs have become a part of the conventional explanation of the factors influencing natural resource availability. We repeat them briefly below:

1. As higher grade deposits of a mineral are exhausted, lower grades are available in greater abundance.
2. With the growing scarcity of a resource, price increases induce the substitution of other resources to achieve the same ends.
3. Price increases accompanying scarcity stimulate exploratory activity and the recycling of natural resources.
4. Technical change reduces the cost of providing constant quality natural resource commodities.[2]

[2] Two points should be noted here. The literature on induced technical change was not widely accepted at the time Barnett and Morse prepared their book. Their discussion of technical change was more in terms of a description of the past patterns of technological change rather than a specific generating mechanism. Nonetheless, it seems clear from their explanations that they did consider the increasing scarcity of natural resources among the motivations for developing new technologies.
    The second aspect of this discussion is what may seem a curious contradiction in the Barnett–Morse reasoning. We noted in the introductory discussion that they adopted a concept of "natural" prices which seemed to offer objective measures of resource availability independent of tastes. These were apparently the long-run tendencies of market prices. It would be difficult to envision how the long-run ad-

With the exception of the first reason, these factors rely on the functioning of perfect markets to reveal indirectly, through the process of exchange, the information necessary to assure an efficient distribution of any resource scarcities.

In evaluating these explanations, then, it is useful to recognize the influence of institutions on market and extramarket resource allocations. While there is an array of institutions which potentially influence the allocation of resources, economists have tended to focus on the market, to the exclusion of many others. The rationale for this attention probably rests with the unique character of the market as an institution for organizing the social interaction involved in the exchange of resources. Virtually all elementary economics texts acknowledge that the perfect market reveals, through the process of exchange between demanders and suppliers, the respective marginal values and costs for the last unit of the good or service exchanged. This attribute is clearly appreciated. However, the role of markets as only one of many possible institutional influences on these interactions is often overlooked. While this simple observation has long been recognized by the institutionalist school in economics, it has not been fully reflected in formal economic analysis. Randall's [6] recent review of the interrelationships between institutionalist school and contemporary economic thought supports this view. Moreover, his review of Commons' development of the role of institutions seems particularly relevant to our argument. He observed that for Commons:

Institutions are defined as collective action in control, liberation, and expansion of individual action. . . . For Commons, the basic unit of analysis is the transaction, which involves alienation and acquisition of the rights of property and liberty created by society and which therefore must be negotiated between the parties concerned before production, exchange, and consumption can take place. The institutional framework makes the transaction feasible by providing the parties with reasonably sure expectations of performance. [6, pp. 3–4]

Buchanan [5] and Mishan [7] also develop arguments which support our position. For example, in an early paper Buchanan discussed the implications of institutional constraints to the definition and use of Pareto optimal criteria. He observed that:

At any particular moment of time, there must exist a set of rules, either legally imposed and enforced by some collectively organized agency or convention-

---

justments described by Barnett–Morse in these three factors are consistent with the existence of objective natural prices existing independent of tastes. Certainly there seems to be some inconsistency in the arguments. However, in fairness to Barnett and Morse we should note that a substantial part of the discrepancy arises from the mechanism postulated to bring the market prices into equality with their natural counterparts.

ally honored, and these rules serve to constrain the behavior of the members of the group as they act in their capacities as private individuals. . . . The set of rules serves to define a "Pareto region," described as the set of all possible positions or points attainable under both these rules and the physical constraints that are present. . . . *Any change in the rules governing private behavior will change the structure of the region.* [5, pp. 342–343]

Our introductory essay and several of the papers in this volume discussed the potential for government policies, in particular the tax and subsidy treatment of the extractive sector, to influence the efficiency of a market-mediated resource allocation. Where impediments arise to the free interaction which characterizes exchange on idealized markets, we cannot claim that the allocations realized will be efficient. As a corollary to this observation, the information provided us by these markets may not reflect the equilibrium sacrifices of demanders and suppliers. There is an element of judgment which must enter any appraisal of the importance of such institutional influences on market allocations. To see this point, one need only compare Stiglitz's (chapter 2) evaluation of the importance of market imperfections for the efficiency of exhaustible resource allocation with Nordhaus' [8] evaluation for a similar set of conditions.[3]

When we turn our attention to those natural resources which do not exchange on organized markets, the services of common property environmental resources, the problems encountered are not simply issues of judgment in evaluating the relative importance of particular external influences. Markets indirectly and other institutions directly influence the allocation of these resources, and unfortunately none of these can be relied upon to provide the information on the marginal valuation of the resources involved in these allocations. Perfect markets offer effective mechanisms for transmitting information on the marginal values and costs of the goods and services exchanged on them. In order to evaluate the properties of any other means of resource allocation, we must have available or obtain an extensive set of information on tastes and technology. It seems logical to ask whether other institutions provide some of this information through their influence on the allocation patterns of common property environmental resources. That is, we noted at the outset of this section that institutions serve to set the ground rules (i.e., in Commons' terms "working rules") directly or indirectly for all allocation processes. We are implicitly asking here whether or not the processes for

---

[3] Stiglitz (chapter 2) concludes that it is unlikely that a Pareto improvement will result from government intervention. Nordhaus [8], on the other hand, concludes that a type of indicative planning is essential because the market mechanism must be regarded as an "unreliable means of pricing and allocating exhaustible appropriable natural resources" (p. 537).

defining these ground rules in a democractic society can be relied on to indirectly reveal something of the character of the population's preferences for nonmarketed goods and services, including views on ethical issues involving intergenerational equity. Randall [6] seems to argue that the Commons' work led to a model that was fundamentally insoluble. That is, he noted:

Institutions, while themselves the creation of man, tend to shape man by influencing his patterns of thought, behavior, and expectations. In aggregate, working rules establish a social framework specifying how economic, social, and spiritual life is organized. Thus, man shapes institutions and is shaped by them. [6, p. 4]

These arguments are true in degrees. There are elements of institutional quiescence which may reduce the jointness in the process of institutional formation and, in turn, the effects of established institutions on individual behavior. Thus Randall's arguments on the ability of institutions to function as mechanisms for recording the collective sentiment may be overly pessimistic.

The principal institutions we can look to for such information are the legislative, public administrative, and judicial systems. One need only look at the legislation concerning air and water pollution to be convinced that the legislative process along with EPA rule making does play a central role in the allocation of environmental common property resources.[4] Unfortunately, social sciences devoted to the study of political processes and budgetary allocations to implement policies have not, as yet, been able to characterize in a very discriminating way the relationship (if any) between the political outcomes represented by a given set of regulations implementing legislation and the underlying preferences of the populace. Thus the information offered by these institutions does not seem to extend beyond a signaling of concern and an attendant need to distribute real (or perceived) scarcities among individuals or groups, and perhaps generations.

An equally important institutional mechanism for allocating common property resources seems to fall to the judicial system. Here again, however, the objectives of the courts tend to limit the information on values and costs obtained through the allocation process. Rosenblum's [11] recent overview of the courts' role in allocating common property resources makes this point clearly. He concluded that:

This scanning of typical cases in which courts make and find law through constitutional and statutory construction and through monitoring the actions

---

[4] For a convenient summary of this legislation, see Kneese and Schultze [9] and Freeman [10].

of administrative bodies evinces an aura of judicial thoroughness and integrity, but *it does not produce uniform policies in the allocation of common property resources . . . the most definitive assertions of role have centered on the essentials of process and methodology to be observed by decision makers. How allocative policies are made more than their goodness or badness is of primary judicial concern.* [11, pp. 141–142; emphasis added]

Thus we are forced to the conclusion that while nonmarket institutions do offer a means for allocating resources, we cannot expect that they will provide the informational signals that are by-products of the exchange activities that a perfect market would. Accordingly, we must consider the kind of information necessary for an efficient allocation of the services of common property environmental resources, and second, the appropriate way to obtain such information, if possible, or to reach prudent decisions in its absence if it is impossible to obtain such information.

III
Potential Physical Constraints on Improvement in Material Well-Being

Our introductory essay described the conventional view of constraints on economic activity. We identified a basic assumption common to most economic analyses of the resource adequacy/stringency issue. This conventional view maintained a specific type of distribution and set of characteristics for the occurrence of mineral elements. We indicated that evidence from the work of geologists and geophysicists suggests there is a question about the reliability of this hypothesis, which holds that as higher grade deposits are exhausted, lower grades are available in greater abundance (Barnett and Morse). This is an area that deserves careful attention in both earth and social science research. Somewhat related to this issue is the fact that some rare elements with peculiar geochemical properties indispensable to advanced technologies (e.g., niobium in prospective fusion reactor technology, helium in cryogenics) are severely limited in supply and lack adequate substitutes.[5]

This leads to the issue of the actual existence of microtechnologies which are assumed to exist when we posit implied substitution for scarce materials on an aggregate scale. That is, given the likelihood of relatively low total capacity for such limitational inputs, there may be significant reasons for doubting the ability of an anticipated backstop technology to attain the level of use implied by substitution in the aggregate. This is an area that requires a much more extensive and intensive exchange

[5] This view of such resource limitations argues that the very attributes which make a particular resource essential in a given use include a geochemistry of resource occurrences that makes substitutes (with similar characteristics) correspondingly rare.

among the scientific, engineering, and economic communities to enhance the realism and relevance of the working assumptions and information that are used in assessing resource adequacy.

In the past, physical constraints were treated as synonymous with materials constraints, so that natural resource availability was gauged only in terms of the goods which exchanged on primary commodity markets. It may be useful to relate the restricted nature of this conceptualization to the prevailing view of the normative significance of price and cost signals flowing from market transactions of only a quarter of a century ago. The effect of market transactions on third parties external to the exchange was considered largely insubstantial and of no practical significance.[6] Today external effects are a pervasive concern and play a central role in a substantial portion of policy applications of microeconomic analysis.

The importance of explicitly treating the external effects of market transactions of individual economic agents exchanging private goods is perhaps best illustrated by a comparison with the conditions required for such actions taken in the aggregate to produce outcomes consistent with a socially optimal set of results. In those cases where there are mechanisms which do take account of such externalities in some fashion, and they are not incorporated in a model of decentralized decision-making affecting resource allocations, we know that the two outcomes will diverge. That is, in the absence of a market or an equivalent mechanism for providing information and incentives, individual actions will not reflect an accounting of the external effects of choice.[7]

These arguments have focused on the static externalities associated with the activities of economic agents. Once we broaden the definition of natural resources to include common property environmental resources and consider these resources as assets, then it must be recognized that their utilization patterns in any one period can result in externalities in that period or in future time periods.[8] A common property resource is

---

[6] Scitovsky [12], writing in the early 1950s, observed that: "The concept of external economies is one of the most elusive in economic literature" (p. 143). It was in this context that he argued that examples of such economies were "somewhat bucolic in nature, having to do with bees, orchards and woods," and that this was not an accident since it was not easy to find examples from industry.

[7] The conventional literature on static externalities calls for a system of effluent charges to provide these signals.

[8] Mohring and Boyd [13] introduced the distinction between the treatment of externalities by Pigou and Knight in terms of the comparison of a "direct interaction" versus an "asset utilization" perspective. The former seems to have dominated much of the economic literature on externalities, which has tended to limit the attention given to these types of intertemporal problems.

one which is equally accessible to all members of society. The allocation of these resources does not take place through market mechanisms, and so the market is not available to provide incentives for individual agents to limit their patterns of consumption or rate of utilization of the resource's services. In our introductory essay we sought to inquire how the presence and use patterns of such resources might affect evaluation of the adequacy of natural resources for economic well-being. If these resources are recognized as natural assets, should they be treated as renewable or exhaustible? Renewability in these cases would imply that the resource has natural regeneration or growth with time so that some mechanism permits the resource to provide, over defined levels of total use, the same quantity of constant quality services in each time period. The answers to these questions must arise out of the physical characteristics of the elements comprising the biosphere and not necessarily the analytical convenience (or lack of it) of the models which might result.

For example, the recent work of Kneese and Schulze [14] and Schulze and coauthors [15] has offered some suggestive empirical evidence indicating that mortality rates related to cancer may be associated with the extent of human intervention in the chemistry of the environment. These analyses candidly acknowledge the difficulties encountered in such econometric studies. The limitations are considerable, ranging from the poor quality of the input data (to the empirical study) to the long latency period generally associated with most carcinogens. Nonetheless, the evidence has been accumulating and can lead to a disconcerting conjecture that the effects of new chemical compounds, combustion processes, heavy use of nitrogenous fertilizers, and halocarbons may reduce certain common property resource services which are associated with human health and well-being.

While we can cite further examples, such as depletion of the ozone layer and its effects on the ultraviolet radiation reaching the earth, one of the central issues addressed here and in our introductory essay is whether such effects are exotic special cases or representative of a pervasive class of externalities.

We should note that our concerns, if correct, seem to call for an alternative institutional mechanism to facilitate the efficient allocation of these resources. One possibility would call for a rather important broadening in the scope of Meade's [16] indicative planning concepts referred to in note 9. He considered a comprehensive set of forward and contingency markets, an indicative plan developed by government as an informational service to individual citizens on the prospective paths of future market prices, and econometric modeling of markets to provide equivalent information.[9] However, a procedure which mimics forward and contingency markets only for those goods and services which exchange on current markets is incomplete. It ignores the role of the nonmarketed goods and services whose exchange, as we have observed, is not mediated through this institutional mechanism. Therefore, we cannot rely on procedures based on the attributes of existing markets to furnish information on marginal costs and valuations of alternative use profiles through time because there are direct physical interdependencies of economic activities and natural systems which are not reflected in market outcomes. Direct information from the engineering, earth, and life sciences is necessary to supplement market-generated information developed through the type of indicative planning called for by Meade. The most constructive form and structuring of this input is itself a research issue.

For the most part, economic evaluations of externalities have implicitly assumed the underlying physical medium serving as their receptacle to be a continuously renewable resource. Moreover, these analyses have also assumed that the rate of utilization of the services of these resources has been below their absorptive capacities, or the physical limit which allows the resource to regenerate its capacity. If these implicit assumptions were an accurate reflection of reality, then comparative static analysis of the implications of externalities would be sufficient to consider the full effects of alternative policy choices. However, once it is acknowledged that the receiving medium may be affected by the level of its use and that there may be cumulative and irreversible effects, then intertemporal analysis similar to that done for exhaustible resources is warranted.

To our knowledge, there are few studies of economic problems that combine direct evidence on the role of common property resources with conventional natural resources.[10] d'Arge and Kogiku [18] appear to be the first economists to consider these problems in an integrated fashion. They evaluated the implications of activities generating stock pollutants which also required the services of a depletable resource. Their model investigated the characteristics of a plan which maximized discounted

---

[9] Meade [16] observed that three approaches offer the means of providing the information consumers would need for efficient decisions—a full set of markets, his indicative planning process, or well-developed econometric models. He suggested that: "The essence of the matter then so far is to find a procedure which will give citizens a foresight of future market prices so that they can make their present plans in the knowledge of what future costs of inputs, selling prices of outputs, and so on will in fact be" (p. 11).

[10] One could also view Krutilla and Fisher's [17] analysis of the allocation problems associated with irreversible decisions for natural environments as addressing these problems.

per capita utility. Society's utility function was assumed in their model to be strongly separable in usable outputs and in the term of the planning horizon. They observed:

Issues emerging from environmental management arise not only from the optimal rate of waste generation in a closed medium but also with regard to the rate of extractive (or renewable) resource exploitation. *If extractive resources are finite in magnitude and can for all practical purposes be exhausted, then optimal environmental management involves a "conjunctive use" type allocation problem where one must consider rates of extraction and rates of waste generation.* Thus, the "pure" pollution problem and questions like these become relevant: which should we run out of first, air to breathe or fossil fuel to pollute the air we breathe? [18, p. 68, emphasis added]

While their model is quite restrictive in several dimensions, it does highlight one view of the indeterminacies in the problem. In short, they demonstrated that the treatment of common property environmental resources *can* affect one's appraisal of resource adequacy.

In related work, Cropper [9] has recently examined the implications of decisions where there is a small probability of large losses, a feature which is often used to characterize the examples we cited above. Her results are important because they provide evidence that the analytical specification of society's objective function and the treatment of uncertainty directly bears on the results we can expect from either optimal planned or decentralized behavior. More specifically, the Cropper model specifies society's planning problem in terms of maximizing its discounted expected utility. In the presence of pollutants which accumulate as a stock and have the potential of preventing further utility-generating activities, we find that the results of conventional optimal planning models must be substantially modified. That is, once we acknowledge that pollution can accumulate as a stock with correspondingly serious implications for sustaining life, then the conclusions of the earlier models which treat pollution as a static phenomenon must be modified:

When the effects of pollution are potentially catastrophic the unique, stable equilibrium which characterizes many pollution control models . . . no longer obtains and multiple equilibria, as well as a no equilibrium solution, are possible. Allowing the pollution stock to enter the utility function directly guarantees the existence of an equilibrium solution but does not rule out the possibility of multiple equilibria. [19, p. 13]

Thus it seems that the limited information we have on the implications of these types of problems for economic analysis of patterns of growth, properties of decentralized decision-making systems, and formulation of optimal centralized plans, all seems to suggest a need for substantial reorientation of our approach to dealing with these issues.

IV
Implications

This volume has raised a number of questions regarding the conventional views developed in *Scarcity and Growth*. We have not offered answers to these questions, but rather have attempted to identify the elements of a research program that is needed to evaluate them. Two of these issues deserve repeating. The first concerns the long-run supply of the physical materials, conventionally treated as synonymous with the full set of natural resources. We have argued, with the support of the literature cited in Brobst's paper (chapter 5), that there are a number of competing hypotheses concerning the long-run availability of materials, particularly our mineral resources. Without a more clear-cut reading of the nature of this supply response, it is difficult to judge whether natural resources will ultimately be a limitational input. Moreover, we must inquire in the same spirit whether the private markets involving these resources are sufficiently free of imperfections and institutional influences to transmit accurately the marginal values and costs of these resources. Beginning with the Internal Revenue Codes of 1916 to the present, public intervention through tax policy affecting the extractive sector has been pervasive. Yet, we have not evaluated the direct and indirect effects of these institutional changes on market transactions and their prices. It may be that in this case, one should not rely on unadjusted market prices as Barnett and Morse did for a part of their empirical analysis.

The second general concern is the consistency between the formulation of economic models and the constraints on man's activities imposed by physical laws. In modeling production processes and specifying the role of the physical environment, the economist's penchant for simplification and partial analysis has often led to a type of "tunnel vision," a failure to fully appreciate the static *and* intertemporal implications of his production and consumption decisions. Physical laws will constrain the constituent elements in production activities. They will limit substitution possibilities in response to increasing scarcity of materials. Moreover, they can place direct limits on the absorptive capacity of environmental systems.

Both of these problems share a recognition of the potential for interactions between the economic system and other noneconomic considerations in our interpretation of the realistic scope of future economic activities. That is, in the first case we must recognize the role of institutional constraints on the social interactions of markets and in the second the interaction between man's production and consumption activities and the physical environment. Ultimately this view is an extension of the concepts of conjunctive management advocated by d'Arge and Kogiku in their discussion of the implications of their model.

As we suggested earlier, the market cannot generate all of the data necessary for the formulation of prudent natural resource policies. Meade's [16] indicative planning is not the complete answer, for it attempts to mimic the function of existing markets. It is necessary to enlist the aid of natural scientists in obtaining information on the nature of interdependencies between the results of market activities and the biosphere's life support processes.

Failure to treat the uses of natural resources conjunctively can lead to economic activities which usurp one or more common property resources without providing any mechanisms for a response by the economic agents involved. Accordingly, a research program addressing these issues must develop analyses of physical, environmental, and institutional constraints on economic behavior that are relevant to the concerns of policy makers who must reconcile the needs of mankind with the earth's supply of resources and society's ability to utilize them.

References

1. E. A. Wrigley, "The Supply of Raw Materials in the Industrial Revolution," *The Economic History Review*, 2nd. Ser., vol. XV, no. 1 (1962) pp. 1–16.
2. W. S. Jevons, *The Coal Question* (London and Cambridge, 1865) p. viii.
3. H. J. Barnett and C. Morse, *Scarcity and Growth: The Economics of Natural Resource Availability* (Baltimore, Johns Hopkins University Press for Resources for the Future, 1963).
4. R. V. Eagly, *The Structure of Classical Economic Theory* (New York, Oxford University Press, 1974).
5. J. M. Buchanan, "The Relevance of Pareto Optimality," *Journal of Conflict Resolution* vol. 6 (December 1962) pp. 341–354.
6. A. Randall, "Property Institutions and Economic Behavior," *Journal of Economic Issues* vol. 12 (March 1978) pp. 1–21.
7. E. J. Mishan, "Pareto Optimality and the Law," *Oxford Economic Papers* vol. 19 (November 1967) pp. 247–280.
8. W. D. Nordhaus, "The Allocation of Energy Resources," *Brookings Papers on Economic Activity* no. 3 (Washington, D.C., Brookings Institution, 1973).
9. A. V. Kneese and C. L. Schultze, *Pollution, Prices, and Public Policy* (Washington, D.C., Brookings Institution, 1975).
10. A. M. Freeman, III, "Air and Water Pollution Policy," in P. Portney, ed., *Current Issues in U.S. Environmental Policy* (Baltimore, Johns Hopkins University Press for Resources for the Future, 1978).
11. V. G. Rosenblum, "The Continuing Role of the Courts in Allocating

Common Property Resources," in E. T. Haefele, ed., *The Governance of Common Property Resources* (Baltimore, Johns Hopkins University Press for Resources for the Future, 1974).

12. T. Scitovsky, "Two Concepts of External Economies," *Journal of Political Economy* vol. 62 (1954) pp. 143–151.

13. H. Mohring and J. H. Boyd, "Analyzing 'Externalities': 'Direct Interaction' vs. 'Asset Utilization' Frameworks," *Economica* vol. 38 (November 1971) pp. 347–361.

14. A. V. Kneese and W. D. Schulze, "Environment, Health and Economics—The Case of Cancer," *American Economic Review, Proceedings* vol. 67 (February 1977) pp. 326–332.

15. W. Schulze, A. Kneese, S. Ben-David, and B. Ives, "Cancer and the Environment: What Cost the Risk," unpublished paper, University of New Mexico, undated.

16. J. E. Meade, *The Theory of Indicative Planning* (Manchester, England, Manchester University Press, 1970).

17. J. V. Krutilla and A. C. Fisher, *The Economics of Natural Environments* (Baltimore, Johns Hopkins University Press for Resources for the Future, 1975).

18. R. C. d'Arge and K. C. Kogiku, "Economic Growth and the Environment," *Review of Economic Studies* vol. 40 (January 1973) pp. 61–78.

19. M. L. Cropper, "Regulating Activities with Catastrophic Environmental Effects," *Journal of Environmental Economics and Management* vol. 3 (June 1976) pp. 1–15.

Index

Adams, Henry, 36
Aggregates: capital input, 223, 258; demand, 162, 238; depletion quotas, 86, 87; economic indexes, 84; growth, 78; optimal consumption, 62; production function, 11–13, 14–15; scarcity indexes, 27; simple economy, 10, 13; substitution, 12, 45–46; throughput, 89; unit cost indexes, 167, 222, 232
Agrarians, 73, 102
Agriculture: environmental effects, 9; growth, 166; labor productivity, 178, 179; relative labor costs, 183–184; prices, 179, 181–183, 224; resource regeneration, 9; resource scarcity, 147, 151, 158; unit costs, 168, 173
Air, 38; pollution, 187, 189, 259; see also Common property resources; pollution abatement
Albers, J. P., 131, 132
Algorithms: future demand, 100
Allais, M., 117, 269
Allocation. See Resource allocation
Aluminum, 109; crustal abundance, 120t, 121, 122, 123t, 144; demand, 145, 148t, 150; distribution, 110t, 123, 124t; energy requirements, 129, 153, 154; marginal supplies, 192; prices, 225t, 226t, 234; substitution, 148, 158, 220, 241; see also Bauxite
Andrews, P. W., 106
Arge, R. C. d', 286, 289
Argon, 157
Arrow, K., 46fn
Arsenic, 149
Asbestos, 109, 110, 111t

Bailly, Paul, 134
Barite, 119, 132

Barium, 119, 122
Barnett, Harold J., 2, 4, 8, 22–23, 24–26, 27, 97, 106, 186, 220–224, 228, 230, 251, 257–259, 261, 277–279
Baumol, William J., 24
Bauxite, 109, 129, 135, 192; adjusted price, 228t
Beckerman, Wilfred, 96, 249
Bell, Frederick W., 175
Bentham, Jeremy, 101
Blaug, Mark, 96
Boron, 109, 110, 111t
Boyd, J. H., 284fn
Brannon, G. M., 27fn
Brevard, J. C., 153
Brobst, Donald A., 17–18, 19, 28, 160
Brooks, D. B., 106
Brown, Gardner M., Jr., 9, 22, 23, 24, 256, 257, 258, 267
Buchanan, J. M., 280

Calcium, 120t
Callahan, J. C., 225
Capital, 80; accumulation, 53fn; productivity, 162
Capital expenditures: tax writeoffs, 58–59
Capital gains tax, 59
Capital inputs, 8, 30, 98, 221, 223, 232; aggregates, 223, 258; mineral prices relative to, 226; pollution abatement, 4fn; substitution, 252, elasticity, 13, 41, 43, 46, 241
Carbon dioxide (CO_2): petrochemicals from, 147, 158
Cartels, 190–192
Chlorine: demand, 146t, 148t
Christy, Francis T., Jr., 220
Chromium, 109, 110, 135; crustal abundance, 123t; demand, 150t

291